FINANCIAL ACCOUNTING

FINANCIAL ACCOUNTING

VOLUME I

Balavant M. Unnibhavi

ATLANTIC
PUBLISHERS & DISTRIBUTORS

Published by
ATLANTIC
PUBLISHERS & DISTRIBUTORS
B-2, Vishal Enclave, Opp. Rajouri Garden,
New Delhi-110027
Phones : 25413460, 25429987, 25466842

Sales Office
7/22, Ansari Road, Darya Ganj,
New Delhi-110002
Phones : 23273880, 23275880, 23280451
Fax : 91-11-23285873
web : www.atlanticbooks.com
e-mail : info@atlanticbooks.com

ISBN 81-269-0421-6 (Vol. I)
ISBN 81-269-0422-4 (Vol. II)
ISBN 81-269-0423-2 (Set)

Printed in India
at Nice Printing Press, Delhi

PREFACE

I am extremely happy to place before the esteemed readers the book entitled *Financial Accounting*. Financial Accounting is said to be the heart of language of business and is more apparent in the Financial Reports. Keeping this in view the two-volume book is designed to cater to the needs of the students of the Indian Universities and those of professional examinations like C.A., I.C.W.A., A.C.S., etc., conducted by the various institutes.

In the best interests of the students who take the different examinations, I have tried to introduce the subject in a simple and lucid manner to enable them to learn and understand the intricacies of accounting in a logical sequence. The concepts have been explained step by step including all minute details and are richly illustrated with graded and appropriate examples, provided in each Chapter, so as to have a concrete understanding of the subject. In addition, short questions, simple problems and practical exercises, selected from the latest question papers of various universities have been given for the benefit of the students. I am optimistic that the book would prove to be a standard textbook on the subject and also worthwhile in enhancing one's knowledge of Accounting.

Although no originality is claimed by me, yet it may be definitely said that it has its own speciality as far as its arrangement, compass and techniques are concerned. I am indebted to all the authors whose works I have referred to and the ideas and thoughts that I have borrowed from.

It would be unjustified if I do not acknowledge the help extended to me by my beloved wife Prof. (Dr.) Pushpa B. Unnibhavi in preparing this book.

I also take this opportunity to express my heartfelt gratitude to Prof. A.G. Sunkad, Head, Department of English, for improving the grammatical standard of the book and for his valuable suggestions which have made the book all the more comprehensive.

I express my profound gratitude to the students, teachers and all my well-wishers whose encouragement has inspired me to bring this book.

Thanks are due to the colleagues and friends of my college for their moral support.

I also thank Dr. K.R. Gupta, Chairman, M/s Atlantic Publishers and Distributors, New Delhi, for taking keen interest in publishing this book.

BALAVANT M. UNNIBHAVI

CONTENTS

VOLUME I

VOLUME II

1

GENERALLY ACCEPTED ACCOUNTING PRINCIPLES AND STANDARDS

Meaning and Definitions of Accounting

A system of recording the business transactions in the books of accounts in accordance with the Principles of Accountancy is known as Accounting or in its elementary stage as Book-keeping. In the earlier stage, accounting was considered simply as a process of recording the business transactions in the books of accounts and the role of accountant as that of record-keeper. But with the lapse of time, more and more was expected from the accounting. At present accounting is more of an information system rather than a mere recording system. In other words, accounting is considered as the language of business which communicates the results of the business operations to various parties interested in the business, *viz.*, owners, investors, creditors, financial institutions, government etc. This has resulted in widening the scope of accounting. The following definitions show how the concept of accounting has undergone a change over a period of time.

In the year 1941, the American Institute of Certified Public Accountants (AICPA) defined the accounting as below :

"Accounting is the art of recording, classifying and summarising in a significant manner and in terms of money, transactions and events which are, in part at least, of a financial character and interpreting the results thereof."[1]

In the year 1966, the American Accounting Association (AAA) defined the accounting as below :

"Accounting is the process of identifying, measuring and communicating economic information to permit informed judgement and decisions by users of the information."

In the year 1970, the Accounting Principles Board (APB) of American Institute of Certified Public Accountants (AICPA) enumerated the accounting functions as below :

1. *Accounting Terminology Bulletin, No. 1*, American Institute of Certified Public Accountants, Committee on Terminology, New York, The Institute, 1953, p. 9.

"The function of accounting is to provide quantitative information, primarily of financial nature, about economic entities, that is needed to be useful in making economic decisions."

Thus, accounting is now defined as the process of recording (in the journal), classifying (in the ledger), summarising (in the trial balance and final accounts), analysing and interpreting the transactions of a financial character and communicating the results thereof to the various parties connected with such information. After analysing the information supplied by the accounting, the users of the same take decisions for the future activities.

Distinction between Book-keeping and Accounting

Although in practical life Book-keeping and Accounting are used interchangeably, there are some differences between two. They are :

1. Book-keeping is the earlier stage of accounting. It is merely concerned with the recording the business transactions in the books of accounts (i.e., journal and ledger). Accounting, on the other hand, is used in a broader sense; it not only includes the recording of business transactions in the books of accounts but also consists of summarising the recorded data, analysing, interpreting and communicating the same to the users, both internal and external, who would like to make use of it for future decisions. Hence, accounting involves book-keeping and book-keeping is the recording branch of accounting.
2. Book-keeping work is mechanical and repetitive in nature. As such, this work is usually entrusted to junior employees who are known as book-keepers. Hence, book-keepers need not possess special skill or special knowledge of accountancy. Whereas, accounting work is more analytical and complicated in nature. Therefore, it requires some skills, experience and imagination. The persons who are engaged with these works are known as accountants. Accountants are required to have a much more knowledge and analytical skill than what are required for book-keepers.

Accounting begins where book-keeping ends. Without book-keeping, accounting is not possible and without accounting, book-keeping has no meaning. Distinction between book-keeping and accounting would be meaningful only in case of big business concerns; but in case of small concerns this distinction would be meaningless as both these works are performed by the same staff.

Distinction between Accountancy and Accounting

In common parlance, the terms accounting and accountancy are used interchangeably. However, there are some differences between two. They are :

1. Accountancy concerns with the creation of principles or rules to be followed while recording the business transactions. Accounting concerns with the recording of business transactions as per the principles or rules of Accountancy.
2. Accountancy concerns with the theoretical aspects. Accounting, on the other hand, concerns with the practical aspects.
3. Accountancy is a science, as it has a set of principles or rules. Whereas accounting is an art, as it records the business transactions in the books of accounts.
4. Accountancy, as a systematised body of knowledge, shows the way to accounting practices and answers the questions in relation to accounting. Whereas accounting follows the accountancy directions.

Branches of Accounting

Different forms of accounting have been developed to satisfy the various users interested in the accounting information. They are :

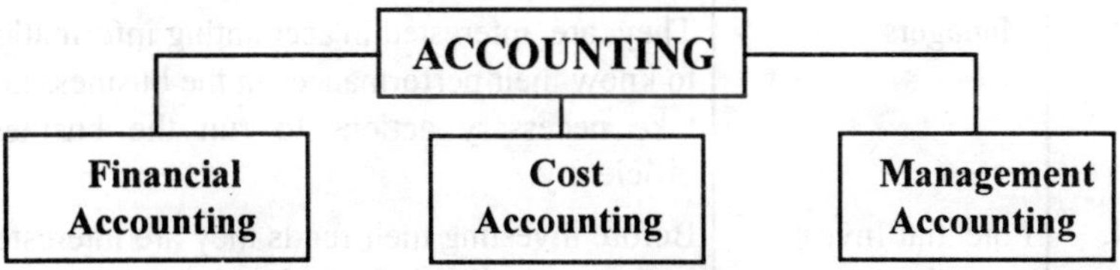

1. Financial Accounting : It is mainly concerned with the preparation of financial statements (*i.e.*, P & L A/c and B/S) and communication of accounting or business information to the external users including share-holders, employees etc. Its aim is to ascertain the profit or loss and to show the financial position of the business. To achieve these objects it is necessary to record all the transactions of a business in the books of accounts in a systematic manner.

2. Cost Accounting : This branch of accounting is developed to overcome the limitations of financial accounting. The object of cost accounting is to ascertain the true cost of goods produced or services rendered by the business. It serves as a guide in fixing the price of product. It helps the businessman in controlling the costs by eliminating or reducing losses or wastes.

3. Management Accounting : Management accounting is concerned with the supply of information which is useful to the management to take decision for the efficient running of the business. It assists the management in formulating policies and controlling the operations of the business. Management accounting provides all accounting information *i.e.*, it not only provides cost information but also financial information.

Users of Accounting Information

There are number of groups who have vested interest in the accounting information of the business. They may be internal users or external users. Following are the some of the users who use the accounting information :

Sl. No.	Users	For the Respective Interest
1.	Owners/Proprietors, and Partners	They are interested to know the financial position of a concern, rate of return on the capital employed, proper and effective utilisation of the scarce resources.
2.	Creditors and other Lending Institutions	Since they have provided the funds, they are eager to get their funds as well as interest thereon. As such, they are naturally interested to know the profitability, real value of assets, short-term and long-term solvency of the business.
3.	Managers	They are interested in accounting information to know their performances in the business and take necessary actions to run the business efficiently.
4.	Potential Investors	Before investing their funds they are interested in the accounting information to know the past and present profitability of the business, because, their investment should always be in safe.
5.	Employees	They are interested in the earning capacity of the business since their salary, bonus, profit-sharing, welfare and social measures depend upon the profitability of business.
6.	Government	Government is interested in the accounts of the firm for ascertaining the income tax, sales tax, excise duty and other taxes.
7.	Consumers	They are interested in the profitability of the business since the price of their purchasing goods depends on it.
8.	Researchers	They are interested in accounting data since they are using them in their research work.

Accounting Principles

Principle is a general law, truth or belief used uniformally everywhere as a base for action. As such accounting principles may be defined as those rules of procedure which are adopted by the accountant universally in recording the accounting transactions.

The American Institute of Certified Public Accountants (AICPA) has defined the word 'principle' as a "general law or rule adopted or professed as a guide to action; a settled ground or basis of conduct or practice". Accounting principles have been defined as the body of doctrine commonly associated with the theory and procedure of accounting, serving as an explanation of current practices and as a guide for the selection of conventions or procedures where alternative exist. Rules governing the formation of accounting axioms, the principles derived from them have arisen from common experiences, historical precedent, statements by individuals and professional bodies and regulations of governmental agencies.[2]

Paton and Littleton, however, prefer to use the term 'standards' in the place of principles. The International Federation of Accountants have constituted the 'International Accounting Standards Committee' which exposed the number of accounting principles. These principles of course, named as 'standards' in order to avoid the confusion. Accounting principles *i.e.*, 'standards' must satisfy three rules *i.e.*, (i) usefulness (relevance) *i.e.*, meaningful to the users, (ii) objectivity *i.e.*, supported and supplemented by the basic facts or data, and (iii) feasibility *i.e.*, practicable or feasible to attain.

Thus, generally accepted accounting principles (GAAPs) are the set of laws, rules, guidelines or concepts used in recording accounting transactions.

Kinds of Accounting Principles

Accounting principles may broadly be classified under two categories *viz.*, concepts and conventions.

1. Accounting Concepts

The term 'concepts' may be considered as postulates, *i.e.*, necessary assumptions or conditions, upon which the accounting is based. Following are the important accounting concepts agreed to by most of the accountants :

(i) Business Entity Concept. According to this concept for accounting purpose the business is treated as a separate unit apart from its owners, creditors and others. In other words, the proprietor of a concern is always considered to be separate from the business which he controls. The transactions of the business should be recorded separately and should not be mixed up with the owner's personal transactions. If the transactions of the business are mixed up

---

2. Canadian Institute of Chartered Accountants (1957).

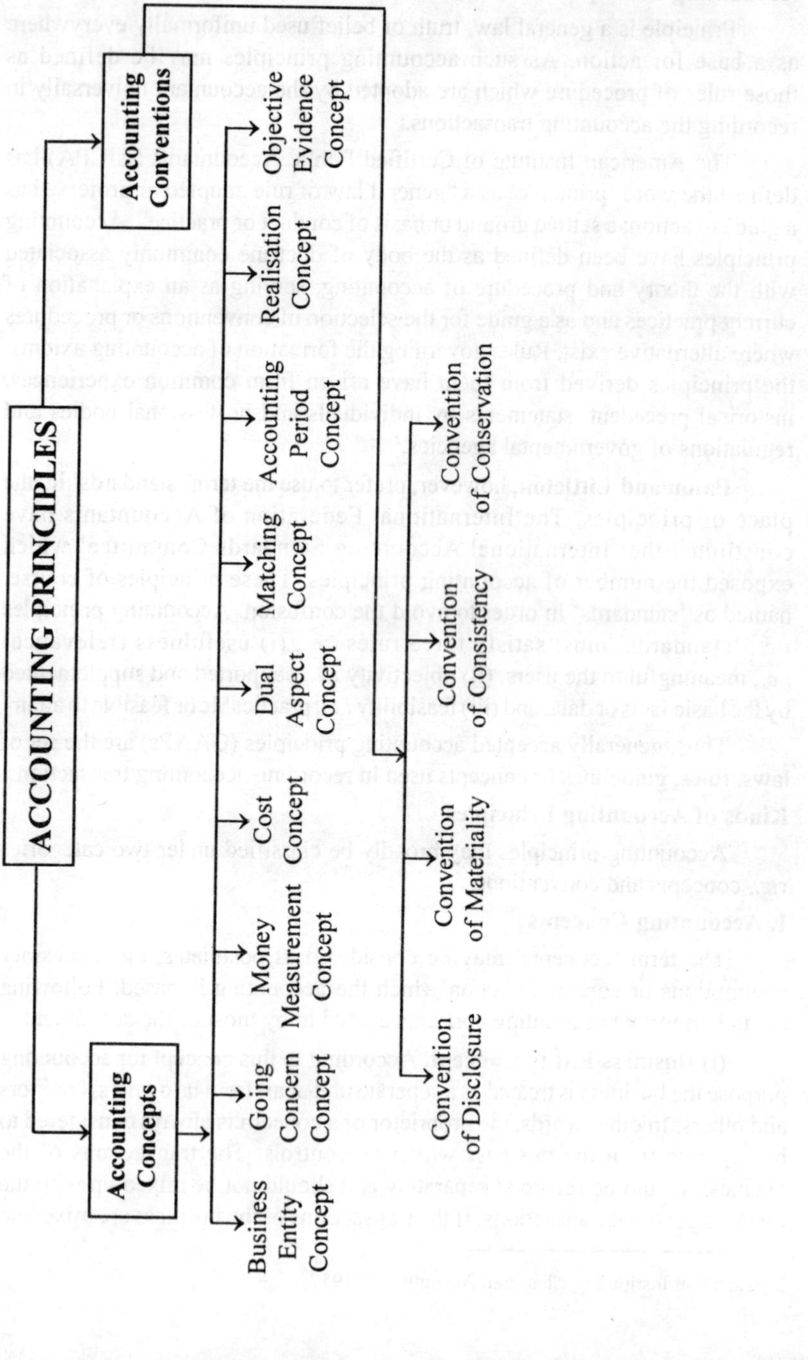
ACCOUNTING PRINCIPLES
Accounting Concepts
Accounting Conventions
Business Entity Concept
Going Concern Concept
Money Measurement Concept
Cost Concept
Dual Aspect Concept
Matching Concept
Accounting Period Concept
Realisation Concept
Objective Evidence Concept
Convention of Disclosure
Convention of Materiality
Convention of Consistency
Convention of Conservation

with the proprietor's personal transactions, the true picture of the business will not be available. The proprietor or owner of the business will be treated as a creditor. For example, if the owner invests Rs. 50,000 in his business, it is deemed that the owner of the business has given that much amount to the business which will be shown as a 'liability' of the business. Similarly, if the owner withdraws Rs. 5,000, it will be debited to his account and the net amount due to him *i.e.*, Rs. 45,000 will be shown as a 'liability' for the business. Because, the proprietor is a creditor of business. This concept helps to give a true picture of the financial conditions of a business. Without this concept the recording of business transactions will not be meaningful.

(ii) Going Concern Concept : It is also known as "the concept of continuity". According to this concept it is assumed that the business will continue for a long time and it is not likely to liquidate in the near future. Kohler defines a going concern as "any enterprise which is expected to continue operating indefinitely in the future". It is with this assumption that the fixed assets are recorded at cost price and are depreciated on the basis of their expected lives without reference to their market values.

(iii) Money Measurement Concept : This concept signifies that only those transactions which can be expressed to terms of money are recorded in the accounting. But, the transactions or happenings which cannot be expressed in terms of money are not recorded. Efficiency of management, honesty of staff, attitude of workers, competitive strength of the concern, customers relations, poor health of the chairman of a concern etc., cannot be expressed in terms of money and thus, are not recorded in the books of account though they are material events. This concept does not give a complete record of all the happenings in the business unit. Because it does not record the non-monetary events. This concept has another limitation *i.e.*, transactions are recorded at its money value on the date of occurrence and the subsequent changes in the money value are ignored. In spite of these limitations, the money measurement concept remains indispensable.

(iv) Cost Concept : This concept is closely related to the going concern concept. According to this concept, fixed assets of the business are ordinarily entered in the books of accounts at their cost price at which they are acquired and not at their current market price since the business is not going to be liquidated but is to be continued for a long time. Cost price is the base for all subsequent accounts for the asset. The change in the value of an asset with passage of time is not recorded in the books of accounts. For example, if a business purchases a piece of land for Rs. 70,000, the asset (land) would be recorded in the books of accounts at Rs. 70,000 even if its market value at that time happens to be Rs. 90,000. Similarly, if a business has not paid anything for an asset which it acquired, then that asset is usually not recorded in the books of accounts. Another point is to be noted that the cost concept does not mean that the asset will always be shown at cost price. It means that the asset is recorded at cost price at the time of its purchase but in the subsequent years it may be reduced in its value by charging depreciation. This concept also suffers from one limitation *i.e.*, it ignores the effect of excessive inflation. Due to this limitation the preparation of accounts and statements become unreliable and irrelevant for judging the true financial position of the business. In order to overcome this limitation, inflation accounting and current values of an assets are to be advocated.

(v) Dual Aspect Concept : This concept is the outcome of entity concept. From the accounting point of view, as the business is treated as a separate entity, the capital invested by the owner represents not merely the initial assets but also a measure of indebtedness to the owner. Therefore, assets acquired, out of the capital, are shown on the asset side of the balance sheet and their equivalent value *i.e.*, capital is shown on the liability side of the balance sheet. Under this concept, every transaction has a dual effect. One is the receiving of benefit and another is the giving of that benefit. When a business firm acquires an asset (receiving of benefit), it must have to pay cash (giving of benefit). Therefore, in the books of the firm two accounts are to be opened *i.e.*, one for receiving the benefit and another for giving the benefit. Thus, there will be a double entry for every transaction *i.e.*, for every debit there must be corresponding credit. This is the principle of double entry which is, in other words, known as the dual aspect concept. The accounting equation *i.e.*, Assets (sources owned by the business) = Equities (claim of various parties *i.e.*, liabilities [outsiders equity] + Capital [owner's equity]) is based on this concept. Therefore, this concept is also known as 'accounting equivalence concept'.

Dual aspect concept can be explained with an example. A starts a business with a capital of Rs. 20,000. Here, the capital of the business is equal to the assets of the business. This expression can be shown in form of the following equation :

Capital = Assets (cash)

Rs. 20,000 = Rs. 20,000

If the business, in the above example, borrows a loan of Rs. 5,000, the assets of the business increase by Rs. 5,000 and liabilities of the business also increase by Rs. 5,000 because of the borrowed loan. The dual aspects of this transactions are as under :

Capital + Liabilities (Loan) = Assets

Rs. 20,000 + Rs. 5,000 = Rs. 25,000

Suppose, the business, in the above example, purchases machinery worth Rs. 25,000 on credit and pays for furniture Rs. 7,000 then the dual aspects are as under :

Capital + Liabilities (Loan + Creditors) = Assets (Cash + Machinery + Furniture)

Rs. 20,000 + Rs. 30,000 (Rs. 5,000 + Rs. 25,000)

= Rs. 50,000 (Rs. 18,000 + Rs. 25,000 + Rs. 7,000)

In this case, machinery is purchased for Rs. 25,000 on credit. Therefore, the assets will increase by Rs. 25,000 and liabilities also increase by Rs. 25,000 on account of the purchase of machinery on credit. Similarly, the business pays the cash Rs. 7,000 for furniture. In this case, one asset (furniture) of the business increases by Rs. 7,000 and the another asset (cash) of the business decreases by Rs. 7,000 without any change in liabilities. Therefore, in both the above transactions dual or two aspects are recorded.

If the business, in the above example, pays Rs. 800 for the creditors, then the dual aspects are as under :

Capital + Liabilities (Loan + Creditors) = Assets (Cash + Machinery + Furniture)

Rs. 20,000 + Rs. 29,200 (Rs. 5,000 + Rs. 24,200)

= Rs. 49,200 (Rs. 17,200 + Rs. 25,000 + Rs. 7,000)

In this case business pays Rs. 800 to the creditors. Therefore, the assets (cash) of the business will decrease by Rs. 800 and creditors of the business also will decrease by Rs. 800.

Hence, the dual aspect concept is the core of the financial accounting.

(vi) Matching Concept : This concept is based on the accounting period concept. According to this concept, the expenses incurred during a specific period should be matched against the revenue realised for that period to ascertain a profit made by the firm for the said period. It means, expenses which are incurred for earning the revenue of the related period should be considered to find out the profit or loss of that period. For example, suppose, the workers are paid the wages in the year 2001 for the work done in the year 2,000, wages paid to the workers in the year 2001 should be taken as the expenses in the year 2000. It means that revenue of 2000 should be matched with the expense incurred for earning that revenue in the year 2000, even though it is paid in the year 2001. Therefore, while preparing the final accounts some adjustments are to be made at the end of the accounting period with regard to outstanding expenses, pre-paid expenses, unearned incomes, accrued incomes etc., for the purpose of matching. This process of relating costs to revenue is called matching process.

(vii) Accounting Period Concept : According to going concern concept, the life of the business is assumed to be indefinite and will continue for a long period. But the proprietor of the business cannot wait for such a long period to study the financial position and measure the income of the business. He is interested to know the progress of the business from time to time. Hence, the accountants choose some shorter period to measure the income or progress of the business. Usually, 12 months period is adopted for this purpose. The accounting period may be calendar year (1st January to 31st December) or financial year (1st April to 31st March) or any other period depending upon the convenience of the business. This time interval is called 'Accounting Period'. At the end of each accounting period, the Income Statement and Balance Sheet are to be prepared to know the performance of the business.

(viii) Realisation Concept : According to this concept, profit is considered only when revenue is realised and revenue is realised only when the sales are made either for cash or some other asset or for a promise to pay the cash in future. In other words, revenue realised/earned during an accounting period should only be taken into account. Unrealised/unearned revenue should not be taken into account. If the order is received and advance payment is also received from the customers, it cannot be treated as revenue realised or earned. If no sales are taken place, no revenues are considered. It should be remembered that revenue is recognised and earned when a firm actually sells the goods to its customers. However, there are some exceptions to this concept. For example, hire purchase transactions, contract accounts etc.

(ix) Objective Evidence Concept : According to this concept the business transactions should be recorded only if they are evidenced and supported by evidentiary documents such as invoice, vouchers, bills, correspondence etc. In other words, there is no place for fictitious transactions in the books of accounts. Evidentiary documents provide the basis for recording the business transactions and for later verification by an auditor.

In addition to the above mentioned concepts, the following should also be noted :

(i) Accounting is a historical record of transactions; it must record only those transactions which have already taken place and not those that are likely to happen.

(ii) Business transactions should be recorded to reflect the true legal position.

2. Accounting Conventions

Accounting conventions means customs, usages, or traditions which are used as a guide to the preparation of accounting statements. In other words, it is a customary practice or an accounting procedure followed on the basis of long-standing customs. Following are the important conventions :

(i) Convention of Disclosure : Convention of disclosure means all the material information or significant facts of the business transactions should be disclosed clearly in the financial statement. For example, in case of assets not only cost price of the assets should be disclosed, but also depreciation written off should be disclosed clearly. The idea behind this convention is to prepare the financial statement honestly. Because, the users of the financial statement are enabled to know as much about the business as is necessary to appraise it.

(ii) Convention of Materiality : According to Kohler's *Dictionary of Accountants*, materiality means 'the characteristic attaching to a statement, fact or item whereby its disclosure or method of giving its expression would be likely to influence the judgement of a reasonable person.' According to this concept, the accountant should attach the importance of each transaction or event to determine its proper treatment. Unimportant items should either be left out or merged with other items. Sometimes items should be shown as footnotes, or in parentheses according to their relative importance. Accountant should ignore insignificant details in preparing the final accounts. An item material for one concern may be immaterial for another. What is material or immaterial depends upon the circumstances and discretion of an accountant.

(iii) Convention of Consistency : According to this convention, accounting rules, methods and practices should remain consistent (unchange) from one year to another unless it becomes absolutely essential to change them. According to Accounting Standard-I 'Consistency is a fundamental assumption and it is assumed that accounting policies are consistent from one year to another.' If the accounting rules or policies are continuously changed from year to year, the comparison of accounting figures from one year to another would be difficult and the conclusions about the progress of the business would also be difficult. Hence, the accounting rules, policies or methods should remain the same from one year to another. If this assumption is not followed, the fact should be disclosed together with reasons.

(iv) Convention of Conservation : Conservatism refers to the principles and practices which are established by way of tradition, reluctance to change from such established principles and practicies, and an inclination to play safe. In short, it is a policy of caution or playing safe and had its origin as a safeguard against possible losses in a world of uncertainty.[3] It means, the

3. Paul S. Kr., *Fundamentals of Accounting,* Calcutta : New Central Book Agency (P) Ltd., 1992, p. 19.

accountant should follow the policy of playing safe while preparing the financial statements. Accountant is expected not to take into account 'anticipated profits' but provide for all possible 'anticipated loses' such as bad debts, discount on debtors, fluctuation in the price of investments etc. In order to protect the interest of various groups the net profits and net assets should not be overstated but may be understated. This means, a firm should not be shown better than what it is.

Accounting Standards

Meaning and Need

Accounting standards are the uniformity in thoughts and application in recording the financial implications. **Kohler** defines accounting standard as 'A mode of conduct imposed on accountants by law, custom or professional body'. The need of an accounting standard is to ensure uniformity in the preparation and presentation of financial statements. Accounting standards, concepts and conventions form a base for accounting theory and practice. They are like grammar of accountancy, which is the language of a business. They have no statutory force. The accountants are free to change any of the accounting assumptions based on conventions. They are being constantly changed, deleted, and/or added in the states and abroad. They provide the accountant with practical and handy rules for the conduct of his or her work. They dominate the accountant's work. The following are the good reasons to establish the accounting standards :

(i) Generate interest in the principles and theories among the interested persons in the accounting disciplines.

(ii) Provide the accounting information about the financial position, performance etc., to the various users.

(iii) Provide the rules of action and guidelines to the public accountants to exercise with due care and independence in selling their expertise.

(iv) Provide the data, based on various variables, to the government to the conduct of taxation, regulation of enterprises, planning and regulation of economy.

In 1894, the American Association of Public Accountants was made an earliest attempt for developing the accounting standards. Since then, American Accounting Association, Accounting Principles Board (USA), Financial Accounting Standards Board (USA), Accounting Standards Committee (England) etc., have made a maximum contribution for the development of accounting standards.

International Accounting Standards

With a view to harmonising the accounting standards and developing the international standards, the International Accounting Standards Committee (IASC) was formed on 29th June, 1973. The Committee consists of 16 principal accounting bodies from nine nations (called as founder members) such as United States, United Kingdom, West Germany, Netherlands, France, Canada, Mexico, Japan and Australia. The Committee has its headquarter at London. The main objectives of the IASC are :

(a) to formulate and publish in the public interest accounting standards to be observed in the presentation of financial statements and to promote their worldwide acceptance and observance, and

(b) to work generally for the improvement and harmonisation of regulations, accounting standards and procedures relating to presentation of financial statements.

These objectives not only help in understanding and exchanging the economic and financial information but also in facilitating a smooth flow of international investment. So far (*i.e.*, as on July 1, 2002), the IASC has published 40 statements of standards with regard to following matters :

IAS-1. Disclosure of accounting policies

IAS-2. Valuation and presentation of inventories

IAS-3. Consolidated financial statements

IAS-4. Depreciation accounting

IAS-5. Information to be disclosed in financial statements

IAS-6. Accounting response to changing prices

IAS-7. Statement of changes in financial position

IAS-8. Unusual and prior period items and changes in accounting policies

IAS-9. Accounting for research and development activities

IAS-10. Contingencies and events occurring after the balance sheet date

IAS-11. Accounting for construction contracts

IAS-12. Accounting for taxes on income

IAS-13. Presentation of current assets and current liabilities.

IAS-14. Reporting of financial information by segments

IAS-15. Information reflecting the effects of changing prices

IAS-16. Accounting for property, plant and equipment

IAS-17. Accounting for leases

IAS-18. Revenue recognition

IAS-19. Accounting for retirement benefits in the financial statement of employers.

IAS-20. Accounting for government grants and disclosure of government assistance.

IAS-21. Accounting for effects of changes in foreign currency rates

IAS-22. Accounting for business combinations

IAS-23. Capitalisation of borrowing costs

IAS-24. Related party disclosers

IAS-25. Accounting for investments

IAS-26. Accounting and reporting by retirement benefit plans

IAS-27. Consolidated financial statements and accounting for investments in subsidiaries.

IAS-28. Accounting for investments in associates

IAS-29. Financial reporting in hyper-inflationary economics

IAS-30. Disclosure in the financial statements of Banks and similar financial institutions.

IAS-31 Financial reporting of interests in joint ventures

IAS-32 Financial instruments, disclosers and presentation

IAS-33 Earnings per share

IAS-34 Interim financial reporting

IAS-35 Discounting operations

IAS-36 Impairment of assets

IAS-37 On provisions, contingent liabilities and contingent assets

IAS-38 Intangible assets

IAS-39 Financial investments, recognition and measurement

IAS-40 Investment property

In this chapter, for the purpose of the study only 'IAS-1. Disclosure of Accounting Policies' has been discussed. The remaining IASs are to be discussed in the concerned subsequent chapters if syllabus permits. Please refer Index-I given at the end of this book for brief idea, modifications, comparative study and recent changes with regard to above IAS.

IAS-1. Disclosure of Accounting Policies

This statement is announced on or after 1st January, 1975. It is issued in June, 1981 and made mandatory in respect of the accounting periods commencing on or after 1-4-1991. It deals with the following standards in respect of disclosure of fundamental accounting assumptions and policies :

Fundamental Accounting Assumptions: They refer to those accounting standards whose acceptance and use are assumed in the preparation of financial statements. The following are recognised by the IASC as fundamental accounting assumptions :

(a) *Going Concern:* The enterprise is normally viewed as going concern, that is as continuing in operation for the foreseeable future. It is assumed that the enterprise has neither the intention nor the necessity of liquidation or of curtailing the scale of its operation.

(b) *Consistency:* It is assumed that the accounting policies are consistent with one period to another.

(c) *Accrual:* Revenues and costs are accrued, *i.e.*, recognised as they are earned or incurred (and not as money is received or paid) and recorded in the financial statements or the periods to which they relate (the consideration affecting the process of matching costs with revenues under the accrual assumption is not dealt with in this statement).

If the above fundamental accounting assumptions are followed in the financial statements, disclosure of such assumptions is not required. In case the above assumptions are not followed, that fact should be disclosed together with reasons.

Accounting Policies: These include principles, bases, conventions, rules and procedures adopted by the management in preparing and presenting the financial statements. There are many different accounting policies in use even in relation to the same subject; judgement is required in selecting and applying those which, in the circumstances of the enterprise, are best suited to present properly its financial position and the results of its operations. The following considerations should govern the selection and application by management of the appropriate accounting policies and preparation of financial statements :

(a) *Prudence:* Uncertainties inevitably surrounded many transactions. This should be recognised by exercising prudence in preparing financial statements. Prudence does not, however, justify the creation of secret or hidden reserves.

(b) *Substance Over Form:* Transactions and other events should be accounted for and presented in accordance with their substance and financial reality and not merely with their legal form.

(c) *Materiality:* Financial statements should disclose all items which are material enough to affect evaluations or decisions.

Accounting policies should normally be disclosed in one place. A change in accounting policy that has a material effect in the current period or may have a material effect in the subsequent periods should be disclosed together with the reasons.

(Indian) Accounting Standards

The Accounting Standard Board (ASB) was established on 21st April, 1977 by the Institute of Chartered Accountants of India in order to :

(i) formulate accounting standards relating to applicable laws, customs, usages, business environment and IASC's standards.

(ii) persuade the related parties to follow the ASB's standard while preparing and presenting their financial statements.

The Institute of Chartered Accountants of India and the Institute of Cost and Work Accountant of India are both members of the International Accounting Standards Committee. They support the standards of the IASC by giving due consideration. The main function of Accounting Standards Board is to develop accounting standards in the light of the conditions and practices prevailing in India. So far (*i.e.*, as on July 1, 2002) the institute has issued the following 28 Accounting Standards :

AS-1. Disclosure of accounting policies

AS-2. Valuation of inventories

AS-3. Changes in financial position

AS-4. Contingencies and events occurring after the Balance Sheet date

AS-5. Prior period and extraordinary items

AS-6. Depreciation accounting

AS-7. Accounting for construction contracts

AS-8. Accounting for research and development

AS-9. Revenue recognition

AS-10. Accounting for fixed assets

AS-11. Accounting for the effects of changes in foreign exchange rates

AS-12. Accounting for government grants

AS-13. Accounting for investments

As-14. Accounting for amalgamations

AS-15. Accounting for retirement benefits in the financial statements of employers.

AS-16. Borrowing costs

AS-17. Segment reporting

AS-18. Related party disclosures

AS-19. "Leases"

AS-20. Earnings per share

AS-21. Consolidated financial statements

AS-22. Accounting for taxes on income

AS-23. Accounting for investments in associates in consolidated financial statements.

AS-24. Discontinuing operations

AS-25. Interim financial reporting

AS-26. Intangible assets

AS-27. Financial reporting of interests in Joint Ventures

AS-28. Impairment of assets.

Note. For brief information with regard to above AS, please refer Index II, given at the end of this book.

In this chapter, only 'AS-1. Disclosure of Accounting Policies' has been discussed for the purpose of study. The remaining ASs will be discussed in the concerned subsequent chapters if syllabus permits.

AS-1. Disclosures of Accounting Policies

This statement is issued in Nov., 1979. It deals with the disclosure of accounting policies, which includes disclosure of fundamental accounting assumptions and policies, followed in the preparation and presentation of financial statements.

Fundamental Accounting Assumptions : Fundamental accounting assumptions include going concern, consistency and accrual (they have already been explained earlier). If the fundamental accounting assumptions are followed in the statements, specific disclosure is not required; because their acceptance and use are assumed. Similarly, if the fundamental accounting assumptions are not followed, the fact should be disclosed.

Accounting Policies : They refer to the specific accounting principles and methods followed in the preparation and presentation of financial statements. There is no single list of accounting policies which is applicable to all the circumstances. In the absence of an accepted list of policies, diverse accounting policies are adopted by the business concerns. The areas in which diverse policies are adopted by different business concerns are : methods of depreciation, depletion and amortisation; treatment of expenditure during the construction; conversion or translation of foreign currency items; valuation of inventories; treatment of goodwill; valuation of investments; treatment of retirement benefits; recognition of profit on long term contracts; valuation of fixed assets; treatment of contingent liabilities etc. Since the accounting policies are not at present regularly and fully disclosed, the purpose of statement is to promote better understanding of financial statements by establishing the accounting standards. Such standards facilitate meaningful comparison of financial statements of different enterprises.

The primary consideration governing the selection of accounting policies by an enterprise is that the financial statements prepared and presented on the basis of such accounting policies should represent a true and fair view of the state of affairs of the enterprise. For this purpose, the major considerations governing the selection and application of accounting policies are : prudence; substance over form and materiality (they have already been explained earlier).

In the case of a change in accounting policies which has a material effect in the current period, the amount by which any item in the financial statements is affected by such change should be disclosed to the extent ascertainable.

When we compare the fundamental accounting assumptions with that of accounting policies, we find some differences in between them. They are :

(i) Fundamental accounting assumptions are assumed to be accepted and used in preparing the financial statements, but no such assumptions are to be made with regard to accounting policies.

(ii) The management has no discretion in adopting the fundamental accounting assumptions. Fundamental accounting assumptions have to be followed by the management. But, in case of accounting policies, the management has discretion in selecting and applying such policies which are best suited to the enterprise.

Systems of Accounting

There are three methods, bases or systems of accounting by which profit or income is measured by an accountant. They are :

1. Cash system or basis
2. Mercantile or accrual basis or system
3. Mixed or hybrid basis or system.

1. *Cash Basis of Accounting*

It is a system in which accounting entries for recording the business transactions are made only when cash is actually received or paid for those transactions. It means, only cash transactions are recorded in this system, but credit transactions are not recorded. Under this system, incomes are supposed to be earned only when they are actually received and expenses are deemed to be incurred only when they are actually paid. All adjustments such as, outstanding and pre-paid expenses, accrued income or income received in advance are not considered under this system. As the items of cash received and cash paid are recorded in this system, it is called as cash system of accounting. Under this system, the difference between the total income received in cash and the total expenditure incurred in cash, will be treated as the profit or loss of a business for a particular accounting period. Government system of accounting is mostly on the basis of cash system. Professional people like lawyers, auditors, engineers, brokers, small traders etc., maintain accounts under this system.

Advantages and Disadvantages

It is very simple method of recording the business transactions since it does not consider the adjusting entries. This method is useful for the individuals and small business concerns. But, it is not useful for the big concerns where there are numerous transactions. This system fails to express profit or loss accurately since it does not consider the necessary adjustments at the closing date.

2. *Mercantile or Accrual Basis of Accounting*

Under this system, all the transactions relating to the period are recorded irrespective of the fact whether the income is received or not or expenditure is incurred or not. In other words, both cash transactions and credit transactions are recorded in the books of accounts. As such the difference between the total incomes earned and the total expenses incurred will be treated as the profit or loss of a business for a particular accounting period. All adjustments *viz.*, outstanding and prepaid expenses, accrued income or income received in advance etc., are considered for ascertaining the true result of a business. This system of accounting is followed by most of the individual and commercial firms.

Advantages

Under this system, correct result of the business operation can be ascertained since it considers the adjustment entries on the periodical account at the closing date. Therefore, the final accounts *viz.*, Profit and Loss Account and Balance Sheet, of the business exhibit a true and fair view of the state of affairs.

3. *Mixed or Hybrid Basis of Accounting*

Under this system, both cash and mercantile systems are followed. In other words, it is a mixer of cash system and mercantile system of accounting. Under this system, some records are maintained under cash system and other records are kept under mercantile system. Generally, incomes are recorded on cash basis whereas expenses are recorded on mercantile basis. This system of accounting is not widely used since it fails to measure the accurate income.

Another Way of Classification

There is another way of classifying the systems of book-keeping. Under this classification, systems of book-keeping are classified into two. They are :

1. Single-entry system of book-keeping
2. Double-entry system of book-keeping

1. *Single Entry System (Incomplete Records)*

It refers to any system of book-keeping where a complete record of each and every transaction is not kept. It means two aspects of each and every transaction are not recorded. In other words, under this system, both aspects of some transactions are not at all recorded, both aspects of some transactions are recorded and only one aspect of most of the transactions is recorded. Since only one aspect of most of the transactions is recorded under this system, it is called 'Single Entry System'. No hard and fast rules are followed for recording the business transactions under this method. For few transactions such as, stock destroyed by fire, depreciation etc., none of the aspects is recorded; for some transactions such as personal accounts of debtors and creditors and cash account, both the aspects are recorded and for most of the transactions such as expenses, incomes, credit purchases, credit sales etc., only one aspect *i.e.*, cash, customers, suppliers etc., account is recorded under this system. There is no uniform method and specific rule for maintaining the records of a business transactions in the single entry system. According to *Eric Kohler* "It is a personal; it is always an incomplete double entry, varying with circumstances."

Because, every businessman follows a way in which it is most convenient to him. This system is followed by only sole-trading concerns and partnership firms.

Advantages

(i) It is more useful for small traders whose turnover is limited.

(ii) It is very simple and easy method of recording the business transactions of a concern.

(iii) It is more economical because, only a few books are maintained for recording the business transactions.

(iv) It is less costly as compared with the double-entry system of book-keeping, because it does not require the qualified staff for applying the rules of double-entry.

Disadvantages

(i) Since the accounts are incomplete, errors and frauds are common and it is difficult to detect and prevent those errors and frauds.

(ii) Since all the nominal accounts are not available, the correct trading results cannot be ascertained.

(iii) In the absence of all the real accounts, balance sheet cannot be prepared. Hence, it is not possible to ascertain the true financial position of the business.

(iv) In the absence of both the aspects of every transaction, the trial balance is not prepared. Hence, arithmetical accuracy of the books cannot be checked.

(v) It is unsystematic, inaccurate and unscientific method of recording the business transactions.

2. *Double Entry System*

It is most common system of book-keeping in which two aspects of every transactions—the giving aspect and the receiving aspect— are recorded in two different accounts for equal value in the opposite directions. Under this system, for every transaction, two entries are required to be made simultaneously in two different accounts for equal value, in the opposite direction and in each party's book. This is most scientific, complete and accurate system of accounting.

Advantages

(i) It provides complete record of all the transactions of a business because both the aspects of each transaction are recorded.

(ii) Arithmetical accuracy of accounting records can be verified easily by preparing the trial balance.

(iii) Correct trading results can be ascertained by preparing the final accounts of a concern.

(iv) True financial position of a business can be ascertained by preparing the balance sheet (*i.e.*, a statement of assets, liabilities and owner's capital).

(v) It helps the businessmen to judge the progress of the business and to correct the wrong way of its working by comparing the position of current year with those of previous years.

(vi) It helps to find out the amount due by the businessman to others and due by the others to the businessman.

(vii) It helps to defect the frauds and errors easily. Then, it will be easy to take to prevent them in future.

(viii) It helps to satisfy the sales tax and income tax authorities about the accuracy of books of accounts.

(ix) It affords all the information which the businessman ordinarily likes to have.

Disadvantages

(i) Under this system, the number of books of accounts are more. Hence, the maintenance of more books of accounts will be costly.

(ii) Under this system, books of accounts will not disclose certain type of errors such as, the compensating errors, omission to make the entry in the subsidiary books etc.

Relationship of Accountancy with Other Disciplines

Accountancy is closely related with the disciplines such as economics, statistics, law, engineering etc. Therefore, the accountant must have the knowledge about these disciplines for effective performance in his duties. The relationship between accounting and other disciplines is discussed as below :

1. Accounting and Economics : The objective of economics is to maximise the wealth of the nation by efficient use of scarce resources. This is also the objective of business organisation; it maximises the wealth of its owners. Hence, accounting and economics have a similarity in optimum utilisation of resources of the concern or nation. Most of the accounting data in terms of money are used by the economist in rational decision making. Similarly, most of the statistical data, which are provided by the economics are used by the accountants in their decision making. Therefore, economist and accountant should know each other's subject. An accountant will understand his own subject better if he knows different economic concepts like cost, value, production cost etc. Similarly, an economist will perform his duties better if he is aware of accounting concepts and conventions. Therefore, one can say that economics and accountancy are closely related with each other.

2. Accounting and Statistics : Statistics is mostly concerned with numerical data and statistical techniques which are used in collecting, classifying, analysing and interpreting the data. In managerial decision making such data are used. The accountant and statisticians perform certain common functions such as, collection of data, tabulation of data, analysis of data and presentation of data. For this purpose they are using diagrams and charts (*viz.* pie chart, bar chart etc.). But, only the difference is that the accountant is interested in data which are expressed in terms of money, whereas statistician is interested in unlimited data since his area is wide. Hence, accounting and statistics are very closely related to each other.

3. Accountancy and Law : Most of the accounting functions can be performed in accordance with the provisions of law. An accountant should possess the sufficient knowledge about the concerned Acts if he wants to maintain the books of accounts of the concerned firm or company. For instance, an accountant should have a sufficient knowledge about the Companies Act to maintain the books of accounts of the joint stock companies. Otherwise his accounting work will not be valid. Similarly, an accountant should know the commercial laws such as sales of goods, sale tax, income tax, partnership law etc., to tackle the problems in relation to those laws. On the contrary, lower or legal adviser should know the sufficient knowledge of accountancy because most of the disputes are related with the accounting transactions and tax-matters. Thus, accountancy and law are inter-related.

4. Accountancy and Engineering : To solve the problems of planning and production department of a concern, an accountant, especially a cost accountant and an engineer should work together. The figures and values, which are provided by an accountant, are used by an engineer for preparing the statement, designs etc. Therefore, an engineer should have a knowledge about the accountancy to perform his duties efficiently. Similarly, an accountant should also possess some knowledge of machineries and their effective working life etc., to perform his duties properly. Hence, there must be a harmony and co-operation between the accountant and engineer to improve the efficiency of the concern. In this way, accounting and engineering are related to each other.

Role of an Accountant

An accountant is an officer of the business organisation who is entrusted for accounting work in the organisation. He is responsible for maintaining and developing the accounting system of the organisation. No doubt, his primary function is to prepare the financial statements, analyse, interpret and audit such statements. At present, he also performs other functions relating to taxation laws, corporated legislations and general problems of the management and the society. Therefore, his area of functions is now vast. He plays an important role as below :

1. Role in the business organisation
2. Role in the society

1. *Role of an Accountant in the Business Organisation*

The services rendered by an accountant to the business organisation in particular, and to the society, in general, are summarised as below :

(i) *Maintaining Books of Accounts* : The primary function of an accountant is to maintain a systematic record of all the transactions of a business. It helps the organisation :

— in ascertaining profit or loss of a business

— in finding out the financial position of a business

— in providing adequate information to the management to plan, control and co-ordinate the activities

— in evaluating the performance of a business

— to provide information to the tax authorities

— in providing the evidences in the court of law

— to fetch a proper price in the event of sale of a business.

(ii) *Auditing of Accounts :* The work of auditing is also performed by an accountant. Auditing is process of verifying the books of accounts to determine the accuracy and reliability of financial statements. Auditor (*i.e.* an accountant who is appointed for audit work) detects any fraud committed by any corner of the accounts. He helps the management to improve the operational efficiency of a business.

(iii) *Proper Tax Planning :* Accountant can also handle tax matters of a business. He assists his management in reducing the tax burden and making proper tax planning. He can settle the tax liabilities of a business with the tax planning. He can settle the tax liabilities of a business with the tax authorities and express his views on tax policies.

(iv) *Financial Services :* Since an accountant has a knowledge of legal, accounting, taxation etc., he can render valuable assistance to the management in respect of financial matters. He can assist the management with regard to investments in different ways; so that the management can earn a maximum return. He can also advise the directors on problems in respect of issue of shares, allotment of shares and also borrowing of money if so needed.

(v) *Management Consultancy Services :* These days accountant can also perform management consultancy services. Such services include proper requirement of working capital and its efficient use; improve productivity, inventory control, credit control, cash management, source and application of funds; corporate planning, computer applications for accounting activities, selection executives, solving the business problems, selection of personnel, placement, training etc.

2. *Role of an Accountant in the Society*

Now-a-days, an accountant has to perform following functions to the society in general in addition to what he does to the owners :

(i) He should supply the accounting information to the investors, creditors, tax authorities etc., who are interested in the accounting information.

(ii) He should design and develop the new accounting procedures/systems/methods for the various sections of the society.

(iii) He must educate the various sections of the society in respect of importance of maintaining proper books of accounts.

(iv) He must advise the people about the various ways of investment in different companies; so that the invester can earn a maximum return.

(v) He can advise the public about the tax planning, tax rates, a ways of reducing the tax etc.

(vi) He can also act as arbitrator to settle the accounting disputes between the parties.

(vii) He can give the legal advise to the promoters for the establishment and registration of companies, partnership firm, sole trading concern etc.

EXAMINATION QUESTIONS

(A) Answer the following questions in one or two sentences each :

(*Each Carrying Two Marks*)

1. Define the term accounting.
2. Give the meaning of accounting.
3. Define the accounting principles.
4. What are concepts?
5. What money measurement concept signifies?
6. What is dual aspect concept?
7. What are accounting conventions?
8. What is materiality?
9. What are accounting standards?
10. Define accounting standards.
11. What is the need of accounting standards?
12. What do you mean by accounting assumptions?
13. What are the accounting policies?
14. Give the meaning of accrual.
15. How many IAS and AS are issued so far?
16. What is the necessity of issuing accounting standards?

    (*B.Com., Hons., Delhi, 1989*)
17. What is the aim of the Accounting Standard Board (ASB)?
18. Give the meaning of cash system of accounting.
19. What is the mercantile system of accounting?
20. Define single entry system.
21. What is double entry system of accounting?
22. Who is an accountant?

(B) Answer the following questions :

(*Each Carrying Eight Marks*)

1. What is accounting? Distinguish between book-keeping and accounting.
2. Distinguish between accounting and accountancy.
3. What are the branches of accounting? Explain.
4. Who are the users of accounting information?

5. Explain the dual aspect concept.
6. Explain the accounting conventions.
7. What are the accounting standards? Give the reasons to establish such standards.
8. Explain IAS-1. Disclosure of Accounting Policies.
9. What is the main function of Accounting Standard Board (ASB)? Distinguish between fundamental accounting assumptions and accounting policies.
10. What are the systems of accounting? Explain.
11. Give the advantages and disadvantages of double entry system of book-keeping.
12. Explain the relationship of accountancy with economics and statistics.

(C) Answer the following questions :

(Each Carrying 16 Marks)

1. What do you understand by accounting concepts? What are they?
2. What are the accounting concepts and conventions? Name them and explain *any two* accounting concepts in detail.

   (B.Com., Delhi, 1991)
3. Explain *any three* of the following accounting concepts :
   (a) Money measurement concept.
   (b) Business entity concept.
   (c) Going concern concept.
   (d) Realisation concept.
   (e) Cost concept. *(B.Com., Hons., Delhi, 1981)*
4. Briefly explain IAS-1 and AS-1. Disclosure of Accounting Policies.
5. What are accounting standards? Name the various accounting standards issued so far by the IASC and ASB.
6. Briefly explain the various systems of accounting.
7. According to the principles of 'Double Entry System; every debit has a corresponding credit'. Explain clearly. Discuss the merits of double entry system also.

   (B.Com., Raj., 1981)
8. Explain the relationship of accountancy with other disciplines.
9. Explain the role of an accountant in the society.

2

SINGLE-ENTRY SYSTEM
(Accounts of Incomplete Records)
(Including Conversion)

Meaning

Single entry system refers to any system of book-keeping where the complete records of each and every transaction are not kept in a systematic manner. Under the single entry system both the aspects of every transaction are not recorded in the books of accounts. Only a single aspect of every transaction is recorded in the books of accounts. Since only one aspect of every transaction is recorded under this system, it is called single entry system. There is no uniform method and specific rule for maintaining the records of the business transactions in the single entry system, because every businessman follows a way in which it is most convenient to him. Therefore, it is called unsystematic, inaccurate and unscientific method of account keeping. The most common method of single-entry system is to maintain the personal accounts of the debtors and creditors and cash account. Real and Nominal Accounts such as, accounts of assets, expenses and incomes are rather completely ignored in the ledger. Thus in the absence of impersonal accounts, the Profit and Loss Account and Balance Sheet cannot be prepared.

Definition

The *Dictionary for Accountants* by Eric Kohler defines the single-entry system as "A system of book-keeping in which as a rule only records of cash and of personal accounts are maintained; it is always incomplete double entry, varying with circumstances."

Important Features of Single-entry System

Following are the important features of single entry system :

(1) It is the reverse of double-entry system.

(2) It is followed by only small concerns such as, sole-trader, partnership organisation etc., which have very few transactions. Joint Stock Companies cannot maintain the books of account under this system because of legal requirements.

(3) It does not provide complete picture of each and every transaction. Hence, it is called 'Defective Double-entry System'.

(4) The most common method of this system is to keep personal accounts and cash accounts only.

(5) Maintenance of real and nominal accounts are completely ignored in the ledger.

(6) Preparation of Trial Balance, Profit and Loss Account and Balance Sheet cannot be possible under this system.

(7) Usually one cash book is maintained which records the personal as well as business transactions of the business.

(8) There is no uniformity in the maintenance of accounts of the business concerns.

Books of Accounts Maintained under Single-entry System

There is no uniform method of maintaining the books of accounts under this method. It depends upon the needs of a particular trader.

(1) Ledger : Some traders are maintaining only a ledger. But they are not maintaining any subsidiary book. The ledger containing only the personal accounts of debtors and creditors. The personal accounts of debtors are maintained for ascertaining the amount due from the various debtors. The personal accounts of creditors are kept for the purpose of ascertaining the amount due to the various creditors.

(2) Ledger and Cash Book : Most of the traders maintain a ledger and only one subsidiary book namely cash book. The cash book is kept for ascertaining the cash in hand and at bank.

(3) Ledger, Cash Book and Some Other Subsidiary Books : A few traders maintain a ledger and more than one Subsidiary book namely purchases book, sales book, purchases returns book, sales returns book, bills receivable book and bills payable book. After making the entries in the subsidiary books, the postings are made only to the personal accounts of debtors and creditors. But other personal accounts, real account and nominal accounts are not maintained under this system.

Types of Single-entry System

The main types of single-entry system are :

1. Pure Single-entry Method : Under this method only the personal accounts of debtors and creditors are maintained. But it does not provide the other information such as, purchases, sales, cash balance, bank balance etc.

2. Simple Single-entry Method : Only the personal and cash accounts are maintained in this method, but other subsidiary books, except cash book, are not maintained.

3. Quasi Single-entry Method : It is a method under which the personal accounts, cash accounts and some subsidiary books are maintained. The main subsidiary books are purchases book, sales book, purchases returns book, sales returns book, bills book and cash book.

Advantages of Single-entry System

Following are the main advantages of Single-entry system :

1. It is more useful for small traders whose turnover is limited.
2. It is very simple and easy method of recording the business transactions of a concern.
3. It is more economical, because only a few books are maintained for recording the transactions.
4. It is less costly as compared with the double-entry system of book keeping. Because it does not require the qualified staff for applying the rules of double-entry.

Disadvantages of Single-entry System

Single-entry system suffers from various limitations, in spite of certain advantages available from it. They are given as below :

1. It is not possible to obtain accurate information regarding the result of the business operation. Because nominal accounts relating to expenses, losses, incomes and gains are not recorded in the ledger.
2. Two-fold aspects *i.e.*, debit and credit of every transaction are not recorded. Only single aspect either debit or credit is recorded. Hence, it is called incomplete system of book-keeping.
3. In the absence of proper checks and controls, frauds are easily committed.
4. As the goods accounts are not maintained, it is not possible to prepare the Trading Account and ascertain the gross profit or gross loss of the business.
5. As the nominal accounts are not maintained, it is not possible to prepare the P & L A/c and ascertain the net profit or net loss of the business.
6. In the absence of real accounts, Balance Sheet cannot be prepared. Hence, it is not possible to ascertain the true financial position of the business.
7. In the absence of both the aspects of every transaction, trial balance cannot be prepared. Hence, arithmetical accuracy of the books cannot be checked.
8. It will be difficult to assess the value of the goodwill at the time of selling of the existing business.

9. It will be difficult to convince the tax authorities at the time of assessment of profit or loss made by the business.
10. It cannot be adopted by the joint stock companies because of legal requirements.

Distinction between Single-entry System and Double-entry System

Single-entry System	Double-entry System
1. Only single aspect of every transaction is recorded in this system.	1. Both the aspects of every transaction are recorded in this system.
2. Only personal accounts of creditors and debtors and cash accounts are maintained in this system.	2. All kinds of accounts such as, personal, real and nominal accounts are maintained in this system.
3. It is incomplete, unsatisfactory and unscientific system of book-keeping.	3. It is complete, satisfactory and scientific system of book-keeping.
4. Trial balance cannot be prepared under this system, because both the aspects of every transaction are not recorded in the ledger.	4. Trial balance can be prepared under this system, because both the aspects of every transaction are recorded in the ledger.
5. There is much scope for frauds or misappropriations under this system, because arithmetical accuracy of the books of accounts cannot be checked by preparing the trial balance.	5. There is no scope for frauds or misappropriations under this system, because arithmetical accuracy of the books of accounts can be checked by preparing the trial balance.
6. As the goods accounts are not maintained, Trading Account cannot be prepared under this system.	6. As the goods accounts are maintained, Trading Account can be prepared under this system.
7. In the absence of Trading Account, gross profit or gross loss cannot be ascertained.	7. In the existence of Trading Account, gross profit or gross loss can be ascertained.
8. As the nominal accounts are not maintained, profit and loss account cannot be prepared.	8. As the nominal accounts are maintained, profit and loss account can be prepared.
9. In the absence of P & L Account, net profit or loss of the business cannot be ascertained.	9. In the existence of P & L Account, net profit or loss of the business can be ascertained.

Single-entry System	Double-entry System
10. In the absence of real accounts under this system, it is not possible to prepare the Balance Sheet and ascertain the true financial position of the business.	10. Under this system real accounts are maintained, hence, it is possible to prepare the Balance Sheet and ascertain the true financial position of the business.
11. It is less costly, because there is no need of maintaining the large number of books of accounts.	11. It is costly, because there is a need of maintaining the large number of books of accounts.
12. It is followed only by small concerns such as, sole traders, partnership firms etc.	12. It is followed by big concerns such as, Joint Stock Companies.

Ascertainment of Profit or Loss under Single-entry System

In the absence of nominal accounts in the ledger of single-entry system, it is not possible to prepare a regular trading and profit and loss account and ascertain exact profit or loss for a particular period of the business. However, the estimated (rough) profit or loss of the business concern can be prepared by one of the following methods :

I. Statement of Affairs Method and

II. Conversion Method.

Let us discuss each of these two methods in detail.

I. Statement of Affairs Method

Statement of affairs means a document or statement in the form of a balance sheet showing the various assets on the right hand side and outside liabilities on the left hand side. The difference between total assets and total outside liabilities represents capital introduced by the proprietor.

Opening capital and closing capital can be ascertained by preparing the statement of affairs. The statement of affairs can be prepared from the facts available in the books of accounts and information provided by the owner. The following items are to be taken up while preparing the statement of affairs :

1. Cash in hand from the Cash Book.
2. Cash at bank from the Pass Book.
3. Sundry Debtors and Creditors from the personal accounts of Debtors and Creditors.
4. Stock in trade by actual stock counting.
5. Real Accounts by physical valuation.
6. Outstanding incomes, outstanding expenses, prepaid expenses and incomes received in advance from memory.

The assets and liabilities are arranged in the statement of affairs in the same manner as those of a Balance Sheet. The excess of assets over liabilities represents capital and excess of liabilities over assets represents deficiency.

Proforma of Statement of Affairs

Statement of Affairs as on ....

Liabilities	Rs.	Assets	Rs.
All Liabilities	xxx	All Assets	xxx
Capital (Balancing Figure)	xxx		
	xxx		xxx

Distinction between Statement of Affairs and Balance Sheet

Statement of Affairs	Balance Sheet
1. It is prepared under the Single-entry System.	1. It is prepared under the Double-entry System.
2. It does not show the true and correct financial position of the concerns.	2. It show the true and correct financial position of the concerns.
3. Usually, it is prepared by the small concerns which have very few transactions.	3. Usually, it is prepared by the big concerns which have big transactions.
4. Value of the assets and liabilities appeared in the statement of affairs are drawn partly from the ledger accounts, partly by physical inspection and partly from the memory.	4. Values of the assets and liabilities appeared in the balance sheet are drawn from ledger accounts.

Ascertainment of Profit or Loss

After preparing the two statement of affairs one at the beginning of the period which represents the capital at the beginning of the period and another at the end of the period which represents the capital at the end of the period. The profit or loss is ascertained by comparing the capital at the beginning of the period with that at the end.

The following procedures can be adopted to ascertain the profit or loss made during the period :

1. Take up the closing capital as a starting point.
2. Add the amount withdrawn, during the period either by way of goods or cash, to the closing capital.

3. Deduct the amount of capital introduced during the period from the closing capital.
4. Deduct capital at the beginning of the period from the adjusted closing capital. The difference will be either gross profit or gross loss. If the adjusted closing capital is more than the capital at the beginning, the difference represents gross profit. On the other hand, if the reverse is the case, the difference represents gross loss.
5. Incomes such as, discount received, interest on drawings, reserve for discount on creditors, prepaid expenses, outstanding incomes etc. should be added to the gross profit. If there is gross loss, then these incomes should be deducted from the gross loss.
6. Expenses such as, proprietor's salary, interest on capital, incomes received in advance, bad debts, discount allowed, depreciation, reserve for discount on debtors, outstanding expenses etc., should be deducted from the gross profit. If there is gross loss, then these expenses should be added to the gross loss.

The difference represents either net profits or net losses of the concern.

Proforma of Statement of Profit or Loss

Statement of Profit or Loss for the year ended ....

	Rs.
Capital at the end of the year	xxx
Add : Drawings during the year	xxx
	xxx
Less : Capital introduced during the year	xxx
Adjusted Closing Capital	xxx
Less : Capital at the beginning of the year	xxx
Balance being Gross Profit or Loss	xxx
Add or *Less* : Adjustments	xxx
Net Profit or Net Loss	xxx

Alternative Method

Statement of Profit of Loss for the year ended ......

	Rs.		Rs.
To All liabilities at the end of the period	xxx	By All assets at the end of the period	xxx
To Closing Capital c/d (Balancing figure)	xxx		
	xxx		xxx

Contd.

Statement of Profit of Loss for the year ended ......(*Contd.*)

	Rs.		Rs.
To Additional capital introduced during the period	xxx	By Closing capital b/d	xxx
To Opening capital	xxx	By Drawing during the period	xxx
To Gross profit c/d	xxx	By Gross loss c/d	xxx
(If credit side is more)	xxx	(If debit side is more)	xxx
To Gross loss b/d	xxx	By Gross profit b/d	xxx
To All expenses	xxx	By All incomes	xxx
To Net profit	xxx	By Net loss	xxx
(If credit side is more)		(If debit side is more)	
Total	xxx	Total	xxx

The statement of profit or loss is prepared in the same manner as profit and loss account. But it is not a profit and loss account. It differs from the profit and loss account in some aspects :

1. A statement of profit or loss does not provide detail information regarding the sources of profits and losses. Hence, it is not possible to ascertain the accurate profit or loss of the concerns. On the other hand, profit and loss account provides the detail information regarding the sources of profits or losses. Hence, it is possible to ascertain the accurate profit or loss of the concern.
2. Closing capitals and opening capitals are to be considered while ascertaining the profits or losses by the statement of profit or loss. But in the case of profit and loss account purchases, sales, returns, and all incomes and expenses are to be considered while ascertaining the profits or losses.
3. Statement of profit or loss is prepared under the single-entry system. On the other hand, profit and loss account is prepared under the double-entry system of book-keeping.
4. Statement of profit or loss is prepared partly from the ledger accounts balances and partly from the memory. But the profit or loss account is prepared from the ledger accounts balances.

Illustration 1

Ishwar started a business on 1st Jan., 1990, with a capital of Rs. 60,000; Rs. 50,000 brought in cash and the balance in the form the machinery. On 1st Sept., 1990, he introduced Rs. 12,000 in the business of which Rs. 7,000 was borrowed from his wife. During the year, he withdrew at the rate of Rs. 1,000 per month.

His position on 31st Dec. 1990 was as follow :

Assets :

Stock in trade	Rs. 40,000	Machinery	Rs. 10,000
Motor-van	Rs. 25,000	Tools	Rs. 5,000
Debtors	Rs. 6,000	Cash in hand	Rs. 500
Cash at Bank	Rs. 2,000		

Liabilities : He owed to creditors Rs. 15,000 and loan to his wife Rs. 3,000.

Prepare a statement showing Ishwar's profit for the year after writing off depreciation at 10% on Machinery, 8% on Motor-van, 5% on Tools and providing a reserve of 5% on Debtors for Bad Debts.

Solution :

Ishwar

Statement of Affairs as at 31st Dec., 1990

(To find out closing stock)

Liabilities	Rs.	Assets	Rs.
Creditors	15,000	Stock in trade	40,000
Loan from wife	3,000	Machinery	10,000
Capital	70,500	Tools	5,000
(Balancing figure)		Motor-van	25,000
		Debtors	6,000
		Cash in hand	500
		Cash at Bank	2,000
	88,500		88,500

Ishwar

Statement of Profit or Loss for the year ended 31-12-1990

		Rs.
Closing capital (31-12-1990)		70,500
Add : Drawings during the year (1,000 × 12)		12,000
		82,500
Less : Additional capital introduced during the year (12,000 – 7,000)		5,000
Adjusted closing capital		77,500
Less : Opening capital (1-1-1990)		60,000
Gross profit		17,500
Less : Reserve for Bad Debts (5% on Closing Debtors)	Rs. 300	
Depreciation :		
Machinery at 10%	Rs. 1,000	
Motor-van at 8%	Rs. 2,000	
Tools at 5%	Rs. 250	3,550
Net profit for the year		13,950

Notes :

(i) Loan taken from his wife is not an additional capital.

(ii) Opening Capital of Rs. 60,000 includes Rs. 50,000 cash and Rs. 10,000 Machinery.

(iii) His drawings during the year amounted to Rs. 12,000.

Illustration 2

Mr. Prabhu keeps his books by single-entry system. His position was as under :

Statement of Affairs as on 31-12-1989

Liabilities	Rs.	Assets	Rs.
Creditors	4,000	Cash in Hand	1,000
Bank Overdraft	2,000	Cash at Bank	2,500
Bills Payable	500	Debtors	10,000
Capital	17,000	Stock	7,000
		Furniture	1,000
		Machinery	2,000
	23,500		23,500

As a result of operations during the year ended 31st December, 1990 :

(i) His Cash in Hand decreased to Rs. 900

(ii) His Cash at Bank increased to Rs. 3,100

(iii) Debtors had increased by Rs. 1,000

(iv) Stocks had decreased by Rs. 3,000

(v) Furniture has decreased by Rs. 600

(vi) Machinery stood at Rs. 1,600

(vii) Creditors and Bank Overdraft appeared at the same figure as at 31st Dec., 1990.

(viii) There were no Bills Payable outstanding

During the year, Mr. Prabhu regularly transferred Rs. 1,200 monthly from his business to his private account. He used foodgrains worth Rs. 6,000 out of business stock for his family purpose. On 1-7-1990, he sold a private scooter for Rs. 6,000 and introduced the proceeds of the same into the business. Provide office rent of Rs. 300 and salary of clerk Rs. 800 for Dec. 1990 was due but not paid. Allow interest on capital at 10%. Debtors include Rs. 500 from a customer who is insolvent and is irrecoverable.

Calculate Mr. Prabhu's Profit or Loss for the year ended 31st Dec., 1990.

Solution :

Mr. Prabhu

Statement of Affairs as on 31-12-1990

(To find out closing capital)

Liabilities	Rs.	Assets	Rs.
Creditors	4,000	Cash in Hand	900
Bank Overdraft	2,000	Cash at Bank	3,100
Capital	15,000	Debtors	11,000
(Balancing figure)		Stock	4,000
		Furniture	400
		Machinery	1,600
	21,000		21,000

Mr. Prabhu

Statement of Profit or Loss for the year ended 31st Dec., 1990

	Rs.	Rs.
Capital as on 31st Dec., 1990		15,000
Add : Drawings : In Cash	14,400	
In goods	6,000	20,400
		35,400
Less : Additional capital introduced		6,000
Adjusted capital as on 31-12-1990		29,400
Less : Opening capital (31-12-1989)		17,000
Profit before adjustments		12,400
Less : Outstanding expenses : Rent	300	
Salary	800	
Interest	1,850	
(10% on Rs. 17,000 and 10% on Rs. 6,000 for six months)		
Bad debts	500	3,450
Net Profit		8,950

Illustration 3

A retail trader does not keep double entry records. His business balance sheet on 1st Jan., 1989 was as follows :

Balance Sheet

Liabilities	Rs.	Assets	Rs.
Creditors	2,100	Cash in hand	450
Bills payable	2,100	Cash at Bank	1,000
Capital	12,500	Debtors	4,000
		Stock	2,200
		Furniture	500
		Machinery	8,000
		Bills receivable	550
	16,700		16,700

His position as at the end of the year 1989 was : Cash in hand Rs. 550; Cash at Bank Rs. 1000; Debtors Rs. 5,000; Stock Rs. 2,000; Bills receivable Rs. 550; Outstanding rent Rs. 200; Creditors Rs. 3,000; Bills payable Rs. 750.

He had withdrawn during the year Rs. 2,100 for his personal use.

Depreciate furniture and machinery at the rate of 10%. Write off bad debts Rs. 250.

Find out the profit or loss made by the trader and prepare the final Statement of Affairs as on 31st Dec., 1989 after charging interest on capital at 6%.

Solution :

Statement of Affairs as at 31st Dec., 1989
(To find out closing capital)

Liabilities	Rs.	Assets	Rs.
Creditors	3,000	Cash in Hand	550
Bills payable	750	Cash at Bank	1,000
Outstanding rent	200	Debtors	5,000
Capital	13,650	Stock	2,000
(Balancing figure)		Bills Receivable	550
		*Furniture	500
		*Machinery	8,000
	17,600		17,600

* In this problem closing position of furniture and machinery are not given. Hence, the opening position of furniture and machinery are considered as the closing position of furniture and machinery, because, as furniture and machinery are fixed assets meant for the use of the business, we have to assume that they are in the business even on the closing date.

Statement of Profit or Loss for the year ended 31st Dec., 1989

	Rs.	Rs.
Capital as at 31st Dec., 1989		13,650
Add : Drawings during the year		2,100
Adjusted capital as at 31st Dec., 1989		15,750
Less : Capital as at 1st Jan., 1989		12,500
Gross profit		3,250
Less : Depreciation on —		
Furniture at 10%	50	
Machinery at 10%	800	
Interest on capital at 6%	750	
Reserve for bad debts	250	1,850
Net profit		1,400

Final Statement of Affairs as on 31st Dec., 1989

Liabilities	Rs.	Rs.	Assets	Rs.	Rs.
Capital :			Cash in Hand		550
Opening Capital	12,500		Cash at Bank		1,000
Add : Net Profit	1,400		Debtors	5,000	
	13,900		*Less* : R.B.D.	250	4,750
Less : Drawings	2,100	11,800	Stock		2,000
Creditors		3,000	Bills Receivable		550
Bills Payable		750	Furniture	500	
Outstanding Rent		200	*Less* : Depreciation	50	450
Outstanding Interest		750	Machinery	8,000	
			Less : Depreciation	800	7,200
		16,500			16,500

Illustration 4

Anand, a trader kept his books under single-entry system. The position of his business at 31st Dec., 1989 was as follows :

Cash at Bank Rs. 13,600; Cash in Hand Rs. 1,100; Stock-in-trade Rs. 19,000; Sundry Debtors Rs. 10,000; Sundry Creditors Rs. 17,400; Furniture and Fixtures Rs. 1,200; Plant and Machinery Rs. 36,000; Land and Buildings Rs. 20,000.

Anand transferred Rs. 600 per month from his business 'Banking Account' to his private 'Banking Account', by way of drawings and has taken

Rs. 400 worth of stock for private use. He introduced Rs. 6,000 as new capital. He paid Rs. 5,000 representing proceeds of realisation of his private property in the business. He has agreed that his plant and machinery should be depreciated by Rs. 3,600; furniture by Rs. 60 and that a provision for doubtful debts be made at 5% on debtors.

His capital on 31st Dec., 1977 was Rs. 51,500. Prepare a Statement of Affairs showing his position at 31st Dec., 1978 and ascertain his profit or loss for the year.

(*CA Inter and Kar. Board, 1979*)

Solution :

Anand

Statement of Affairs as at 31st Dec, 1978

(To find out closing capital)

Liabilities	Rs.	Assets	Rs.
Creditors	17,400	Cash in Hand	1,100
Capital	83,500	Cash at Bank	13,600
(Excess of assets over liabilities)		Sundry Debtors	10,000
		Stock-in-trade	19,000
		Furniture & Fixtures	1,200
		Plant & Machinery	36,000
		Land & Buildings	20,000
	1,00,900		1,00,900

Statement of Profit or Loss for the year ended 31st Dec., 1978

	Rs.	Rs.
Capital as at 31st Dec., 1978		83,500
Add : Drawings during the period		7,600
(Rs. 600 p.m. for 12 months + Rs. 400 worth of stock)		91,100
Less : Additional capital introduced		6,000
		85,100
Less : Proceeds of realisation of private property		5,000
Adjusted capital as at 31st Dec., 1978		80,100
Less : Capital on 31st Dec., 1977		51,500
Gross profit		28,600
Less : Depreciation on :		
Plant and Machinery	3,600	
Furniture	60	
Reserve for doubtful debts	500	4,160
Net profit		24,440

Illustration 5

Shridar maintained his books of accounts under single-entry system, from which the following information is available :

	1-1-1990	31-12-1990
	Rs.	Rs.
Stock of goods	2,000	4,000
Office furniture	4,000	4,000
Bills receivable	5,000	7,000
Creditors	6,000	8,000
Machinery	10,000	10,000
Motor-van (30-6-1990)	Nil	20,000
Fixtures	3,000	5,000
Bank overdraft	2,500	3,500
Loan from his friend	3,000	Nil
Outstanding salary	Nil	700
Investments	18,000	20,000
Debtors	16,000	21,000
Cash in Hand	400	800
Cash at Bank	1,500	4,500

During the year 1990, he had withdrawn Rs. 4,000 for his personal use and Rs. 2,500 for brother's marriage. Out of the business funds he had also purchased a residential building amounted to Rs. 20,000 which is not shown in the above records. Depreciate fixtures by 10%, machinery by 8% and motor-van by 7%. Write off Rs. 500 from the value of furniture. As regards to Debtors, it is ascertained that Rs. 1,000 for bad and a reserve 5% for doubtful debts is to be created. A reserve of Rs. 800 in respect of bills receivable is to be made. He informs you that the interest on the amount borrowed from his friend was Rs. 200. He had forgotten to pay the rent of his shop amounting to Rs. 300. During the year, he had given a gift Rs. 5,000 to his daughter. He has invested Rs. 6,000 at par on 1-7-1990 12% debentures which is to be now treated as business asset. The interest on the same is still due.

Ascertain his profit during the year and prepare the revised statement of affairs.

Solution :

Shridar

Statement of Affairs as at 1st Jan., 1990

(To find out opening capital)

Liabilities	Rs.	Assets	Rs.
Creditors	6,000	Stock	2,000
Bank overdraft	2,500	Furniture	4,000
Loan of friend	3,000	Bills receivable	5,000
Outstanding salary	—	Machinery	10,000
Capital	48,400	Motor-van	—
(Balancing figure)		Fixtures	3,000
		Investments	18,000
		Debtors	16,000
		Cash in Hand	400
		Cash at Bank	1,500
	59,900		59,900

Statement of Affairs as at 31st Dec, 1990

(To find out closing capital)

Liabilities	Rs.	Assets	Rs.
Creditors	8,000	Stock	4,000
Bank overdraft	3,500	Furniture	4,000
Outstanding salary	700	Machinery	10,000
Capital	90,100	Motor-van	20,000
(Balancing figure)		Fixtures	5,000
		Investment	20,000
		Debtors	21,000
		Bills receivable	7,000
		Cash in Hand	800
		Cash at Bank	4,500
		12% Debentures	6,000
	1,02,300		1,02,300

Statement of Profit or Loss for the year ended 31st Dec., 1990

	Rs.	Rs.
Capital as at 31st Dec., 1990		90,100
Add : Drawings (4,000 + 3,500 + 20,000 + 5,000 gift to daughter)		32,500
		1,22,600
Less : Capital introduced (debentures)		6,000
		1,16,600
Less : Capital as on 1st Jan., 1990		48,400
Gross profit		68,200
Add : Interest on debenture (12% on 6,000 for six months)		360
		68,560
Less : Depreciation :		
Fixtures	500	
Furniture	500	
Machinery	800	
Motor-van (for six months)	700	
Bad debts	1,000	
Reserve for doubtful debts (on good debtors *i.e.*, Rs. 20,000)	1,000	
Reserve for bills receivable	800	
Interest on loan	200	
Outstanding rent	300	5,800
Net profit		62,760

Revised Statement of Affairs as at 31st Dec., 1990

Liabilities	Rs.	Rs.	Assets	Rs.	Rs.
Creditors		8,000	Stock		4,000
Bank Overdraft		3,500	Machinery	10,000	
Interest on Loan		200	*Less :* Depreciation	800	9,200
Outstanding Salary		700	Furniture	4000	
Outstanding Rent		300	*Less :* Depreciation	500	3,500
Capital :			Motor-van	20,000	
Opening capital	48,400		*Less* : Depreciation	700	19,300
Add : Additional Capital	6,000		Fixtures	5,000	
Add : Net Profit	62,760		*Less :* Depreciation	500	4,500
	1,17,160		Investments		20,000
Less : Drawings	32,500	84,660			

(*Contd.*)

Revised Statement of Affairs as at 31st Dec, 1990 (*Contd.*)

		12% Debentures	6,000	
		Add : Interest	360	6,360
		Bills Receivable	7,000	
		Less : Reserve	800	6,200
		Debtors	21,000	
		Less : Bad Debt	1,000	
			20,000	
		Less : R.D.D.	1,000	19,000
		Cash in Hand		800
		Cash at Bank		4,500
	97,360			97,360

Note : The debentures treated as business assets. It is also capital introduced during the year. It should be taken on the asset side of the closing statement of affairs as an unrecorded asset.

Illustration 6

Umesh, Mahesh and Prakash are equal partners in a business in which the books are kept by single-entry. Their position on 1st Jan., 1989 was as under :

	Rs.		Rs.
Sundry creditors	7,000	Cash in Hand	3,000
Bills payable	2,000	Cash at Bank	2,000
Umesh's capital	33,000	Debtors	16,000
Mahesh's capital	27,000	Stock	9,000
		Machinery	20,000
		Furniture	10,000
		Prakash's capital	9,000
	69,000		69,000

On 31st Dec., 1989 the following was the state of affairs :

Cash in Hand Rs. 1,300; Cash at Bank Rs. 2,000; Debtors Rs. 19,000; Stock Rs. 13,100; Creditors Rs. 8,000; Bills payable Rs. 1,600. The drawings of three partners were : Umesh Rs. 4,000; Mahesh Rs. 3,800; and Prakash Rs. 3,900. Interest at 10% should be allowed on the capitals as at the commencement of each year, and Interest of Rs. 1,200 should be charged upon Prakash's overdraft.

Find out the result of the business for the year ended 31st Dec., 1989.

Solution :

Statement of Affairs as at 31st Dec., 1989

(To find out closing capital)

Liabilities	Rs.	Assets	Rs.
Creditors	8,000	Cash in Hand	1,300
Bills payable	1,600	Cash at Bank	2,000
Capital	55,800	Debtors	19,000
(Balancing figure)		Stock	13,100
		Machinery	20,000
		Furniture	10,000
	65,400		65,400

Statement of Profit or Loss for the year ended 31st Dec., 1989

	Rs.	Rs.
Capital as at 31st Dec., 1989		55,800
Add : Drawings–		
Umesh	4,000	
Mahesh	3,800	
Prakash	3,900	11,700
Adjusted closing capital		67,500
Less : Opening capital–		
Umesh	33,000	
Mahesh	27,000	
Prakash	(Dr) 9,000	51,000
Gross profit for the year		16,500
Less : Interest on capital–		
Umesh	3,300	
Mahesh	2,700	
Prakash	(Dr) 1,200	4,800
Net profit for the year		11,700
Share in Net profit–		
Umesh 1/3		3,900
Mahesh 1/3		3,900
Prakash 1/3		3,900

Revised Statement of Affairs for the year ended 31st Dec., 1989

Liabilities	Rs.	Rs.	Assets	Rs.	Rs.
Creditors		8,000	Cash in Hand		1,300
Bills payable		1,600	Cash at Bank		2,000
Capital Accounts :			Debtors		19,000
Umesh's capital	33,000		Stock		13,100
Add : Net profit	3,900		Machinery		20,000
Add : Interest	3,300		Furniture		10,000
	40,200		*Capital Accounts :*		
Less : Drawings	4,000	36,200	Prakash's capital	9,000	
Mahesh's capital	27,000		*Add* : Interest on		
Add : Net profit	3,900		overdraft	1,200	
Add : Interest	2,700			10,200	
	33,600		*Less* : Net profit	3,900	
Less : Drawings	3,800	29,800		6,300	
			Add : Drawings	3,900	10,200
		75,600			75,600

Illustration 7

Shridar, Shashidar and Shivadar were the partners sharing profit and loss in the ratio of 1/2 : 1/3 : 1/6. They kept their books on single-entry system. Their position as on 31st Dec., 1990 was as under :

Liabilities		Rs.	Assets	Rs.
Creditors		10,000	Cash in Hand	3,200
Bank overdraft		4,000	Cash at Bank	4,000
Bills payable		2,500	Debtors	10,300
Capital Accounts :			Stock	20,000
Shridar	13,500		Furniture	4,320
Shashidar	9,000		Machinery	1,800
Shivadar	4,500	27,000	Advance payments	105
Current Accounts :			*Current Accounts :*	
Shridar	435		Shivadar	510
Shashidar	300	735		
		44,235		44,235

Their position as on 31st Dec., 1990 was as follows : Cash in Hand Rs. 3,000; Cash at Bank Rs. 6,600; Debtors Rs. 9,775; Stock Rs. 20,000;

Advance payment Rs. 75; Creditors Rs. 14,000; Bank overdraft Rs. 2,000; Bills payable Rs. 2,120. The drawings of three partners were — Shridar Rs. 4,000; Shashidar Rs. 3,200; and Shivadar Rs. 1,950. Furniture is to be depreciated by 10% p.a. and Machinery at 7½%. Interest at 5% is to be allowed on capital.

Prepare a statement of profit or loss for the year ended 31st Dec., 1990 and statement of affairs as at that date.

Solution :

If the partners' current accounts are given in the problem, the partners' capitals are to be fixed. When the capitals are fixed, the profit or loss has to be ascertained by comparing the opening balance of current account with that of closing balance.

Statement of Affairs as at 31st Dec, 1990

Liabilities		Rs.	Assets	Rs.
Creditors		14,000	Cash in Hand	3,000
Bank overdraft		2,000	Cash at Bank	6,600
Bills payable		2,120	Debtors	9,775
Capital Accounts : (Fixed)			Stock	20,000
Shridar	13,500		Furniture	4,320
Shashidar	9,000		Machinery	1,800
Shivadar	4,500	27,000	Advance payments	75
Combined Closing Current Account (Balancing figure)		450		
		45,570		45,570

Statement of Profit or Loss for the year ended 31st Dec., 1990

	Rs.	Rs.
Combined closing current account balance		450
Add : Partners' drawings : Shridar	4,000	
Shashidar	3,200	
Shivadar	1,950	9,150
Adjusted combined closing current a/c balance		9,600
Less : Combined opening current a/c balance :		
Shridar	435	
Shashidar	300	
Shivadar	(Dr.) 510	225
Gross profit for the year		9,375

Contd.

			Rs.	Rs.
Gross profit for the year (c/f)		Rs.		9,375
Less : Depreciation —	Furniture	432		
	Machinery	135	567	
Interest on capital —	Shridar	675		
	Shashidar	450		
	Shivadar	225	1,350	1,917
Net profit for the year				7,458
Share in Net profit of Shridar				3,729
Share in Net profit of Shashidar				2,487
Share in Net profit of Shivadar				1,242

Revised Statement of Affairs for the year ended 31st Dec., 1990

Liabilities	Rs.	Rs.	Assets	Rs.	Rs.
Creditors		14,000	Cash in Hand		3,000
Bank overdraft		2,000	Cash at Bank		6,600
Bills payable		2,120	Debtors		9,775
Capital Accounts :			Stock		20,000
Shridar	13,500		Furniture	4,320	
Shashidar	9,000		*Less :* Depreciation	432	3,888
Shivadar	4,500	27,000	Machinery	1,800	
			Less : Depreciation	135	1,665
Current Accounts :			Advance payments		75
Shridar :			*Current Account :*		
Opening balance	435		Shivadar :		
Add : Interest	675		Opening balance	510	
Add : Profit	3,729		*Add*: Drawings	1,950	
	4,839			2,460	
Less : Drawings	4,000	839	*Less :* Interest on		
Shashidar :			capital 225		
Opening balance	300		Profit 1,242	1,467	993
Add : Interest	450				
Add : Profit	2,487				
	3,237				
Less : Drawings	3,200	37			
		45,996			45,996

Illustration 8

The Balance Sheets of 'A' as at 31st Dec., 1983 and 1984 are set out below : He does not understand as to what has happened to the profit of Rs. 1,20,000 as disclosed by the 1984 Balance Sheet as he does not find it in his Bank Balance.

Draw up a statement which will explain to him as to how the profit may me accounted for.

	1983 Rs.	1984 Rs.		1983 Rs.	1984 Rs.
Capital : Balance			Cash at Bank	10,000	10,000
at 31st Dec., 1983	2,30,000	2,30,000	Sundry Debtors	1,40,000	1,60,000
Add : Profit for			Stock-in-trade	60,000	1,00,000
1984		1,20,000	Motor Vehicles	20,000	16,000
		3,50,000	Plant & Machinery		
Deduct Drawings			at cost less		
during 1984		24,000	Depreciation	1,60,000	1,40,000
		3,26,000			
Mortgage on			Freehold Property	2,00,000	2,00,000
Freehold Property	1,60,000	1,20,000			
Sundry Creditors	2,00,000	1,80,000			
	5,90,000	6,26,000		5,90,000	6,26,000

(Calcutta, B.Com., Hons.)

Solution :

Statement of Profit for the year ended 31st Dec., 1984

	Rs.	Rs.
Appreciation in the value of assets :		
Sundry Debtors	20,000	
Stock	40,000	
Add : Reduction in the value of liabilities :		
Mortgage	40,000	
Creditors	20,000	1,20,000
Less : Depreciation in value of assets :		
Plant & Machinery	20,000	
Motor Vehicles	4,000	24,000
		96,000
Add : Drawings		24,000
Profit for the year 1984		1,20,000

II. Conversion of Single-entry into Double-entry

Under the single-entry system, twofold aspects of each and every transaction are not recorded. Hence, a Trial Balance is not prepared and also the information necessary for the preparation of trading account and profit and loss account is not available. If the profit or loss of the concern is to be ascertained by preparing the final accounts, then it is better (necessary) to convert the Single-entry records into Double-entry records.

Conversion of Single-entry into Double-entry refers to preparation of final accounts with Trial Balance. This method involves the complete process of journalising, posting and preparation of Trial Balance. Though this may be possible and practicable in the actual business, but it is not practicable from the examination point of view. Hence, it is not necessary to make out the complete process of journalising, posting and preparation of Trial Balance. In other words, final accounts are to be prepared directly with the scattered information which is equivalent to Trial Balance. Final accounts consist of preparing the trading account, profit and loss account and balance sheet.

The following procedure is to be followed in the conversion of Single-entry into Double-entry (*i.e.*, preparation of final accounts) for the examination purpose.

1. Preparation of Statement of Affairs : It is prepared to find out any missing figures of assets and liabilities such as, Capital, Creditors, Stock, Debtors, Cash Balance etc.

2. Preparation of Cash Book : It is prepared to find out any missing figures of items such as, Cash in Hand and at Bank at the beginning of the year, Cash in Hand and at Bank at the end of the year, Cash sales, Cash purchases, Bills receivable received, Bills payable paid, Incomes such as Interest, Dividend, Rent etc., Expenditures such as Salaries, Wages, Rent, Telephone charges, Telegrams etc., other incomes, other expenditure etc.

Dr. **Cash Book** Cr.

Liabilities	Rs.	Assets	Rs.
To Cash in hand (opening)	xxx	By Cash paid to creditors	xxx
To Cash at Bank (opening)	xxx	By Cash paid on purchases	xxx
To Cash received from cash sales	xxx	By Cash paid on B/P	xxx
To Cash received from debtors	xxx	By Cash paid on purchase of any assets	xxx
To Cash received on B/R	xxx	By Rent	xxx
To Cash received from the sale of any assets	xxx	By Salary	xxx
To Other receipts	xxx	By Wages	xxx
		By Other expenses	xxx
		By Cash at Bank (closing)	xxx
		By Cash in Hand (closing)	xxx
	xxxx		xxxx

(It may be noted that anyone of the items in the above account may be missing, the balancing figure should be considered as the missing figure.)

3. Preparation of Other Accounts : Other accounts such as, Total Debtors, Total Creditors, Bills Receivable and Bills Payable Accounts are prepared to find out the Credit Purchases, Credit Sales at the beginning and at the end of the year and other information.

The Total Debtors Account is to be prepared to find out the missing figures of credit sales or the closing balance of the debtors or cash received from the debtors or opening balance of debtors in the following manner :

Dr. **Total Debtors Account** Cr.

Liabilities	Rs.	Assets	Rs.
To Opening balance	xxx	By Cash received from	
To Credit sales	xxx	Customers	xxx
To B/R dishonoured	xxx	By B/R received	xxx
To Cash returned to customers	xxx	By Sales returns	xxx
To Creditors (B/R endorsed to creditors)	xxx	By Discount or rebate allowed	xxx
To Interest or any other expenses charged	xxx	By Allowances given to customers	xxx
To Customers	xxx	By Bad debts	xxx
		By Transfer to creditors	xxx
		By Closing balance	xxx
	xxxx		xxxx

(It may be noted that anyone of the items in the above account may be missing, the balancing figure should be considered as the missing one)

Items do not concern to the Debtors Account :

(i) Cash sales

(ii) Bad debts recovered

(iii) Reserve for discount on debtors

(iv) B/R discounted

(v) B/R honoured

The Total Creditors Account is to be prepared in the same manner as Total Debtors Account to find out the missing figures of credit purchases or closing balance of creditors or cash paid to creditors or opening balance of creditors as given below :

Total Creditors Account

Dr.	Rs.		Cr. Rs.
To Cash paid to creditors	xxx	By Opening balance	xxx
To B/P issued to creditors	xxx	By Credit purchases	xxx
To Purchases returns	xxx	By B/P dishonoured	xxx
To Discount or rebate received	xxx	By Cash received from creditors	xxx
To B/R endorsed to creditors	xxx	By Interest and expenses credited to creditors	xxx
To Allowances received from Creditors			
To Transfer from debtors	xxx		
To Closing balance	xxx		
	xxxx		xxxx

(It may be noted that any one of the items in the above account may be missing, the balancing figure should be considered as the missing one)

Items do not concern to the Creditors Account :

(i) Cash purchases (ii) Reserve for discount on creditors (iii) B/P honoured

Bills Payable and Bills Receivable Accounts are to be prepared in order to find out the opening or closing balance of Bills Payable and Bills Receivable in the following manner :

Bills Payable Account

Dr.	Rs.		Cr. Rs.
To Cash paid (*i.e.*, B/P paid)	xxx	By Balance b/d (opening balance)	xxx
To Sundry creditors (B/P dishonoured)	xxx	By Sundry creditors (B/P issued or accepted during the year)	xxx
To Balance c/d (closing balance)	xxx		
	xxxx		xxxx

Bills Receivable Account

Dr.	Rs.		Cr. Rs.
To Balance b/d (Opening balance)	xxx	By Cash received (B/R honoured)	xxx
To Sundry debtors (B/R received during the year)	xxx	By Sundry debtors (B/R dishonoured)	xxx
		By Sundry creditors (B/R endorsed to creditors during the year)	xxx
		By Balance c/d (Closing balance)	xxx
	xxxx		xxxx

Note : In the above two accounts some items may be missing, the balancing figure should be considered as the missing figure.

4. Calculation of Total Sales and Purchases : The total purchases and total sales can be calculated by adding cash purchases to the credit purchases and also cash sales to the credit sales.

5. Preparation of Trading Account, P & L Account and Balance Sheet : After preparing the above accounts, the Trading account, P & L Account and Balance Sheet are to be prepared at the end of the trading period in the usual manner.

How to find out the required information?

The following procedure should be followed in order to find out the required information for the preparation of final accounts :

Final Accounts	**Items required**	**Source of information**
1. Trading Account	(a) Opening Stock	Opening Statement of Affairs.
	(b) Purchases	Cash purchases from cash book and credit purchases from the total creditors account or from the given information.
	(c) Returns Outwards	From the total creditors account or from the other information.
	(d) Expenses such as wages freight, carriage, octroi etc.	From the payment side of book or from the given information.
	(e) Sales	Cash sales from the cash book and credit sales from the total debtors account or from the other information.
	(f) Returns Inwards	From the total debtors account or from the other information.
	(g) Closing Stock	Closing statements of affairs or other information.
(2) Profit and Loss Account	(a) Expenses such as salaries, rent, printing, stationery, advertising, bad debts, depreciation etc.	From the payment side of cash book or from the given information.
	(b) Gross Profit	From the trading account
	(c) Incomes such as commission received, discount received, interest on investments, reserve on creditors etc.	From the receipt side of the cash book or from the adjustments and other information.

(3) Balance Sheet	(a) Assets such as Cash in Hand & at Bank, debtors, bills receivable, land and building, machinery, furniture etc.	From the receipts and payments side of the cash book or from the total debtors account and total bills receivable account or from the opening and closing statement of affairs or from the other information.
	(b) Liabilities such as Bank overdraft, creditors, bills payable, outstanding creditors etc.	From the cash book or from the total creditors account and total bills payable account or from the opening statement of affairs or from the other information.
	(c) Capital	Opening capital from opening statement of affairs, additional capital from the receipts side of the cash book.
	(d) Interest on Capital and Drawings	From the other information.
	(e) Net Profit or Net Loss	From the Profit and Loss A/c.

Objects of Converting Single-entry into Double-entry

Following are the important objects of converting Single-entry into Double-entry :

(1) To record both the aspects of each and every transaction of the business.

(2) To verify the arithmetical accuracy of the books of accounts.

(3) To ascertain the true net profit or loss of the business through and trading and profit and loss account.

(4) To know the correct financial position of the business through the balance sheet.

(5) To avoid the misappropriation and frauds in the single-entry system.

Illustration 1

From the particulars of Mr. 'X' who keeps his accounts under single-entry system, ascertain the opening stock :

Purchases	Rs. 40,000	Purchases Returns	Rs. 5,000
Sales	Rs. 80,000	Manufacturing Expenses	Rs. 5,000
Closing Stock	Rs. 5,000	Rate of gross profit on cost $33^1/_3$%	

Solution :

When the rate of gross profit is given, the opening stock will be ascertained by preparing the Memorandum Trading Account.

Dr. **Memorandum Trading Account** Cr.

	Rs.		Rs.
To Opening stock (Balancing figure)	25,000	By Sales	80,000
		By Closing stock	5,000
To Purchases 40,000 *Less* : Returns 5,000	35,000		
To Manufacturing expenses	5,000		
To Gross profit (80,000 × ¼)	20,000		
	85,000		85,000

Note : $33\frac{1}{3}$% on cost or $\frac{1}{3}$ on cost is $\frac{1}{4}$ on selling cost.

Illustration 2

Calculate the stock at the end.

Opening stock	10,000
Cash sales	30,000
Credit sales	20,000
Purchases	35,000

Rate of gross profit on sales 25%.

Solution :

Dr. **Memorandum Trading Account** Cr.

	Rs.			Rs.
To Opening stock	10,000	By Sales :		
To Purchases	35,000	Cash	30,000	
To Gross profit (25% of Rs. 50,000)	12,500	Credit	20,000	50,000
		By Closing stock (Balancing figure)		7,500
	57,500			57,500

Illustration 3

Calculate the total sales from the following details :

Opening stock	Rs. 10,000	Direct expenses	Rs. 8,000
Closing stock	Rs. 4,000	Purchases	Rs. 50,000

Rate of gross profit on the sale is 20%.

Solution :

Dr. **Memorandum Trading Account** Cr.

	Rs.		Rs.
To Opening stock	10,000	By Sales	80,000
To Purchases	50,000	(Balancing figure)	
To Direct Expenses	8,000	By Closing stock	4,000
To Gross profit	16,000		
(As shown below)			
	84,000		84,000

Note : 20% on sales or 1/5 on sales is 1/4 on cost. The cost of goods sold is Rs. 64,000. This is arrived as below :

Cost of goods sold = Opening stock + Purchases + Direct expenses – Closing stock

10,000 + 50,000 + 8,000 – 4000 = 64,000

therefore, the gross profit is Rs. 16,000 (*i.e.*, 64,000 × ¼)

Illustration 4

From the following details find out the credit sales :

	Rs.
Bills Receivable 1-1-97	8,200
Debtors 1-1-97	23,000
Bills Receivable encashed during 1997	12,000
Cash received from debtors	20,000
Bad debts written off	400
Returns inwards	500
Bills Receivable dishonoured	1,800
Bills Receivable 31-12-97	7,000
Debtors 31-12-97	18,000

Solution :

Dr. **Bills Receivable Account** Cr.

	Rs.		Rs.
To Balance b/d	8,200	By Cash	12,000
To Sundry Debtors	12,600	By Sundry Debtors	1,800
(Bills received)		(Bills dishonoured)	
		By Balance c/d	7,000
	20,800		20,800

Dr. **Total Debtors Account** Cr.

	Rs.		Rs.
To Balance b/d	23,000	By Cash received	20,000
To B/R dishonoured	1,800	By B/R received	12,600
To Credit sales	26,700	By Bad debts	400
(Balancing figure)		By Returns inwards	500
		By Balance c/d	18,000
	51,500		51,500

Illustration 5

From the following details find out the credit purchases and total purchases:

Cash purchases	30,000
Opening balance of bills payable	9,000
Opening balance of creditors	18,000
Closing balance of bills payable	4,500
Closing balance of creditors	20,000
Cash paid to creditors	23,000
Allowances from creditors	900
Purchases returns	1,100
Bills payable paid during the year	12,000
Bills payable dishonoured	500

Solution :

Dr. **Bills Payable Account** Cr.

	Rs.		Rs.
To Cash	12,000	By Balance b/d	9,000
To Sundry creditors	500	By Sundry creditors	8,000
(B/P dishonoured)		(B/P accepted)	
To Balance c/d	4,500		
	17,000		17,000

Dr. **Total Creditors' Account** Cr.

	Rs.		Rs.
To Cash paid	23,000	By Balance b/d	18,000
To B/P accepted	8,000	By B/P dishonoured	500
To Allowance received	900	By Credit purchases	34,500
To Purchases return	1,100	(Balancing figure)	
To Balance c/d	20,000		
	53,000		53,000

Total purchases = Cash purchases + Credit purchases

30,000 + 34,500 = 64,500

Illustration 6

From the following particulars prepare total debtors account, total creditors account, bills payable account and bills receivable account and also find out the total sales and purchases :

	Rs.
Opening balance of debtors	18,800
Opening balance of creditors	8,400
Opening balance of bills receivable	6,500
Opening balance of bills payable	4,200
Bills receivable received from debtors	?
Credit sales	?
Bills payable issued to creditors	?
Credit purchases	?
Cash sales	69,000
Cash purchases	55,800
Cash received from debtors	55,250
Cash paid to creditors	42,300
Sales returns	2,750
Purchases returns	2,700
Bad debts	2,500
Bills receivable dishonoured	2,200
Bills payable discharged during the year	10,500
Cash received on bills receivable	15,800
Closing balance of debtors	43,000
Closing balance of creditors	8,400
Closing balance of bills receivable	7,000
Closing balance of bills payable	8,700

Solution :

Bills Receivable Account

(To find out B/R received from debtors)

Dr. Cr.

	Rs.		Rs.
To Balance b/d	6,500	By Cash received on B/R	15,800
To Debtors (B/R received from the debtors during the year) (Balancing figure)	18,500	By Debtors (B/R dishonoured)	2,200
		By Balance c/d	7,000
	25,000		25,000

Total Debtors' Account

Dr. (To find out credit sales) Cr.

	Rs.		Rs.
To Balance b/d	18,800	By Cash received from debtors	55,250
To Bills Receivable (B/R dishonoured)	2,200	By B/R received	18,500
To Credit sale		By Bad debts	2,500
(Balancing figure)	1,01,000	By Sales returns	2,750
		By Balance c/d	43,000
	1,22,000		1,22,000

Total Sales = Cash Sales + Credit Sales
= 69,000 + 1,01,000 = Rs. 1,70,000

Bills Payable Account

Dr. (To find out B/P issued to creditors) Cr.

	Rs.		Rs.
To Cash (B/P discharged)	10,500	By Balance b/d	4,200
		By Creditors	15,000
To Balance c/d	8,700	(B/P issued during the year) (Balancing figure)	
	19,200		19,200

Total Creditors' Accounts

Dr. (To find out credit purchases) Cr.

	Rs.		Rs.
To Cash paid to creditors	42,300	By Balance b/d	8,400
To Bills payable issued	15,000	By Credit purchases	60,000
To Purchases returns	2,700	(Balancing figure)	
To Balance c/d	8,400		
	68,400		68,400

Total Purchases = Cash purchases + Credit purchases
= 55,800 + 60,000 = 1,15,800

Illustration 7

From the following information, prepare Total Debtors Account, Total Creditors Account, Bills Receivable Account and Bills Payable Account :

	Rs.
Opening Debtors	8,000
Opening Creditors	5,000
Opening Bills Receivable	2,000
Opening Bills Payable	1,000
Credit Sales	38,000
Credit Purchases	33,000
Bills Receivable received during the year	12,000
Bills Payable issued during the year	7,000
Cash received from debtors	31,000
Cash paid to creditors	18,000
Cash paid to customers	300
Discount allowed to customers	200
Discount allowed by suppliers	100
Allowances given to customers	100
Allowances received from suppliers	50
Bad debts written off	1,000
Bills Receivable endorsed to creditors	3,000
Bills Receivable dishonoured by customers	1,000
Bills Receivable endorsed to creditors dishonoured	500
Bills Receivable honoured by customers	6,000
Bills Payable honoured	4,000
Bills Payable dishonoured	1,000
Interest charged to customers	100
Bill Receivable discounted for (Discount charge Rs. 30)	970
Bills Receivable discounted dishonoured	1,000
Bad debts recovered	50
Purchases returns	100
Sales returns	300
Reserve for doubtful debts	200

(*C.A. Inter*)

Solution :

Dr. **Total Debtors' Account** Cr.

	Rs.		Rs.
To Balance b/d	8,000	By Bills Receivable (Received during the year)	12,000
To Cash paid to customers	300	By Cash received from debtors	31,000
To Credit sales	38,000	By Discount allowed to customers	200
To B/R (*i.e.*, B/R in the hand dishonoured)	1,000	By Allowances given to customers	100
To Sundry Creditors (B/R endorsed to creditors dishonoured)	500	By Bad debt written off	1,000
To Interest charged to customers	100	By Sales returns	300
To Cash (*i.e.*, B/R discounted dishonoured)	1,000	By Balance c/d (Balancing figure)	4,300
	48,900		48,900

Dr. **Bills Receivable Account** Cr.

	Rs.		Rs.
To Balance b/d	2,000	By Sundry Creditors (B/R endorsed to creditors)	3,000
To Sundry Debtors (B/R received during the trading period)	12,000	By Sundry Debtors (B/R in hand dishonoured by customers)	1,000
		By Cash (B/R honoured)	6,000
		By Cash	970
		By Discount	30
		By Balance c/d (Balancing figure)	3,000
	14,000		14,000
To Balance b/d	3,000		

Total Creditors' Account

Dr.	Rs.		Cr. Rs.
To Bills Payable (issued during the year)	7,000	By Balance b/d (opening creditors)	5,000
To Cash paid to creditors	18,000	By Credit Purchases	33,000
To Discount (received from creditors)	100	By Sundry Debtors (B/R endorsed to creditors dishonoured)	500
To Bills Receivable (B/R endorsed to creditors)	3,000	By Bills Payable (B/P dishonoured)	1,000
To Purchases Returns	100		
To Allowance (received from creditors)	50		
To Balance c/d (closing creditors)	11,250		
	39,500		39,500
		By Balance b/d	11,250

Bills Payable Account

Dr.	Rs.		Cr. Rs.
To Cash (B/P honoured)	4,000	By Balance b/d (opening B/P)	1,000
To Sundry creditors (B/P dishonoured)	1,000	By Sundry Creditors (B/P issued during the trading period)	7,000
To Balance c/d (Balancing figure)	3,000		
	8,000		8,000
		By Balance b/d	3,000

Note : Bad debts recovered and reserve for doubtful debts will not be appeared in the total debtors' account, as they do not affect the debtors' account.

Illustration 8

Rajan keeps his books by single-entry. An analysis of Cash Book for the year ended 31st Dec., 1990, given the following particulars :

Debit side	Rs.
Opening balance (1-1-1990)	3,990
Received from Debtors	1,23,750
Loan from Nanda (taken on 1-6-1990 at 15% p.a.)	3,000

Credit side

	Rs.
Payments to creditors	96,510
Salaries	7,500
Light and power	1,000
Wages	8,000
Paid for private expenses of proprietor	4,680
Printing and stationery	1,680
Carriage and freight	2,520
Rent	1,170
Purchase of new machinery	2,000
Closing balance (31-12-1990)	5,680

Other assets and liabilities were as follows :

	1st Jan., 1990	31st Dec., 1990
Sundry Debtors	Rs. 3,000	Rs. 4,500
Sundry Creditors	Rs. 7,500	Rs. 6,000
Stock	Rs. 12,000	Rs. 10,500
Plant and Machinery	Rs. 27,000	Rs. 27,000

Prepare Trading and Profit and Loss Account for the year ending 31st Dec., 1990 and a Balance Sheet as on that date.

Solution :

In this problem first we have to find out opening capital by preparing the Opening Statement of Affairs and Credit Sales and Credit Purchases by preparing the Total Debtors' Account and Total Creditors' Account. Finally, we have to prepare the Trading, Profit and Loss Account and Balance Sheet.

Rajan

Statement of Affairs as on 1st Jan., 1990

Liabilities	Rs.	Assets	Rs.
Creditors	7,500	Cash	3,990
Opening Capital	38,490	Debtors	3,000
(Balancing figure)		Stock	12,000
		Plant & Machinery	27,000
	45,990		45,990

Dr. **Total Debtors' Account** Cr.

	Rs.		Rs.
To Opening balance	3,000	By Cash (received)	1,23,750
To Credit sales (Balancing figure)	1,25,250	By Closing balance	4,500
	1,28,250		1,28,250

Dr. **Total Creditors' Account** Cr.

	Rs.		Rs.
To Cash (paid)	96,510	By Opening balance	7,500
To Closing balance	6,000	By Credit purchases (Balancing figure)	95,010
	1,02,510		1,02,510

Trading and Profit and Loss Account

for the year ended 31st Dec., 1990

	Rs.		Rs.
To Opening stock	12,000	By Sales	1,25,250
To Purchases	95,010	By Closing stock	10,500
To Wages	8,000		
To Light and power	1,000		
To Carriage and freight	2,520		
To Gross profit c/d	17,220		
	1,35,750		1,35,750
To Salary	7,500	By Gross profit b/d	17,220
To Rent	1,170		
To Printing & stationery	1,680		
To Interest on loan	225		
To Depreciation :			
On Machinery	2,000		
To Net profit (transferred to capital)	4,645		
	17,220		17,220

Balance Sheet as at 31st Dec., 1990

Liabilities		Rs.	Assets		Rs.
Creditors		6,000	Cash		5,680
Capital :			Debtors		4,500
Opening Capital	38,490		Stock		10,500
Add : Net profit	4,645		Plant & Machinery		
	43,135			27,000	
Less : Drawings	4,680	38,455	*Add* : Additions	2,000	
Loan from Nanda		3,000		29,000	
Outstanding interest on loan		225	*Less* : Depreciation	2,000	27,000
		47,680			47,680

Calculation of depreciation on machinery :	Rs.
Book value of the machinery as on 1-1-1990	27,000
Add : Addition of new machinery during the year	2,000
	29,000
Less : Book value of the machinery as on 31-12-1990	27,000
Balance being depreciation	2,000

Illustration 9

Rahim carries on a retail business. He does not keep his books on double entry basis. The following particulars have been extracted from his book :

	1st Jan., 1990 Rs.	31st Dec., 1990 Rs.
Capital	80,000	—
Stock	26,000	17,500
Debtors	42,500	30,000
Creditors	31,000	8,000
Furniture	2,500	2,500
Building	35,000	35,000
Cash	5,000	14,000

His Bank transactions for the year ending 31st Dec., 1990 were :

Paid to Creditors	Rs. 37,500
Received from Debtors	Rs. 49,000
Personal drawings	Rs. 3,000
Salaries	Rs. 13,000
Received from cash sales	Rs. 30,000
Paid for cash purchases	Rs. 5,000
Rent	Rs. 11,500

Furniture and building are to be depreciated at 5%, reserve Rs. 1,500 for doubtful debts and allow 5% interest on capital.

From the above materials, prepare a Trading and Profit and Loss Account for the ended 31st Dec.,1990 and Balance Sheet as on that date.

Solution :

Total Debtors' Account

Dr. (To find out credit sales) Cr.

	Rs.		Rs.
To Opening balance	42,500	By Cash (received)	49,000
To Credit sales (Balancing figure)	36,500	By Closing balance	30,000
	79,000		79,000

Total Creditors' Account

Dr. (To find out credit purchases) Cr.

	Rs.		Rs.
To Cash (paid)	37,500	By Opening balance	31,000
To Closing balance	8,000	By Credit purchases (Balancing figure)	14,500
	45,500		45,500

Trading and Profit and Loss Account

Dr. For the year ended 31st Dec., 1990 Cr.

		Rs.			Rs.
To Opening stock		26,000	By Sales :		
To Purchases :			Cash	30,000	
Cash	5,000		Credit	36,500	66,500
Credit	14,500	19,500	By Closing stock		17,500
To Gross profit c/d		38,500			
		84,000			84,000
To Salaries		13,000	By Gross profit b/d		38,500
To Rent		11,500			
To Interest on capital at 5%		4,000			
To Reserve for doubtful debts		1,500			
To Depreciation on :					
Furniture	125				
Building	1,750	1,875			
To Net profit (transferred to capital)		6,625			
		38,500			38,500

Balance Sheet as at 31st Dec., 1990

Liabilities		Rs.	Assets		Rs.
Creditors		8,000	Cash		14,000
Capital :			Debtors	30,000	
Opening capital	80,000		*Less* : R.D.D.	1,500	28,500
Add: Interest	4,000		Stock		17,500
Add: Net profit	6,625		Furniture	2,500	
	90,625		*Less:* Depreciation	125	2,375
Less: Drawing	3,000	87,625	Building	35,000	
			Less: Depreciation	1,750	33,250
		95,625			95,625

Illustration 10

'X' started a business with a capital of Rs. 20,000 on 1-1-1990. He immediately brought furniture for Rs. 6,000. During the year he borrowed Rs. 1,000 from his friend and introduced a further capital of Rs. 3,000. He had withdrawn Rs. 500 at the end of each month for family expenses.

From the following particulars obtained from his book which does not confirm strictly to double-entry principle, you are required to prepare the trading and profit and loss account for the year ending 31-12-1990 and Balance Sheet as on that date:

	Rs.
Sales (inclusive of cash sales Rs. 20,000)	80,000
Purchases (inclusive of cash purchases Rs. 25,000)	60,000
Wages	500
Lighting and power	500
Discount earned	300
Salaries to Staff	5,000
Stationeries	200
Rent and taxes	700
Bad debts written off	500

The owner of the firm used goods worth Rs. 2,000 for private purposes and paid Rs. 1,000 to his son which were not recorded anywhere.

On 31-12-1990 his debtors were Rs. 40,000 and creditors Rs. 20,000. Stock on that date was worth Rs. 12,000.

Provide 10% depreciation on furniture and 5% reserve for doubtful debts on debtors.

Solution :

Total Debtors' Account

Dr. (To find out cash received from debtors) Dr.

	Rs.		Rs.
To Balance b/d	—	By Cash (received) (Balancing figure)	19,500
To Credit sales (80,000 – 20,000)	60,000	By Bad Debts	500
		By Balance c/d	40,000
	60,000		60,000

Total Creditors' Account

Dr. (To find out cash paid to creditors) Cr.

	Rs.		Rs.
To Cash (paid) (Balancing figure)	14,700	By Balance b/d	—
To Discount (earned)	300	By Credit purchases (60,000 – 25,000)	35,000
To Balance c/d	20,000		
	35,000		35,000

Cash Account

Dr. (To find out closing cash balance) Cr.

	Rs.		Rs.
To Capital	20,000	By Furniture	6,000
To Additional capital	3,000	By Drawings (500 × 12)	6,000
To Loan of friend	1,000	By Cash purchases	25,000
To Cash sales	20,000	By Creditors (as per Creditors A/c)	14,700
To Debtors (as per debtors account)	19,500	By Drawings (goods taken for personal use)	2,000
		By Drawings (paid to son)	1,000
		By Wages	500
		By Lighting and power	500
		By Salaries	5,000
		By Stationeries	200
		By Rent and taxes	700
		By Balance c/d (Balancing figure)	1,900
	63,500		63,500

Trading and Profit and Loss Account

Dr. For the year ending 31-12-1990 Cr.

		Rs.			Rs.
To Opening stock		—	By Sales :		
To Purchases :			Cash	20,000	
Cash	25,000		Credit	60,000	80,000
Credit	35,000	60,000	By Closing stock		12,000
To Wages		500			
To Lighting and power		500			
To Gross profit c/d		31,000			
		92,000			92,000
To Salaries		5,000	By Gross profit b/d		31,000
To Stationeries		200	By Discount earned		300
To Rent & taxes		700			
To Bad debts	500				
Add : Provision	2,000	2,500			
To Depreciation on furniture		600			
To Net profit (transferred to capital)		22,300			
		31,300			31,300

Balance Sheet as at 31-12-1990

Liabilities	Rs.	Rs.	Assets	Rs.	Rs.
Capital	20,000		Furniture	6,000	
Add: Additional capital	3,000		*Less* : Depreciation	600	5,400
Add : Net profit	22,300		Debtors	40,000	
	45,300		*Less* : R.D.D.	2,000	38,000
Less : Drawings (6,000+2,000+1,000)	9,000	36,300	Stock		12,000
Creditors		20,000	Cash		1,900
Loan of friend		1,000			
		57,300			57,300

Illustration 11

From the following particulars furnished by a trader who keeps his books of account on single-entry system. Prepare his trading and profit and loss account for the year ending 31-12-1990 and balance sheet as on that date.

(1) Statement of Affairs as on 1-1-1990

Liabilities	Rs.	Assets	Rs.
Capital	80,000	Land & Building	60,000
Creditors	30,000	Machinery	20,000
Bank overdraft	5,000	Furniture	5,000
Bills payable	8,000	Debtors	20,000
		Bills receivable	8,000
		Stock	7,000
		Cash in Hand	3,000
	1,23,000		1,23,000

(2) Summary of Cash Transactions for the year 1990

	Rs.		Rs.
To Opening Balance	3,000	By Cash Purchases	40,000
To Cash Sales	60,000	By Creditors	85,000
To Debtors	70,000	By Bills Payable	20,000
To Bills Receivable	35,000	By Purchase of Machinery (on 1-7-1990)	2,000
		By Wages	3,000
		By Carriage Inwards	2,000
		By Salaries	4,000
		By Advertisement	500
		By Sundry Expenses	1,000
		By Drawings	8,500
		By Closing Balance	2,000
	1,68,000		1,68,000

(3) Other information for the year 1990

	Rs.		Rs.
Credit sales	1,30,000	Returns outwards	4,500
Credit purchases	1,00,000	Bills payable accepted	20,000
Discount allowed	2,000	Bills receivable received	30,000
Discount earned	3,000	Bad debts written off	1,000
Returns inwards	4,000	Stock of goods on 31-12-90	20,000

Depreciate machinery and furniture at 10%. Make provision for doubtful debts at 5% on debtors.

Solution :

Total Debtors' Account

Dr. (To find out closing debtors) Cr.

	Rs.		Rs.
To Balance b/d	20,000	By Cash (received)	70,000
To Credit sales	1,30,000	By Discount (allowed)	2,000
		By Returns inwards	4,000
		By B/R (received)	30,000
		By Bad debts	1,000
		By Balance c/d (Balancing figure)	43,000
	1,50,000		1,50,000

Bills Receivable Account

Dr. (To find out closing bills receivable) Cr.

	Rs.		Rs.
To Balance b/d	8,000	By Cash (received)	35,000
To Debtors	30,000	By Balance c/d (Balancing figure)	3,000
	38,000		38,000

Total Creditors' Account

Dr. (To find out closing creditors) Cr.

	Rs.		Rs.
To Cash (paid)	85,000	By Balance b/d	30,000
To Discount (earned)	3,000	By Credit purchases	1,00,000
To Returns outwards	4,500		
To B/P (accepted)	20,000		
To Balance c/d (Balancing figure)	17,500		
	1,30,000		1,30,000

Bills Payable Account

Dr. (To find out closing bills payable) Cr.

	Rs.		Rs.
To Cash (paid)	20,000	By Balance b/d	8,000
To Balance c/d (Balancing figure)	8,000	By Creditors	20,000
	28,000		28,000

Trading and Profit and Loss Account
for the year ending 31-12-1990

Dr. Cr.

		Rs.			Rs.
To Opening stock		7,000	By Sales :		
To Purchases :			Cash	60,000	
Cash	40,000		Credit	1,30,000	
Credit	1,00,000			1,90,000	
	1,40,000		*Less* : Returns	4,000	1,86,000
Less : Returns	4,500	1,35,500	By Closing stock		20,000
To Wages		3,000			
To Carriage inwards		2,000			
To Gross profit c/d		58,500			
		2,06,000			2,06,000
To Salary		4,000	By Gross profit b/d		58,500
To Advertisement		500	By Discount earned		3,000
To Discount allowed		2,000			
To Sundry expenses		1,000			
To Bad debts	1,000				
Add : Provision	2,150	3,150			
To Depreciation on :					
Machinery	2,100				
Furniture	500	2,600			
To Net profit (transferred to capital)		48,250			
		61,500			61,500

Balance Sheet as on 31-12-1990

Liabilities		Rs.	Assets		Rs.
Capital	80,000		Land & Building		60,000
Add : Net profit	48,250		Machinery	20,000	
	1,28,250		*Add* : Additions	2,000	
Less : Drawings	8,500	1,19,750	*Less* : Depreciation	2,100	19,900
Creditors		17,500	Furniture	5,000	
Bank overdraft		5,000	*Less* : Dep.	500	4,500
Bills payable		8,000	Debtors	43,000	
			Less : Provision	2,150	40,850
			Bills Receivable		3,000
			Stock		20,000
			Cash in Hand		2,000
		1,50,250			1,50,250

Illustration 12

Mr. Arun does not keep his books of account properly. From such books and other records given below prepare his Trading and Profit and Loss Account for the year ending 31-12-1990 and Balance Sheet as on that date.

(1) The balances as on 1-1-1990 were as under :

Cash in Hand	10,000
Cash at Bank	3,000
Machinery	10,000
Furniture	5,000
Stock	15,000
Creditors	12,000
Debtors	20,000
Capital	40,000
Current Account	11,000

(2) During the year 1990 the Debtors paid Rs. 20,000 in cash and Rs. 60,000 by cheque and the creditors were paid Rs. 25,000 in cash and Rs. 40,000 by cheques. At the close of the year the balance of debtors and creditors stood at Rs. 9,000 and at Rs. 20,000 respectively.

(3) All the expenses charged to profit and loss account were paid by cheques except the expenses amounting to Rs. 2,000 which were paid in cash. At the close of the year the outstanding rent and salary stood at Rs. 800 and Rs. 700 respectively.

(4) After debiting all the above expenses and also depreciation at 8% on machinery and 7% on furniture, the net profit for the year ending 31-12-1990 amounted to Rs. 6,000.

(5) During the year Arun's drawings were Rs. 2,000 in cash and Rs. 3,000 by cheques.

(6) The stock as on 31-12-1990 was valued at Rs. 45,000.

Solution :

Total Debtors' Account

Dr. (To find out credit sales) Cr.

	Rs.		Rs.
To Balance b/d	20,000	By Cash	20,000
To Credit sales	69,000	By Bank	60,000
(Balancing figure)		By Balance c/d	9,000
	89,000		89,000

Total Creditors' Accounts

Dr. (To find out credit purchases) Cr.

	Rs.		Rs.
To Cash	25,000	By Balance b/d	12,000
To Bank	40,000	By Credit purchases	73,000
To Balance c/d	20,000	(Balancing figure)	
	85,000		85,000

Cash Book

Dr. (To find out closing cash and bank balance) Cr.

Particulars	Cash	Bank	Particulars	Cash	Bank
	Rs.	Rs.		Rs.	Rs.
To Balance b/d	10,000	3,000	By Creditors	25,000	40,000
To Debtors	20,000	60,000	By Drawings	2,000	3,000
			By Expenses	2,000	15,350
			By Balance c/d (Balancing figure)	1,000	4,650
	30,000	63,000		30,000	63,000

Trading and Profit and Loss Account
for the year ending 31-12-1990

Dr. Cr.

		Rs.		Rs.
To Opening stock		15,000	By Sales (credit)	69,000
To Purchases (credit)		73,000	By Closing stock	45,000
To Gross profit c/d		26,000		
		1,14,000		1,14,000
To Expenses (Balancing figure)	17,350		By Gross profit b/d	26,000
Add : Outstanding :				
Rent 800				
Salary 700	1,500	18,850		
To Depreciation on :				
Machinery	800			
Furniture	350	1,150		
To Net profit (transferred to capital)		6,000		
		26,000		26,000

Balance Sheet as on 31-12-1990

Liabilities		Rs.	Assets		Rs.
Capital		40,000	Machinery	10,000	
Current Account :			*Less :* Depreciation	800	9,200
Opening balance	11,000		Furniture	5,000	
Add : Net profit	6,000		*Less :* Depreciation	350	4,650
	17,000		Debtors		9,000
Less : Drawings	5,000	12,000	Stock		45,000
Creditors		20,000	Cash in Hand		1,000
Outstanding rent		800	Cash at Bank		4,650
Outstanding salary		700			
		73,500			73,500

Working Note :

Calculation of expenses paid by cheque :		Rs.
Total expenses debited to P & L Account (Rs. 18,850 + Rs. 1,150)		20,000
Less : Non-cash expenses :		
Outstanding rent and salary	1,500	
Depreciation on machinery and furniture	1,150	2,650
Expenses paid in cash and cheques		17,350
Less : Expenses which are paid in cash		2,000
Balance being expenses paid by cheques		15,350

Illustration 13

Mr. Sundar keeps his books under single-entry system. He started a business with a capital of Rs. 40,000 and acquired a retail business on 1-1-1990.

Of the acquisition price Rs. 8,000 was for goodwill, Rs. 6,000 to furniture, Rs. 20,000 to stock and Rs. 6,000 were retained as working capital of which Rs. 3,000 were paid into bank. Further, Sundar withdrawn Rs. 2,000 from the bank for office use.

Of the total cash sales of Rs. 85,000 Sundar paid Rs. 70,000 into the bank and remainder being utilized for cash payments. The following were the payments in cash as well as by cheques during the year :

	Rs.
Purchases	70,000
Wages	1,500
Lighting and power	500
Carriage inward	200
Salary	5,000

		Rs.
Stationery		300
Payments for domestic expenses		2,500
Rent and taxes :		
Business proportion	3,500	
Personal	500	4,000
Total payments		84,000

On 31-12-1990 his stock was of the value of Rs. 28,000. A sum of Rs. 8,000 was due to his suppliers of good and there was owing to him for goods sold to customers Rs. 5,000. The bank balance was Rs. 6,000.

Provide Rs. 200 for doubtful debts on debtors and depreciate furniture at 10%.

From the above information prepare trading and profit and loss account for the year ending 31-12-1990 and balance sheet as on that date.

Solution :

Cash Book

Dr. (To find out closing cash and Bank balance) Cr.

Particulars	Rs. Cash	Rs. Bank	Particulars	Rs. Cash	Rs. Bank
To Capital	40,000	—	By Goodwill	8,000	—
To Cash (C) (Deposited)	—	3,000	By Furniture	6,000	—
			By Stock	20,000	—
To Bank (C) (Withdrawn)	2,000	—	By Bank (C) (Deposited)	3,000	—
To Sales	85,000	—	By Cash (C) (Withdrawn)	—	2,000
To Cash (C) (Deposited)	—	70,000	By Bank (C) (Deposited)	70,000	—
			By Payments (Cheques) (Balancing figure)	—	65,000
			By Payments (Cash) (84,000 – 65,000)	19,000	—
			By Balance c/d (Balancing figure)	1,000	6,000
	1,27,000	73,000		1,27,000	73,000

Trading and Profit and Loss Account

for the year ending 31-12-1990

Dr.	Rs.			Cr. Rs.
To Opening stock	20,000	By Sales - Cash	85,000	
To Purchases – Cash 70,000		Credit	5,000	90,000
Credit 8,000	78,000	By Closing stock		28,000
To Wages	1,500			
To Lighting & Power	500			
To Carriage inwards	200			
To Gross Profit c/d	17,800			
	1,18,000			1,18,000
To Salary	5,000	By Gross Profit b/d		17,800
To Rent & taxes (Business proportion)	3,500			
To Stationery	300			
To Provisions for bad debts	200			
To Depreciation on furniture	600			
To Net Profit (transferred to capital)	8,200			
	17,800			17,800

Balance Sheet as on 31-12-1990

Liabilities	Rs.	Rs.	Assets	Rs.	Rs.
Capital	40,000		Goodwill		8,000
Add : Net profit	8,200		Furniture	6,000	
	48,200		*Less* : Depreciation	600	5,400
Less : Drawings :			Debtors	5,000	
Domestic Exp. 2,500			*Less* : R.D.D.	200	4,800
Rent & taxes			Stock		28,000
personal 500	3,000	45,200	Cash in Hand		1,000
Creditors		8,000	Cash at Bank		6,000
		53,200			53,200

Illustration 14

Ashok and Arun are in partnership and keep their books by single-entry. They share profits in the proportion of Ashok 3/5 and Arun 2/5. You are required to prepare their trading and profit and loss account for the year ending 31st Dec., 1990 and their Balance Sheet on that date from the following information :

Dr. **Cash Account for the year 1990** Cr.

	Rs.		Rs.
To Balance b/d	8,000	By Paid to creditors	60,000
To Received from Trade Debtors	91,200	By Paid against Bills Payable	16,000
To Received against Bills Receivable	16,090	By Ashok's Drawings	9,000
To Cash Sales	31,620	By Arun's Drawings	6,000
To Bank Overdraft	3,000	By Salaries	10,000
		By Wages	22,000
		By Trade Expenses	26,510
		By Balance c/d	400
	1,49,910		1,49,910

The respective capital of Ashok and Arun on 1-1-1990 were Rs. 80,000 and Rs. 20,000. Particulars of other assets and liabilities were :

	1-1-1990 Rs.	31-12-1990 Rs.
Debtors	50,000	38,710
Stock	39,600	50,000
Bills Payable	6,000	Nil
Bills Receivable	10,000	14,000
Furniture	2,400	2,400
Premises	40,000	40,000
Creditors	44,000	14,000

Interest on capital is to be allowed at 5%. Interest on Drawings has been agreed as for Ashok Rs. 120 and Arun Rs. 60. Arun is also to be credited with a commission of 6% on the Net profit remaining after charging such commission. Allow 5% depreciation on premises and furniture and create a provision for bad debts amounting to Rs. 2,650.

Solution :

Bills Receivable Account

Dr. (To find out B/R received during the year) Cr.

	Rs.		Rs.
To Balance b/d	10,000	By Cash received	
To Debtors (B/R received	20,090	against B/R	16,090
during the year)		By Balance c/d	14,000
	30,090		30,090

Total Debtors' Account

Dr. (To find out credit sales) Cr.

	Rs.		Rs.
To Balance b/d	50,000	By Cash received	91,200
To Credit sales	1,00,000	By B/R received during	
(Balancing figure)		the year	20,090
		By Balance c/d	38,710
	1,50,000		1,50,000

Bills Payable Account

Dr. (To find out B/P accepted during the year) Cr.

	Rs.		Rs.
To Cash paid against Bills		By Balance b/d	6,000
Payable	16,000	By Creditors	10,000
		(B/P accepted during	
		the year)	
	16,000		16,000

Total Creditors' Account

Dr. (To find out credit purchases) Cr.

	Rs.		Rs.
To Cash paid	60,000	By Balance b/d	44,000
To B/P accepted during		By Credit purchases	40,000
the year	10,000	(Balancing figure)	
To Balance c/d	14,000		
	84,000		84,000

Trading and Profit & Loss Account

for the year ended 31st Dec., 1990

Dr.		Rs.	Cr.		Rs.
To Opening stock		39,600	By Sales :		
To Purchases		40,000	Cash	31,620	
To Wages		22,000	Credit	1,00,000	1,31,620
To Gross profit c/d		80,020	By Closing stock		50,000
		1,81,620			1,81,620
To Salaries		10,000	By Gross profit b/d		80,020
To Trade expenses		26,510	By Interest on drawings :		
To Interest on capital :			Ashok	120	
Ashok	4,000		Arun	60	180
Arun	1,000	5,000			
To Provision for bad debts		2,650			
To Depreciation on :					
Furniture	120				
Premises	2,000	2,120			
To Arun's commission*		1,920			
To Net profit :					
Ashok	19,200				
Arun	12,800	32,000			
(transferred to Capital A/c)					
		80,200			80,200

***Arun's Commission is calculated as follows :**

Net profit before charging commission Rs. 33,920

If a commission of 6% is to be given there must be a profit of Rs. 106

$$\left(i.e.,\ 33,920 \times \frac{6}{106}\right) = 1,920$$

Balance Sheet as on 31st Dec., 1990

Liabilities		Rs.	Assets		Rs.
Creditors		14,000	Debtors	38,710	
Bank overdraft		3,000	*Less* : R.D.D.	2,650	36,060
Capital :			Stock		50,000
Ashok :			Bills receivable		14,000
Opening capital	80,000		Furniture	2,400	
Add : Interest	4,000		*Less* : Depreciation	120	2,280
Add : Net profit	19,200		Premises	40,000	
	1,03,200		*Less* : Depreciation	2,000	38,000
Less : Drawings			Cash in Hand		400
& interest	9,120	94,080			
Arun :					
Opening capital	20,000				
Add : Interest	1,000				
Add : Net profit	12,800				
Add : Commission	1,920				
	35,720				
Less : Drawings					
and interest	6,060	29,660			
		1,40,740			1,40,740

Illustration 15

Dr. King George did not keep regular accounts for the year 1980 but he is able to furnish the following information :

(1) All receipts and payments were by cheques. The particulars of his bank transactions are as follows :

	Rs.		Rs.
Bank balance on 1st Jan., 1980	700	Furniture purchased	1,000
Medicines purchased	3,000	Equipment purchased	5,000
Salaries paid	2,500	Rent and taxes (Including Rs. 500 for 1981)	4,500
Printing & Stationery	1,200	General Expenses	2,000
Subscriptions paid	200		
Drawings (personal)	2,400		

He is not able to ascertain the amount of deposits but he is certain that all deposits in the bank were cheques received from his patients. The amounts received included Rs. 8,300 being the outstandings of 1979.

(2) The fees earned by him in 1980 were Rs. 19,600 of which Rs. 5,300 were not received during the year.

(3) The expenses outstanding were as follows :

	As on 1-1-1980 Rs.	As on 31-12-1980 Rs.
Salaries	500	1,000
Printing & stationery	—	300
Subscriptions	100	—
Rent and taxes	1,500	—
General expenses	—	700
	2,100	2,000

(4) As on 1st January, 1980 his fixed assets were as follows :

Furniture Rs. 2,000 and equipment Rs. 20,000

(5) Provide for depreciation of Rs. 300 on furniture and Rs. 2,000 on equipment.

You are required to prepare the Balance Sheet as at 1st Jan., 1980, profit and loss account for the year 1980 and balance sheet as on 31st December, 1980, from the particulars given above.

(*Mysore, B.Com., 1986*)

Solution :

Dr. King George

Statement of Affairs as on 1-1-1980

Dr. (To find out opening capital) Cr.

Liabilities		Rs.	Assets	Rs.
Outstanding expenses :			Cash at Bank	700
(of 1979)			Equipments	20,000
Salaries	500		Furniture	2,000
Subscriptions	100		Outstanding fees (of 1979)	8,300
Rent & taxes	1,500	2,100		
Capital (Balancing figure)		28,900		
		31,000		31,000

Bank Account
(To find out closing Bank balance)

Dr.	Rs.		Cr. Rs.
To Balance b/d	700	By Medicines purchased	3,000
To Outstanding fees of 1979 received during the year	8,300	By Furniture purchased	1,000
To Fees of 1980 received (19,600 – 5,300)	14,300	By Equipment purchased	5,000
		By Salaries	2,500
		By Printing & stationery	1,200
		By Subscriptions paid	200
		By Drawings	2,400
		By Rent and taxes	4,500
		By General expenses	2,000
		By Balance c/d (Balancing figure)	1,500
	23,300		23,300

Profit and Loss Account
for the year ended 31st Dec., 1980

Dr.		Rs.		Cr. Rs.
To Medicines purchased		3,000	By Fees earned & due (*i.e.*, 14,300 + 5,300)	19.600
To Salary	2,500			
Less : Previous year outstanding	500			
	2,000			
Add : Current year outstanding	1,000	3,000		
To Printing & stationery	1,200			
Add : C.Y.O.S.	300	1,500		
To Subscriptions	200			
Less : P.Y.O.S.	100	100		
To Rent & taxes	4,500			
Less : P.Y.O.S.	1,500			
	3,000			
Less : Prepaid	500	2,500		
To General expenses	2,000			
Add : C.Y.O.S.	700	2,700		
To Dep. : Furniture	300			
Equipment	2,000	2,300		
To Net profit (transferred to capital)		4,500		
		19,600		19,600

Balance Sheet as at 31st Dec., 1980

Liabilities		Rs.	Assets		Rs.
Capital :			Furniture	2,000	
Opening capital	28,900		*Add* : Additions	1,000	
Add : Net profits	4,500			3,000	
	33,400		*Less* : Depreciation	300	2,700
Less : Drawings	2,400	31,000	Equipment	20,000	
Outstanding expenses :			*Add* : Additions	5,000	
Salary	1,000			25,000	
Printing & stationery	300		*Less* : Depreciation	2,000	23,000
General expenses	700	2,000	Prepaid rent & taxes		500
			Dues from patients		5,300
			Cash at Bank		1,500
		33,000			33,000

Illustration 16

Mr. Slipshod started business as a provision merchant on 1st Jan., 1979. He opened a bank account for the business with Rs. 25,000 and immediately spent Rs. 12,500 on fixtures and fittings. The only records kept were of cash sales which amounted in 1979 to Rs. 37,500 and in 1980 to Rs. 45,000. There were no credit sales. Following facts were ascertained :

(a) All expenses of the business had been met by cheques and an analysis of the Bank Pass Book showed the following payment in the two years.

Purchases (of which Rs. 37,000 related to 1979)	Rs. 63,750
Rent and Taxes	Rs. 5,100
Salaries	Rs. 11,000
Advertising	Rs. 1,400
Other expenses	Rs. 2,880

(b) The value of the stock on 31st Dec., 1980 was Rs. 15,000. No Stock was taken on 31st Dec., 1979, but a uniform rate of gross profit may be assumed.

(c) Liabilities outstanding at 31st Dec., 1980 were :

Purchases	Rs. 7,500
Advertising	Rs. 500
Other expenses (light, heat, etc.)	Rs. 170

(d) Amounts paid in Advance at 31st Dec., 1980 were :

Rates	Rs. 100
Other expenses (Insurance)	Rs. 50

(e) All business expenses arose equally in the two periods.

(f) Goods were taken from stock for private consumption, the estimated cost being Rs. 500 in 1979 and Rs. 750 in 1980.

(g) Private drawings amounting to Rs. 6,620 were met out of cash receipts and the balance was banked.

(h) Private income of Rs. 2,250 had been paid into the bank. The fixtures and fitting are to be written off over 10 years in equal instalments. On the basis of the foregoing, you are required to prepare:

(i) Trading and Profit and Loss account for each of the years 1979 and 1980.

(ii) Balance Sheet as at 31-12-1980.

(B.Com., Madurai & C.A. Final)

Solution :

In this problem, the stock on 31st Dec., 1979 is not given. This stock can be found out only if the normal rate of gross profit on sales is known. Therefore, we have to prepare a combined trading account for the two years 1979 and 1980 to ascertain the combined gross profit for the years 1979 and 1980 and find out the rate of gross profit on sales in two years because rate of gross profit will help us in ascertaining the closing stock of 1979.

Combined Trading Account for the years 1979 and 1980

Dr. (To find out the rate of gross profit on sales) Cr.

	Rs.		Rs.
To Purchases for the year 1979 & 1980 :		By Sales :	
Cash purchases 63,750		1979 37,500	
Credit purchases for the year 1980 7,500		1980 45,000	82,500
71,250		By Closing stock for the year 1980	15,000
Less : Goods taken by the proprietor for private consumption (500 + 750) 1,250	70,000		
To Gross profit for the year 1979 and 1980 (Balancing figure)	27,500		
	97,500		97,500

Rate of gross profit on sales : $\frac{\text{Combined G/P of 1979 \& 1980}}{\text{Combined sales of 1979 \& 1980}} \times 100$

i.e., $\frac{27,500}{82,500} \times 100 = 33\frac{1}{3}\%$

Combined Bank Account for the years 1979 & 1980)
(To find out the bank balance as on 31-12-1980)

Dr.		Rs.		Cr. Rs.
To Capital A/c		25,000	By Fixtures & fittings	12,500
To Cash sales (37,500 + 45,000)	82,500		By Purchases	63,750
Less : Drawings out of cash sales	6,620	75,880	By Rent & taxes	5,100
To Capital A/c (Private income deposited into bank)		2,250	By Salaries	11,000
			By Advertising	1,400
			By Other expenses	2,880
			By Balance c/d (Balancing figure)	6,500
		1,03,130		1,03,130
To Balance b/d		6,500		

Trading and Profit and Loss Account
for the years ended 31st Dec., 1979 and 1980

	1979	1980	1979 Rs.	1980 Rs.		1979 Rs.	1980 Rs.
To Opening Stock (*i.e.*, Closing stock of the year 1979)				11,500	By Sales	37,500	45,000
To Purchases	37,000	34,250			By Closing Stock (Balancing figure for 1979)	11,500	15,000
Less : Goods taken for personal use	500	750	36,500	33,500			
To Gross profit c/d (33-1/3% of sales)			12,500	15,000			
			49,000	60,000		49,000	60,000
To Salaries			5,500	5,500	By Gross profit	12,500	15,000
To Rent & taxes	5,100						
Less : Prepaid	100		2,500	2,500			
To Advertising	1,400						
Add : Outstanding	500		950	950			
To Other expenses	2,880						
Add : Outstandings	170						
	3,050						
Less : Prepaid	50		1,500	1,500			
To Depreciation on fixtures & fitting : 10% on Rs. 12,500			1,250	1,250			
To Net profit (transferred to capital)			800	3,300			
			12,500	15,000		12,500	15,000

Balance Sheet as on 31st Dec., 1980

Liabilities			Rs.	Assets		Rs.
Creditors for purchases				Cash at Bank		6,500
as on 31-12-1980			7,500	Closing stock		15,000
Outstanding Liabilities for				Prepaid Expenses:		
expenses as on				Rate	100	
31-12-1980 :		Rs.		Insurance	50	150
Advertising		500		Fixtures & fittings :		
Other expenses		170	670	Cost	12,500	
Capital :				*Less* : Depreciation :		
Introduced on 1-1-79		25,000		10% p.a. for		
Add : Private income				two years	2,500	10,000
paid in		2,250				
Add : Net profit 1979		800				
1980		3,300				
		31,350				
Less : Drawings :						
Cash	6,620					
Goods	1,250	7,870	23,480			
			31,650			31,650

Examination Questions

(A) Answer the following questions in not exceeding 4 lines each.

(Each Carries 2 Marks)

(1) What is single entry system of book keeping?

(Bangalore, April, 1984)

(2) Define single entry system?

(3) What do you mean by pure single entry system?

(4) What is simple single entry system?

(5) What do you understand by quasi-single entry system?

(6) Mention the classification of single entry system.

(7) Mention the four advantages of single entry system.

(8) Mention any two defects of single entry book keeping.

(Bangalore, Nov., 1982 & April, 1982)

(9) Mention any four demerits of single entry system.

(Karnatak, April, 1995)

(10) Mention two differences between single entry system and statement of affairs.

(11) What is statement affairs?

(Karnatak, Oct., 1996)

(12) Mention two differences between statement of affairs and balance sheet.

(13) Mention any two objectives of converting single entry into double entry.

(Bangalore, April, 1993)

(14) How do you ascertain credit sales and credit purchases in single entry system?

(Karnatak, April, 1996)

(15) How to you ascertain Bills Payable issued and Bill Receivable received in single entry system?

(16) What is single entry system? State any two advantages of its system?

(Karnatak, Oct., 1997)

(17) How do you find out profit in single entry system?

(Karnatak, April, 1998)

(18) How do you find out the value of credit purchases while converting single entry into double entry?

(Bangalore, April, 1997)

(19) What are the demerits of single entry book keeping?

(Bangalore, April, 1998)

(B) Answer the following questions/problems :

(Each Carries 16 marks)

(1) What is single entry system? Explain its features.

(2) What are the types of single entry system?

(3) Explain the drawbacks of single entry system.

(Karnatak, 1980)

(4) Distinguish between statement of affairs and Balance Sheet.

(Bangalore, April, 1985)

(5) What is Statement of Affairs? Explain the steps to be taken in preparing the same.

(M.K.U., Oct., 1992)

(6) Explain the steps to be taken to convert single entry into double entry.

(Shivaji, April, 1989)

(7) What are the objectives of converting the single entry into double entry system?

(8) Correctly write the following after deleting the words that are not applicable :

(i) Single-entry system of book keeping is a scientific/crude way of writing accounts.

(ii) Single-entry system is generally adopted by petty shopkeepers/ large traders.

(iii) Under single-entry, the net profits of the concern can/cannot be easily and accurately obtained.

(iv) Whenever additional capital is brought in, it is a added/deducted out of the capital as at the end of the year, to know the profits.

(v) Single-entry system can be/cannot be converted into double-entry system.

(vi) Under single-entry system partnership business is possible/not possible.

(Shivaji, April, 1992)

Ans. : (i) Crude way, (ii) Petty shopkeeper, (iii) Cannot be easily obtained, (iv) Deducted, (v) Can be converted, (vi) Impossible.

(9) Smt. Kanta keeps her accounts on Single-entry Method. Following are the particulars available of her assets and liabilities as on 1-1-1996 and 31-12-1996.

	1-1-1996	31-12-1996
	Rs.	Rs.
Cash in Hand	200	300
Cast at Bank	500	800
Loan from Bank	2,000	3,000
Debtors	3,000	2,000
Furniture	1,500	2,600
Creditors	1,000	1,400

Find out her opening and closing apital balances.

Ans. : Opening Capital Rs. 2,000; Closing Capital Rs. 1,300.

(10) Vijay, a trader keeps his books under single entry system. His opening capital is Rs. 13,250. During the year he introduced Rs. 2,500 as further capital. He had withdrawn Rs. 375 per month. On 31-12-1994 his financial position was as follows :

Cash at Bank Rs. 1,000; Cash in Hand Rs. 150; Stock in trade Rs. 9,500; Debtors Rs. 7,000; Furniture Rs. 750; Machinery Rs. 13,500 and Creditors Rs. 14,500. From the above particulars prepare a statement showing the profit or loss for the year ended 31-12-1994.

(*M.K.U., Oct., 1995*)

Ans. : Profit Rs. 6,150; Closing Capital Rs. 17,400.

(11) From the following particulars ascertain the sales : Opening stock Rs. 6,000; Closing stock Rs. 9,000; Purchases Rs. 40,000; Direct expenses Rs. 3,000; Rate of Gross profit 20% on sale.

(*Bangalore, April, 1989*)

Ans. : Sales Rs. 50,000. Cost of goods sold Rs. 40,000.

Note : 20% on sales is 25% on cost.

(12) From the following facts you are required to calculate total purchases:

	Rs.
Opening balance of bills payable	5,000
Opening balance of creditors	6,000
Closing balance of bills payable	7,000
Closing balance of creditors	4,000
Cash paid to creditors during the year	30,200
Bills payable discharged during the year	8,900
Returns outwards	1,200
Cash purchases	25,800

(*B.Com.* (*Pass*), *Delhi, 1975*)

Ans. : Creditors being bills accepted during the year Rs. 10,900
Credit purchases Rs. 40,300; Total purchases Rs. 66,100.

(13) From the following information, prepare the Total Debtors & Total Creditors Account :

	Rs.		Rs.
Sundry debtors on 1-1-84	12,000	Discount allowed	350
Sundry debtors on 31-12-84	9,800	Discount received	250
Cash received from debtors	6,400	Bill received from debtors	2,500
Sundry creditors on 1-1-84	7,600	Acceptance given to creditors	5,870
Sundry creditors on 31-12-84	9,030	Bad debts	300
Cash paid to creditors	1,750	Bills dishonoured by debtors	400

(*Kar. Board, April, 1985*)

Ans. : Credit Sales Rs. 4,150; Credit purchases Rs. 9,300.

(14) From the following prepare Total Debtors Account and Total Creditors Account and find out Credit Sales and Credit Purchases :

	Rs.		Rs.
Debtors as on 1st January	5,000	Bad debts written off	1,200
Creditors as on 1st January	4,000	Bad debts recovered	300
Debtors as on 31st December	4,000	Bill receivable endorsed to creditors	4,000
Creditors as on 31st December	6,000		
Bills receivable received during the year	10,000	Bills receivable dishonoured by customers	1,000
Bills payable issued during the year	8,000	Endorsed bills receivable dishonoured	500
Cash received from customers	30,000	Bills receivable discounted	2,000
Cash returned to customers	500	Discounted bills receivable dishonoured	700
Cash paid to suppliers	20,700		
Discount allowed by suppliers	270	Sales returns	600
Discount allowed to customers	150	Purchases returns	200

(*Bangalore, B.Com., 1971*)

Ans. : Credit sales Rs. 30,250; Credit purchases Rs. 34,670

Note : B/R discounted and Bad Debt recovered shall not affect the Total Debtors Account.

(15)(a) From the following details, find out credit sales by preparing Total Debtors Account :

	Rs.		Rs.
Opening Balance of Debtors	40,000	Cheques from debtors dishonoured	1,000
Cash received from Debtors	3,60,000	Bad Debts written off	5,000
Cheque received from Debtors	50,000	Sales returns	4,000
B/R received during the year	10,000	B/R dishonoured during the year	100
B/R honoured during the year	5,000	Provisions for doubtful debts	500
		Closing Balance	48,000

(b) From the following particulars, find out closing balance by preparing Total Creditors' Account :

Opening Balance of creditors	1,80,000	Bills payable dishonoured	500
Payment by cheques	4,50,000	Cheques issued to creditors dishonoured	100
Payment in cash	50,000		
Bills payable issued	10,000	Discount allowed by creditors	400
Returns to creditors	600	Purchases	3,35,000
Bills payable honoured	2,000		

(*Mysore, B.Com.*)

Ans. : (a) Credit sales Rs. 4,35,900, (b) Closing balance of creditors Rs. 4,600

Note : (i) B/R honoured and provision for doubtful debts will appear in the Total Debtors' Account.

(ii) Bills payable honoured will not appear in the Total Creditors' Accounts.

(16) Ascertain credit sales and purchases from the following :

		Rs.
(a)	Opening debtors	10,000
(b)	Opening creditors	7,000
(c)	Cheques and cash received from debtors	28,000
(d)	Cheques and cash paid to creditors	21,000
(e)	Discount allowed by creditors	1,000
(f)	Discount allowed to debtors	1,500
(g)	Returns inwards	2,000
(h)	Returns outwards	1,500
(i)	Provision for doubtful debts	1,000
(j)	Bills accepted for creditors	5,000
(k)	Bills accepted by debtors	8,000
(l)	Cheques issued to creditors returned unpaid	500
(m)	Cheques and bills dishonoured by debtors	1,000

(n) Closing debtors	8,000
(o) Closing creditors	5,000

(*Karnatak, April, 1995*)

Ans. : Credit sales Rs. 36,500; Credit purchases Rs. 26,000.

Note : (i) Provision for doubtful debts is omitted.

(ii) Cheques returned unpaid means cheques dishonoured.

(17) From the following particulars prepare the total debtors' account and total creditors' account.

	Rs.
Sundry debtors on 1-1-1994	12,800
Sundry debtors on 31-12-1994	9,800
Sundry creditors on 1-1-1994	7,600
Sundry creditors on 31-12-1994	9,030
Cash received from debtors	6,400
Cash paid to creditors	1,750
Discount allowed	350
Discount received	250
Bills received from debtors	2,500
Acceptances given to creditors	5,870
Bad debts	300
Bills dishonoured by debtors	400
Credit purchases	?
Credit sales	?

(*Karnatak, Oct., 1995*)

Ans. : Credit sales Rs. 6,150; Credit purchases Rs. 9,300.

(18) From the following prepare Debtors and Bills Receivable Accounts :

	Rs.
Balance of total debtors as on 1-1-1995	12,700
Balance of total debtors as on 31-12-1995	15,000
Balance of bills receivable as on 1-1-1995	6,000
Balance of bills receivable as on 31-12-1995	9,000
Credit sales	?
Cash received from debtors	41,000
Bills receivable received from debtors	?
Bills receivable dishonoured	300
Cash received against bills	16,700
Goods returned from debtors	2,000
Discount allowed	1,300
Bad debts	700

(*Karnatak, Oct., 1996*)

Ans. : Bills receivable received from debtors Rs. 20,000; Credit sales Rs. 67,000.

(19) From the following particulars of Mr. X, who keeps his books under single-entry system, calculate the total sales :

	Rs.
Opening balance of bills receivable	25,000
Opening balance of sundry debtors	39,000
Closing balance of bills receivable	35,000
Closing balance of sundry debtors	25,400
Bills receivable encashed during the year	1,00,000
Cash received from debtors	2,87,000
Returns inwards	5,600
Bad debts written off	7,000
Bills receivable dishonoured	5,000
Cash sales	70,000

(*Bangalore, April, 1990*)

Ans. : Bill receivable received from debtors (as per Bills Receivable A/c) Rs. 1,15,000: B/R, A/c Total Rs. 1,40,000; Credit sales Rs. 3,96,000; Total Debtors A/c Total Rs. 4,40,000 and Total Sales Rs. 4,66,000 (Cash sales Rs. 70,000 + Credit Sales Rs. 3,96,000).

(20) From the following particulars you are required to prepare Closing Balance for Debtors; Creditors; Bill Receivables and Bills Payable.

	Rs.
Total Debtors on 1st Jan., 1989	44,250
Total Creditors on 1st Jan., 1989	26,910
Bills Receivable on 1st Jan., 1989	16,000
Bills Payable on 1st Jan., 1989	5,000
Credit Sales	2,06,310
Credit Purchases	1,12,830
Cash received from Debtors	1,72,350
Discount allowed	1,740
Bad debts	2,550
Returns from Customers	3,450
Payment to Creditors	89,340
Discount allowed by Creditors	1,290
Returns outwards	1,560
B/R accepted by Customers	28,800
Bills payable accepted	19,200

Cash received against B/R	30,000
Cash paid against B/P	14,000

(*Bangalore, October, 1990*)

Ans. : Closing balance of Total Debtors' Account Rs. 41,670
Closing balance of Total Creditors' Account Rs. 28,350
Closing balance of Bill Receivable Account Rs. 14,800
Closing balance of Bill Payable Account Rs. 10,200

(21) From the following particulars available from the books of Mr. Ravath, you are required to determine the total purchases for the year 1990 :

	Rs.
Total creditors balance on 1-1-90	39,200
Bills payable balance on 1-1-90	9,345
Discount earned	1,455
Cash purchases	4,800
Cash paid to creditors (including payment to a supplier of a sum of Rs. 1,800 towards the cost of furniture)	23,532
Returns outwards	1,156
Bills payable balance on 31-12-90	14,345
Payment made against bills payable	14,000
Bills receivable endorsed to creditors	2,057
Total creditors balance on 31-12-90	33,000

(*Bangalore, April, 1994*)

Ans. : Credit purchases Rs. 37,745; Bills Payable accepted during the year Rs. 19,000 and cash paid to Creditors Rs. 21,732 (*i.e.*, 23,532 – 1,800).

(22) From the following information, calculate the total purchases :

	Rs.
Bills payable 1-1-1994	12,000
Creditors 1-1-1994	10,000
Bills payable 31-12-1994	16,000
Creditors 31-12-1994	12,000
Bills payable paid during the year	17,800
Cash paid to creditors	60,400
Returns outwards	2,400
Cash purchases	41,600
Discount allowed by creditors	200

(*Bangalore, April, 1995*)

Ans. : Bills payable issued to creditors (as per Bills Payable Account) Rs. 21,800; Credit purchases Rs. 86,800 and Total purchases Rs. 1,28,400 (Cash purchases Rs. 41,600 + Credit purchases Rs. 86,800).

(23) From the following particulars available from the books of Mr. Prem Kumar, you are required to determine the total sales for the year 1997 :

	Rs.
Total Debtors balance on 1-1-97	1,30,000
Cash received from Debtors	1,90,000
Discount allowed	4,000
Bills receivable received	16,000
Bills receivable dishonoured during the year	2,000
Bad debts	1,000
Cash sales	13,000
Returns inward	5,200
Returns outward	7,500
Discount earned	2,200
Total Debtors' balance on 31-12-97	65,000

(Bangalore, April, 1998)

Ans. : Total Debtors' Account Total Rs. 2,81,200;
Credit sales Rs. 1,49,200;
Total sales Rs. 1,62,200 (*i.e.*, 1,49,200 + Cash sales Rs. 13,000).

(C) Solve the following problems :

(Each Carries 16 Marks)

Statement of Affairs Method

(1) Laxman commenced business on 1-1-81 with a capital of Rs. 40,000. Rs. 36,000 brought in cash and the balance in the form of furniture. On 1-8-81 he introduced Rs. 8,000 in the business of which Rs. 5,000 was borrowed from his wife. During the year, he withdrew at the rate of Rs. 750 per month. His position on 31-12-81 was as follows :

Assets : Stock of goods Rs. 24,000; Sundry debtors Rs. 20,000; Furniture Rs. 4,000; Cash at Bank Rs. 6,000; Cash in Hand Rs. 400; Bills receivable Rs. 3,600 and Plant Rs. 22,000.

Liabilities : He owed to sundry creditors Rs. 16,000 and loan to his wife Rs. 5,000.

Ascertain his profit for the year ending 31st Dec., 1981.

(Karnatak Board, 1983)

Ans. : Closing capital Rs. 59,000 and Gross profit Rs. 25,000
Note : Loan from wife is not an additional capital.

(2) A and B who share profits and losses in the ratio of 3 : 2 keep their books by single-entry. On 1st July, 1985, their financial position was as follows : Cash Rs. 498; Bank Rs. 2,308; Stock Rs. 4,972; Furniture Rs. 1,480; B/R Rs. 1,309; Patents Rs. 1,300; Debtors Rs. 1,386; B/P Rs. 3,924; Creditors Rs. 1,329; A's Capital Rs. 5,000; B's Capital Rs. 3,000.

On 30th June, 1986, their Statement of Affairs was as follows : Cash Rs. 327; Bank Rs. 428; B/R Rs. 2,908; Stock Rs. 1,227; Debtors Rs. 2,460; Furniture Rs. 1,480; Patents Rs. 1,300; B/P Rs. 1,369; Creditors Rs. 2,497. Ascertain the profit or loss for the year ended 30th June, 1986, after allowing 6% interest on capital and charging depreciation 10% on patents and 7½% on Furniture. Create a Reserve for doubtful debts at 5% on debtors. During this period A withdrew for personal use Rs. 420 and B Rs. 390. Prepare also a Statement of Affairs as on 30th June, 1986.

(Rajasthan Board)

Ans. : Net loss Rs. 1,770; Statement of Affairs total Rs. 9,766.

(3) Raju kept his books under single-entry system. From the following details ascertain his profit or loss for the year ending 30th June, 1975. Also prepare a final statement of affairs :

Particulars	**1-7-1974**	**30-6-1975**
Stock in trade	16,700	18,500
Sundry Creditors	15,400	14,000
Sundry Debtors	11,200	10,500
Cash in Hand	250	1,200
Bills Receivable	15,050	14,200
Bank overdraft	20,200	19,400
Fixtures	1,500	1,500
Motor-van	1,900	1,900

Drawings during the year amounted to Rs. 2,600. Depreciate fixture by 10%. Write off Rs. 300 from the value of the motor-van. As regards to debtors, it is ascertained that Rs. 500 for bad and a reserve 5% for doubtful debts is to be credited. Further, a reserve of Rs. 700 in respect of Bills receivable is to be made.

(Kar. Board, April, 1979 and Oct., 1980 modified)

Ans.: Opening capital Rs. 11,000; Closing capital Rs. 14,400; Net profit Rs. 3,850; Revised Statement of Affairs Total Rs. 45,650.

(4) A, B and C entered into partnership on 1st April, 1973 and contributed as capital Rs. 20,000; Rs. 15,000 and Rs. 10,000 respectively. They agreed to share profits and losses in the same proportion after charging interest on capital at 5% per annum. The firm kept their books by single-entry during the year ending 31st March, 1974, when they decided to convert to double-entry system. For this purpose, a Statement of Affairs was prepared which showed :

	Rs.		Rs.
Cash	150	Bank	4,680
Debtors	30,000	Bills Receivable	3,500
Stock	20,000	Plant	8,600
Furniture	2,000	Creditors	10,200
Bills payable	3,000		

These items were agreed subject to a provision of Rs. 1,500 for doubtful debts and depreciation on plant at 10% and on furniture at 5%. Prepare a Statement of Profit for the year and Statement of Affairs as on 31-3-1974

(*Mysore, B.Com., 1973*)

Ans. : Closing Capital Rs. 55,730; N/P Rs. 6,020 (A-2,675.56; B-2,006.66; C-1,337.78); Revised statement of Affairs Total Rs. 66,470.

(5) Angel and Lucas were in partnership sharing profit and losses in the proportion of the 3/5 and 2/5 respectively. The firms books were kept by single-entry and the following Statement of Affairs was prepared on 31st March, 1984 :

	Rs.		Rs.
Capital :		Lease	2,075
Angle	18,000	Plant & Machinery	4,940
Lucas	10,000	Stock	9,673
Creditors	3,170	Sundry Debtors	15,550
Bills Payable	2,150	Cash	1,082

On 31st March, 1985, investigation disclosed that Lucas had introduced a further Rs. 1,000 capital on September 30, 1984; that Rs. 500 had been spent upon new machinery and that the partners cash drawings during the year had been Angel, Rs. 950 and Lucas, Rs. 630. It was ascertained that Angle had Rs. 75 worth of goods out of the business for his private use. Statements were prepared on the same date showing :

Sundry Debtors	Rs. 14,640
Sundry Creditors	Rs. 2,039
Bills Payable	Rs. 1,775

The stock was valued on 31st March, 1985 at Rs. 11,417 and the cash amounted to Rs. 917. You are required to prepare statement of profit and statement of affairs as on 31st March, 1985, taking into consideration the following: 5% to be reserved on sundry debtors for bad debts. 7½% to be written off plant and machinery, Rs. 125 to be written off the lease. Interest at 5% p.a. to be credited to partners in respect of their capital in the business.

(B.Com., Bombay)

Ans. : Net Profit Rs. 677.50; Statement of Affairs Total Rs. 33,261.50.

(6) X and Y are equal partners in a business in which the books are kept by single entry. The position of affairs on 1st January was as under :

Liabilities	Rs.	Assets	Rs.
Bills Payable	646	Cash in Hand	27
Sundry Creditors	2,029	Cash at Bank	220
Capital Accounts :		Bills Receivable	407
X	7,340	Sundry Debtors	4,868
Y	7,340	Stock	3,285
		Plant	8,018
		Furniture	530
	17,355		17,355

The following was the state of affairs on 31st December: Cash in hand Rs. 40; Cash at Bank Rs. 584; Debtors 5,629; Bills Receivable Rs. 684; Stock Rs. 3,673; Creditors Rs. 2,147; Bills Payable Rs. 595. The partners had drawn Rs. 450 each and were further entitled to interest on their capital at 5% per annum. It was agreed to depreciate plant at the rate of 10% and furniture at 5%. Draw up the final accounts.

(B.Com., Panjab)

Ans. : Combined closing capital of A & B Rs. 15,587; Profit Rs. 1,073.

(7) Mr. A does not maintain complete double entry books of accounts. From the following details determine the profits for the year and Statement of Affairs at the end of the year.

Rs. 1,000 (cost) furniture was sold for Rs. 5,000 on 1-1-1977; 10% depreciation is to be charged on furniture. Mr. A has drawn Rs. 1,000 per month. Rs. 2,000 was invested by Mr. A in 1977.

	1-1-1977	31-12-1977
Stock	40,000	60,000
Debtors	30,000	40,000
Cash	2,000	1,000
Bank	10,000	5,000 (O.D)
Creditors	15,000	25,000
Outstanding expenses	5,000	8,000
Furniture (cost)	3,000	2,000

Bank balance on 1-1-1977 is as per cash book, but the bank overdraft on 31-12-1977 is as per bank statement. Rs. 2,000 cheque drawn in December 1977 has not been encashed within the year.

(*B.Com., Madras, March, 1977*)

Ans. : Opening capital Rs. 65,000; Closing capital Rs. 63,000; Net profit Rs. 78,000; Revised Statement of Affairs Total Rs. 1,02,800.

Note : Overdraft as per bank Rs. 5,000
Add : Cheques unpresented Rs. 2,000
Overdraft as per cash book Rs. 7,000

(It should be taken on the liability side of the balance sheet at the end.)

(8) Dwarkadas keeps his books by the single-entry system. His financial position as on 31st Dec., 1988 was as follows :

	Rs.		Rs.
Cash in Hand	180	Sundry Debtors	6,300
Cash in Bank	2,250	Machinery & Plant	15,000
Stock in Trade	9,630	Fittings & Fixtures	1,200
Sundry Creditors	15,560		

During the year, Dwarkadas drew from business for his household expenses Rs. 6,000 and paid Rs. 500 for premium on his life policy. On 31st Dec, 1989, his financial position stood as follows :

	Rs.		Rs.
Cash in Hand	225	Sundry Debtors	10,950
Overdraft at Bank	7,500	Machinery & Plant	20,000
Stock in Trade	14,000	Fixture & Fittings	1,200
Sundry Creditors	20,000		

From the above particulars prepare a statement showing the profits made by Dwarkadas for the year ended 31st Dec., 1989, and his Balance sheet at that date. Write off depreciation on Machinery at 5% per annum and on Fittings and Fixtures at 10% per annum. Allow interest on Capital at 5% per annum (ignoring interest on drawing.)

(*B.Com., Bombay*)

Ans. : Net profit Rs. 3,555; Balance sheet total Rs. 45,505.

(9) Kumar, Krishna and Keshava in partnership, kept their books by single-entry. Their capitals on 1st Jan., 1980 were Rs. 20,000, Rs. 15,000 and Rs. 5,000 respectively. Interest at 5% was payable on the capital as at the commencement of each year. Krishna and Keshava were entitled to salary of Rs. 200 and Rs. 300 respectively every month. They shared profits and losses as follows : Kumar 1/2, Krishna 1/3, and Keshava 1/6. In the six months ending

30th June, 1980, Krishna and Keshava had drawn the salary and the drawings were : Kumar Rs. 500; Krishna Rs. 750 and Keshava Rs. 1,000.

On 30th June, 1980 the position was :

	Rs.		Rs.
Creditors	5,000	Cash	1,250
Bills Payable	750	Plant	9,000
		Building	8,000
		Debtors	10,000
		Stock	27,000
			55,250

Prepare the capital accounts and the Balance sheet as on 30th June, 1980.

(*B.Com., Kurukshetra*)

Ans. : Closing capital Rs. 49,500; Net profit Rs. 10,750 (Kumar Rs. 5,375.00; Krishna Rs. 3,583.33; Keshava Rs. 1,791.67).
Capital A/c Balance : Kumar Rs. 25,375.00; Krishna Rs. 18,208.33; Keshava Rs. 5,916.67.
Balance Sheet Total Rs. 55,250.

(10) 'R' keeps his books on the single-entry system. His statement of Assets & Liabilities as at Dec., 31, 1983 is as follows :

Liabilities	Rs.	Assets	Rs.
Sundry Creditors	65,000	Land & Buildings	20,000
Loan from Moneylender	56,600	Furniture & Fixtures	3,000
Sundry Other Liabilities	13,400	Plant & Machinery	55,000
		Stock	9,200
		Sundry Debtors	75,500
		Cash	8,300
	1,35,000		1,71,000

His drawings during the year amounted to Rs. 3,000. Land and Buildings are to be depreciated by 2%, Furniture & Fixtures by 5% and Plant & Machinery by 10%. Sundry Debtors are to be reduced by 2%. He has used Rs. 800 worth of stock of his business for private purposes. During the year 1983 he sold some of his household furniture for Rs. 1,000 and paid this into his business Bank Account. His capital at the beginning of the year was Rs. 30,000. Draw up his statement of profit & loss for the year ended December 31, 1983.

(*Calcutta, B.Com., Hons., 1984*)

Ans : Closing capital Rs. 36,000; Net profits Rs. 1,240.

(11) The following information is available from Ram's records.

Particulars	1-7-1969	30-6-1970
Creditors	5,000	8,000
Bank overdraft	—	15,000
Bank balance	10,000	—
Plant & Machinery	10,000	20,000
Furniture	4,000	4,000
Debtors	30,000	52,000
Stock of goods	34,000	28,000

Ram had withdrawn Rs. 5,000 for personal expenses and Rs. 4,000 for son's marriage, out of the business funds he had also purchased a residential building costing Rs. 20,000 which is not shown in the above balance. Additions to machinery were made on 1st July, 1969. Depreciation at 10% p.a. should be provided on plant and machinery.

Please find out Ram's net profit for the year ended 30th June, 1970.

(*B.Com., Bangalore, 1971*)

Ans. : Opening capital Rs. 83,000; Closing capital Rs. 81,000; Net profit Rs. 25,000; Total drawings Rs. 29,000.

(12) The following balances appear in the Mr. Jacob's books which are kept under single-entry system :

	31-12-1970 Rs.	31-12-1971 Rs.
Creditors	39,803	41,538
Furniture	4,000	4,000
Stock	51,304	46,217
Debtors	34,511	37,622
Bank balance	2,420	2,306
Motor-car	—	12,350
Bills payable	—	6,750

Jacob has been regularly transferring Rs. 900 per month by cheques from his banking account to his private use. He has also taken goods worth Rs. 1,384 for his private use.

Calculate Mr. Jacob's profit or loss for the year ended 31st Dec., 1971 and also the Statement of Affairs as on that date after providing depreciation on furniture and motor car (which was brought on 30th June, 1971) at 5% each. Office rent Rs. 150 and salary to the office stenographer Rs. 325 for the month of Dec., 1971 were yet due.

(*Kar. Board, Oct., 1973*)

Ans. : Opening Capital Rs. 54,432; Net profit Rs. 12,975.25 Revised Statement of Affairs Total Rs. 1,01,986.25.

(13) 'R' had Rs. 3,00,000 in Bank on 1st January, 1969 when he started his business. He closed his accounts on 31st March, 1970. His single-entry books (in which he did not maintain any account for the bank) showed his position as follows :

	31-3-69 Rs.	31-3-70 Rs.
Cash in Hand	2,000	3,000
Debtors	1,000	2,000
Stock in trade	19,000	29,000
Creditors	5,000	3,000

On 1st February, 1969 he began drawing Rs. 700 per month for his personal expenses from the cash box of the business.

His account in the Bank had the following entries :

	Deposits Rs.	Withdrawals Rs.
1-1-1969	3,00,000	—
1-1-1969 to 31-3-1969	—	2,23,000
1-4-1969 to 31-3-1970	2,30,000	2,70,000

The above withdrawals included payments by cheques of Rs. 2,00,000 and Rs. 60,000 respectively during the periods from 1st January, 1969 to 31st March, 1969 and from 1st April, 1969 to 31st March, 1970 for the purchase of machinery for the business; and the deposits after 1st January, 1969 consisted wholly of sale price received from customers by cheques.

Draw up 'R's Statement of Affairs as on 31st March, 1969 and 31st March, 1970 respectively and workout his profit or loss for the year ended 31st March, 1970.

(Institute of Company Secretaries, Inter, 1970 and B.Com., Osmania)

Ans. : Opening Capital Rs. 2,94,000; Closing Capital Rs. 3,28,000; Opening Cash at Bank Rs. 77,000 (3,00,000 – 2,23,000); Closing Cash at Bank Rs. 37,000 (77,000 + 2,30,000 – 2,70,000); Opening Machinery Rs. 2,00,000; Closing Machinery Rs. 2,60,000; Net Profit Rs. 42,400.

(14) A, B and C were in partnership and towards the end of 1988, most of their books and records were destroyed in fire. The Balance sheet of the firm as on 31-12-1987 was as follows :

		Rs.		Rs.
Creditors		11,000	Cash at Bank	4,800
Capital A/cs :	Rs.		Debtors	7,200
A	9,000		Stock	13,000
B	6,000		Machinery & Plant	2,880
C	3,000	18,000	Fixture & Furniture	1,200
Current A/cs :	Rs.		Advance Payments	70
A	290		Current A/c :	
B	200	490	C	340
		29,490		29,490

The partners' drawings during 1988 were : A Rs. 2,800; B Rs. 2,000; and C Rs. 1,300. On 31st Dec., 1988, the cash at Bank was Rs. 6,400; Debtors Rs. 8,050; Stock Rs. 11,800; Advance Payments Rs. 50; and Creditors Rs. 12,080.

Machinery is to be depreciated at 10% and Fixtures & Furniture at 7½%. 5% interest is to be allowed on Capital. The partners' share profits in the respective proportions of 1/2, 1/3 and 1/6.

You are required to prepare a statement showing net profit for the year 1988, and the division of the same between the partners, together with the Balance Sheet as at 31-12-1988.

(B.Com., Calcutta and Banaras)

Ans. : Closing Capital Rs.18,300; Net Profit Rs. 4,972 (A - Rs. 2,486; B - Rs. 1,657 and C - Rs. 829).

Revised Statement of Affairs Total Rs. 30,663.

Conversion Method

(1) Roshan keeps his books on Single-entry. He gives you the following information :

Particulars	31-12-1977 Rs.	31-12-1978 Rs.
Furniture	5,000	6,000
Stock	3,000	1,000
Debtors	10,000	7,000
Cash	1,100	300
Creditors	4,000	7,000

Receipts and Payments during the year 1978 :

Receipts from debtors	Rs. 21,000
Paid to creditors	Rs. 10,000
Drawings	Rs. 12,000
Business expenses	Rs. 18,000
Furniture purchased for cash	Rs. 1,000

There was a considerable amount of cash sales. Prepare Trading and Profit and Loss Account for the year ended 31st Dec., 1978 and the Balance Sheet as on that day after providing for bad debts at 10%.

(*Gulbarga, April,1990*)

Ans. : Opening Capital Rs.15,100; Credit Sales Rs. 18,000; Credit Purchases Rs. 13,000; Cash Sales Rs. 19,200; Gross Profit Rs. 22,200; Net Profit Rs. 3,500; Balance Sheet Total Rs. 13,600.

(2) You are able to obtain the following information from the books of Mr. Firmfoot. Prepare therefrom an account to ascertain the profit for the year ending 31st December, 1982 and a balance sheet on that date.

Position on 1st Jan., 1982 :

Fixed Assets	Rs. 1,085;	Cash	Rs. 422
Book Debts	Rs. 1,561;	Creditors	Rs. 307

The analysis of cash transactions for the year showed Receipts from Debtors Rs. 7,080; Drawings of Proprietor Rs. 2,720; Payments to Creditors Rs. 3,012; Business Expenses Rs. 1,053.

There was no stock at the beginning or at the end of the year on 31st December, 1982, Mr. Firmfoot owed Rs. 535 for goods bought and his customers owed him Rs. 1,890 for goods supplied to them.

Provide 5% depreciation on fixed assets and raise a reserve of 10% on debtors.

(*Adapted from Mysore University I, B.Com., Oct., 1968*)

Ans. : Gross Profits: Rs. 4,169; Opening Capital Rs. 2,761; Net Profits: Rs. 2,872.75; Closing Cash Balance Rs. 717; Closing Capital Rs. 2,913.75; Closing Balance Sheet Total Rs. 3,448.75.

(3) The books of 'H' and 'S' on 31st December, 1975, showed the following position :

Capital Rs. 1,600; Profit Rs. 1,161; Creditors Rs. 307; Goodwill Rs. 618; Furniture Rs. 467; Debtors 1,561 and Bank Rs. 422. In the six months ending 30-6-1976, the accounts had been imperfectly kept and the bank transactions showed the following :

Receipts from customers Rs. 7,080; Drawings of partners Rs. 2,720; Salary paid Rs. 610; Payments to creditors Rs. 3,012; Rent, etc. paid Rs. 315 and Miscellaneous expenses Rs. 128. No account was taken of the stock, but a schedule of the debtors totalled Rs. 1,890 and that of the Creditors Rs. 535.

Prepare the Bank Account, the Trading and Profit and Loss Account and the Balance Sheet as on 30-6-1976.

(*Bangalore University, March, 1968*)

Ans.: Closing Bank Balance Rs. 717; Closing Capital Rs. 3,157; Gross Profits Rs. 4,169; Net Profits Rs. 3,116; Closing Balance Sheet Total Rs. 3,692.

(4) Mr. Shrikant did not maintain proper Books of Accounts, with the help of the records available, he requests you to prepare Final Accounts and the Balance Sheet. Following are the figures extracted from the books maintained by him during the period up to 31-12-1980.

You are required to Prepare Trading A/c, P & L A/c and Balance Sheet as on 31-12-1980.

I.

	1-1-1980 Rs.	31-12-1980 Rs.
Cash at Bank	1,500	2,700
Stock	22,500	19,500
Sundry Debtors	18,750	21,750
Machinery	30,000	30,000
Sundry Creditors	15,000	13,875

II. Receipts	**Rs.**	**Payments**	**Rs.**
Balance b/d	1,500	Payment to creditors	41,250
Received from Debtors	64,875	Wages	7,575
Miscellaneous Income	150	Salaries and Expenses	4,950
Cash Sales	3,150	Building Purchased	11,250
Loan from Mr. Laxmipati		Private Payments (Drawings)	3,450
@ 6% on 1-7-1980	1,500	Balance c/d	2,700
	71,175		71,175

III. Adjustments

(a) Expenses Outstanding Rs. 600; (b) Depreciate Machinery at 5% p.a.

(c) Write off Bad Debts Rs. 375.

(*KUD, Oct., 1981*)

Ans. : Credit Sales Rs. 67,875; Credit Purchases Rs. 40,125; Opening Capital Rs. 57,750; Gross Profit Rs. 20,325; Net Profit Rs. 10,005; Balance Sheet Total Rs. 80,325.

Note : Interest on loan for 6 months is calculated as follows :

$$1{,}500 \times \frac{6}{100} \times \frac{6}{12} = \text{Rs. } 45$$

(5) Mr. Nisher carries on a grocery business and does not keep his books on double-entry basis. The following particulars have been extracted from his books :

	1st July, 1962 Rs.	30th June, 1963 Rs.
Plant and Machinery	25,000	25,000
Stock	22,000	19,500
Sundry Debtors	8,000	25,500
Sundry Creditors	12,500	10,000
Cash in Hand	400	800
Bank Balance	6,250	*7,000

*Overdraft.

The following cash transactions took place during the year ending 30th June, 1963 :

	Rs.		Rs.
Received on account of Cash Sales	31,250	Payment for Purchases	28,850
		Payment of Sundry Creditors	1,32,000
Received from Sundry Debtors	1,60,000	General Expenses of Business	21,450
		Wages	15,000
		Drawings	6,800
	1,91,250		2,08,100

During the year, Nisher had taken goods from the business for his own consumption which amounted to Rs. 1,950 and not paid any money into the business for them, you are required to prepare :

(1) The Profit and Loss A/c for the year ending 30th June, 1963 after charging 10% depreciation on Plant and Machinery and also (2) The Balance Sheet as at 30th June, 1963.

(*B.U., November, 1966*)

Ans. : Credit Sales Rs. 1,77,500; Credit Purchases Rs. 1,29,500; Opening Capital Rs. 49,150; Gross Profit Rs. 34,150; Net Profit Rs. 10,900; Balance Sheet Total Rs. 68,300.

(6) Anand keeps his books of account on Single Entry System. He gives you the following information :

Assets and Liabilities as on :

	1-1-1981 Rs.	31-12-1981 Rs.
Cash	2,500	2,800
Stock	15,000	18,300
Sundry Debtors	16,000	20,000
Bills Receivable	6,400	4,800
Investments	—	5,000
Sundry Creditors	15,000	12,000

Summary of cash transactions during the year ending 31st Dec., 1981 :

Receipts	Rs.	Payments	Rs.
Balance b/d	2,500	Payment to Creditors	18,000
Received from debtors	40,000	Payment against Bills Payable	9,600
Received against Bills Receivable	10,000	Salaries	3,400
Interest on Investment	600	Rent and Taxes	2,000
		Purchases	12,300
		Investments	5,000
		Balance c/d	2,800
	53,100		53,100

(a) Provide reserve for doubtful debts at 5% on Debtors.

(b) Prepare

(1) total debtors account

(2) total creditors account

(3) bills receivable account

(4) bills payable account

(5) trading account and profit and loss account for the year ended 31-12-1981.

(6) balance sheet as on 31-12-1981.

(K.U.D., Oct., 1982 & 1997)

Ans. : (i) Opening Capital Rs. 24,900; (ii) Credit Sales Rs. 52,400; (iii) Credit Purchases Rs. 24,600; (iv) Gross Profit Rs. 18,800; (v) Net Profit Rs. 13,000; (vi) Balance Sheet Total Rs. 49,900.

(7) The books of Nayak and Bhat showed the following figures :

	1-1-82 Rs.	31-12-82 Rs.
Fixed Assets	3,000	3,000
Debtors	30,000	35,000
Creditors	23,400	18,500
Stock	22,000	25,000
Cash	3,400	19,950
Nayak's Capital	18,500	
Bhat's Capital	16,500	

Analysis of Cash Book for 1982 :

	Rs.
Collection from Debtors	1,35,000
Cash Sales	16,000
Discounts Allowed	1,400
Additional Capital from Bhat	2,000
Business Expenses	17,850
Drawings of Nayak	3,600
Payments of Creditors	1,12,000
Drawings of Bhat	3,000
Discounts received	1,200

Outstanding expenses at the end of the year amounted to Rs. 145. Reserve 5% for doubtful debts. Fixed assets were to be depreciated by 20%.

Prepare the Trading and Profit and Loss Accounts and the Balance Sheet of the firm, assuming that the Partners' share in Profits and Loss is equally.
(*Adapted from Mysore University, B.Com., Oct., 1971 & May, 1985 Modified*)

Ans. : Gross Profit Rs. 52,100; Net Profit Rs. 31,555; Closing Balance Sheet Total Rs. 80,600.

(8) Shri Angadi kept his accounts by Single-entry System. From the following particulars prepare Trading Account and Profit and Loss account for the year ended 31st March, 1972 and also Balance Sheet as on that date.

Receipts	Rs.
Fresh Capital brought in cash in business	15,000
Private dividend paid to Bank	200
Amount received from Debtors	22,000
Cash sales	1,200

Payments	Rs.
Paid to Creditors	28,200
Wages	1,500
Salaries	800
Rent	1,200
Purchase of cycle for his son	300
Private payments (Drawing)	3,000

The assets and liabilities were as follows :

	31-12-1972 Rs.	31-12-1971 Rs.
Sundry Debtors	1,400	2,000
Sundry Creditors	2,730	3,000
Stock	2,000	12,000
Land and Building	4,000	4,000
Furniture	1,000	1,000
Cash at bank	800	1,400
Cash in hand	30	830

Depreciate Land and Building by 5% and Furniture by 10%. Provide Reserve for Doubtful Debts 5% on Debtors.

(*Poona, 1960 & Karnatak, 1976*)

Ans. : Credit Sales Rs. 22,600; Credit Purchases Rs. 28,470;
Gross Profit Rs. 3,830; Net Profit Rs. 1,430;
Balance Sheet Total Rs. 22,830.

(9) Aravind did not keep a complete set of double entry records but was able to provide you with following information on December 31st, 1970 :

	1st July, 1970 Rs.	31st Dec., 1970 Rs.
Trade Debtors	4,884	5,580
Prepaid Insurance	—	150
Trade Creditors	2,580	2,772
Rent owing to Landlord	—	750
Sundry expenses unpaid	360	450
Stock in Trade	6,480	7,395
Machinery	13,500	15,150

Aravind deposited all cash into the Bank and made all payments by cheque and the following figures are available in respect of transactions with the Bank.

	Rs.		Rs.
Balance at Bank 1-1-1970	786	Insurance	750
Cash Sales	49,968	Payments to Creditors	51,048
Cash received from Debtors	24,486	Wages	8,001
Loan from Rajendra	3,000	Rent	2,250
		New Machinery	3,000
		Sundry Expenses	4,878
		Personal Drawings	6,240
		Balance at Bank (31-12-70)	2,073
	78,240		78,240

Further details which come to notice that a customer who owed Rs. 1,260 died leaving no assets behind. Discount Rs. 945 had been allowed on the receipts from debtors and discount of Rs. 1,962 had been deducted from the payments made to creditors.

You are required to prepare Trading and Profit and Loss Account for the year ended 31st December, 1970 and Balance Sheet as on 1-1-1970 and 31-12-1970.

(Shivaji University, 1971 & Calcutta, B.Com., 1967 Modified)

Ans. : Opening Capital Rs. 22,710; G.P. Rs. 17,067; N.P. Rs. 6,906, B/S Rs. 30,348.

Hints : (1) Sundry expenses outstanding at the beginning are to be deducted and the closing are to be added.

(2) Rs. 1,260 are bad debt.

(10) You are given below :

(a) Information about assets and liabilities of Mr. Single.

(b) Cash transactions for 12 months to 31st March, 1968.

(c) A summary of the additional information :

(i) Assets of Mr. Single— Bills receivable Rs. 25,000; Sundry debtors Rs. 39,000; Stock-in-trade Rs. 75,300; Plant and machinery Rs. 47,000; Land and buildings Rs. 70,000; Cash in Hand Rs. 700; Liabilities of Mr. Single— Bank overdraft Rs. 5,000; Sundry creditors Rs. 36,000; Bills payable Rs. 16,000.

(ii) **Cash transactions :** Receipts from debtors Rs. 2,90,000, bills receivable encashed Rs.1,00,000;

Payments : Salaries 12,000; Wages Rs. 15,800; Bills payable Rs. 1,43,000; Payments to creditors Rs. 1,47,000; General expenses Rs. 8,000; Drawings Rs. 45,000; Cash in Hand at the end Rs. 2,400.

(iii) Other information :

	Rs.		Rs.
Total sales (all credit)	4,07,000	Bills receivable received during the year	1,09,000
Discount to customers	2,000		
Purchases (all credit)	3,00,000	Stock of goods on 31st March, 1968	53,000
Discount received from Suppliers	1,000	Create provision for doubtful debts on debtors @ 5%	
		Bills payable issued during the year	1,50,000

Depreciate plant at 5% and building at 2½%. You are required to prepare a Trading and Profit and Loss Account for the year ended 31st March 1968 and Balance sheet as on that date.

(Bombay, B.Com., 1971)

Ans. : Closing Debtors Rs. 45,000; Closing Creditors Rs. 38,000; Closing Bills Receivable Rs. 34,000; Closing Bills Payable Rs. 23,000; Closing Cash Balance Rs. 12,500; Gross Profit Rs. 68,900; Net Profit Rs. 41,550; Balance Sheet Total Rs. 2,57,550.

(11) The following information is extracted from the incomplete records of the partnership of Hussain and Rajan :

	1st January, 1980 Rs.	31st December, 1980 Rs.
Machinery	1,000	—
Furniture	7,500	—
Stock	11,275	10,180
Debtors	12,750	—
Cash	1,975	3,535
Creditors	—	6,370

Purchases and sales during the year amounted to Rs. 61,510 and Rs. 80,190 respectively and compared to Hussain's Capital, Rajan's Capital is more by Rs. 5,000 as at 1st January, 1980. Cash transactions during the year were as follows :

Receipts	Rs.	Payments		Rs.
To Trade Customers	72,740	By Suppliers		63,960
To Hussain's Capital		By Salaries		8,750
(additional)	5,000	By Rent for 6 months		
		up to 30-6-80		3,000
		By Rates and Taxes		3,000
		(for 6 months up to 31-3-81)		
		By Advertising		870
		By Electric Charges		1,250
		By Delivery Charges		680
		By Repairs		1,810
		By Sundry Expenses		700
		By Drawings :		
		Hussain	2,760	
		Rajan	2,125	4,885

On 31st December, 1980 outstanding liabilities also included Electricity Charges Rs. 260, Advertising Rs. 130 and Sundry Expenses Rs. 200.

Depreciate Furniture and Machinery by 5% and 20% respectively. Provide 4% for Bad debts. Cash Purchases are not made.

Prepare Final Accounts for the year ended 31st December, 1980.

(*B.Com.* [*Hons.*], *Delhi & Calcutta*)

Ans. : Cash Sales Rs. 12,725; Credit Sales Rs. 67,465 (80,190 – 12,725); Closing Debtors Rs. 7,475; Opening Creditors Rs. 8,820; Opening Capital Rs. 25,680; Hussain's Capital Rs. 10,340 (25,680 – 5,000 = 20,680 × ½ = 10,340); Rajan's Capital Rs. 15,340 (20,680 × ½ = 10,340 + 5,000); Net Loss : Hussain's Rs. 2,719.50; Rajan's Rs. 2,719.50; Balance Sheet Total Rs. 30,316.

(12) From the following particulars prepare a Trading and Profit and Loss Account for the year ended 31st March, 1973 and a Balance Sheet as at that date :

(a) Balance Sheet as on 31st March, 1973 :

	Rs.			Rs.
Capital	2,00,000	Buildings		1,00,000
Fixed Deposits	50,000	Plant		68,250
Creditors	16,262	Stocks		67,750
Overdraft	2,167	Debtors	10,700	
		Less : R.B.D.	1,070	9,630
		P & L A/c		22,799
	2,68,429			2,68,429

(b) Cash Summary :

	Rs.		Rs.
To Sales	10,626	By Bank O/D	2,167
To Debtors	1,21,004	By Creditors	92,636
		By Wages	10,607
		By Trade Expenses	15,206
		By Interest on Fixed Deposits	2,100
		By Balance	8,914
	1,31,630		1,31,630

(c) The books disclosed the following total :

Discounts allowed Rs. 3,202; Discounts received Rs. 2,006; Purchases Rs. 95,585; Sales Rs. 1,24,756; Closing Stock Rs. 70,100; Depreciation to be written off on Plant 10%; Keep a reserve of 10% on Debtors. Insurance Premium of Rs. 62 has been paid in advance and included in Trade Expenses.

(*Adapted from My. U.I., B.Com., April, 1973*)

Ans. : Gross Profits Rs. 31,540; Net Profits Rs. 6,220;
Closing Balance Sheet Total Rs. 2,50,626.

(13) Premlal carries on a small business, but he does not maintain a complete set of account books. He banks all receipts and makes all payments only by means of cheques. He maintains properly a Cash Book, a Sales Ledger and a Purchases Ledger. He also makes a proper record of the assets and liabilities as at the close of every accounting year. From such records you are able to gather the following facts :

Receipts for the year ended 31-12-1983 :	Rs.
From Sundry Debtors	17,625
Cash Sales	4,125
Paid in by Premlal the Proprietor	2,500
	24,250

Payments made for the year ended 31-12-1983 :	Rs.
New Plant Purchased	625
Drawings	1,500
Wages	6,725
Salaries	1,125
Interest paid	75
Telephone	125
Rent	1,200
Light and Power	475

Sundry Expenses	2,125
Sundry Creditors	7,625
	21,600

Assets and Liabilities

	As at 31-12-1982 Rs.	As at 31-12-1983 Rs.
Sundry Creditors	2,525	2,400
Sundry Debtors	3,750	6,125
Bank	625	—
Stock	6,250	3,125
Plant	7,500	7,315

From the above data prepare the Profit and Loss Account for the year ended 31st December,1983 and the Balance Sheet as on that date.

(Adapted from Mysore University, B.Com., 1986 and Bangalore, April, 1990; Oct., 1991 & 1992 Mod.)

Ans. : Opening Capital Rs. 15,600; Closing Bank Balance Rs. 3,275; Credit Sales Rs. 20,000; Credit Purchases Rs. 7,500; Depreciation charged on Plant & Machinery Rs. 810 (7,500 + 625 – 7,315); Net Profit Rs. 840; Closing Capital Rs. 17,440; Balance Sheet Total Rs. 19,840.

(14) You are given :

(a) The Balance Sheet of Mr. Raj Kumar as at 31st March, 1979

(b) A Cash Account for the year ended 31st March, 1980 and

(c) Additional information.

You are required to prepare a Trading and Profit and Loss Account for the year ended 31st March, 1980 and a Balance Sheet as on that date.

Balance Sheet as on 31-3-1979

	Rs.		Rs.
Creditors	20,000	Cash	5,000
Bill Payable	40,000	Bank	10,000
Capital	1,00,000	Bills Receivable	20,000
		Debtors	25,000
		Stock-in-trade	20,000
		Furniture	10,000
		Plant	70,000
	1,60,000		1,60,000

Cash Account for the year ended 31-3-1980

	Rs.	Rs.		Rs.	Rs.
Balance : Cash	5,000		Drawings		12,000
Bank	10,000	15,000	Wages		20,000
Cash Sales		35,000	Payments to Creditors		35,000
Collection from debtors		80,000	Bills Payable		60,000
			Sundry Expenses		30,000
			Rent, Rates and Taxes		20,000
Bills Receivable		75,000	Balance : Cash	3,000	
			Bank	25,000	28,000
		2,05,000			2,05,000

Additional Information :

	Rs.
Debtors on 31st March, 1980	40,000
Creditors on 31st March, 1980	25,000
Bills receivable on 31st March, 1980	30,000
Bills payable on 31st March, 1980	50,000
Stock in trade on 31st March, 1980	30,000
Bills receivable in hand dishonoured during the year	5,000
Bills payable dishonoured	2,000
Bills receivable endorsed	15,000
Bills receivable endorsed dishonoured	2,000
Discount allowed	1,000
Discount received	2,000

(*C.A. Inter & Gulbarga, 1983 Modified*)

Ans. : B/R received during the year Rs. 1,05,000; B/P issued duringt the year Rs. 72,000; Credit sales Rs. 1,94,000; Credit purchases Rs. 1,25,000; Gross profit Rs. 94,000; Net profit Rs. 45,000; B/S Total Rs. 2,08,000.

(15) Mr. Jamshedji a retail trader who kept his books under single entry system, started his business with a capital of Rs. 30,000 and acquired a retail business on 1-1-1978.

Of the acquisition price Rs. 7,500 was for goodwill; Rs. 2,500 for furniture; Rs. 17,500 for stock and Rs. 2,500 was retained as working capital of which Rs. 2,000 was paid into the Bank. Of the total Cash sales of Rs. 1,15,000, Jameshedji paid Rs. 1,09,000 into the Bank and remainder being utilized for cash payments. The following are the cash and cheque payments during the year :

		Rs.
Purchase of goods		78,000
Salary of the Manager		2,500
Wages		8,200
Sundry expenses		3,600
Rent and taxes :		
Business proportion	2,960	
Personal	1,480	4,440
Domestic expenses of proprietor		1,200
Drawing during the year		12,000

The stock on 31-12-1978 was valued at Rs. 18,750. A sum of Rs. 6,750 was due to supplier of goods. Rs. 7,500 was owing to him from his customers. Bank balance on 31-12-1978 was Rs. 2,750. Furniture was to be depreciated by 5%. Provide Rs. 500 on debtors for doubtful debts.

Prepare the Trading and Profit and Loss Account for the year ending 31-12-1978 and the Balance Sheet as on that date.

(Karnatak, Oct., 1980; Mysore, B.Com., 1972; Modified, Madras, 1960 & G.D.A. 1978)

Ans. : G/P Rs. 30,800; N/P Rs. 21,115; B/S total Rs. 43,185.

Hints : Credit sales Rs. 7,500; Credit purchases Rs. 6,750; Balancing figure in bank account (*i.e.*, payments by cheques) Rs. 1,08,250 (*i.e.* 1,11,000 – 2,750 Bank balance); Payments in cash Rs. 1,690 (*i.e.* payments in cash and cheques Rs.10,994 – 1,08,250 payments in cheques); Closing cash balance Rs. 4,810.

(16) Prepare the trading and profit and loss account for the year ending 31-12-1982 and the balance sheet of Mr. Arun from the following information:

(i) The balance as on 1-1-1982 were :

	Rs.
Cash in hand	4,000
Cash at Bank	28,000
Creditors	15,000
Debtors	23,000
Stock	35,000
Fixed Assets	20,000
Arun's Capital	75,000
Arun's Current Account	20,000

(ii) During the year the creditors were paid Rs. 26,000 in cash and Rs. 1,55,000 by cheques while the debtors paid Rs. 55,000 in cash and Rs. 1,90,000 by cheques. The balance at the close of the year stood at : Debtors Rs. 27,000 and Creditors Rs. 35,000.

(iii) All the expenses debited to profit and loss account were disbursed by cheques except the petty expenses amounting to Rs. 7,500 which were paid in cash. The outstanding expenses at the close of the year amounted to Rs. 2,000.

(iv) The net profit for the year ended was Rs. 41,000 after providing 10% depreciation on fixed assets.

(v) The closing stock was valued at Rs. 75,000.

(vi) Arun's drawings during the year were Rs. 10,000 in cash and Rs. 14,000 by cheques.

(*Karnatak, Oct.,1984 & Institute of Company Secretary, 1970*)

Ans. : Credit sales Rs. 2,49,000; Credit purchases Rs. 2,01,000; Closing cash balance Rs. 15,500; Closing Bank balance Rs. 13,500; G.P. Rs. 88,000; N.P. Rs. 41,000; Total expenses debited to P & L A/c Rs. 47,000 (*i.e.* G/P Rs. 88,000 – N/P Rs. 41,000 = 47,000 *i.e.* Rs. 43,000 paid by cheques and cash + 2,000 outstanding + Rs. 2,000 depreciation); B/S Total Rs. 1,49,000.

Note : Balance of expenses paid by cheques Rs. 35,500 (*i.e.* total expenses debited to P & L A/c Rs. 47,000 – Rs. 4,000 outstanding and depreciation – Rs. 7,500 petty exp. paid in cash).

(17) You are given below the following information of Mr. Singh :

Assets and Liabilities as on 1-4-1981 :

	Rs.
Bills receivable	25,000
Sundry debtors	39,000
Stock	75,300
Plant and machinery	47,000
Land and buildings	70,000
Cash in Hand	700
Bank overdraft	5,000
Sundry creditors	36,000
Bills payable	16,000

Cash transactions for 12 months to 31-3-1982 :

Receipts from debtors	2,90,000
Bills receivable encashed	1,00,000
Salaries	12,000
Wages	15,800
Paid against bills payable	1,43,000

Payments to creditors	1,47,000
General expenses	8,000
Drawings	45,000
Cash in Hand at the end	2,400

Other information :

Total sales (all on credit)	4,07,000
Discount to customers	2,000
Purchases (all on credit)	3,00,000
Discount earned	1,000
Bills receivable received during the year	1,09,000
Stock of goods on 31-12-1982	53,000
Bills payable issued during the year	1,50,000

Create provision for doubtful debts on debtors at 5%. Depreciate plant at 5% and land and building at 2½%.

You are required to prepare the trading and profit and loss account for the year ending 31-12-1982 and the balance sheet as on that date.

(Gulbarga, Oct., 1983)

Ans. : Gross profit Rs. 68,900; Net profit Rs. 41,550; Balance Sheet Total Rs. 2,57,550; Closing balances : Debtors Rs. 45,000; Creditors Rs. 38,000; Bills receivable Rs. 34,000; Bills payable Rs. 23,000; Cash in Hand Rs. 2,400. Cash at Bank Rs. 12,500 and Opening capital Rs. 2,00,000.

(18) A client submits to you the following figures relating to his business in respect of the year ending 31 December, 1977. Prepare a Trading and Profit and Loss Account and Balance Sheet as on that date. Any difference in the cash balance is assumed to be drawings. As the trader lives in his business premises, 1/3 of the lighting and heating, and of the rent and rates is to be treated as personal expenses and thus charged as drawings.

	Rs.
Cash paid into bank	8,690
Private dividends paid into the business (cash)	200
Private payments out of bank	750
Business payments to creditors by cash and cheques	7,950
Cash and cheques from debtors	11,700
Wages	1,500
Delivery expenses	600
Rent and rates	135
Lighting and heating	90

General expenses	250
Bank interest received	10

The assets and liabilities are as follows :

	1-1-1977	31-12-1977
	Rs.	Rs.
Stock	600	750
Bank Balance	800	1,000
Cash in Hand	30	20
Trade Debtors	750	1,050
Trade Creditors	1,200	1,400
Investments	3,000	3,000

(*Karnatak, April, 1993*)

Ans. : Opening capital Rs. 3,980; Credit sales Rs. 12,000; Credit purchases Rs. 8,150; Gross profit Rs. 2500; Net profit Rs. 1,510; B/S Total Rs. 5,820.

Hints : Payments to creditors by cheques Rs. 7,750. Payments to creditor by cash Rs. 200. Drawings in the cash column Rs. 445.

(19) The following information is supplied from which you are required to prepare Trading and Profit and Loss Account for the year ended 31st December, 1980 and a Balance Sheet as on that date.

Assets and Liabilities :

	1-1-1980	31-12-1980
	Rs.	Rs.
Creditors	15,770	12,400
General Expenses Owing	600	330
Sundry Assets	11,610	12,040
Stock	8,040	11,120
Cash in Hand and at Bank	6,960	8,080
Debtors	?	17,870
Other transactions :		
Cash and discount credited to debtors		64,000
Return from debtors		1,450
Bad debts		420
Sales— Cash and Credit		71,810
Discount allowed by creditors		700
Returns to creditors		400
Capital introduced (paid into bank)		8,500
Receipts from debtors (paid into bank)		62,500

Cash purchases	1,030
Expenses paid by cash	9,570
Purchase of machinery by cheque	430
Cash payments into banks	5,000
Drawings by cheque	3,180
Withdrawn from bank into cash	9,240
Cash in Hand at the end	1,200
Payments to creditors by cheque	60,270

(*Adapted from My. U.I., B.Com., Oct., 1970 & Karnatak, Oct., 1983*)

Ans. : Opening Capital Rs. 26,770; Opening Debtors Rs. 16,530; Credit Sales Rs. 67,210 (71,810 – 4,600); Credit Purchases Rs. 58,000; G/P Rs. 14,810; N/P Rs. 4,290; B/S Total Rs. 49,110.

Hints : Discount allowed to creditors Rs. 1,500 (64,000 – 62,500); Opening Cash Rs. 2,960 (6,960 – 4,000); Opening bank balance Rs. 4,000 [80,000 (430 + 9,240 + 60,270 + 6,880) – 76,000 (8,500 + 62,500 + 5,000)]; Closing cash Rs. 1,200; Closing bank balance Rs. 6,880.

(20) A trader, who has not kept a complete set of books, asks you to prepare his final accounts for the year ended 31st Dec., 1980. You are, however, able to obtain the following information :

Summary of his cash book:

Balance of cash on 1st January, 1980 Rs. 5,170; Cash sales Rs. 42,050; Personal drawings Rs. 3,000; Purchases Rs. 32,400; Salaries Rs. 2,500; Rent Rs. 1,200; Electricity Charges Rs. 350; Printing and Stationery Rs. 250; Advertising Rs. 450.

His other assets and liabilities were :

	31st December, 1979	31st December, 1980
	Rs.	Rs.
Debtors	3,350	5,100
Creditors	1,400	3,500
Rent outstanding	100	100
Electricity charges outstanding	20	15
Advertising outstanding	—	250

The stock on 31st December, 1980 was valued at Rs. 4,500 but the trader has no record of the stock on 31st December, 1979. He informs you, however, that he invariably sells his goods at cost plus 33-1/3%.

Prepare his Profit and Loss Account for the year ended 31st December, 1980 and his Balance Sheet as on that date.

(*Adapted from My. U.I., B.Com., April, 1969 & G.D.A.*)

Ans. : Credit sales Rs. 1,750; Credit purchases Rs. 2,100; Opening capitals Rs. 9,850; Closing cash balance Rs. 7,070; G/P Rs. 10,950; N/P Rs. 5,955; B/S Total Rs. 16,670.

Hints : Opening stock of Rs. 2,850 is calculated as below :

Sales (Cash sales Rs. 42,050 + Credit sales Rs. 1,750) =	43,800
Less : Gross profit on sales $43{,}800 \times \frac{1}{4}$ i.e., $\left(\frac{33.3}{133.3}\right)$	10,950
Cost of goods sold	32,850
Add : Closing stock	4,500
	37,350
Less : Purchases (32,400 + 2,100)	34,500
Opening stock	2,850

(21) The Books of Kalyani showed the following figures :

	1-1-1973 Rs.	31-12-1973 Rs.
Creditors	5,000	10,000
Debtors	6,000	6,600
Provision for doubtful debts	300	400
Buildings	30,000	24,000
Furniture	14,000	14,200
Bills payable	2,400	3,400
Commission received in advance	100	200
Rent due but not received	300	1,400
Unpaid salaries	1,500	1,600
General expenses owing	400	500
Stock	—	10,000

The analysis of the cash book showed the following :

Receipts	Rs.	Payments	Rs.
To Op. Balance b/d	7,400	By General expenses	1,000
To Sales (cash)	16,000	By Salaries	2,400
To Rent received	1,400	By Bills Payable	10,000
To Commission received	1,000	By Furniture	4,000
To Debtors	10,000	By Creditors	12,000
To Sale of fold furniture	100	By Investments	4,000
		By Balance c/d	2,500
	35,900		35,900
To Balance b/d	2,500		

The stock is valued on the closing date but no stock was taken on 1-1-1973. The rate of gross profit is 25% on sales. Prepare Trading & Profit and Loss A/c and Balance Sheet as at 31-12-1973.

(*B'lore, B.Com., 1983 & 1982 Modified*)

Ans.: B/P issued during the year Rs. 11,000; Credit purchases Rs. 28,000; Credit sales Rs. 10,600; Opening capital Rs. 49,950; Net loss Rs. 3,350; Balance Sheet Total Rs. 62,300.

Hint : Opening stock Rs. 1,950 [Sales Rs. 26,600 – G/P Rs. 6,650 (*i.e.*, 20% on 26,600) + Closing Stock Rs. 10,000 – Purchases Rs. 28,000].

(22) A Merchant, who keeps his books on Single-entry, requests you to prepare his Trading and Profit and Loss Account for the year ending 30-9-1984 and the Balance Sheet as on that date :

(I) Summary of cash book for 1983-84	Rs.
Bank overdraft on 1-10-1983	7,400
Drawings	3,000
Manager's salary	4,500
Staff salary	3,500
Trade expenses	2,000
Wages	15,500
Paid to suppliers	25,000
Received from customers	60,000
Cash sales	5,000
Balance at bank on 30-9-1984	4,000
Cash in Hand on 30-9-1984	100

(II) Other assets and liabilities	1-10-1983	30-9-1984
	Rs.	Rs.
Stock	22,000	19,000
Debtors	53,000	88,000
Creditors	15,000	19,500
Machinery	20,000	20,000
Furniture	1,400	1,400

(III) Other information :

(1) Make provision for doubtful debts at 5% on debtors.

(2) Depreciate machinery by 20%.

(3) The manager is entitled to a commission at 5% on the net profit after charging such commission. Make provision for this commission.

(*Karnatak, April, 1988 & Oct., 1991 and Gulbarga, Oct., 1994 Modified*)

Ans. : Credit sales Rs. 95,000; Credit purchases Rs. 29,500; Opening capital Rs. 74,000; G/P Rs. 52,000; N/P Rs. 32,000; B/S Total Rs. 1,24,100;

Manager commission Rs. $1{,}600 \left(i.e., 33{,}600 \times \frac{5}{105} \right)$.

(23) You are instructed by X who keeps his book by single-entry to prepare a Trading and Profit and Loss Account for the year ended 30th September, 1978, together with a Balance Sheet as at that date.

On an analysis of the cash book for the year, you find the following :

	Rs.
Bank Overdraft on 1st October, 1977	80,000
Interest on above and bank charges	2,000
X's drawings	40,000
Manager's salary	20,000
Salaries and wages	1,50,000
Other business expenses	1,58,000
Paid to trade creditors	3,00,000
Balance at Bankers, 30th September, 1978	48,500
Balance in hands of cashier	1,500
Received from trade debtors	5,00,000
Received from cash sales	3,00,000
X's capital on 1st October, 1977	7,00,000

His stock on hand on 1st October, 1977 was Rs. 1,80,000 and on 30th September, 1978 Rs. 2,04,400.

His creditors on 1st October, 1977 were Rs. 1,60,000 and on 30th September, 1978 Rs. 1,10,000.

His debtors on 1st October, 1977 were Rs. 4,40,000 and on 30th September, 1978 Rs. 6,00,000.

His furniture on 1st October, 1977 were Rs. 20,000 and on 30th September, 1978 Rs. 20,000.

His business premises on 1st October, 1977 were Rs. 3,00,000 and on 30th September, 1978 Rs. 3,00,000.

You are to allow 5% interest on the balance of capital at 1st October, 1977, to reserve Rs. 30,000 for doubtful debts and to charge 5% depreciation on business premises and furniture.

In addition to the salary of Rs. 20,000 already paid to the manager, he is entitled to a commission of 5% upon the net profits after charging such salary and commission.

Make provision for this commission and prepare the accounts as instructed.

(*Adapted from Madras University & Madhurai, 1972*)

Ans. : G/P Rs. 7,34,400; N/P Rs. 3,08,000; Closing Balance Sheet Total Rs. 11,28,400; Manager's Commission Rs. 15,400.

(24) From the following information furnished by Shri Basu. Prepare the Trading and Profit and Loss Account for the year ending 31-3-1988 and the Balance Sheet as on that date :

Assets and liabilities :

	31-3-1988 Rs.	31-3-1987 Rs.
Creditors	30,500	25,800
Stock	30,000	25,000
Furniture	1,500	1,000
Debtors	28,000	23,000
Cash in Hand	5,200	500
Cash at Bank	800	200

The following further details of the transactions for the year ended 31-3-1988 are available from the incomplete records :

	Rs.
Cash received from debtors and banked	60,000
Discount allowed to debtors	1,200
Payments to creditors by cheques	50,000
Discount allowed by creditors	1,000
Returns from debtors	5,000
Returns to creditors	4,000
Bad debts written off	1,500
Cash and credit purchases	67,300
Cash sale of land and cash used for business	10,000
Cash sales	5,000
Sundry expenses paid by cheques	1,500
Withdrawals by cheques from bank for office use	3,000
Salary paid by cheques	3,000
Rent paid in cash	1,000
Cash paid into Bank	5,000
Purchase of furniture by cheque	500
Drawings by cheque	6,400

(*Gulbarga, April, 1993*)

Ans. : Opening Capital Rs. 23,900 (49,700 – 25,800); Closing Capital Rs. 35,000 (23,900 + 10,000 + 7,500 – 6,400); Credit Purchases Rs. 59,700; Credit Sales Rs. 72,700; Cash Purchases Rs. 7,600 (67,300 – 59,700); Gross Profit Rs. 14,400; Net Profit Rs. 7,500 & B/S Total Rs. 65,500.

Notes : (i) Sale proceeds of land Rs. 10,000 is added to Capital.

(ii) Even though the opening and closing balances are given, Cash Book with Cash and Bank Columns is to be prepared. The difference of Rs. 300 in cash column is treated as sundry income.

(25) Shri Mohan maintains his books under Single-entry System. He supplied to you the following information to prepare final accounts for the year 1988.

(a) Statements of affairs as on 1-1-1988 :

	Rs.		Rs.
Sundry creditors	18,000	Bills Receivable	12,500
Bills Payable	8,000	Sundry Debtors	19,500
Bank overdraft	2,500	Cash in hand	350
Mohan's Capital	1,00,000	Stock	37,650
		Plant & Machinery	23,500
		Land & Buildings	35,000
	1,28,500		1,28,500

(b) Summary of cash transactions for 12 months :

Receipts	Rs.	Payments		Rs.
To Balance on 1-1-1988	350	By Bank overdraft		2,500
To Receipts from debtors	1,45,000	By Salaries		6,000
To Bills receivable	50,000	By Wages		3,000
		By Carriage inwards		4,000
		By Rent		900
		By Office expenses		3,000
		By Advertisement		1,000
		By Bills payable		71,500
		By Payments to creditors		73,500
		By Drawings		22,500
		By Balance on 31-12-1988 :		
		In hand	1,200	
		At bank	6,250	7,450
	1,95,350			1,95,350

(c) Summary of the remaining transactions :

	Rs.
Sales	2,03,500
Discount to customers	1,000
Purchases	1,50,000
Discount from suppliers	500
Bills receivable received during the year	54,500
Bills payable issued during the year	75,000
Stock of goods on 31-12-1988	26,500

Provide deprecation at 10% on land and buildings and for bad debts at 5% on debtors.

(*Karnatak, Oct., 1995*)

Ans. : Closing capital Rs. 96,825; Closing B/R Rs. 17,000; Closing B/P Rs. 11,500; Closing Debtors Rs. 22,500; Closing Creditors Rs. 19,000; Gross Profit Rs. 35,350; Net Profit Rs. 19,325 and B/S Total Rs. 1,27,325.

(26) Mr. Anand, who keeps his books under Single-entry System, gives you the following information for the year 1992.

Cash Book

	Rs.		Rs.
To Balance at Bank	4,350	By Anand's Drawings	7,520
To Sunday Debtors	38,400	By Sundry Creditors	27,100
To Bills Receivable	12,000	By Bills Payable	9,300
To Commission	1,500	By Wages	12,000
To Cash Sales	8,600	By Salaries	6,500
To Balance c/d	3,350	By Rent	4,400
		By Insurance	800
		By Advertising	580
	68,200		68,200

Other assets and liabilities on :	1-1-1992	31-12-1992
	Rs.	Rs.
Stock	18,700	23,400
Sundry Debtors	12,000	14,000
Sundry Creditors	9,000	1,500
Bills Receivable	4,000	5,000
Bills Payable	1,000	200
Furniture	600	600
Building	12,000	12,000

Adjustments

(a) Provide Rs. 1,450 for doubtful debts on debtors.
(b) Outstanding expenses were : Wages Rs. 3,000; Salaries Rs. 1,200.
(c) Prepaid insurance was Rs. 250.
(d) Depreciate building by 5%.

Prepare trading and profit and loss account for the year ended 31-12-1992 and balance sheet as on that date

(*Gulbarga, April, 1996*)

Ans. : Opening Stock; Rs. 41,650; and Closing Stock Rs. 43,950; (41,650 + 9,820 – 7,520); Credit Purchases Rs. 28,100 and Credit Sales Rs. 53,400; Closing Bank Overdraft Rs. 3,350; Gross Profit Rs. 23,600; Net Profit Rs. 9,820 and B/S Total Rs. 53,200.

(27) Shri Vijaykumar, who keeps his books under single-entry, gives you the following information.

Balance Sheet as on 1-1-1988

Liabilities	Rs.	Assets	Rs.
Capital	22,000	Machinery	7,000
Creditors	2,000	Bills Receivable	2,000
Bills Payable	1,000	Debtors	6,000
		Stock	5,000
		Bank	4,000
		Cash	1,000
	25,000		25,000

Cash Book for the year 1988

Receipts	Rs.	Payments	Rs.
Balance b/d	1,000	Creditors	10,000
Bank (withdrawn)	1,000	Machinery (on 1-10-1988)	600
Capital (on 1-7-1988)	3,000	Bills Payable	1,000
Debtors	12,000	Drawings	1,000
Cash Sales	2,000	Deposited in Bank	3,000
Bills Receivable	2,500	Freight & Carriage	500
Miscellaneous income	400	Wages & Salaries	3,000
		Rent & Taxes	200
		Office Expenses	700
		Balance c/d	1,900
	21,900		21,900

Other information

(1) Balance on 31-12-1988 :

	Rs.
Debtors	8,000
Creditors	4,000
Stock	5,000
Bills Receivable	3,000
Bills Payable	2,000

(2) Credit purchases during the year Rs. 14,000, credit sales during the year Rs. 17,500.

(3) Allow interest on capital at 5% p.a.

(4) Depreciate machinery by 10% p.a.

Prepare the Trading and Profit and Loss Account for the year ending 31-12-1988 and the Balance Sheet as on that date.

(*Karnatak, Oct., 1996*)

Ans. : Closing Bank balance Rs. 6,000 (4,000 + 3,000 – 1,000); Gross profit Rs. 2,000; Net loss Rs. 390, and B/S Total Rs. 30,785.

Notes : (1) Depreciation is calculated for one year on Rs. 7,000 and for 3 months on Rs. 600.

(2) Interest on capital is calculated for one year on Rs. 22,000 and for 6 months on Rs. 3,000.

(3) Wages and sales are debited to trading account.

(28) Sri Rajiv does not maintain regular accounts. From the following information provided by him. Prepare the Trading and Profit and Loss Account for the year ended 31st December, 1990, and also a Balance Sheet as on that date.

Balance as on 1-1-1990

	Rs.
Cash in Hand	4,000
Cash at Bank	28,000
Sundry creditors	15,000
Sundry debtors	23,000
Stock	35,000
Fixed assets	20,000

During the year creditors were paid Rs. 26,000 in cash and Rs. 1,55,000 by cheques. Debtors paid in cash Rs. 55,000 and Rs. 1,90,000 by crossed cheques. The balances on 31-12-1990—Debtors Rs. 27,000 and Sundry Creditors Rs. 35,000.

All expenses chargeable to Profit and Loss Account were disbursed by cheques, except petty expenses amounting to Rs. 7,500 paid in cash. Outstanding expenses at close were Rs. 2,000.

Closing stock on 31st December, 1990 was Rs. 75,000. Net profit for the year was Rs. 41,000 after allowing 10% depreciation on fixed assets.

Sri Rajiv's drawings during the year were Rs. 10,000 in cash and Rs. 14,000 by cheques.

(*Bangalore, April, 1991*)

Ans. : Opening capital Rs. 95,000; Credit sales Rs. 2,49,000; Credit purchases Rs. 2,01,000; Closing cash balance Rs. 15,500; Closing Bank balance Rs. 13,500; Indirect expenses Rs. 35,500; Gross profit Rs. 88,000; and Balance Sheet Total Rs. 1,49,000.

Note : Indirect expenses are ascertained as below :

	Rs.
Gross profit as per trading account	88,000
Less: Items debited to profit and loss account (Petty expenses Rs. 7,500 + O/s expenses Rs. 2,000 + Depreciation Rs. 2,000 + Net profit Rs. 41,000)	52,500
Indirect Expenses	35,500

(29) Mr. Raju started his business on 1-1-89 with a capital of Rs. 25,000. He bought furniture of Rs. 4,000. He borrowed Rs. 5,000 from his wife and introduced further capital of Rs. 3,000. He withdrew Rs. 600 every month. From the following information prepare his Trading and Profit and Loss Account and the Balance Sheet as on 31-12-89 :

	Rs.
Sales (including cash sales Rs. 30,000)	1,00,000
Purchases (including cash purchases Rs. 10,000)	75,000
Carriage inwards	700
Wages	300
Discount allowed to debtors	800
Salary paid	6,200
Bad debts written off	1,500
Trade Expenses	1,200
Advertisement	2,200

Mr. Raju used goods worth Rs. 1,300 for private purposes and paid Rs. 500 to his son, which is not recorded. On 31-12-1989, his debtors were worth Rs. 21,000 and creditors Rs. 15,000. Stock in trade was valued at Rs. 10,000 on that date. Furniture is to be depreciated by 10% p.a.

(*Bangalore, April, 1992*)

Ans. : Credit sales Rs. 70,000; Cash received from debtors Rs. 46,700; Credit purchases Rs. 65,000; Cash paid to creditors Rs. 50,000; Closing cash balance Rs. 27,400; Cash Book total Rs. 1,09,700; Gross profit Rs. 35,300; Net profit Rs. 23,000 and Balance Sheet Total Rs. 62,000.

Notes : (i) Amount paid to son from the business should be recorded as drawings. Therefore, it should be credited to cash book and deducted from capital.

(ii) Goods used for private purpose should be taken as drawings. Hence, it should be deducted from purchases and capital.

(30) Rama commenced business, as a cloth merchant on 1st January, 1983 with a capital of Rs. 10,000. On the same day, he purchased furniture and fittings for cash Rs. 3,000. From the following particulars obtained from his books kept by single entry, you are asked to prepare a Trading and Profit and Loss Account for the year ending 31st December, 1983 and the Balance Sheet as on that date :

	Rs.
Sales (inclusive of cash Rs. 7,000)	17,000
Purchases (inclusive of cash Rs. 4,000)	15,000
Rama's drawings	1,200
Salaries of staff	2,000
Bad debts written off	500
Business expenses	700

Rama took cloth worth Rs. 500 from the shop for private use and paid Rs. 200 to his son but omitted to record these transactions in his books. On 31st December, 1983 his sundry debtors were Rs. 5,200 and sundry creditors Rs. 3,600. Stock in hand on 31st December, 1983 was Rs. 6,500.

(*Bangalore, November, 1993*)

Ans. : Credit sales Rs. 10,000; Cash received from debtors Rs. 4,300; Credit purchases Rs. 11,000; Cash paid to creditors Rs. 7,400; Closing cash balance Rs. 2,800; Cash book total Rs. 21,300; Gross profit Rs. 9,000; Net profit Rs. 58,000 and Balance Sheet Total Rs. 17,500.

Note : Goods used for private purpose should be deducted from purchases and capital. Amount paid to son should be credited to cash book and deducted from capital.

(31) Arjun carries on a grocery business and does not keep his books on a double-entry basis. The following particulars have been extracted from the his books :

	1-1-1993	31-12-1993
	Rs.	Rs.
Plant and Machinery	18,000	18,000
Stock	8,000	7,000
Sundry Debtors	2,000	3,000
Sundry Creditors	5,000	4,000
Cash	4,660	?

Analysis of his cash book for the year ending 31-12-1993 showed the following :

	Rs.
Wages	6,000
Sundry expenses	2,500
Advertising	1,120
Rent and rates	2,500
Carriage inwards	2,460
Cash received from debtors	82,500
Cash paid to creditors	64,340
Drawings	3,120

During the year, Arjun had taken from his business for his own consumption goods which amounted to Rs. 780. Purchases returns during the year were Rs. 2,000 and sales returns were Rs. 1,000. Depreciate machinery by 5%.

Prepare Trading and Profit and Loss Account for the year ending 31st December, 1993 and a Balance Sheet as at that date.

(Bangalore, April, 1994)

Ans. : Opening capital Rs. 27,660; Credit sales Rs. 84,500; Credit purchases Rs. 65,340; Closing cash balance Rs. 5,120; Gross profit Rs. 11,480; Net profit Rs. 4,460 and Balance Sheet Total Rs. 32,220.

(32) Mr. Srinivas carries on a small business, but he does not maintain a complete set of account books. He banks all receipts and makes all payments by cheques. The following are the particulars obtained from the records.

Receipts and Payments for the year ended 31st December, 1994 :

Receipts	Rs.	Payments	Rs.
Cash from debtors	32,250	Furniture	1,250
Cash sales	8,250	Drawings	3,000
Additional capital	5,000	Wages	13,450
		Salaries	2,650
		Rent	2,400
		Sundry expenses	5,200
		Paid to creditors	15,250

Assets and Liabilities :

	As on 1-1-1994 Rs.	As at 31-12-1994 Rs.
Furniture	15,000	15,500
Sundry debtors	7,500	12,250
Stock	12,500	6,250
Sales returns	—	4,000
B/R dishonoured during the year	—	100
Bank	1,250	?
Sundry creditors	5,050	4,800

Provide reserve for doubtful debts Rs. 500.

From the above particulars, prepare Trading and Profit and Loss Account for the year ended 31st December, 1994 and the Balance Sheet as on the date.

(Bangalore, April, 1995)

Ans. : Opening capital Rs. 31,200; Credit sales Rs. 37,000; Credit Purchases Rs. 15,000; Closing Bank balance Rs. 3,550; Gross profit Rs. 10,550; Net loss Rs. 950 and Balance Sheet Total Rs. 37,050.

(33) The following is the position of Mr. Satish on 1-1-1988 :

Liabilities	Rs.	Assets	Rs.
Creditors	75,000	Furniture	20,000
Capital	80,000	Debtors	90,000
		Stock	40,000
		Bank	5,000
	1,55,000		1,55,000

His Bank transactions during the year were :

	Rs.
Receipt from customers	3,50,000
Drawings for personal expenses	60,000
Payment of salaries	30,000
Payment to creditors	2,20,000
Payment of rent	15,000
Miscellaneous expenses	4,000

On 31st December, 1988, debtors stood at Rs. 95,000 and creditors at Rs. 64,000. No inventory or stock was taken on 31st December, 1988. But the gross profit was estimated at 40% on turnover made during the year. Prepare Bank Account, Trading and Profit and Loss Account for the year and Balance Sheet as on 31st December, 1988.

(Bangalore, April, 1993 & Oct., 1995)

Ans. : Credit sales Rs. 3,55,000; Credit purchases Rs. 2,09,000; Closing Bank balance Rs. 26,000; Closing stock Rs. 36,000; Gross profit Rs. 1,42,000 (40% of sales of Rs. 3,55,000); Net profit Rs. 93,000 and Balance Sheet total Rs. 1,77,000.

(34) Mr. Sachin keeps his books under single-entry system. From the following information, prepare Trading and Profit and Loss Account for the year ending December 31, 1997 and Balance Sheet as on that date.

	1-1-97 Rs.	31-12-97 Rs.
Sundry Debtors	15,000	9,000
Stock	6,880	4,000
Machinery	15,500	15,500
Sundry Creditors	12,500	11,700
Rent Payables (outstanding)	250	150

Analysis of the Cash book for the year ending 31st December, 1997 :

	Rs.		Rs.
To Balance b/d (1-1-97)	1,875	By Sundry creditors paid	14,500
To Sundry debts collected	20,600	By Wages	1,400
To Cash sales	16,000	By Rent	600
To Interest on Fixed Deposits	300	By Salaries	7,500
		By Son's education expenses	2,200
		By Fixed Deposits made on 1-7-97 @ 10% p.a.	10,000
		By Balance c/d (31-12-97)	2,575
	38,775		38,775

Depreciate machinery by 10% p.a., provide for reserve for doubtful debts at 5% on sundry debtors.

(*Karnatak, April, 1998*)

Ans. : Opening capital Rs. 26,505; Credit sales Rs. 14,600; Credit purchases Rs. 13,700; Gross profit Rs. 12,620; Net profit Rs. 3,120 and Balance Sheet Total Rs. 39,275.

Notes : (i) Rent debited to P&L A/c Rs. 500 (i.e., 600 + 150 – 250).

(ii) Outstanding interest on Fixed Deposit is Rs. 200. Because, out of Rs. 500 $\left(10,000 \times \frac{10}{100} \times \frac{6}{12}\right)$ Rs. 300 is already received.

(35) The following information is obtained from the books of Mr. Mahesh, who maintained the same under single-entry system.

(1) Receipts for the year ending 31-12-97 :

	Rs.
From Debtors	1,76,250
Cash Sales	41,250
Paid by Mr. Mahesh	25,000

Payments under during the year :

	Rs.
New Plant bought	6,250
Drawings	15,000
Salaries	11,250
Wages	67,250
Interest paid	750
Rent paid	13,250
Light and Power	4,750
Sundry Expenses	21,250
Sundry Creditors	76,250

Mr. Mahesh banks all receipts and makes payments by means of cheques.

(2) Assets and Liabilities :

	1-1-1997 Rs.	31-12-1997 Rs.
Sundry Creditors	25,250	24,000
Sundry Debtors	37,500	61,250
Bank	6,250	?
Stock	62,500	31,250
Plant	75,000	73,150

Prepare Trading and Profit and Loss A/c and Balance Sheet.

(*Bangalore, April, 1990 & 1998*)

Ans. : Credit Sales Rs. 2,00,000; Credit Purchases Rs. 75,000; Closing Bank Balance Rs. 32,750; Bank A/c Total Rs. 2,48,750; Opening Capital Rs. 1,56,000; Gross Profit Rs. 63,000; Net Profit Rs. 8,400 and Balance Sheet Total Rs. 1,98,400.

3

CONSIGNMENT ACCOUNTS

Meaning

In order to increase the sales, many manufacturers and traders appoint their agents at different places in the country or abroad. Such agents exploit the sales opportunities in the country, and in the foreign market. Generally, the persons who are knowing the marketing conditions will be appointed as agents. These agents are usually local people. The agents do not buy the goods from the open market, but only they undertake to sell the goods received from the manufacturers or traders on their behalf in return for commission. Agents are not responsible for the loss or damage. All expenses incurred by the agents are borned by the manufacturers or traders. Agents do their duties according to the instructions given by the manufacturers or traders. Manufacturers or traders supply the goods to their agents to sell the goods in different areas. This method of supplying the goods to the agents for the purpose of sale is termed as 'Consignment'. In other words, the term consignment refers to despatch of goods by one person to another to be sold on behalf and at the risk of sender in return for commission. Consignment also be defined as "a contract between the two parties by which one party undertakes to sell the goods supplied by another on the sender's behalf and at the sender's risk".

The goods so sent are called as "Goods Sent on Consignment". The person who sends goods to agents for sale is called as 'consignor' and the person who receives goods from the consignor for sale is called as 'consignee'. The accounts relating to consignment transactions are called 'Consignment Accounts'. The consignment of goods becomes 'outward consignment' from the consignor's point of view and 'inward consignment' from the consignee's point of view.

Main Features of Consignment

1. Consignment of goods is not a sale. The ownership of the goods remains with the consignor, the consignee gets only the physical possession of goods.
2. The relationship between the consignor and consignee is that of principal and agent. Consignor is the principal and consignee is the agent.

3. Consignee sells the goods at the risk of the consignor. Consignee is not responsible for any loss or destruction of goods.
4. The expenses incurred by the consignee in connection with consignment should be paid later by the consignor.
5. Consignee does not get any share in the profits earned by the consignor. Consignee gets only commission for his work.
6. Consignee is not a debtor of the consignor. He will be responsible to pay the price of the goods only when he sells the goods.

Distinction between Sale and Consignment

Sale	Consignment
1. Ownership of the goods sold is transferred to the buyer of the goods.	1. Ownership of the goods sold is not transferred to the buyer of the goods.
2. Risk connected with the goods is transferred to buyer.	2. Risk connected with the goods is not transferred to the buyers.
3. Relation is that of a creditor and debtor.	3. Relation is that of a principal and an agent.
4. Goods once sold cannot be taken back from the customer.	4. Goods once sold can be taken back from the consignee.
5. Goods will be supplied only against the order of customer.	5. Goods will be forwarded even there is no order from the consignee.

Distinction between Consignment and Goods on Sale or Return

Consignment	Goods on Sale or Return
1. In consignment, goods are sent to an agent of the sender.	1. In sale or return, goods are sent to the optional or potential buyer.
2. In consignment, consignor pays commission to the consignee.	2. In sale or return, no commission is payable to the optional buyer.

Some Important Terms

1. Commission. Remuneration or reward payable to the consignee for selling the goods is termed as 'commission'. Generally, it is payable on the basis of gross sale proceeds of goods.

2. *Del credere* Commission. It is an additional commission allowed to consignee for undertaking the risk of bad debts arising out of credit sales. If the consignee agrees to take the *del credere* commission, he should bear the loss on account of bad debts. When the consignor paid such special commission to the consignee, he receives the total amount of gross sales proceeds whether actually recovered by the consignee or not. Such commission is payable on the total sales unless it is specifically stated that the same is to be paid on credit sales.

3. Over-riding Commission. It is also an additional commission payable to the consignee to push up the sales of a new product in the market.

4. Proforma Invoice. It is a statement giving the particulars of goods consigned. It gives the particulars as to the description, quantity, quality, price of the goods and other necessary information. It is sent by the consignor to the consignee along with the goods. It may be prepared either at cost price or at invoice price. Generally, it is prepared at higher price in order to enable the consignee to sell the goods at maximum profits. It looks like a regular invoice, but it does not make the consignee responsible to pay the amount as in case of regular invoice for sales.

Specimen of Proforma Invoice

Proforma Invoice

Tele { Gram.... / Phone.... Consignor's Address..............

Date...............

Consignee's Address ....

....

Sl. No.	Particulars	Rate Rs.	Quantity	Amount Rs.
1.	Accountancy Vol. II by Prof. Balavant M.U.	80	15	1,200.00
2.	Text Book of Commerce by Prof. V.N. Mugali	50	10	500.00
3.	Vanijyashastra Bhag II by Prof. Balavant M.U.	50	10	500.00
				2,200.00
	Less : 10% trade discount			220.00
				1980.00
	Less : Other expenses : packing, forwarding etc.			80.00
	(Rupees nineteen hundred only)			1,900.00

E. & O.E. Sd/-

Signature of the Consignor

5. Non-recurring Expenses. Non-recurring expenses are those which are incurred for bringing the goods from the place of consignor to the place of business or godown of the consignee. These are also be called 'Direct Expenses'. Non-recurring expenses are given as below :

(a) Non-recurring expenses of consignor are packing, carriage, octroi, loading charges, freight, insurance, dock dues and other forwarding expenses.

(b) Non-recurring expenses of consignee are unloading, railway dues, dock dues, import or customs duty, octroi, carriage to his godown etc.

The above expenses should be added to the original price of the goods consigned.

6. Recurring Expenses. Recurring expenses are those which are incurred after the goods have reached the place of business or godown of the consignee. They are given as below :

(a) Recurring expense incurred by the consignor are—bank charges for discounting the bills, drafts and cheques received from the consignee, bad debt, expenses of damaged goods received back etc.

(b) Recurring expenses incurred by the consignee are—godown charges, insurance (fire), brokerage, advertisement, salary to salesmen, expenses on goods returned and damaged, commission etc.

(c) Commission taken by the consignee.

The above expenses also be called as 'indirect expenses' or 'selling expenses'. These expenses are not taken into consideration while calculating the value of abnormal loss and closing stock.

7. Advance by the Consignee. When the goods are consigned to the consignee, consignor may ask the consignee to deposit some money with him as a security in respect of the goods sent on consignment. This is called an 'Advance on Consignment' or 'Advance from Consignee'. Such an advance is not a part of sales proceeds. Therefore, it should not be credited to the consignment account. It should be posted to the credit side of the consignee's personal account. The advance may be made by the consignee by way of accepting the bill of exchange drawn by the consignor. If the consignor needs funds, he may discount such bill with the banker and get the cash to meet his liabilities. The amount of such discount is treated in two different ways : (1) If the consignor's business is centred only on consignment basis, the amount of discount should be treated as consignment expenses and should be debited to consignment account. (2) If the consignment is only a part of the consignor's business, such discount should not be treated as consignment expenses, it should be treated as an ordinary financial expenses and should be charged to Profit and Loss Account.

8. Account Sales. On the completion of sales or at periodical intervals, the consignee sends to the consignor a statement stating the details of the goods sold. Such a statement is called 'Account Sales'. It shows the details of sale proceeds, expenses incurred for receiving and selling the goods, commission of the consignee, advance paid to the consignor and the balance due to the consignor. The consignee sends the cheque, draft or bill to the consignor for the ultimate balance due to him. When account sale is submitted by the foreign consignee, it will be necessary to convert the figures of foreign currency into consignor currency as per the rate prevailing on the date of receipt of the Account Sale. The following is specimen of Account Sale :

Sheela Book Depot

Bangalore

Dated : 10th Oct., 2001

600 books received from Sushila Publishers, Delhi-5 to be sold on commission.

Account Sales

	Rs.	Rs.
300 Books sold @ Rs. 20 each		6,000
100 Books sold @ Rs. 10 each		1,000
		7,000
Less : Expenses :		
Carriage	100	
Freight and insurance	120	
Selling expenses	180	
Godown rent	100	
Commission at 10% of sales	700	1,200
Net proceeds		5,800
Less : Advance given or draft accepted		2,000
Balance due, Bank draft enclosed		3,800

E. & O. E.

For Sheela Book Depot

Vasanti

Manager

Distinction between Proforma Invoice and Account Sales

Proforma Invoice	Account Sales
(i) It is prepared and sent by the consignor to the consignee.	(i) It is prepared and sent by the consignee to the consignor.
(ii) It contains the particulars of goods to be sold by the consignee.	(ii) It contains the details of goods sold by the consignee.
(iii) It is prepared only once.	(iii) It is prepared periodically or the completion of sales.
(iv) It does not make the consignee responsible to the consignor.	(iv) It makes the consignee responsible to the consignor.
(v) It does not serve as the basis of book-keeping entries.	(v) It serves as the basis of book-keeping entries.

Recording Procedure of Consignment Transactions

There are mainly two parties in the consignment transactions *viz.*, consignor and consignee. Therefore, consignor and consignee should record the consignment transactions in their own books to know the trading result of their transactions.

(I) Recording in the Books of Consignor

Consignor should maintain the following accounts to record the consignment transactions in his books :

1. Consignment Account. In order to ascertain the exact profit or loss in respect of each consignment, the consignor opens consignment account for each consignment. It is just like Trading and Profit and Loss Account. In other words, it is nominal account. This account is debited with the value of goods sent on consignment, expenses of consignor, expenses of consignee and commission payable to the consignee. It is credited with the value of sales, value of goods returned and value of closing consignment stock, if any. The difference between the totals of two sides represents either profit or loss which is transferred to the General Profit and Loss Account. Specimen of consignment account is given below :

Dr. **Consignment Account** Cr.

	Rs.		Rs.
To Goods Sent on Consignment A/c (Cost of goods sent)	xx	By Consignee's A/c (Sale proceeds)	xx
To Bank or Cash A/c (Expenses of consignor)	xx	By Consignment Stock A/c (Value of unsold stock)	xx

Contd.

Dr. **Consignment Account** *(Contd.)* Cr.

	Rs.		Rs.
To Consignee's Account (Expenses of consignee)	xx	By Profit and Loss A/c (Loss)	xx
To Consignee's Account (Commission due to consignee)	xx		
To Profit and Loss Account (Profit)	xx		
	xxx		xxx

2. Goods Sent on Consignment Account. It is real account. In other words, it is just like sales account which is credited with the value of goods sent and debited with the value of goods returned, if any. The balance of this account should be transferred to the trading account at the end of the accounting period. The specimen of Goods Sent on Consignment Account is given below :

Dr. **Goods Sent on Consignment Account** Cr.

	Rs.		Rs.
To Consignment A/c (Cost of goods returned)	xx	By Consignment A/c (Cost of goods sent)	xx
To Trading A/c (Balancing figure)	xx		
	xxx		xxx

3. Consignee's Account. It is prepared to know the amount due from the consignee. It is personal account. It is debited with the sale proceeds of goods and credited with the expenses incurred by consignee, commission payable to consignee and advance received from the consignee. The balance represents the net amount due from the consignee. The debit balance in the consignee's account represents that the consignee is a debtor of consignor. The specimen of Consignee's Account is given below :

Dr. **Consignee's Account** Cr.

	Rs.		Rs.
To Consignment A/c (Sale proceeds)	xx	By Consignment A/c (Expenses incurred by consignee)	xx
		By Bank or Cash or B/R (Advance received from consignee)	xx
		By Consignment A/c (Commission to consignee)	xx
		By Bank or Cash (When balance received)	xx
	xxx		xxx

4. Consignment Stock Account. All goods sent on consignment to consignee may not sold by him within the accounting period of the consignor. Therefore, the stock of goods remained unsold with the consignee is called 'Consignment Stock'. This stock should be properly valued and credited to the Consignment Account to find out the correct profit or loss on consignment. It will show a debit balance. Consignment Stock Account balance will appear on the assets side of the balance sheet of the consignor.

5. Valuation of Stock. The unsold goods lying with the consignee should be valued at cost price or market price whichever is lower. In this context, cost price means value of goods (cost price or invoice price of goods) unsold plus non-recurring or direct expenses incurred both by the consignor and consignee. Recurring or indirect expenses should not be added to value of unsold stock.

Journal entries in the Books of Consignor

(1) When the goods are sent on consignment :

Consignment A/c	Dr.	With the value
To Goods Sent on Consignment A/c		of the goods

(2) When consignor is incurred some expenses in sending the goods :

Consignment A/c	Dr.	With the amount
To Bank or Cash A/c		of expenses

(3) When consignee is incurred some expenses on the consignment :

Consignment A/c	Dr.	With the amount
To Consignee's A/c		of expenses

(4) When cash, cheque or acceptance (*i.e.*, bill) is received from the consignee as advance :

Cash or Bank or B/R A/c	Dr.	With the amount of
To Consignee's A/c		cash, cheque or B/R

(5) When B/R is discounted by the consignor :

Bank or Cash A/c	Dr.	With amount received
Discount A/c	Dr.	With discount charge
To Bills Receivable A/c		With full value of B/R

(6) When consignee sells the goods :

Consignee's A/c	Dr.	With the amount
To Consignment A/c		of total sale proceeds

(7) When commission is payable to the consignee :

Consignment A/c	Dr.	With the total amount of commission (*i.e.* ordinary, *del credere* and over-riding commission).
To Consignee's A/c		

(8) When goods are returned by the consignee :

Goods Sent on Consignment A/c Dr. } With the value of
To Consignment A/c } goods returned

(9) For adjustment of bad debts :

(a) When *del credere* commission is not given :

Consignment A/c Dr. } With the amount of
To Consignee's A/c } bad debts

(b) When *del credere* commission is given :

When the *del credere* commission is given to the consignee, he has to bear the loss of bad debts. Therefore, no entry should be passed in this case.

(10) When the value of unsold stock with the consignee is taken into account:

Consignment Stock A/c Dr. } With the value of
To Consignment A/c } closing stock

(11) When the final balance is received from the consignee by cash, cheque or acceptance (*i.e.*, bill) :

Cash, Bank or B/R A/c Dr. } With amount of final
To Consignee's A/c } balance

(12) For transferring the profit or loss on consignment to the profit and loss account :

(a) When there is profit :

Consignment A/c Dr. } With the amount of
To Profit and Loss A/c } profit

(b) When there is loss :

Profit and Loss A/c Dr. } With the amount of
To Consignment A/c } loss

(13) When the balance in the goods sent on consignment account is transferred to trading account :

Goods Sent on Consignment A/c Dr. } With the amount of
To Trading A/c } balance

(II) Recording in the Books of Consignee

When a consignment of goods is received by the consignee, he has to keep proper records of stock of goods in the memorandum book called 'Consignment Stock Book' or 'Consignment Inward Book'. Consignee should specially open the personal account of the consignor in his book for the settlement of his dues. He may maintain the other accounts like Debtors, Cash, Bills Payable, Expenses Accounts etc. which are of less importance.

Consignor's Account. It is personal account. This account is prepared to find out the balance due to the consignor by the consignee. This account is debited with the advance paid by the consignee, expenses incurred by the consignee and commission due to the consignee. This account is credited with the sale proceeds of the goods. The balance of this account represents the balance due to the consignor. Specimen of consignor account is given below :

Dr. **Consignor's Account** Cr.

	Rs.		Rs.
To Bank or Cash (Expenses by consignee)	xx	By Cash or Bank or Debtors or Purchase (Sale proceeds either for cash or on credit or for goods purchased)	xx
To Commission (Commission from consignor)	xx		
To Cash or Bank or B/P (Advance to consignor)	xx		
To Cash or Bank or B/P (Payment of Balance)	xx		
	xxx		xxx

Journal Entries in the Books of Consignee

(1) When the consignee receives goods from consignor :

No entry should be passed, because, the consignee does not purchase the goods. However, he may record the details of the goods received in a Consignment Inward Book.

(2) When consignor incurs expenses on consignment :

No entry should be passed, because, consignee is not affected by this transaction.

(3) When cash, cheque or acceptance (*i.e.*, bill) is given to the consignor as advance :

Consignor's A/c	Dr.	With the amount of advance paid
To Cash or Bank or B/P A/c		

(4) When consignee returns goods to the consignor :

No entry should be passed, because, these returned goods have not been recorded in the consignee book when they were received from the consignor.

(5) When consignee incurs expenses on consignment :

Consignor's A/c	Dr.	With the amount of expenses
To Bank or Cash A/c		

(6) When sale is made by the consignee :

Cash or Bank or Debtors or Purchases A/c	Dr.	With the total amount of sale
To Consignor's A/c		

(7) When commission is due to the consignee :

Consignor's A/c	Dr.	With the total amount of commission (*i.e.* ordinary, *del credere* & over-riding commission)
To Commission A/c		

(8) For the adjustment of bad debts on the consignment debtors :

(i) When *del credere* commission is receivable :

Bad Debts A/c	Dr.	With the amount of bad debts
To Debtor's A/c		

(ii) When *de credere* commission is not receivable :

No entry should be passed, because, it is borned by the consignor.

(9) When there is closing stock with consignee :

No entry should be passed, because, closing stock is not the property of consignee.

(10) For the profit or loss on consignment :

No entry should be passed, because, consignee is not concerned with the profit or loss on consignment.

(11) When the final balance due to the consignor is paid by the consignee by cash, cheque or acceptance (*i.e.*, bill) :

Consignor's A/c	Dr.	With the balance amount paid
To Cash or Bank or B/P A/c		

Accounting for Loss of Goods Sent on Consignment

Goods sent on consignment may be lost or damaged either in the course of transit or after they reach the consignee's godown. Such loss may be normal or abnormal.

Normal Loss. It arises due to natural causes such as evaporation, leakage, loading and unloading, breaking in the bulk, dusting, weighment etc. This loss cannot be avoided. It is not shown in the consignment account. It is a part of the cost of consignment. This is considered in calculating the cost of stock remained unsold with the consignee. Value of closing stock will be increased proportionately due to such normal loss. Following formula is used for ascertaining the cost of closing stock when there is normal loss :

$$\frac{\text{Total value of goods sent (cost price/invoice price)} + \text{Non-recurring expenses}}{\text{Total quantity of goods sent} - \text{Quantity of normal loss}} \times \text{Quantity of closing stock}$$

The above formula will clear from the following example :

'A' consigned 1000 tonnes of coal at Rs. 20 per tonne to 'B' of Bangalore. He paid Rs. 1,000 as freight and cartage. 10 tonnes are lost due to unloading. 'B' paid Rs. 1,500 as unloading charges. 200 tonnes are lying unsold with 'B'. Calculate the value of closing stock.

$$\frac{20{,}000 + 2{,}500}{1{,}000 - 10} \times 200 = \text{Rs. } 4{,}545.45$$

Value of the closing stock will be Rs. 4,545.45. When there is no normal loss, the value of the closing stock will be Rs. 4,500 $\left(\frac{20{,}000 + 2{,}500}{1{,}000} \times 200\right)$.

If there is a normal loss of 10 tonnes of coal, the value of closing stock will be increased by Rs. 45.45.

Abnormal Loss. Abnormal losses are those which are arised due to fire, theft, flood, earthquakes etc. This loss can be avoided by taking the more care. Usually, such loss arising from carelessness and improper handling of goods. Abnormal loss is calculated in the same way as the value of unsold stock on consignment after adding the proportionate non-recurring expenses incurred up to the stage that such loss had been occurred. Formula of calculating abnormal loss is given as below :

Abnormal Loss = Cost price of goods + Proportionate non-recurring expenses (NRE) incurred upto the stage of loss

It is clear from the following example :

'X' sent to 'Y' 200 articles costing Rs. 300 per article. He paid Rs. 2,000 as freight and cartage. In the course of transit 50 articles were destroyed. 'Y' received 150 articles and paid 1,500 as unloading and carriage. 'Y' sold 100 articles at Rs. 400 per article. Calculate the value of abnormal loss and stock.

Value of Abnormal Loss

		Rs.
Cost price of 50 articles at Rs. 300 each		15,000
Add : Non-recurring expenses incurred upto damage on 50 articles *i.e.*,	$\frac{50}{200} \times 2{,}000$ =	500
	Abnormal Loss =	15,500

Value of Closing Stock

Cost price or invoice price of 50 articles (*i.e.*, units of closing stock) (50 × 300)		15,000
Add : (i) Non-recurring expenses incurred by the consignor on 50 articles *i.e.*,	$\frac{50 \times 2000}{200}$ =	500
(ii) Non-recurring expenses incurred by the consignee on 50 articles *i.e.*,	$\frac{50 \times 1500}{150}$ =	500
	Value of Stock	16,000

Abnormal loss should be credited to the consignment account to know the usual profit on the particular consignment. The entries relating to abnormal loss are given below :

(1) When the abnormal loss is not insured and not recoverable :

(i) Abnormal Loss A/c Dr. To Consignment A/c		With the value of abnormal loss
(ii) Profit and Loss Account Dr. To Abnormal Loss A/c		With the value of abnormal loss transferred to P & L Account.

(2) When the abnormal loss is insured and recoverable fully :

(i) Abnormal/Accidental Loss A/c Dr. To Consignment A/c		With the total value of abnormal loss
(ii) Insurance Co./Cash A/c Dr. To Abnormal/Accidental Loss A/c		With the amount of loss transferred to insurance Co. or loss recovered in cash

(3) When the abnormal loss is insured and partly recoverable :

(i) Abnormal/Accidental Loss A/c Dr. To Consignment A/c		With the total amount of abnormal loss
(ii) Insurance Co./Bank A/c Dr. Profit and Loss A/c Dr. To Abnormal/Accidental Loss A/c		With the amount of loss partly recoverable and balance transferred to P & L Account

Normal and Abnormal Losses. Sometimes, there may be a possibility of normal as well as abnormal losses. In such cases, the abnormal losses are to be ascertained in the same manner at cost plus proportionate non-recurring expenses incurred up to the stage of such losses. The amount of abnormal loss should be deducted from the total value (*i.e.*, cost plus all non-recurring expenses) of goods consigned. The remaining balance represents the value of goods available for sale. Then, the value of closing stock will be ascertained as below :

$$\text{Value of Closing Stock} = \frac{\text{Units in Closing Stock}}{\text{Units Available for Sale}} \times \text{Value of Goods available for sale}$$

Example. 'A' supplied 8,000 Kgs of oil at Rs. 20 per Kg to 'B' on consignment. He paid Rs. 4,000 as packing and forwarding expenses. 500 Kgs of oil was stolen in transit. 'B' sold 4,500 Kgs of oil at Rs. 25 per Kg. He reported that there was a 5% loss of oil due to evaporation during storing. Ascertain (a) Abnormal Loss; and (b) Value of Closing Stock.

Solution :

(A) Calculation of Abnormal Loss :

	Rs.
Cost price of 500 Kgs of oil at Rs. 20 per Kg	10,000
Add : Proportionate expenses of consignor *i.e.*, $\frac{500 \times 4,000}{8,000}$	250
Abnormal Loss =	10,250

(B) Calculation of Value of Closing Stock

	Rs.
Cost price or invoice price of 8000 Kgs of oil (8000 × 20)	1,60,000
Add : Non-recurring expenses	4,000
Total cost of 8000 Kgs of oil	1,64,000
Less : Abnormal loss of 500 Kgs of oil	10,250
Cost of 7500 Kgs will be cost of 7125 Kgs (*i.e.*, 7,500 – 375 *i.e.*, normal loss)	1,53,750

Therefore, cost of 2625 Kgs of closing stock will be $= \frac{2,625 \times 1,53,750}{7,125} =$ Rs. 56,645

(8,000 – 5,375 *i.e.*, 500 + 4,500 + 375)

Note : Normal loss of oil is 375 Kgs (*i.e.*, 5% of 7500 Kgs)

Accounting Methods

Following are the main three methods of accounting of consignment transactions :

I. Cost Price Method

II. Invoice Price Method

III. Memorandum Columns Method

I. Cost Price Method

Under this method of accounting, goods are forwarded by the consignor at cost without adding any margin of profit. But the consignee is expected to sell the goods at higher price than the cost price so that the consignor will earn profit. Following are the problems relating to cost price method.

Illustration 1 (Without Closing Stock) :

Sham of Mumbai consigned to Sundar of Bangalore 320 goods costing Rs. 180 per good to be sold on consignment. He paid Rs. 500 for loading, Rs. 300 for carriage and Rs. 200 for insurance. A bill for Rs. 12,000 was received from Sundar as advance. This bill was discounted by Sham at Rs. 11,800.

Sundar paid Rs. 600 for unloading, Rs. 300 for cartage and Rs. 300 for advertisement. He returned 20 defective goods to Sham. He sold remaining goods for Rs. 64,000. He is entitled to a commission of 6½% on gross sales. He settled his account through a Bank Draft.

Pass the journal entries in the books of Sham and Sundar and prepare the necessary accounts in the books of both parties.

Solution :

In the Books of Sham (Consignor)

Journal Entries

Sl. No.	Particulars		L.F.	Debit Rs.	Credit Rs.
1.	Consignment to Bangalore A/c	Dr.		57,600	
	To Goods Sent on Consignment A/c				57,600
	(Being goods sent to Sundar of Bangalore)				
2.	Consignment to Bangalore A/c	Dr.		1,000	
	To Cash Account or Bank A/c				1,000
	(Being paid for loading, carriage and insurance charges)				
3.	Bills Receivable A/c	Dr.		12,000	
	To Sundar's A/c				12,000
	(Being received his acceptance as advance on goods consigned to him)				
4.	Bank A/c	Dr.		11,800	
	Discount A/c	Dr.		200	
	To Bills Receivable A/c				12,000
	(Being the bill is discounted and discount charge is debited to Consignment A/c)				
5.	Consignment to Bangalore A/c	Dr.		1,200	
	To Sundar's A/c				1,200
	(Being expenses incurred by him on unloading, cartage and advertisement)				
6.	Consignment to Bangalore A/c	Dr.		4,160	
	To Sundar's A/c				4,160
	(Being commission at 6½% on Rs. 64,000 due to him)				
7.	Sundar's A/c	Dr.		64,000	
	To Consignment to Bangalore A/c				64,000
	(Being sale proceeds of goods sold by him)				

(Contd.)

Journal Entries *(Contd.)*

Sl. No.	Particulars		L.F.	Debit Rs.	Credit Rs.
8.	Goods Sent on Consignment A/c	Dr.		3,600	
	To Consignment to Bangalore A/c				3,600
	(Being value of goods returned by Sundar)				
9.	Consignment to Bangalore A/c	Dr.		3,440	
	To Profit and Loss A/c				3,440
	(Being profit on consignment transferred)				
10.	Bank Account	Dr.		46,640	
	To Sundar's A/c				46,640
	(Being Bank Draft received from Sundar for settlement of his account)				
11.	Goods Sent on Consignment A/c	Dr.		54,000	
	To Trading A/c				54,000
	(Being balance transferred to trading account)				

Ledger

Consignment to Bangalore Account

Dr. Cr.

		Rs.		Rs.
To Goods Sent on Consignment A/c		57,600	By Sundar : Sale Proceeds	64,000
To Bank : Loading	500		By Goods Sent on Consignment A/c (Returns)	3,600
Carriage	300			
Insurance	200	1,000		
To Discount		200		
To Sundar : Unloading	600			
Cartage	300			
Advertisement	300	1,200		
To Sundar : Commission (6½% on 64,000)		4,160		
To Profit and Loss A/c (Profit transferred)		3,440		
		67,600		67,600

Goods Sent on Consignment Account

Dr. Cr.

	Rs.		Rs.
To Consignment to Bangalore A/c (Returns)	3,600	By Consignment to Bangalore A/c	57,600
To Trading A/c (Transfer)	54,000		
	57,600		57,600

Sundar's Account (Consignee)

Dr.	Rs.			Cr. Rs.
To Consignment to Bangalore A/c:		By Bills Receivable (advance)		12,000
Sale Proceeds	64,000	By Consignment to Bangalore :		
		Unloading	600	
		Cartage	300	
		Advertisement	300	
		Commission	4,160	5,360
		By Bank (balance received)		46,640
	64,000			64,000

Journal Entries in the Books of Sundar (Consignee)

Sl. No.	Particulars		L.F.	Debit Rs.	Credit Rs.
1.	Sham's A/c	Dr.		12,000	
	To Bill Payable A/c				12,000
	(Sent our acceptance as advance against consignment from him)				
2.	Sham's A/c	Dr.		5,360	
	To Cash A/c				5,360
	(Paid for unloading cartage, advertisement and commission due from him)				
3.	Cash A/c	Dr.		64,000	
	To Sham A/c				64,000
	(Received on sale of goods of Sham)				
4.	Sham A/c	Dr.		46,640	
	To Bank A/c				46,640
	(Sent Bank Draft in settlement of his account)				

Ledger

Sham's Account (Consignor)

Dr.	Rs.		Cr. Rs.
To Bills Payable (advance)	12,000	By Cash	64,000
To Cash (expenses of sales including commission)	5,360	(Sale proceeds)	
To Bank (balance paid)	46,640		
	64,000		64,000

Illustration 2 (With Closing Stock):

Lalita of Nagpur sent to Mamata of Chennai 400 bags of wheat costing Rs. 350 each bag to be sold on consignment. She spent Rs. 3,000 for carriage and insurance for sending the goods. She received Rs. 20,000 from Mamata as advance. Thc consignee is entitled to a commission of 10% on gross sale proceeds. Consignee sent a cheque for the amount due together with an account sales as given below :

Account Sale

	Rs.	Rs.
Sale Proceeds :		
100 bags at Rs. 450 each	45,000	
200 bags at Rs. 400 each	80,000	1,25,000
Less : Advance paid	20,000	
Custom duty	2,000	
Carriage	1,000	
Insurance	200	
Selling expenses	300	
Commission 10%	12,500	36,000
	Net amount due	89,000

The unsold goods were valued at Rs. 42,000. Show the necessary accounts in the books of Lalita and Mamata.

Solution :

In the Books of Lalita (Consignor)

Dr. **Consignment to Chennai Account** Cr.

		Rs.		Rs.
To Goods Sent on Consignment A/c		1,40,000	By Mamata : (Sale proceeds)	1,25,000
To Bank : Carriage and Insurance		3,000	By Consignment stock	42,000
To Mamata :				
Custom Duty	2,000			
Carriage	1,000			
Insurance	200			
Selling expenses	300	3,500		
To Mamata :				
Commission at 10%		12,500		
To Profit and Loss A/c (Profit transferred)		8,000		
		1,67,000		1,67,000

Dr. **Mamata's Account (Consignee)** Cr.

	Rs.			Rs.
To Consignment to Chennai :		By Cash (Advance)		20,000
Sale Proceeds	1,25,000	By Consignment to Chennai :		
		Custom duty	2,000	
		Carriage	1,000	
		Insurance	200	
		Selling expenses	300	
		Commission	12,500	16,000
		By Bank (Balance received)		89,000
	1,25,000			1,25,000

Dr. **Goods Sent on Consignment Account** Dr.

	Rs.		Rs.
To Trading Account (Transfer)	1,40,000	By Consignment to Chennai	1,40,000
	1,40,000		1,40,000

In the Books of Mamata (Consignee)

Dr. **Lalita's Account (Consignor)** Cr.

	Rs.		Rs.
To Bank (Advance)	20,000	By Cash :	
To Cash (Selling expenses)	3,500	Sale Proceeds	1,25,000
To Commission	12,500		
To Bank (Balance paid)	89,000		
	1,25,000		1,25,000

Illustration 3

Shri Sukumar of Sagar sends a consignment of the value of Rs. 1,00,000 to Shri Tukaram of Tumkur. Sukumar incurred Rs. 1,000 for freight, Rs. 500 for carriage and Rs. 200 for insurance. Tukaram clear the goods by paying Rs. 200 for loading charges, Rs. 100 for octroi charges and Rs. 150 for carriage to warehouse. Tukaram sells on credit half of the consignment for Rs. 75,000 of which he received only Rs. 20,000, his bad debts amounting to Rs. 1,000 and discount being Rs. 300. Half of the remaining consignment is sold for cash at Rs. 50,000. Towards the close of the year, suddenly a new type of goods appeared in the market and there was no possibility of selling the balance of goods at a higher price. The unsold goods were held by them. Tukaram incurred recurring expenses amounted to Rs. 600 and he is paid 4% ordinary commission, 1% over-riding commission and 7½ *del credere* commission. Tukaram remits the balance due to Sukumar by Bank Draft.

Open the necessary accounts in the books of Sukumar.

Solution :

In the Books of Sukumar of Sagar

Dr. Consignment to Tumkur Account Cr.

		Rs.			Rs.
To Goods Sent on Consignment		1,00,000.00	By Tukaram :		
To Bank : Freight	1,000		Credit Sales	75,000	
Carriage	500		Cash Sales	50,000	1,25,000.00
Insurance	200	1,700.00	By Consignment Stock :		
To Tukaram :			Cost of Stock	25,000.00	
Loading Charges	200		*Add* : Prop. expenses	537.50	25,537.50
Octroi Charges	100				
Carriage	150				
Cash Discount	300				
Recurring Expenses	600	1,350.00			
To Tukaram : Commission (ordinary 4%, over-riding 1% and *del credere* commission 7½ on Rs. 1,25,000)		15,625.00			
To P & L A/c (Profit transferred)		31,862.50			
		1,50,537.50			1,50,537.50

Dr. Tukaram's Account (Consignee Account) Cr.

		Rs.			Rs.
To Consignment to Tumkur :			By Consignment to Tumkur :		
Credit Sales	75,000		Loading Charges	200	
Cash Sales	50,000	1,25,000	Octroi Charges	100	
			Carriage	150	
			Cash Discount	300	
			Recurring expenses	600	1,350
			By Consignment to Tumkur : Commission		15,625
			By Bank (Balance received)		1,08,025
		1,25,000			1,25,000

Dr. Consignment Stock Account Cr.

	Rs.		Rs.
To Consignment to Tumkur	25,537.50	By Balance c/d	25,537.50
	25,537.50		25,537.50

Dr. Goods Sent on Consignment Account Cr.

	Rs.		Rs.
To Trading Account (Transfer)	1,00,000	By Consignment to Tumkur	1,00,000
	1,00,000		1,00,000

Working Notes

(i) Calculation of Value of Stock

		Rs.
Value of goods sent		1,00,000.00
Less : 50% credit sales		50,000.00
	Balance	50,000.00
Less : 50% of the balance as cash sales		25,000.00
Cost of Stock		25,000.00
Add : Proportionate non-recurring expenses incurred by both Sukumar and Tukaram		
i.e., $\frac{25,000}{1,00,000} \times 2,150$ (*i.e.*, 1,700 + 200 + 100 + 150)		537.50
	Value of Closing Stock =	25,537.50

(ii) When the *del credere* commission is paid to the consignee, he must bear the risk of bad debt. Therefore, bad debts is a loss to the consignee.

(iii) Cash discount is an expense and not a loss, hence, it should debited to the consignment account whether the *del credere* commission is paid or not paid to the consignee.

Illustration 4

The consignment stock account in respect of consignment to Anda of Bagalkot in the Books of Chanda of Chandigarh showed a debit balance of Rs. 7,000 in the beginning of the year. During the year Chanda sent a further consignment of 300 bags of rice at Rs. 400 each to Anda of Bagalkot. She incurred Rs. 200 for insurance and Rs. 900 for freight. Chanda drew a bill of exchange on Anda for Rs. 30,000 and after receiving the acceptance from her, Chanda discounted the bill with her bank for Rs. 29,800. Anda sold entire old stock for Rs. 10,000 and sold 200 bags at Rs. 500 each on credit and 80 bags at Rs. 450 each for cash and took 5 bags at Rs. 450 each for her own use in the second portion of consignment. She received from debtors cash Rs. 4,000, allowed discount Rs. 100 and incurred bad debts Rs. 600 and her other expenses were : rent Rs. 800 and carriage outward Rs. 500. Anda has collected Rs. 300 by sale of empty bags. Anda is entitled for a commission of 10% on sales price.

Anda sent a cheque for the balance due. The cheque was encashed by Chanda by paying Rs. 100 as bank charges.

Show the important Ledger Accounts in the books of Chanda.

Solution :

In the Books of Chanda of Chandigarh

Consignment to Bagalkot Account

Dr.		Rs.			Rs. Cr.
To Consignment Stock :			By Anda : Sale		10,000
Opening Stock		7,000	By Anda :		
To Goods Sent on Consignment		1,20,000	Credit Sales	1,00,000	
(300 bags × Rs. 400 each)			Cash Sales	36,000	
To Bank : Expenses :			Sales to Herself	2,250	1,38,250
Insurance	200		By Anda (Sale of empty bags)		300
Freight	900	1,100	By Consignment Stock :		
To Discount on Bill		200	Cost of Stock	6,000	
To Anda : Discount allowed	100		*Add* : Prop. Exps.	55	6,055
Bad Debts	600	700			
To Anda : Rent	800				
Carriage Outward	500	1,300			
To Anda : Commission		14,825			
(10% on 1,38,250 + 10,000)					
To Bank Charges A/c :					
Collection Charges of Cheque		100			
To Profit and Loss A/c		9,380			
(Profit transferred)					
		1,54,605			1,54,605

Anda's Account (Consignee)

Dr.	Rs.			Rs. Cr.
To Consignment to Bagalkot :		By Bills Receivable (Advance)		30,000
Sale of Old Stock	10,000	By Consignment to Bagalkot :		
Sale of New Goods	1,38,250	Discount Allowed	100	
Sale of Empty Bags	300	Bad Debts	600	
		Rent	800	
		Carriage Outward	500	
		Commission	14,825	16,825
		By Bank (Cheque)		1,01,725
	1,48,550			1,48,550

Goods Sent on Consignment Account

Dr.	Rs.		Rs. Cr.
To Trading Account (Transfer)	1,20,000	By Consignment to Bagalkot	1,20,000
	1,20,000		1,20,000

Dr. **Consignment Stock Account** Cr.

	Rs.		Rs.
To Balance b/d	7,000	By Consignment to Bagalkot	7,000
To Consignment to Bagalkot	6,055	By Balance c/d	6,055
	13,055		13,055

Dr. **Bills Receivable Account** Cr.

	Rs.		Rs.
To Anda's A/c (Advance)	30,000	By Bank	29,800
		By Discount	200
	30,000		30,000

Working Notes

(i) Calculation of Value of Closing Stock : Rs.

Cost of Closing Stock (15 bags × Rs. 400 each) 6,000

Add : Proportionate Non-recurring Expenses $\left(\frac{1,100 \times 15}{300}\right)$ 55

Value of Closing Stock = 6,055

(ii) Sale of empty bags is an additional income and should be credited to Consignment Account. However, commission should not be debited to this account.

(iii) Commission will also be charged on value of the goods taken by the consignee.

(iv) Since the consignee is not paid *del credere* commission, the bad debt should be borned by the consignor. Therefore, it should be debited to the Consignment Account.

Illustration 5 (with normal and abnormal loss) :

X Oil Mills of Srinagar consigned 6000 Kgs of sweet oil to 'Y' of Meenanagar. The cost of oil was Rs. 12 per Kg. The consignor paid Rs. 6,000 for carriage, Rs. 1,000 for octroi and Rs. 1,500 for insurance.

During transit 300 Kgs of oil was accidentally destroyed for which insurance company paid Rs. 3,500 in full settlement of the claim directly to the consignor.

'Y' took delivery of the consignment and accepted the bill drawn on him for Rs. 30,000. He sold 5,060 Kgs at Rs. 16 per Kg the expenses being godown rent Rs. 600, advertisement Rs. 400 and salesman's salary Rs. 800. He is entitled to a commission of 6% and 4% *del credere* commission.

'Y' reported a loss of 40 Kgs due to leakage. He also settled the amount due.

Prepare the necessary accounts in the books of the consignor.

Solution

In the books of X Oil Mills of Srinagar

Consignment to Meenanagar Account

Dr. Cr.

		Rs.		Rs.
To Goods Sent on Consignment (600 Kgs × Rs. 12 per Kg)		72,000	By Y : Sales (5060 Kgs × Rs. 16 per Kg)	80,960
To Bank : Carriage	6,000		By Abnormal loss	4,025
Octroi	1,000		By Consignment Stock	8,107
Insurance	1,500	8,500		
To Y : Godown Rent	600			
Advertisement	400			
Salesman's Salary	800	1,800		
To Y : Commission (6% + 4% on Rs. 80,960)		8,096		
To Profit and Loss A/c (Profit transferred)		2,696		
		93,092		93,092

Y's Account (Consignee)

Dr. Cr.

	Rs.			Rs.
To Consignment to Meenanagar (Sale proceeds)	80,960	By Bill Receivable		30,000
		By Consignment to Meenanagar :		
		Godown Rent	600	
		Advertisement	400	
		Salesman's Salary	800	1,800
		By Consignment to Meenanagar : Commission		8,096
		By Bank (Balance received)		41,064
	80,960			80,960

Goods Sent on Consignment Account

Dr. Dr.

	Rs.		Rs.
To Trading Account (Transfer)	72,000	By Consignment to Meenanagar	72,000
	72,000		72,000

Abnormal Loss Account

Dr. Cr.

	Rs.		Rs.
To Consignment to Meenanagar	4,025	By Bank (claim received)	3,500
		By Profit and Loss A/c (net loss transferred)	525
	4,025		4,025

Dr. **Consignment Stock Account** Cr.

	Rs.		Rs.
To Consignment to Meenanagar	8,107	By Balance c/d	8,107
	8,107		8,107

Working Notes

(i) Calculation of Abnormal Loss

	Rs.
Cost price of 300 Kgs oil at Rs. 12 each	3,600
Add : Proportional Non-recurring Expenses $\left(\frac{300 \times 8,500}{6,000}\right)$	425
Value of Abnormal Loss =	4,025

(ii) Calculation of Value of Closing Stock :

Cost of 6000 Kgs of oil at Rs. 12 each	72,000
Add : Non-recurring expenses	8,500
Total value of oil sent	80,500
Less : Cost of abnormal loss of 300 Kgs of oil	4,025
Cost of 5700 Kgs of oil reaching consignee	76,475
Less : 40 Kgs of oil being normal loss	Nil
5660 Kgs of oil cost	76,475

Value of Closing Stock = $\left(\frac{7,6475 \times 600}{5,660}\right)$ = Rs. 8,107

(*i.e.*, 6,000 – 5,400 *i.e.*, 300 + 40 + 5,060)

Therefore, value of 600 Kgs of oil (*i.e.*, 600 Kgs of oil sent – 5400 *i.e.*, 300 Kgs of oil abnormal loss + 40 Kgs of oil normal loss + 5060 Kgs of oil sold); Closing stock is Rs. 8,107.

(iii) In this problem there is Non-recurring expenses of consignee.

Illustration 6

A Cotton Mill of Bangalore sends regular consignment of cloth to Messrs. Kolarappa and Sons, Kolar, who are the agents for selling the cloth and are entitled to a commission of 20 paise per metre of cloth sold. This includes *del credere* commission. Stock of cloth with the agents at the beginning—20,000 metres costing Rs. 60,000. Quantity of cloth consigned—1,60,000 metres at Rs. 4 per metre. Total quantity of cloth sold—1,50,000 metres at Rs. 5 per metre. Total remittances by the agents Rs. 6,25,000. Transportation charges paid by the agents were Rs. 10,000. Of the sales, Messrs. Kolarappa and Sons could not collect Rs. 12,000 due to the insolvency of the customer. 5,000 metres of cloth were damaged by the transport company for which the agents recovered Rs. 8,000. The damaged goods were sold for Rs. 5,000.

Prepare the Consignment Account and Kolarappa and Sons Account in the books of the Cotton Mill.

(*Mysore, B.Com., April, 1981*)

Solution :

In the Books of Cotton Mill Bangalore

Consignment to Kolar Account

Dr. Cr.

	Rs.		Rs.
To Consignment Stock A/c (Opening Stock)	60,000.00	By Kolarappa and Sons : Sales (1,50,000 × 5)	7,50,000.00
To Goods Sent on Consignment (1,60,000 × 4)	6,40,000.00	By Kolarappa and Sons : Compensation Recovered from Transport Company	8,000.00
To Kolarappa and Sons : Transportation Changes	10,000.00	By Kolarappa and Sons : Sale of Damaged Goods	5,000.00
To Kolarappa and Sons : Commission (1,50,000 × 1/5)	30,000.00	By Abnormal Loss	8,312.50
To Profit and Loss A/c (Profit transferred)	1,32,875.00	By Consignment Stock A/c (Closing Stock)	1,01,562.50
	8,72,875.00		8,72,875.00

Kolarappa and Son's Account

Dr. Cr.

	Rs.		Rs.
To Consignment to Kolar : Sales	7,50,000	By Consignment to Kolar : Transportation Charges	10,000
To Consignment to Kolar : Compensation Recovered from Transport Company	8,000	By Consignment to Kolar : Commission	30,000
To Consignment to Kolar : Sale of Damage Goods	5,000	By Bank (Remittances)	6,25,000
		By Balance c/d (Balancing Figure)	98,000
	7,63,000		7,63,000

Working Notes

(i) Calculation of Abnormal Loss

		Rs.
Cost of goods damaged (5,000 metres × Rs. 4 per metre)		20,000.00
Add : Proportionate non-recurring expenses on damaged goods $\left(\frac{10,000}{1,60,000} \times 5,000\right)$		312.50
Total cost of damaged goods		20,312.50
Less : Compensation recovered	8,000	
Sale proceeds of damaged goods Rs. 5,000 minus agent's commission on the sale of damaged goods Rs. 1,000	4,000	12,000.00
Abnormal Loss		8,312.50

(ii) Calculation of Value of Closing Stock Rs.

	Rs.
Cost of 25,000 metres of cloth in stock at Rs. 4 per metre	1,00,000.00
Add : Proportionate non-recurring expenses on the closing stock $\left(\frac{10,000}{1,60,000} \times 25,000\right)$	1,562.50
Value of closing stock	1,01,562.50

(iii) Transportation charge is assumed as non-recurring expense incurred on 1,60,000 metres of cloth.

Illustration 7

The following two given statements represent :

(i) Consignment sent out by R & Co., of Mumbai to S & Co., of Chennai.

(ii) The Account sales of the goods as rendered by S & Co.

You are required to prepare the necessary accounts in the books of R & Co., Mumbai.

(i) Invoice

		Rs.
8 Cases of Indigo each weighing 480 Kgs. at Rs. 5 per Kg.		19,200
Charges thereon :		
Freight paid at Rs. 35 per case	280	
Insurance on Rs. 20,000 at 1½%	300	
Packing charges	100	
Duty, bill of lading etc.	40	720
		19,920

E. & O.E. R & Co., Mumbai

14-10-1980

(ii) Account Sales

Goods sold by S & Co., Chennai for and on account of R & Co., Mumbai.

		Rs.
4 Cases of Indigo of 480 Kgs at Rs. 6 per Kg		11,520
2 Cases of Indigo of 480 Kgs at Rs. 7 per Kg		6,720
Gross sales		18,240
Deduct : Lading charges, dock dues etc.	180	
Wharfage etc.	60	
Commission on gross sales at 5%	912	
Advance paid by cheque	12,000	13,152
Balance sent herewith by sight draft		5,088

E. & O.E. S & Co., Chennai

31-12-1980

Further it was reported by S & Co., Chennai that one case of Indigo was damaged in transit and one case is in stock. Insurance company settled the claim for Rs. 2,100 for damaged case of Indigo.

(*Kar., B.Com., Oct., 1981*)

Solution :

In the Books of R & Co., Mumbai

Consignment to Chennai Account

Dr.	Rs.			Rs. Cr.
To Goods Sent on Consignment	19,200	By S & Co. : Sale Proceeds		18,240
To Bank : Expenses	720	By Abnormal Loss		2,490
To S & Co. : Expenses and Commission	1,152	By Stock on Consignment : Cost of Stock	2,400	
To Profit and Loss A/c (Profit transferred)	2,187	*Add* : Prop. Exps.	120	2,539
	23,269			23,269

S & Company Account (Consignee)

Dr.	Rs.		Rs. Cr.
To Consignment to Chennai : Sales	18,240	By Consignment to Chennai : Expenses and Commission	1,152
		By Bank (Advance)	12,000
		By Bank (Balance received)	5,088
	18,240		18,240

Goods Sent on Consignment Account

Dr.	Rs.		Rs. Cr.
To Trading Account (Transfer)	19,200	By Consignment to Chennai	19,200
	19,200		19,200

Consignment Stock Account

Dr.	Rs.		Rs. Cr.
To Consignment to Chennai	2,520	By Balance c/d	2,520
	2,520		2,520

Abnormal Loss Account

Dr.	Rs.		Rs. Cr.
To Consignment to Chennai	2,490	By Bank (Claim)	2,100
		By P & L Account (Balance transferred)	390
	2,490		2,490

Working Notes

(i) Calculation of Value of Abnormal Loss

	Rs.
Cost of 1 case of 480 Kgs at Rs. 5 per Kg	2,400
Add : Proportionate non-recurring expenses	
on damaged indigo *i.e.,* $\left(\frac{1 \times 720}{8}\right)$	90
Value of abnormal loss	2,490

(ii) Calculation of Value of Closing Stock

	Rs.
(a) Cost of 1 case of 480 Kgs at Rs. 5 per Kg	2,400
Add : Proportionate non-recurring expenses of consignor $\frac{1 \times 720}{8}$	90
(b) Proportionate non-recurring expenses	
of consignee $\frac{1 \times 340\ (180 + 160)}{7}$	49
Value of Closing Stock	2,539

II. Invoice Price Method

Sometimes goods are sent to the consignee at a price higher than cost price. In other words, certain percentage of profit is added in the cost price. Such price is called 'Invoice Price' or 'Selling Price'. The main object of sending the goods at invoice price is not to disclose to the consignee the profits made by the consignor on the consignment.

Loading. In the invoice price method, goods are consigned to the consignee by adding certain percentage of profit on cost price. The price charged over and above the cost price is called 'Loading'. In other words, the difference between the 'Invoice Price' and the 'Cost Price' of the goods is known as loading. Such loading is found only in the following items :

(i) Consignment stock at the beginning

(ii) Goods sent on consignment

(iii) Goods returned by the consignee and

(iv) Consignment stock at the end.

At the end of the financial or accounting period, before closing the consignment account, the following four adjustments should be made to cancel or remove the loading in each of the above items in order to ascertain the true profit on consignment.

(i) For removing loading (excess amount) in opening stock :

Stock Reserve A/c	Dr.	With the amount of
To Consignment A/c		loading in opening stock

(ii) For removing loading in goods sent on consignment :

Goods Sent on Consignment A/c	Dr.	With the amount of
To Consignment A/c		loading in goods sent

(iii) For removing loading in goods returned by consignee :

Consignment A/c	Dr.	With the amount of
To Goods Sent on Consignment A/c		loading in goods returned

(iv) For removing loading in closing stock :

Consignment A/c	Dr.	With the amount of
To Stock Reserve A/c		loading in closing stock

Note : Stock reserve account is also known as stock suspense account.

Methods of Calculating Loading

1. When cost price is given and invoice price is fixed at certain percentage above the cost price

In this case, given percentage should be added to the cost price of the goods to arrive the invoice price. The percentage that is added is called loading.

Example. The 'Cost price' of the goods sent is Rs. 40,000 and the 'Invoice price' is 50% above cost price. The loading and invoice price are calculated as below :

If cost price is Rs. 100, then loading is Rs. 50, when cost price is Rs. 40,000, then loading will be Rs. 20,000 $\left(\textit{i.e.,}\ \frac{50 \times 40{,}000}{100}\right)$.

Therefore, invoice price will be Rs. 60,000 (cost price + loading).

2. When cost price and percentage of loading on the invoice price are given

In this case invoice price is to be calculated first. Then, the loading is to be calculated on the invoice price.

Example. The cost of goods sent is Rs. 40,000 and invoice price is to be fixed to give a profit of $33\frac{1}{3}\%$ on selling price (i.e., invoice price). The calculation of invoice price and loading is as under :

If invoice price (selling price) is Rs. 100, then, profit or loading required is Rs. $33\frac{1}{3}$.

Therefore, cost price is Rs. $66\frac{2}{3}$ (*i.e.*, $100 - 33\frac{1}{3}$), and loading is at

50% on cost $\left(i.e., \dfrac{33\frac{1}{3} \times 100}{66\frac{2}{3}}\right)$

Therefore, loading is Rs. 20,000 $\left(i.e., \dfrac{4{,}000 \times 33\frac{1}{3}}{66\frac{2}{3}}\right)$

Invoice price comes to Rs. 60,000 (i.e., 40,000 + 20,000).

3. When invoice price and certain percentage of loading (Profit) on cost price are given

In this case cost price is not given. Hence, cost price is to be calculated first. Then loading is to be calculated.

Example. The goods are invoiced at Rs. 60,000 which is 50% above cost price. The calculation of loading is as below :

If cost price is Rs. 100, then loading is Rs. 50.

Therefore, invoice price is Rs. 150 (*i.e.*, Rs. 100 + Rs. 50).

The percentage of loading on invoice price comes to $33^1/_3$ $\left(i.e., \dfrac{50 \times 100}{150}\right)$ or $\frac{1}{3}$ of invoice price. Therefore, loading is Rs. 20,000 $\left(i.e., \dfrac{60{,}000 \times 50}{150}\right)$ or ($33\frac{1}{3}$% of 60,000).

4. When invoice price and cost price are given

In this case, loading is the difference between invoice price and cost price. For example, if invoice price is Rs. 60,000 and cost price is Rs. 40,000, then loading is Rs. 20,000 (i.e., Rs. 60,000 – 40,000).

From the above, the following equations can be created :

Invoice price = Cost price + Loading (60,000 = 40,000 + 20,000)

Cost Price = Invoice price – Loading (40,000 = 60,000 – 20,000)

Loading = Invoice price – Cost price (20,000 = 60,000 – 40,000)

It means, loading is $33\frac{1}{3}$ % on invoice price $\left(i.e., \dfrac{20{,}000 \times 100}{60{,}000}\right)$ and it is 50% on cost price $\left(i.e., \dfrac{20{,}000 \times 100}{40{,}000}\right)$. Therefore, the following are the comparative percentages :

$16\frac{1}{3}\%$ on invoice price = 20% on cost price

20% on invoice price = 25% on cost price

25% on invoice price = $33\frac{1}{3}\%$ on cost price

$33\frac{1}{3}\%$ on invoice price = 50% on cost price

50% on invoice price = 100% on cost price.

Illustration 8

M/s Motilal & Co., of Munirabad sent 200 boxes of tea powder at Rs. 80 per box to Kantilal of Kolhar. The boxes were invoiced at Rs. 100 per box. They spent Rs. 200 for carriage and Rs. 120 per insurance and Rs. 100 on miscellaneous heads. M/s Motilal & Co., drew a bill for three months for Rs. 15,000 which was duly accepted by Kantilal. Kantilal sold 100 boxes at Rs. 120 each for cash and 90 boxes at Rs. 150 each on credit. Kantilal returned 10 boxes as they were unsalable. Motilal paid Rs. 100 as freight on the returned goods. Kantilal incurred Rs. 800 as selling expenses. Kantilal was entitled to 4% commission and 2% *del credere* commission on total sale proceeds. One customer who had bought goods worth Rs. 500 on credit from Kantilal failed to pay the due amount. Kantilal remitted the balance of M/s Motilal & Co., and settled the account.

Prepare the necessary ledger accounts.

Solution :

In the Books of Motilal & Co.,

Consignment to Kolhar Account

Dr. Cr.

		Rs.			Rs.
To Goods Sent on Consignment		20,000	By Kantilal :		
To Bank : Carriage	200		Cash Sales	12,000	
Insurance	120		Credit Sales	13,500	25,500
Miscellaneous expenses	100	420	By Goods Sent on Consignment (Returns)		1,000
To Kantilal : Selling Expenses		800	By Goods Sent on Consignment (Loading on goods sent)		4,000
To Bank : Expenses on Goods returned		100			
To Kantilal : Commission (4% + 2% on 25,500)		1,530			
To Goods Sent on Consignment (Loading on returns)		200			
To Profit & Loss Account (Profit transferred)		7,450			
		30,500			30,500

Dr. Kantilal's Account (Consignee's Account) Cr.

		Rs.			Rs.
To Consignment to Kolhar :			By Bills Receivable (Advance)		15,000
Cash Sales	12,000		By Consignment to Kolhar :		
Credit Sales	13,500	25,500	Selling Expenses	800	
			Commission	1,530	2,330
			By Bank (Balance received)		8,170
		25,500			25,500

Dr. Goods Sent on Consignment Account Cr.

	Rs.		Rs.
To Consignment to Kolhar (Invoice price of goods returned)	1,000	By Consignment to Kolhar (Invoice price of goods sent)	20,000
To Consignment to Kolhar (Loading on goods sent)	4,000	By Consignment to Kolhar (Loading on goods returned)	200
To Trading Account (Balance transferred)	15,200		
	20,200		20,200

In the Books of Kantilal

Dr. M/s. Motilal and Co., Account (Consignor Account) Cr.

	Rs.		Rs.
To Bills Payable (Advance)	15,000	By Bank and Debtors :	
To Bank (Expenses)	800	Sale Proceeds	25,500
To Commission	1,530		
To Bank (Balance sent)	8,170		
	25,500		25,500

Note : Since consignee gets *del credere* commission, he alone is liable for bad debts.

Illustration 9

On 1-1-1990 V. Vishal of Vijayawada dispatched to K. Kushal of Kanakapur 200 tyres at an invoice price of Rs. 400 each which was 25% above the cost price. He paid Rs. 400 for carriage and Rs. 100 for insurance. He draws 3 months bill for Rs. 40,000 and discounted the same for Rs. 39,700.

K. Kushal received the consignment on 20-1-1990 and incurred Rs. 150 for unloading and Rs. 300 for salesman salary and Rs. 400 for selling expenses. Consignee returned 10 tyers and sold 100 tyers at Rs. 450 each for cash and 80 tyers at Rs. 500 each on credit. K. Kushal sent a draft for the balance due after deducting expenses and commission at 5% on sale and *del credere* commission 2% on credit sales on 30th March, 1990.

All money due was collected from debtors except Rs. 800 from Mr. Nishal.

Prepare the Consignment Account and pass Journal Entries in the books consignee.

Solution :

In the Books of Vishal

Dr. **Consignment to Kanakapur Account** Cr.

		Rs.			Rs.
To Goods Sent on Consignment		80,000	By K. Kushal :		
To Bank : Carriage	400		Cash Sales	45,000	
Insurance	100	500	Credit Sales	40,000	85,000
To Discount on Bill		300	By Goods Sent on Consignment (Returns 10 × 400)		4,000
To K. Kushal : Unloading	50		By Consignment Stock (Closing Stock)		4,033
Salary	300				
Selling Exp.	400	850			
To K. Kushal :			By Goods Sent on Consignment (Loading on goods sent $\frac{80,000 \times 25}{125}$)		16,000
Commission 5% on sales	4,250				
Del credere commission 2% on credit sales	800	5,050			
To Goods Sent on Consignment (Loading on goods returned $\frac{4,000 \times 25}{125}$)		800			
To Stock Reserve (Loading on Closing Stock $\frac{4,000 \times 25}{125}$)		800			
To Profit and Loss Account (Profit transferred)		20,733			
		1,09,033			1,09,033

In the Books of K. Kushal (Consignee)

Journal Entries

Sl. No.	Particulars	L.F.	Debit Rs.	Credit Rs.
1.	V. Vishal Account Dr.		40,000	—
	To Bills Payable Account			40,000
	(Being bill accepted drawn by V. Vishal)			
2.	V. Vishal Account Dr.		850	
	To Bank Account			850
	(Being expenses paid for unloading, salesman's salary and selling expenses)			
3.	Bank Account Dr.		85,000	
	To V. Vishal Account			85,000
	(Being Tyers sold for cash and credit)			
4.	V. Vishal Account Dr.		5,050	
	To Commission Account			5,050
	(Being commission due at 5% on sales and 2% on credit sales)			
5.	V. Vishal Account Dr.		39,100	
	To Bank Account			39,100
	(Being final remittance made by draft)			

Working Notes

(i) Valuation of Closing Stock

	Rs.
Invoice price of 10 (200 – 190 *i.e.*, 100 + 80 + 10) unsold tyers at Rs. 400 each	4,000
Add : Proportionate non-recurring expenses $\left(\frac{10 \times 650 \text{ (} i.e., 500 + 150\text{)}}{200}\right)$	33
Value of Closing Stock	4,033

(ii) Loading on closing stock will be calculated on the invoice price of the stock of tyers.

(iii) Bad debts will not appear in the books as *del credere* commission is allowed to consignee.

(iv) If cost price is 100, loading is 25, then invoice price would be 125.

Illustration 10

Marimallappa of Mangalore consigned 200 sewing machines costing Rs. 1,60,000 to their agent Karimallappa of Kanpur at 20% above the cost, to be sold on behalf of them. Marimallappa incurred Rs. 100 for packing, carriage and other charges on each machine.

Karimallappa received consignment by paying Rs. 1,200 as railway charges and spent Rs. 800 for carriage to godown. He accepted one month bill for Rs. 50,000 as advance. He rendered an account sales showing that :

100 machines realised at Rs. 98,000 for cash.

60 machines sold on credit at Rs. 1,000 each.

20 machines taken for his own stock at Rs. 975 each.

Consignee remitted the balance after deducting his commission at 7% on invoice price of goods sold and 12% on any excess money realised.

Prepare the important Ledger Accounts in the books of Marimallappa.

Solution :

In the Books of Marimallappa

Consignment to Kanpur Account

Dr. Cr.

		Rs.			Rs.
To Goods Sent on Consignment (200 × 960)		1,92,000	By Karimallappa :		
			Cash Sales	98,000	
To Bank :			Credit Sales	60,000	
Packing, Carriage and			Self Use	19,500	1,77,500
Other charges (200 × 100)		20,000	By Consignment Stock :		
To Karimallappa :			Invoice price (20 × 960) =	19,200	
Railway charges	1,200		*Add* : Proportionate		
Carriage to godown	800	2,000	N.R.E. $\left(\frac{20 \times 22,000}{200}\right)$	2,200	21,400
To Karimallappa :			By Goods Sent on Consignment		32,000
Commission 7% on			(Loading on goods sent		
Rs. 1,72,800 (180 × 960)	12,096		*i.e.*, 1,92,000 – 1,60,000)		
Special Commission					
12% on Rs. 4,700					
(1,77,500 – 1,72,800)	564	12,660			
To Stock Reserve		3,200			
(Loading on closing stock					
i.e., 19,200 – 16,000)					
To Profit and Loss Account		1,040			
(Profit transferred)					
		2,30,900			2,30,900

Dr. Goods Sent on Consignment Account Cr.

	Rs.		Rs.
To Consignment to Kanpur	32,000	By Consignment to Kanpur	1,92,000
To Trading Account (Transfer)	1,60,000		
	1,92,000		1,92,000

Dr. Consignment Stock Account Cr.

	Rs.		Rs.
To Consignment to Kanpur	21,400	By Balance c/d	21,400
	21,400		21,400

Dr. Karimallappa's Account (Consignee's A/c) Cr.

		Rs.		Rs.
To Consignment to Kanpur :			By Bills Receivable (Advance)	50,000
Cash Sales	98,000		By Consignment to Kanpur (Exp.)	2,000
Credit Sales	60,000		By Consignment to Kanpur (Commission)	12,660
Self Use	19,500	1,77,500		
			By Bank (Balance received)	1,12,840
		1,77,500		1,77,500

Note : Loading is 20% on above the cost. Therefore, loading on each machine is Rs. 160 (*i.e.* 960 – 800).

Illustration 11

'X' consigned 10,000 bricks to 'Y' at an invoice price of 75 paise per brick which is 50% above cost by spending Rs. 200 for carriage and Rs. 100 for other expenses.

Consignee realised 9,000 bricks at a profit of 100% on cost price by spending Rs. 200 as godown rent and Rs. 300 for selling and other expenses. Consignee reported the loss of 100 bricks due to unloading and rough handling which is expected. Consignee is entitled to 8% commission. There was bad debt of Rs. 200.

You are required to prepare consignment account and consignee account.

Dr. **Consignment to 'Y' Account** Cr.

		Rs.		Rs.
To Goods Sent on Consignment		7,500	By 'Y' : Sale Proceeds (9,000 × 100 paise *i.e.*, 100% on cost price *i.e.* 50 + 50)	9,000
To Bank : Carriage	200		By Consignment Stock	709
Other Charges	100	300	By Goods Sent on Consignment (Loading on goods sent) (7500 – 5000)	2,500
To 'Y' : Godown Rent	200			
Selling and Other Exp.	300	500		
To 'Y' : Commission 8%		720		
To 'Y' : Bad Debts		200		
To Stock Reserve (Loading on closing stock 675 – 450)		225		
To Profit and Loss Account (Profit transferred)		2,764		
		12,209		12,209

Dr. **Consignee's Account** Cr.

	Rs.		Rs.
To Consignment to 'Y'	9,000	By Consignment to 'Y' : Expenses	500
		By Consignment to 'Y' : Commission	720
		Bad Debts	200
		By Bank (Balance received)	7,580
	9,000		9,000

Workings

(i) Closing Stock : When there is a normal loss, closing stock is calculated as below :

$$\frac{\text{Value of goods sent + N.R.E.} \times \text{Quantity of closing stock}}{\text{Quantity of goods sent} - \text{Quantity of normal loss}}$$

$$= \frac{7{,}500 + 300 \times 900}{10{,}000 - 100} = \text{Rs. } 709$$

(ii) Loading is calculated as below

If cost is 100, loading is 50, then invoice price is 150. Therefore, the percentage of loading will be 33-1/3 on invoice price or 1/3 of invoice price.

(iii) Loading on Closing Stock Rs.

		Rs.
Invoice price of 900 bricks × 75 paise =	Rs. 675	
Less : Cost price of 900 bricks × 50 paise =	Rs. 450	225

(iv) Loading on Goods Sent

Invoice price of 10,000 bricks = 10,000 × 75 paise =	7,500	
Less : Cost price of 10,000 bricks = 10,000 × 50 paise =	5,000	2,500

(v) Bad debt is debited to the consignment account, because *del credere* commission is not given to the consignee.

Illustration 12

Mr. Siri of Sholapur sent goods on consignment to Mr. Giri of Gulburga at a proforma invoice price which is 20% of sales. He sent 1,000 goods of the cost of Rs. 40 each and paid Rs. 2,000 as freight and insurance. Giri is entitled to a commission of 8% and 2% *del credere* commission. He has to bear all the expenses after the goods reached to his godown.

25 goods were totally damaged in transit for which the consignor received a claim of Rs. 800 from the insurance company.

Giri took delivery of the rest of the goods by paying Rs. 1,000 for octroi and carriage to his godown. Subsequently he paid Rs. 800 as godown rent and selling expenses. He sold 900 goods at Rs. 70 each of which 400 goods were sold on credit. But, the proceeds of 5 goods could not be recovered because of insolvency of debtors. He remitted the amount due to the consignor by bank draft.

Prepare the necessary accounts in the books of Siri of Sholapur.

Solution :

In the Books of Siri

Dr. **Consignment to Gulburga Account** Cr.

	Rs.			Rs.
To Goods Sent on Consignment (1000 × 50)	50,000	By Giri :		
		Cash Sales	35,000	
To Bank : Freight & Insurance	2,000	Credit Sales	28,000	63,000
To Giri : Octroi & Carriage	1,000	By Abnormal Loss		1,050
To Giri : Commission (8% + 2% on 63,000)	6,300	By Consignment Stock (Closing Stock)		3,977
To Stock Reserve (Loading on Closing Stock 75 × 10)	750	By Goods Sent on Consignment (Loading on Goods Sent 1,000 × 10)		10,000
To Profit and Loss Account (Profit transferred)	17,977			
	78,027			78,027

Dr. **Goods Sent on Consignment** Cr.

	Rs.		Rs.
To Consignment to Gulburga	10,000	By Consignment to Gulburga	50,000
To Trading Account (Transfer)	40,000		
	50,000		50,000

Abnormal Loss Account

Dr.	Rs.		Cr. Rs.
To Consignment to Gulburga	1,050	By Bank (Insurance)	800
		By Profit and Loss A/c (Net loss transferred)	250
	1,050		1,050

Consignment Stock Account

Dr.	Rs.		Cr. Rs.
To Consignment to Gulburga	3,977	By Balance c/d	3,977
	3,977		3,977

Giri's Account (Consignee's Account)

Dr.	Rs.			Cr. Rs.
To Consignment to Gulburga	63,000	By Consignment to Gulburga :		
		Expenses	1,000	
		Commission	6,300	7,300
		By Bank (Balance received)		55,700
	63,000			63,000

Working Notes

(i) Calculation of Abnormal Loss

		Rs.
Cost price of 25 destroyed goods (*i.e.*, 25 × 40)		1,000
Add: Proportionate N.R.E. up to the stage of damage $\left(i.e., \frac{25 \times 2,000}{1,000}\right)$		50
Total Abnormal Loss		1,050

(ii) Calculation of Closing Stock

		Rs.
Invoice price of 75 (i.e., 1,000 – 25 = 975 – 900) goods (75 × 50)		3,750
Add : Proportionate N.R.E. of Consignor $\left(i.e., \frac{75 \times 2,000}{1,000}\right)$	150	
Proportionate N.R.E. of Consignee $\left(i.e., \frac{75 \times 1,000}{975}\right)$	77	227
Value of Closing Stock		3,977

(iii) Since consignee gets *del credere* commission he alone is liable for bad debts.

(iv) Godown rent and selling expenses of Rs. 800 paid by consignee are not debited to consignment account as they are incurred after the goods are reached to the godown of consignee as per the agreement in between the consignor and consignee.

Illustration 13

On 1-9-1979 goods costing Rs. 33,000 were consigned by 'A' to his agent 'B' at a proforma invoice price of 20% profit on cost. 'A' paid Rs. 1,250 towards insurance and freight. 'B' was allowed Rs. 1,000 for cost of establishment. 'B' was entitled to 5% commission on gross sales and 3% *del credere* commission. He was also allowed 5% of the net profit as extra commission after charging such commission.

'B' incurred expenses of Rs. 350 as loading charges. He sold ¾ of the goods at $33^1/_3$% profit on cost, half of which were credit sales. Further it was informed that ½ of the balance of goods were destroyed by fire and a claim lodged for Rs. 4,000 was settled at a discount of 20%.

Your are required to prepare Consignment Account and Abnormal Loss Account in the books of 'A'.

(*Kar., B.Com., April, 1981 Mod.*)

Solution :

In the Books of 'A'

Dr. **Consignment to B Account** Cr.

		Rs.		Rs.
To Goods Sent on Consignment (33,000 + 6,600)		39,600	By B : Sales [6/8 of goods (*i.e.*, 2,450 sold at 33½% profit on cost]	33,000
To Bank : Insurance & Freight		1,250	By Abnormal Loss (1/8 of goods lost)	4,325
To 'B': Establishment Charges	1,000		By Consignment Stock (1/8 of goods in stock)	5,150
Loading Charges	350	1,350	By Goods Sent on Consignment (Loading on goods sent)	6,600
To 'B' : Commission 8% (*i.e.*, 5% + 3%) on Rs. 33,000		2,640		
To Stock Reserve (Loading on closing stock 4,950 − 4,125)		825		
To Balance c/d		3,410		
		49,075		49,075
To 'B' : Special Commission $\left(\frac{5 \times 3,410}{105}\right)$		162	By Balance b/d (Profit before commission)	3,410
To Profit and Loss Account (Profit after charging commission)		3,248		
		3,410		3,410

Dr. **Abnormal Loss Account** Cr.

	Rs.		Rs.
To Consignment to 'B'	4,325	By Bank (Insurance) (4,000 – 20% Discount)	3,200
		By Profit and Loss Account (Net loss transferred)	1,125
	4,325		4,325

Workings

(i) **Calculation of Abnormal Loss**

	Rs.
Cost price of 1/8 goods (*i.e.*, 1/8 × 33,000 cost)	4,125
Add : Proportionate N.R.E. upto loss : 1/8 of 1,600 (*i.e.*, 1,250 + 350)	200
Value of Abnormal Loss	4,325

(ii) **Calculation of Closing Stock**

Invoice price of 1/8 goods (*i.e.*, 1/8 × 39,600)	4,950
Add : Proportionate N.R.E. of consignor and consignee : 1/8 × 1,600 (*i.e.*, 1,250 + 350)	200
Value of Closing Stock	5,150

(iii) Goods are destroyed in the godown of consignee.

III. Memorandum Columns Method

Under this method two amount columns are maintained on each side of consignment account. The first column is used for recording the memorandum price i.e., the price at which invoice price is prepared and second column is used for recording the cost of goods consigned. If the entries are made on the basis of invoice price, the necessary adjustments are to be made to remove the loading in goods sent, goods returned, opening stock and closing stock. But under this method, even though the accounting entries are made on the basis of invoice price in the memorandum columns, necessary adjustments are not made to remove the loading. In fact memorandum columns are not important for the accounting purpose. But these columns are meant merely for the sake of information or memory. The accounting entries are made in the cost price columns as usual to ascertain the profit or loss on consignment.

Illustration 14

Premadas of Panjab consigned 200 toys to Ramadas of Rameshwaram at a invoice price of Rs. 60 each (cost price Rs. 50 each). He spent Rs. 1,000 for forwarding charges including insurance and drawn a bill on Ramadas for Rs. 5,000 at 60 days. 30 toys were destroyed in transit and Ramadas received 80% of the cost price in full satisfaction of the claim from insurance company.

Ramadas sold 150 toys at invoice price and spent Rs. 200 for selling the toys. He returned 10 defective toys by paying return freight of Rs. 50. He deducted commission at 4% on sales and paid the balance to Premadas.

Prepare Consignment Account, Consignment Stock Account and Accidental Loss Account in the books of Premadas under Memorandum Columns Method.

Solution :

In the Books of Premadas

Consignment to Rameshwaram Account

Dr. Particulars		Memo-randum Rs.	Actual Rs.	Particulars Cr.	Memo-randum Rs.	Actual Rs.
To Goods Sent on Consignment		12,000	10,000	By Ramadas : Sales (150 × 60)	9,000	9,000
To Bank : Forwarding Charges including Insurance		1,000	1,000	By Abnormal Loss	1,650	1,650
To Ramadas : Selling Exp.	200			By Goods Sent on Consignment(Returns)	600	500
Freight on Goods Returned	50	250	250	By Consignment Stock (Closing Stock)	650	550
To Ramadas : Commission		360	360	By Profit & Loss A/c (Loss transferred)	1,710	
To Profit & Loss A/c (Profit transferred)		—	90			
		13,610	11,700		13,610	11,700

Accidental Loss Account

Dr.	Rs.	Rs.	Cr.	Rs.	Rs.
To Consignment to Rameshwaram	1,650	1,650	By Bank (Received by Ramadas from Insurance Company (80% of cost price of goods damaged $= \frac{80 \times 1,500(30 \times 50)}{100}$)	1,200	1,200
			By Profit & Loss A/c (Loss transferred)	450	450
	1,650	1,650		1,650	1,650

Dr. **Consignment Stock Account** Cr.

	Rs.	Rs.		Rs.	Rs.
To Consignment to Rameshwaram	650	550	By Balance c/d	650	550
	650	550		650	550

Notes :

(i) Calculation of Abnormal Loss

	Rs.
Cost price of 30 damaged toys of Rs. 50 each	1,500
Add : Proportionate N.R.E. upto the stage of damage $\left(i.e., \dfrac{30 \times 1,000}{200}\right)$	150
Value of Abnormal Loss	1,650

(ii) Calculation of Closing Stock

(a) Invoice price of 10 toys of Rs. 60 each	600
Add : Proportionate N.R.E. $\left(i.e., \dfrac{10 \times 1,000}{200}\right)$	50
Value of Closing Stock on Invoice Price	650
(b) Cost price of 10 toys of Rs. 50 each	500
Add : Proportionate N.R.E. $\left(i.e., \dfrac{10 \times 1,000}{200}\right)$	50
Value of Closing Stock on Cost Price	550

(iii) Memorandum column shows loss because loading in invoice price is ignored.

(iv) Advance of Rs. 5,000 will appear in the consignee and consignor account.

(v) There is no change in the remaining accounts of consignor and consignee.

EXAMINATION QUESTIONS

(A) Answer the following questions in not exceeding 4 lines each :

(*Each Carries Two Marks*)

(1) What is consignment? (*K.U.D., April, 1996*)

(2) Why *Del credere* commission is given? (*K.U.D., Oct., 1995*)

(3) What is over-riding commission?

(4) What is proforma invoice? (*K.U.D., Oct., 1996*)

(5) Give four examples of recurring expenses of consignor and consignee.

(6) Give four examples of non-recurring expenses of consignor. (*K.U.D., April, 1995*)

(7) Give any four examples of recurring expenses paid by consignee. (*K.U.D., Oct., 1996*)

(8) What do you understand by *del credere* commission? (*K.U.D., April, 1995*)

(9) What do you mean by advance on consignment?

(10) What is account sales?

(11) What is normal loss?

(12) What is the formula for ascertaining the cost of closing stock when there is normal loss?

(13) What do you mean by abnormal loss?

(14) Give the formula for calculating the abnormal loss.

(15) How do you calculate the value of goods lost in a consignment? (*K.U.D., Oct., 1995*)

(16) What do understand by cost price? (*Madras, Oct., 1989*)

(17) What is invoice price?

(18) What is loading?

(19) How do you treat bad debts in consignment? (*K.U.D., April, 1996*)

(20) What do you mean by memorandum price?

(21) Why does the consignor sends goods to consignee at invoice price?

(22) How do you treat the loss of consignment stock by accident?

(23) How do you consider the closing stock used for advertising? (*I.C.W.A., Inter, 1995*)

(24) How do you treat normal loss and abnormal loss in the books of consignor? (*K.U.D. & Gulbarga, Oct., 1990*)

(25) Who is consignor?

(26) Who is consignee?

(27) What is outward consignment?

(28) What is inward consignment?

(29) How do you treat the loss of consignment stock due to natural cause?

(30) How do you treat bad debts when *del credere* commission is given?

(31) What is normal loss and abnormal loss?

(K.U.D., April, 1997)

(32) What are non-recurring expenses? Give four examples of such expenses paid by consignor. *(K.U.D., April, 1998)*

(B) Answer the following questions/problems :

(Each Carries eight Marks)

(1) Distinguish between a sale and a consignment.

(2) What are differences between a 'consignment and goods on sales or returns?

(3) Explain the following terms :

(a) Account sale
(b) Proforma invoice
(c) *Del credere* commission
(d) Over-riding commission

(Osmania, April, 1986)

(4) What are recurring and non-recurring expenses in consignment?

(Shivaji, Oct., 1981)

(5) What are the differences between proforma invoice and account sales?

(6) What are methods of calculating the loading?

(7) On 1-1-1997 'A' consigned goods to 'B' amounting to Rs. 1,00,000. 'A' incurred the expenses of Rs. 4,000 for consigning the goods. On 1-7-1997 an account sale was received from 'B' which showed that the entire goods were sold for Rs. 1,50,000. His expenses were Rs. 30,000. He was entitled to a commission of 10% on sales. He sent an advance Rs. 80,000. Make out an account sales assuming that 'B' remitted a bank draft for the balance on 30-7-1997.

(Simla, April, 1983)

Ans. : Balance remitted by bank draft Rs. 25,000.

(8) Find out the value of closing stock from the following :

1. Goods sent on consignment; 1,000 Kgs at Rs. 20 per Kg.
2. Normal loss; 5% in weight while in transit.
3. Non-recurring expenses paid by the consignor Rs. 900.
4. Quantity sold; 800 Kgs.

(K.U.D., Oct., 1996)

Ans. : Value of Closing Stock Rs. 3,300.

(9) 'X' sent 200 Kgs. of oil at a cost of Rs. 350 per Kg to 'Y'. He paid the non-recurring expenses of Rs. 425 for consigning the oil. 'Y' sold 178 Kgs of oil incurring Rs. 200 as selling expenses and reported that there was a loss of 2 Kgs due to normal leakage. Calculate the value of closing stock.

(*M.K.U., April, 1989*)

Ans. : Value of Closing Stock Rs. 750.

(10) 'M' consigned to 'N' 100 cases of tea costing Rs. 100 per case. He paid Rs. 1,000 as freight and cartage. 'N' could take delivery of only 90 cases since 10 cases were lost in transit. He paid Rs. 2,000 as unloading and carriage charges. At the end of the year he reported that he has sold away 80 cases at Rs. 150 per case. Calculate the value of closing stock and abnormal loss.

(*C.A. Inter, 1985*)

Ans. : Value of closing stock Rs. 1,322.
Value of abnormal loss Rs. 1,100.

(11) Ascertain (a) Abnormal loss; and (b) Value of closing stock.

Oil supplied 6,000 Kgs at Rs. 18 per Kg.

Packing and forwarding expenses – Rs. 6,000.

Oil stolen in transit 1,000 Kgs.

Oil sold by consignee 4,500 Kgs at Rs. 25 per Kg.

Loss of oil due to evaporation during storing 5%.

(*K.U.D., April, 1996*)

Ans. : Abnormal Loss Rs. 19,000; Value of closing stock Rs. 5,000.

Note : Normal Loss of oil is 250 Kgs (*i.e.*, 5% of 5,000 Kgs).

(12) Pass the journal entries in the books of Mohan :

(a) Mohan of Mysore sent goods worth Rs. 2,00,000 to Shyam for sale on commission.

(b) Mohan incurred Rs. 2,100 on freight and insurance.

(c) Shyam sold all the goods for Rs. 3,20,000 and he paid Rs. 1,100 for carriage etc.

(d) Shyam was entitled to a commission of 5% on sales. He remitted the amount due to Mohan by bank draft.

(*Baroda, Oct., 1979*)

Note : Amount due received from Shyam Rs. 3,02,900; Profit on consignment Rs. 1,00,800.

(13) 'A' consigned goods of the cost of Rs. 20,000 to 'B'. The consignor paid freight Rs. 1,000 and insurance Rs. 500 and received an advance of Rs. 10,000 by cheque from 'B'. The consignee paid carriage Rs. 300 and octroi Rs. 200. He sold all the goods for Rs. 30,000 and sent an account sales. He also sent a cheque to 'A' for the amount due after deducting his expenses along with commission at 10% on the gross sale proceeds. Pass the journal entries in the books of consignee.

(*Gorakhpur, April, 1989*)

Note : Final remittance in settlement Rs. 16,500.

(14) Pass the entries relating to abnormal loss under the following circumstances :

(a) When the abnormal loss is not insured and not recoverable.

(b) When the abnormal loss is insured and recoverable fully.

(c) When the abnormal loss is insured and partly recoverable.

(15) Compute commission and abnormal loss from the following :

(a) Cost of goods sent on consignment Rs. 60,000.

(b) Loading on goods at 25% on invoice price.

(c) Commission at 10% on sales plus 20% on excess amount realised over invoice price of goods sold.

(d) Expenses paid by the consignor are freight and insurance Rs. 4,000.

(e) Expenses paid by the consignee are octroi and duty Rs. 1,000, advertisement and rent Rs. 1,300.

(f) Goods sold are 80% of the consignment for Rs. 70,000.

(g) Half of the remaining goods are destroyed by fire at consignee's warehouse.

(*K.U.D., April, 1995*)

Ans. : Total commission Rs. 8,200 (7,000 *i.e.,* 10% on 70,000 plus Rs. 1,200 *i.e.,* 20% on 6,000 *i.e.,* 70,000 – 64,000). Abnormal loss Rs. 6,500 (cost price 6,000 *i.e.,* 60,000 × 1/10 plus proportional non-recurring expenses Rs. 500 *i.e.,* 5,000 × 1/10).

Note : 25% on invoice price is $33^1/_3$% *i.e.,* 1/3 on cost price.

(16) Calculate the value of closing stock and of abnormal loss from the following particulars :

(a) 5,000 Kgs oil consigned at Rs. 16 per Kg.

(b) Freight Rs. 2,000 and insurance Rs. 3,000 paid by consignor.

(c) Consignee's expenses : Rs. 700 for advertisement and Rs. 200 for godown rent.

(d) 750 Kgs of oil lost in transit and the insurance company paid Rs. 10,000 for it to the consignor.

(e) Sales : 3,000 Kgs at Rs. 18 per Kg.

(f) Commission at 5% on sales.

(g) Stock with the consignee was 1,000 Kgs.

(h) Normal loss 250 Kgs.

(*K.U.D., Oct., 1995*)

Ans. : Abnormal loss Rs. 12,750 (cost price Rs. 12,000 plus Rs. 750 proportionate non-recurring expenses); Value of closing stock Rs. 18,062.50 $\left(i.e., \frac{72,250 \times 1,000}{4,000}\right)$

(17) From the following particulars, find out the values of abnormal loss and closing stock.

(a) Goods sent on consignment—200 pieces of glass-wares at Rs. 50 per piece.

(b) Expenses incurred by the consignor Rs. 1,000.

(c) Goods lost in the transit—10 pieces.

(d) Expenses incurred by the consignee—Octroi Rs. 710 and selling expenses Rs. 500.

(e) Goods sold by the consignee—170 pieces.

(f) Goods damaged at consignee's place—2% of the total goods consigned (which is permissible)

(*Kar., April, 1998*)

Ans. : Abnormal loss Rs. 550 (11,000 × 10/200); Value of closing stock Rs. 960 (11,160 × 16/186); Goods available for sale 186 (200 – 14 *i.e.,* 10 + 4); Value of goods available for sale Rs. 11,160 (10,000 + 1,000 – 550 + 710).

(C) Solve the following problems :

(*Each Carries 16 Marks*)

On Cost Price Method

(1)

15-6-1973 Tej & Co., of Mumbai sent a consignment of 200 sewing machines to Bhaskar of Chennai with a proforma invoice amounting to cost of Rs. 8,000.

15-6-1973 He paid freight and insurance there on amounting to Rs. 1,000.

4-7-1973 Bhaskar received the goods and paid loading charges Rs. 150 and cartage and rent Rs. 210.

25-7-1973 Tej & Co., received from Bhaskar a draft for Rs. 3,500 against the consignment.

10-8-1973 Bhaskar sold the entire lot and realised Rs. 15,000. He also incurred sales expenses amounting to Rs. 500.

7-9-1973 He sent account sales and a sight draft for the balance due to Tej & Co., after deducting his commission at 7.5% on the gross proceeds.

15-9-1973 Tej & Co., received the account sales and draft.

Pass the necessary journal entries in the books of the consignor and show the Consignor's Account in the books of Bhaskar.

(*Karnatak, B.Com., Oct., 1975*)

Ans. : Consignment profit Rs. 4,015; Final remittance Rs. 9,515.

(2) 'A' sends out a consignment of the value of Rs. 5,000 to 'B' drawing on the later for Rs. 4,000 as an advance against the same. 'A' also pays Rs. 475 for freight etc. 'B' clears the goods paying Rs. 250 for duty, dock dues, etc. He sells on credit half the lot for Rs. 4,200 and half of the remaining is sold for cash at Rs. 2,000. 'B' remuneration is 2.5% on gross proceeds.

'B' sends out an Account Sales and a draft to 'A' for the balance as shown therein. Rs. 1,250 worth of goods are on hand with 'B'.

Open the necessary accounts in the books of 'A' and 'B' respectively recording the above transactions.

(*Bombay, University*)

Ans. : Profit on consignment Rs. 1,751.25

(3) A & Co., of Mumbai sent on October 10, 1987 two consignments of goods to B & Co., of Kolkata, invoiced at Rs. 16,000 and Rs. 12,000 respectively. The consignor's expenses were Rs. 314 for insurance, Rs. 117 for freight and Rs. 16 for miscellaneous charges. On November 15, 1987, B & Co., advised having sold the first lot of Rs. 22,000 and half of the second lot for Rs. 7,000. They had incurred the following expenses; for the first lot— Rs. 119 for insurance, Rs. 72 for storage and Rs. 31 for incidentals; and for the second lot— Rs. 92 for insurance, Rs. 49 for storage and Rs. 12 for incidentals. They charge commission at 5% on gross sale proceeds payable at one month. The accounts of A & Co., are closed on Nov. 30, 1987 by which date the remaining stock lying with B and Co., could not be sold. The expenses incurred by A & Co., should be divided equally between the two consignments. Show in the books of A & Co., how these transactions will be recorded.

(*Calcutta, B.Com., 1988*)

Ans. : Profit on consignment Rs. 4,626.25; Value of closing stock Rs. 6,188.25; Final remittance Rs. 26,885.00

(4) Khatau of Mumbai consigned goods, value Rs. 16,500 to M. Kimberley of East Borneo and the consignor paid freight and dues of Rs. 650, while the insurance cost him Rs. 490. A draft was drawn on M. Kimberley at six months for Rs. 5,500 and this was immediately discounted with the Bank for Rs. 4,520. In due course an Account Sales was received from the consignee stating that part of the goods had been sold for Rs. 10,000. Whilst expenses were Rs. 370 and commission Rs. 500, and a draft was enclosed for the balance (Rs. 5,500 previously drawn being a payment on account). The unsold stock was valued at cost price at Rs. 10,500. You are required to give the journal entries necessary to record these details in the books of the consignor and write up the ledger accounts.

(Bombay University)

Ans. : Profit on consignment Rs. 1,990.

(5) 'X' of Mumbai consigned 200 radios at Rs. 400 each to 'Y' of Kolkata and paid for packing and forwarding charges Rs. 400, freight Rs. 1,000 and insurance Rs. 600. 'X' drew 3 months bill for Rs. 6,000 on 'Y' which the later accepted. The bill was discounted in the bank for Rs. 5,900.

'X' received an account sales from 'Y' from which it appeared that 136 radios were sold at Rs. 600 each for cash and 20 radios at 640 each to Sen & Co., on credit and 'Y' took 4 radios at Rs. 600 each for his own use. 'Y' paid for advertisement Rs. 600, rent and taxes Rs. 1,000 and charged commission at 5% and *del credere* commission at 1% on gross receipts. The balance amount was remitted by bank draft.

Prepare the Consignment Account and Consignee's Account in the books of the Consignor and Consignor's Account in the books of the consignee.

(Karnatak, B.Com., Oct., 1978)

Ans. : Value of closing stock Rs. 16,400 (16,000 + 400); Profit on consignment Rs. 23,692; Final remittance Rs. 83,392.

(6) Chhotamull Ltd. of Kolkata, shipped in Nov. 1985 to their agents, Badamull Ltd. of Rangoon, 140 cases of goods, costing Rs. 1,29,000. Badamull Ltd. were to sell the goods on account of the consignors and were to receive a commission of 5% of the gross proceeds with a further 2% as *del credere* commission. Chhotamull Ltd. incurred the following charges in connection with the consignment :

	Rs.
Carriage	280
Insurance and Freight	3,290
Landing Charges	210
Cables and Expenses	40

Badamull Ltd., sold 140 cases for an average Rs. 1,500 per case incurring Bad Debts of Rs. 4,310 and paid the following expenses :

	Rs.
Landing Charges	470
Warehousing and Insurance	1,300
Packing and Selling Expenses	1,580

Raise the necessary accounts in the books of Chhotamull Ltd. To record the above transactions.

(*Calcutta, B.Com., 1987*)

Ans. : Consignment profit Rs. 59,130; Final remittance Rs. 1,91,950.

(7) Mr. Prakash of Bangalore sends Silk Sarees costing Rs. 20,000 to Mr. Arvind of Mumbai for sale on consignment basis. Prakash incurred expenses of Rs. 200 and paid it.

Mr. Arvind renders an account sales to the consignor showing the sales as Rs. 22,000. Arvind incurred expenses towards freight Rs. 800, godown rent Rs. 300 and insurance premium Rs. 200. The stock of unsold goods was valued at Rs. 8,000. Arvind is to get 10% commission on sales.

Draw the account sales and pass the journal entries in the books of Prakash and also show the Consignment Account.

(*Kar., B.Com., Oct., 1983*)

Ans. : Profit on Consignment Rs. 6,450; Final remittance Rs. 8,500.

On Cost Price with Normal and Abnormal Loss

(8) Rahim of Kolkata consigned 100 cases of medicine costing Rs. 1,000 per case to Karim of Kanpur on 1-1-1987. The goods were to be sold at 25% above cost. Any deficiency in selling price was to be borne by Karim. Karim was however entitled to a special commission at 25% of any surplus price realised. Karim was further entitled to an ordinary commission of 5% and *del credere* commission of 22½% on all sales.

Rahim incurred the following expenses :

	Rs.
Packing charges	6,000
Lorry hire	12,000
Loading charges	1,000
Railway freight	21,000

The cases were received by Karim on 15-1-87. The account sales received from Karim on 30-6-1987 revealed the following :

40 cases sold on 21-3-1987 at Rs. 1,500 per case, 30 cases sold on 24-5-1987 at Rs. 1,200 per case, 10 cases sold on 15-6-1987 at Rs. 1,300 per case, 5 cases of medicine were stolen by a dishonest employee. A compensation

of Rs. 2,000 was realised from him. Karim incurred unloading charges of Rs. 2,000 and warehouse rent Rs. 3,000. Karim enclosed a bank draft for the balance due.

Write up necessary accounts in the books of Rahim.

(*Calcutta, B.Com., Hons., 1988*)

Ans. : Loss on Consignment Rs. 16,900; Consignment Stock Rs. 21,300; Abnormal Loss Rs. 7,100.

(9) Somesh of Kolkata consigned 100 cases of candles to Sailesh of Bankura, which costs him Rs. 30 per case. He incurred the following costs : packing Rs. 40, carriage Rs. 20 and railway freight (paid in advance Rs. 40). Some of the cases were damaged in transit and Sailesh took delivery of 90 cases only. He (Sailesh) spent Rs. 10 for cartage and Rs. 40 for godown rent and sold the consignment at Rs. 35 per case. He sent the net amount to Somesh after deducting his expenses and commission at the rate of 5% on the sale proceeds together with his Account Sales. Somesh also received Rs. 80 from the railway as damages. Show how the transactions would appear in the books of Somesh.

(*B.Com., Panjab*)

Ans. : Profit on Consignment Rs. 152.50; Accidental Loss Rs. 310.00; Final remittance Rs. 2,942.50

(10) The Mumbai Mills Ltd. of Mumbai consigned to their Calcutta office Rs. 5,000 worth of piece goods (100 bales in all) drawing on Calcutta for the amount.

They paid charges, freight and insurance on the consignment amounting to Rs. 400 and discount the bill with cost Rs. 100.

The goods were realised in Calcutta and in due course Account Sales were received as follows :

Account sales of 100 bales of piece goods from Mumbai Mills Ltd. :

	Rs.	Rs.
80 bales of piece goods at Rs. 80		6,400
Delivery Cartage	250	
Godown Rent	35	
Insurance	40	
Sundry Charges	9	
Commission	353	687
		5,713
Draft paid		5,000
Balance herewith		713

The consignee also informs that out of the remaining 20 bales in stock, 5 were damaged and the insurance company had admitted a claim of Rs. 200 only. The balance were in good condition.

Pass journal entries in the books of both the parties and show the ledger accounts.

(*Bangalore, B.Com., 1980 and Mysore, B.Com., 1973*)

Ans. : Profit on Consignment Rs. 1,393; Value of Damaged Goods Rs. 270; Final Remittance Rs. 713.

(11) Neel Cycle Enterprises, Gadag consigned 100 Cycles costing Rs. 300 each to their agents at Bijapur. They paid Rs. 2,000 for freight and insurance.

During transit 5 cycles were totally damaged and the insurance company accepted the claim for Rs. 1,400 only.

The agents took delivery of the rest of the cycles and paid Rs. 570 to take the goods to their showroom and subsequently Rs. 300 as godown rent and sales expenses.

They sold 80 cycles of Rs. 400 each. They are entitled to a commission at 5% on gross sales. They also sent a bank draft in settlement of account.

Prepare the necessary accounts in the books of both the parties.

(*Nagpur, B.Com. and Karnatak, B.Com., Oct., 1985*)

Ans. : Profit on Consignment Rs. 4,020

Abnormal Loss Rs. 1,600

Value of Stock Rs. 4,890

(4,500 + 300 Expenses of Consignor + 90 Expenses of Consignee *i.e.*, $\frac{15 \times 570}{95}$

Final Remittance Rs. 29,530

(12) Mr. Rao consigned 400 packets of lip-sticks, each packet containing 100 lip-sticks. The cost price of each packet was Rs. 300. He spent Rs. 5 per packet as cartage, insurance and forwarding commission. 10 packets were lost on the way and Mr. Rao lodged claim with the insurance company and could get only Rs. 2,700 as claim on average basis.

The consignee took delivery of the rest of the packets and spent Rs. 780 as non-recurring expenses and Rs. 1,250 as recurring expenses. He sold 370 packets at the rate of Rs. 5 per lip-stick. He was entitled to 2% commission on sales + 1% *del credere* commission.

Prepare the Consignment Account and Consignee's Account in the books of Mr Rao.

(*Gulbarga, B.Com., 1984 and Poona, B.Com.*)

Ans. :		
	Profit on Consignment	Rs. 64,610
	Value of Closing Stock (6,000 + 140)	Rs. 6,140
	Abnormal Loss (3,000 + 50)	Rs. 3,050
	Final Remittance	Rs. 1,77,420
	Balance of Abnormal Loss Account	Rs. 350

(13) Satish of Gulburga consigned 100 cases of biscuits each costing Rs. 500, to his agent Girish of Bidar to be sold at his risk.

Satish paid Rs. 1,000 towards freight and insurance. On the way 10 cases were destroyed due to accident. Insurance company paid compensation of Rs. 4,000 directly to Satish.

Girish took delivery of the remaining cases at Bidar paying unloading charges and octroi Rs. 270. His other expenses were : rent Rs. 60 and selling expenses Rs. 40. He sold 80 cases at Rs. 650 per case. He was entitled to a commission at 5% on sales.

You are required to prepare (a) Consignment Account, (b) Girish's Account and (c) Goods Sent on Consignment Account in the books of Satish.

(*Madurai, B.Com., Kerala, B.Com. & Gulbarga, B.Com., 1982*)

Ans. :		
	Profit on Consignment	Rs. 8,260
	Value of Closing Stock (5,000 + 100 Exp. of Consignor + 30 Exp. of consignee *i.e.*, 10 × 270/90)	Rs. 5,130
	Abnormal Loss (5,000 + 100 Exp.)	Rs. 5,100
	Final Remittance	Rs. 47,030.

(14) Sri S.B. Oil Mills, Gulbarga consigned 20,000 Kgs of Sweet Oil to Patil of Poona. The cost of the Oil was Rs. 4 per Kg. The consignor paid Rs. 10,000 as freight and insurance.

During transit 500 Kgs of oil was accidentally destroyed for which the insurance company paid Rs. 2,000 in full settlement of the claim directly to the consignor.

Patil took delivery of the consignment and accepted the bill drawn on him for Rs. 30,000. He reported that 15,000 Kgs were sold at Rs. 6 per Kg the expenses being Rs. 400 on godown rent, Rs. 2,000 on advertisement and Rs. 4,000 salesmen's salaries. He is entitled to a commission of 3% and 1½% *del credere* commission.

Patil reported a loss of 200 Kgs due to leakage. He also settled the amount due.

Prepare the necessary accounts in the books of the consignor.

(*Karnatak, B.Com., 1978, Madras, B.Com., 1985*)

Ans. : Profit on Consignment Rs. 11,350

Abnormal Loss (2,000 + 250 Exp.) Rs. 2,250

Final Remittance Rs. 49,550

Balance of Abnormal Loss Account Rs. 250

Value of Closing stock Rs. 19,550

(*i.e.*, Cost of 20,000 Kgs sweet oil)	Rs. 80,000
Add : N.R.E. of consignor	Rs. 10,000
Total Value of Goods Sent	Rs. 90,000
Less : Abnormal Loss of 500 Kgs	Rs. 2,250
Value of 19,300 Kgs	Rs. 87,750
(*i.e.*, 20,000 – 500 = 19,500 – 200 normal loss)	

∴ Value of closing stock of 4,300 Kgs (19,300 – 15,000 sold)

of sweet oil Rs. 19,550 $\left(i.e., \dfrac{87,750 \times 500}{19,300}\right)$

On Invoice Price Method

(15) M/s Sundar and Co. consigned 1,000 tins of ghee costing Rs. 60 per tin to their agents Bansal Stores at Kolkata. The tins were invoiced at proforma Rs. 80 per tin. The agents sold 400 tins at Rs. 80 per tin for cash, 400 tins at Rs. 82 per tin on credit and they took over the balance to their own stock at Rs. 82 per tin. M/s Sundar & Co., paid freight and carriage Rs. 500 and miscellaneous Rs. 200. They drew on Bansal Stores at 3 months for Rs. 45,000 which was duly accepted by the later. The expenses incurred by the Bansal Stores were : carriage Rs. 50, octroi Rs. 40, storage Rs. 110, miscellaneous Rs. 100. They were entitled to 5% commission and 2% *del credere* commission on total gross sale proceeds. They sent their Account Sales to their principal showing as a deduction therefrom their commission and the various expenses incurred by them. A month later all the debtors except one who owed Rs. 200, paid cash and the Bansal Stores remitted the amounts due on consignment.

Pass the Journal Entries and

prepare the necessary accounts in the books of the Consignor and Consignee.

(*Calicut, B.Com. & Mysore, B.Com., 1970*)

Ans. : Profit on Consignments Rs. 14,516

(16) Shri Hegade of Bangalore consigned goods to Shri Jayakumar of Mumbai at a proforma invoice price of Rs. 2,00,000 which is 25% above the cost price. He paid Rs. 10,000 towards freight and Rs. 6,000 towards insurance and other charges.

Jayakumar took delivery of the goods and paid unloading charges, carriage, etc. Rs. 2,000. His other expenses were godown rent Rs. 1,000 and selling expenses Rs. 2,000. He sold ¾ of the goods for Rs. 2,00,000. He was entitled to an usual commission at 5% and a *del credere* commission at 2% on gross sale proceeds. He sent a draft for the balance to Hegade.

Prepare (a) Consignment Account, (b) Goods Sent on Consignment Account and (c) Consignee's Account in the books of the consignor.

(*Gulbarga, B.Com., April, 1985*)

Ans. : Profit on Consignment	Rs. 49,500
Value of Stock	Rs. 54,500
(¼ of 2,00,000 = 50,000 + ¼ of N.R.E. of Rs. 18,000 = 4,500)	
Loading on goods sent	Rs. 40,000
Loading on Closing Stock	Rs. 10,000
Final Remittance	Rs. 1,81,000

(17) Desai & Co., sent goods on consignment to Babu of Mumbai at a proforma invoice price which is 20% on sales. Desai & Co., sent goods costing Rs. 20,000 and paid for freight and other charges amounting to Rs. 1,200.

The terms are that Babu shall receive 10% commission on the invoice price and 20% of any price realised above the invoice price. Babu shall have to bear all the expenses himself incurred by him. Desai & Co., draws one month bill for Rs. 5,000 on Babu and Babu accepted bill which was discounted for Rs. 4,850 by Desai & Co.

Babu paid for rent Rs. 150, advertisement charges Rs. 100. He sold 4/5 of the goods for Rs. 24,000 which includes Rs. 15,200 being goods sold on credit. Babu paid the balance amount by draft.

Show the necessary accounts in the books of the consignor and consignee.

(*Kar., B.Com., 1982*)

Ans. : Profit on Consignment	Rs. 4,090
Commission (10% of 20,000 = 2,000 + 20% of 4,000 (24,000 – 20,000) = 800)	Rs. 2,800
Loading on goods sent	Rs. 5,000
Loading on closing stock	Rs. 1,000
Value of closing stock (5,000 + 240)	Rs. 5,240
Final Remittance	Rs. 16,200

(18) Vishal Traders of Shimoga consigned goods to Prabhu & Co., of Mysore to be sold at or above invoice price. Prabhu and Co. are to get 5% commission on sales at invoice price plus 25% of any surplus price realised, the account being settled by bank draft immediately on sale.

A three months bill was drawn by Vishal Traders on Prabhu and Co. for Rs. 1,50,000, which was discounted at 9% p.a.

During 1986, Vishal Traders consigned to Prabhu and Co., goods worth (including freight) Rs. 1,80,000; the invoice price of which was Rs. 2,50,000. Sales by Prabhu & Co. during the year amounted to Rs. 2,15,000. Goods unsold on 31st Dec., 1986 with Prabhu & Co., were of invoice price Rs. 75,000 (cost including freight Rs. 50,000), Vishal Traders had received from Prabhu & Co., bank drafts during the year Rs. 40,000, certain remittances being in transit on 31st Dec., 1986.

Show the Accounts in the books of Vishal Traders and Prabhu & Co.

(*Mysore, B.Com. & Hyderabad, B.Com.*)

Ans. : Loss on Consignment

Discount on bill $\left(1,50,000 \times \frac{9}{100} \times \frac{3}{12}\right)$		Rs. 3,375
Commission :		
5% on invoice price of Rs. 1,75,000 (Goods consigned Rs. 2,50,000 – Stock Rs. 75,000)	= 8,750	
25% on the surplus price of Rs. 40,000 (Sales Rs. 2,15,000 – Invoice price of goods sold Rs. 1,75,000)	= 10,000	18,750
Value of Stock		Rs. 75,000
Final Remittance		Rs. 6,250

(19) Mazda & Co. of Sri Lanka consigned goods to Rama & Bros. of Lahore at the value of Rs. 5,000 and invoiced the same proforma at 20% above cost plus freight etc. They paid thereon Rs. 120 for freight and cartage, and Rs. 80 for insurance. They drew on Rama & Bros for Rs. 2,000 as advance against the consignment and sold the bill for Rs. 1,950. They received account sales showing that ¾ of the goods were sold for Rs. 5,200 and Rama & Bros. expenses amounted to Rs. 175 and their commission to Rs. 300. The unsold stock was valued at actual cost and a two months' draft was received from Rama & Bros. in settlement of account to date.

Show the transactions in the books of both the parties.

(*Bombay, B.Com. & Poona, B.Com.*)

Ans. : Profit on Consignment Rs. 825.

(20) Bharat Exports Co. of Kolkata consigned 400 bales of Cotton goods to Sri M. Inam of Mysore on 1st Nov., 1987. The cost price was Rs. 600 per bale but the consignment invoice was made out at a figure to show a gross profit of 20% on sales. Sri Inam reported on 31st January, 1988 that he had sold ¾th of the consignment at a profit of 25% on sales and he had incurred Rs. 2,500 by way of freight and loading charges etc., and also Rs. 1,500 by way of godown rent etc. exclusive of his commission. Consignor spent Rs. 1,200 earlier as expenses in despatching the goods. Sri Inam was entitled to a commission of 5% on sales and 20% of the net proceeds as bonus after charging up both commission and bonus. On 1st Feb., 1988, Sri Inam sent a Bank Draft for the amount so far due from him.

Show the important Ledger Accounts in the books of the consignor and ascertain the profit on consignment up to 31st Jan., 1988.

(Calcutta, B.Com., 1988)

Ans. :	Profit on consignment	Rs.	6,392
	Value of stock (75000 + 925)	Rs.	75,925
	Final Remittance	Rs.	1,86,667

Note : Bonus at 20% on the net proceeds after charging commission and bonus is as under :

Gross proceeds	Rs.	2,40,000
Less : Charges	Rs.	16,000
Net proceeds	Rs.	2,24,000
Bonus $\left(\dfrac{2,24,000 \times 20}{120}\right)$	Rs.	37,333

(21) Bala consigned 40 machines to Rama on 1st January, 1980 on the following terms :

(a) All machines were to be sold 20% above the cost of Rs. 10,000. Any deficit in selling price is to be borne by Ram, while Ram is to retain 50% of any surplus realised.

(b) Ram is to be paid 3% commission and *del credere* commission on all sales.

Bala incurred freight charges of Rs. 40,000 in a consigning the machines. Ram sent Account Sale on 31st Dec., 1980 disclosing :

10 Machines sold for Rs. 12,000 each
15 Machines sold for Rs. 10,000 each
15 Machines sold for Rs. 14,000 each.

Ram had incurred unloading charges of Rs. 4,000 and selling expenses of Rs. 6,000. He had collected the entire sale proceeds except Rs. 3,000 which had become a bad debt. Ram sent a bank draft for the net amount due to Bala.

On 30th June, 1981, Ram sent a further Account Sale disclosing :

10 machines sold at Rs. 12,000 each, selling expenses were Rs. 1,500. He also sent a draft for the net amount due.

Bala closes his books on 31st December each year. Write up the ledger accounts in the books of Bala recording the above transactions.

(*Adapted from C.A. Inter*)

Ans. : Profit on Consignment Rs. 1,500
Value of Stock Rs. 1,11,000
Remittance on Dec., 1980 Rs. 3,46,000
Remittance on June, 1981 Rs. 1,12,500

Note : Calculation of Rama's commission on 31-12-1980 :

5% (3 + 2) on sales of Rs. 3,80,000	Rs. 19,000
Add : 50% of surplus sale price realised on 15 machines sold at Rs. 14,000 each as against Rs. 12,000 (*i.e.*, 2,000 × 15 = 30,000 × 50/100)	Rs. 15,000
	Rs. 34,000
Less : Deficit in sale price on 5 machines sold at Rs. 10,000 each as against Rs. 12,000 each to be met by Rama (*i.e.*, 2,000 × 5)	Rs. 10,000
Net Commission Due	Rs. 24,000

Calculation of commission of Rama on 30-6-1981 :

5% (3 + 2) on sale of 10 machines costing Rs. 1,20,000 = Rs. 6,000

On Invoice Price with Normal and Abnormal Loss

(22) On 1st Jan., 1985 P, a manufacturer of electric fans of Kolkata, consigned 80 fans costing Rs. 200 each to Q, the consignee at Mumbai. The invoice price was stated at Rs. 240 each. P paid Rs. 500 as packing expenses, Rs. 300 as insurance and Rs. 200 as railway freight while despatching the fans. On the same date P also drew a three months' bill for Rs. 10,000 which was accepted by Q by way of advance remittance against the consignment. During transit 20 fans were totally damaged in an accident for which Rs. 3,000 was received as claim realised on 1-3-85 from the Insurance Company. On 4th March, 1985, Q sent his account sales reporting sale of 50 fans at Rs. 12,500 of which Rs. 500 was unrealisable. Q who was entitled to an ordinary commission at 10% on sales, spent Rs. 300 as carriage to godown, Rs. 100 as godown rent and Rs. 250 as advertisement cost.

Give journal entries to record the above transactions in the books of P.

(*Calcutta, B.Com., 1975*)

Ans. : Loss on Consignment Rs. 475

Value Stock $(2{,}400 + 125 + 50 \left(\frac{300 \times 10}{60}\right)$ Rs. 2,575

Abnormal Loss (4,000 + 250) Rs. 4,250

Balance of Abnormal Loss Account Rs. 1,250

(23) Shri Joshi of Kumta consigned 100 boxes of wine to Shri Nayak of Karwar at on invoice price of Rs. 225 per box which is 50% above cost. He incurred the following expenses :

Packing Rs. 200; Insurance Rs. 100 and Freight Rs. 200.

Ten boxes were totally damaged in transit for which the consignor received Rs. 700 from the insurance company.

Shri Nayak took delivery of 90 boxes and paid Rs. 45 for carriage inwards and Rs. 200 as godown charges. He sold 80 boxes at Rs. 250 per box and was to get commission at 6% + 2% *del credere* commission. There was a bad debt of Rs. 200. The accounts were settled.

Show the necessary accounts in the books of both the parties.

(*Kar., B.Com., April, 1985 & Kerala, B.Com., 1970*)

Ans. : Profit on Consignment Rs. 5,760

Abnormal Loss (1,500 + 50 Exp. of consignor) Rs. 1,550

Value of Stock (2,250 + 50 N.R.E. of consignor + 5 N.R.E. of consignee) Rs. 2,305

Loading on Goods Sent Rs. 7,500

Loading on Closing Stock Rs. 750

Final Remittance Rs. 18,155

Balance of Abnormal Loss Account Rs. 850

(24) On Ist June, 1980, Shenoy and Co., of Mangalore consigned 100 cases of toys to Iyer and Co. of Chennai. The cost of consignment amounted to Rs. 7,500 but the goods were charged at proforma invoice price so as to show a profit of 25% on sales. The consignor paid Rs. 600 towards freight and insurance. An acceptance for Rs. 3,000 was received from the consignee and it was discounted for Rs. 2,900. The consignee had paid Rs. 1,000 towards import duty and Rs. 200 towards dock dues. One case was lost in transit and Rs. 50 was received from the Insurance Company by the consignee in full settlement of the claims. The consignee had sold 80 cases for cash Rs. 12,000. The consignee is entitled to a commission of 5% on sale proceeds. The consignee enclosed a Bank Draft for the balance due.

Prepare the necessary Ledger Accounts in the books of both the parties.

(*My. Uni., B.Com., I (R.R.), 1975*)

Ans. : Profit on Consignment Rs. 3,950

Final Remittance Rs. 7,250.

(25) On 1st September, 1982 goods cost price of which was Rs. 66,000 were consigned by Shri Lakshmi Das of Delhi to agent Sardar Ram Singh in Amritsar at a proforma invoice price of 20% above cost. Sardar Ram Singh paid freight and other forwarding charges amounting to Rs. 2,000. He was allowed Rs. 1,000 per annum towards establishment cost; 5% commission on gross sales and 3% *del credere* commission. Sardar Ram Singh paid Rs. 500 as rent of godown for the 3 months ended 31-12-1982.

Three-fourths of the goods were sold at $33^1/_3$% profit on cost, half of which were credit sales. Half the balance of goods was stolen, but the stock being insured, a claim lodged for Rs. 7,000 was settled for Rs. 6,900. Balance of stock was valued at proforma invoice price.

Write up the consignment account and stock lost on consignment account as on 31st December 1962 in the books of Seth Lakshmi Dass.

(*B.Com., Delhi, 1964*)

Ans. :	Profit on Consignment	Rs. 8,970
	Sales (cash Rs. 33,000 + credit Rs. 33,000)	Rs. 66,000
	Value of Stock [Unsold stock (1/4 × 79,200 *i.e.*, invoice price of goods sent) 19,800 and ½ of the stock unsold lost in transit *i.e.*, 19,800 × ½]	Rs. 9,900
	Loading on Closing Stock (9,900 – 8,500 *i.e.*, cost of 1/8 stock)	Rs. 1,400
	Loading Goods Sent (79,200 × $^1/_6$)	Rs. 13,200

(26) M/s Dev & Co., of Dadar manufactures sewing machines at a cost of Rs. 1,200 per machine. On 1-1-1891 they consigned 200 machines at an invoice price of Rs. 1,500 each to Shri Kittur of Hubli to be sold on behalf of M/s Dev & Co.

Shri Kittur is entitled to a commission of 8% on sales + 2% *del credere* commission. He was to bear all the expenses after the machines reach his godown.

M/s Dev & Co., incurred Rs. 5,000 as forwarding expenses and insurance. 10 machines were damaged in transit for Dev & Co., received Rs. 10,500 from the Insurance Company.

Shri Kittur took delivery of the remaining machines paying Rs. 11,400 as freight and octroi. Subsequently he also paid Rs. 5,000 as storage and other charges. He sold 160 machines at Rs. 1,800 each of which 100 of them on credit out of which, the proceeds of 5 machines could not be recovered because of insolvency of the debtors. He remitted the amount due to Dev & Co.

Show the Consignment Account and Consignee's Account in the books of M/s Dev & Co.

(*Sagar, B.Com., 1968 and Kar., B.Com., Oct., 1984*)

Ans. :	Profit on Consignment	Rs. 53,600
	Abnormal Loss (12,000 + 250 Exp. of consignor)	Rs. 12,250
	Value of Stock (45,000 + 750 Exp. of consignor + 1,800 Exp. of consignee)	Rs. 47,550
	Final Remittance	Rs. 2,47,800
	Loading on Goods Sent	Rs. 60,000
	Loading on Closing Stock	Rs. 9,000
	Balance of Abnormal Loss Account	Rs. 1,750

Note : Storage and other charges of Rs. 5,000 are incurred after the goods reached the godown. Hence, they are not debited to Consignment Account as agreed before.

(27) Hegade of Srinagar consigned goods costing Rs. 40,000 to his agent Bhat of Mumbai at a proforma invoice price of 20% profit on cost. He paid Rs. 1,200 towards freight and insurance. Bhat was allowed Rs. 550 for establishment expenses like salesman's salary, rent etc. He was entitled to a commission of 3% and 2% *del credere* commission after charging such commission.

Bhat took delivery of the goods paying Rs. 400 as octroi. He sold ¾ of the goods at 50% profit on cost. He reported that ½ of the balance of goods were destroyed by fire and a claim was lodged for Rs. 6,000. It was settled at a discount of 25% and claim amount was received directly by the consignor.

Prepare the necessary accounts in the books of consignor.

(*Panjab and Nagpur, B.Com. and C.A. Inter*)

Ans. :	Profit on Consignment	Rs. 10,000
	Bhat Commission (11,000 × 10/100)	Rs. 1,000
	Abnormal Loss [5,000 (40,000 × $^1/_8$) + 200 (1,200 + 400 × $^1/_8$)]	Rs. 5,200
	Value of Stock (6,000 (48,000 × $^1/_8$) + 200 (1,200 + 400 × $^1/_8$)]	Rs. 6,200
	Final Remittance	Rs. 40,800
	Loading on Goods Sent	Rs. 8,000
	Loading on Closing Stock	Rs. 1,000

On Memorandum Columns Method

(28) 'D' in Chennai consigned to 'J' in Trichy, goods to the value of Rs. 60,000 (cost Rs. 40,000) paying freight and insurance Rs. 4,000 and draws a bill on 'J' for Rs. 40,000 at 60 days 9/10ths of the consignment was sold by 'J' for Rs. 70,000 and expenses of Rs. 4,000 was incurred. 'J' is also entitled to a commission of 10% on sales. J remitted to D, the net amount held for his account by means of a sight draft. Show the ledger accounts in the books of both the parties on memorandum column method.

(*Calcutta and Delhi, B.Com.*)

Ans. : Profit on consignment in invoice price column Rs. 1,400
Profit on consignment in cost price column Rs. 19,400.

Additional Problems

(29) Shri Rajesh of Mysore sent a consignment of goods to Shri Rakesh of Bangalore to be sold at his risk. Shri Rakesh was to receive a commission of 10% on the invoice price of goods sold and 20% on any excess price realised over and above the invoice price. The commission was considered to include *del credere* commission also.

Shri Rajesh sent goods costing Rs. 25,000 at an invoice price of Rs. 30,000 and spent Rs. 500 for packing and Rs. 500 for forwarding.

On receiving the goods Rakesh accepted a draft in favour of Rajesh for Rs. 12,000. He also incurred the following expenses :

Octroi Rs. 200 and godown rent Rs. 300.

He sold 4/5 of the goods for Rs. 32,000. There is a bad debt of Rs. 600.

Prepare the necessary accounts in the books of Rajesh.

(*Gulbarga, April, 1990*)

Ans. : Profit on Consignment Rs. 6,740; Value of Closing Stock Rs. 6,240 (6,000 + 240 *i.e.*, 1/5 of Rs. 1,000 plus 1/5 of Rs. 200); Loading on Goods Sent Rs. 5,000 and on Closing Stock Rs. 1,000; Total Commission Rs. 4,000 (2,400 *i.e.*, 10% of 24,000 plus 1,600 *i.e.*, 20% of 8,000); Final Remittance Rs. 15,500.

Note : Bad debt is borne by the consignee since he gets *del credere* commission.

(30) Ashok Ltd. consigned 100 sewing machines costing Rs. 50,000 to M/s Bharat Agencies of Hubli at 20% on cost, to be sold on their behalf.

The consignor incurred Rs. 4,000 for packing charges and Rs. 1,000 for other expenses and drew a bill for Rs. 20,000 on Bharat Agencies which was duly accepted.

Bharat Agencies received the consignment by paying Rs. 500 for railway freight and spent Rs. 50 for carriage to godown.

They rendered an account sales as under :

(a) 50 machines sold at Rs. 600 each for cash.

(b) 20 machines sold at Rs. 700 each on credit.

(c) 10 machines taken for their own use at Rs. 600 each.

The consignee remitted the balance after deducting his commission at 5% on total sales and 15% on any excess amount realised over the invoice price of the goods sold.

Prepare the necessary ledger accounts in the books of both the parties.

(*Karnatak, April, 1992*)

Ans. : Profit on Consignment Rs. 2,760; Value of Closing Stock Rs. 13,110 (invoice price Rs. 12,000 + expenses Rs. 1,000 + Rs. 110); Loading on Goods Sent Rs. 10,000 and on Stock Rs. 2,000; Total Commission Rs. 2,800 (2,500 *i.e.*, 5% on 50,000 + 300 *i.e.*, 15% on 2,000); Final Remittance Rs. 26,650; Total Sales Rs. 50,000.

(31) Vishal Traders of Dharwad consigned goods to Prabhu & Co., of Belgaum to be sold on their behalf at or above invoice price. Prabhu & Co., are to get 5% commission on sales at invoice price plus 25% of any surplus realised, the account being settled by bank draft immediately on sale.

A three months bill for Rs. 1,50,000 was drawn by Vishal Traders on Prabhu & Co., which was duly accepted.

During the year 1990 Vishal Traders consigned to Prabhu & Co. goods (including freight) amounting to Rs. 1,80,000, the invoice price was fixed at Rs. 2,50,000.

Total sales by Prabhu & Co., during the year amounted to Rs. 2,15,000. Goods unsold on 31-12-1990 with Prabhu & Co., were valued at invoice price for Rs. 75,000 (cost including freight amounted to Rs. 50,000).

Vishal Traders received the bank draft from Prabhu & Co., in full settlement of their account.

Prepare the necessary accounts in the books of Vishal Traders.

(*Mysore & Karnatak, April, 1993*)

Ans. : Profit on Consignment Rs. 66,250; Value of Closing Stock Rs. 75,000; Loading on Goods Sent Rs. 70,000 (2,50,000 – 1,80,000); Loading on Stock Rs. 25,000 (75,000 – 50,000); Total Commission Rs. 18,750 (8,750 *i.e.*, 5% on 1,75,000 + 10,000 *i.e.*, 25% on 40,000).

(32) Sameer Sports of Surat consigned sports goods of the cost price of Rs. 30,000 to Praveen of Poona, invoiced at a profit on $33^1/_3$% on cost. They paid Rs. 3,000 on packing, cartage and insurance. 10% of the consignment was found damaged in transit which were returned to the consignors at Rs. 200 freight which was paid by them. Nothing could be received from the insurance company and these goods were sold by the consignor for cash Rs. 2,000.

The consignee received the balance of consignment and paid Rs. 900 for unloading and carriage to shop. His further expenses on rent, advertisement, etc. amounted to Rs. 2,100. He found 10% of the goods received by him being defective and by incurring expenses of Rs. 1,800 on repairs he sold this quantity for Rs. 3,000. He sold 80% of the goods received by him for Rs. 35,000. There was a bad debt of Rs. 500. Consignee's commission was :

(a) 10% on invoice price of goods sold (except defective goods) plus 5% on the amount of sale price over the invoice price.

(b) 10% on the sale price of the defective goods.

The consignee settled his account by sending a sight draft for the balance due by him.

Prepare the necessary accounts in the books of both the parties.

(*Karnatak, Oct., 1993*)

Ans. : Profit on Consignment 2,370; Value of Closing Stock Rs. 3,960 (invoice price Rs. 3,600 [*i.e.*, 40,000 – 36,400 (*i.e.*, 4,000 + 28,800 + 3,600) plus N.R.E. Rs. 270 + 90]; Loading on Goods Sent Rs. 10,000 and on Closing Stock Rs. 900; Total Commission 3,490 (2,880 *i.e.*, 10% of 28,800 plus 310 *i.e.*, 5% of 6,200 plus 300 *i.e.*, 10% of 3,000); Final Remittance Rs. 29,210.

Note : Sale proceeds of damaged goods Rs. 2,000 is credited to abnormal loss account and the balance is transferred to P&L A/c.

(33) Prakash Ltd. of Kolkata despatched 1,000 radio sets costing Rs. 150 each to Ramesh of Mumbai on 25-3-1982. The following expenses were paid by the company on the consignment.

Freight Rs. 7,500, Cartage Rs. 150 and Insurance Rs. 2,000.

The proforma invoice to the agents was for Rs. 2,00,000 and the remuneration was fixed at 5% on the gross sale proceeds. The agent accepted a bill for Rs. 50,000 drawn on them as advance. 50 sets were stolen in transit to Mumbai and insurance claim of Rs. 7,000 was received in final settlement. On 31-12-1982 the company received on account sales from the agent as under :

		Rs.
Sale proceeds of 800 sets		1,60,000
Less : Cleaning charges	1,900	
Storage	3,100	
Commission	8,000	13,000
Balance		Rs. 1,47,000

They remitted a sight draft for the balance after deducting the amount of bill already accepted.

Show the ledger accounts in the books of the consignor.

(*Karnatak, Oct., 1994*)

Ans. : Profit on Consignment Rs. 19,580; Value of Closing Stock Rs. 31,748 (Invoice price Rs. 30,000 plus N.R.E. Rs. 1,448 + Rs. 300); Loading on Goods sent Rs. 50,000 and Stock Rs. 7,500; Abnormal Loss Rs. 7,982

$\left(\text{Rs. } 7,500 + 482 \ i.e., \dfrac{9,650 \times 50}{1,000}\right)$; Final remittance Rs. 97,000.

Note : After crediting the insurance claim of Rs. 7,000 to Abnormal Loss A/c the balance of Rs. 982 is transferred to P & L A/c.

(34) On 1-1-1992 Ravindra of Rajnagar despatched to Surendra of Sholapur 500 tyres of an invoice price of Rs. 300 each which was 25% above the cost price. He paid Rs. 200 for packing and Rs. 300 for carriage and insurance. He draws 3 months bill for Rs. 50,000 and discounted the same for Rs. 49,800.

Surendra received the consignment on 15-1-1992 and incurred Rs. 100 for unloading and carriage; Rs. 500 for selling expenses and Rs. 1,000 for salesman's salary.

The consignee returned 50 tyres and sold 200 tyres at Rs. 330 each and 200 tyres at Rs. 350 each on credit. Surendra sent draft for the balance due after deducting his expenses and commission at 10% on sales and *del credere* commission at 3% on credit sales, on 30-3-1992. Market value of tyres was Rs. 250 each.

All the money due was collected from debtors except Rs. 2,000 from Mr. Mahesh.

Prepare ledger accounts in the books of consignor and pass the journal entries in the books of consignee.

(*Karnatak, April, 1995*)

Ans. : Profit on Consignment Rs. 20,087; Value of Closing Stock Rs. 15,067 (invoice price Rs. 15,000 plus N.R.E. Rs. 67 *i.e.*, 600 × 50/450); Loading on Goods Sent Rs. 30,000, on Goods Returned Rs. 3,000 and on Closing Stock Rs. 3,000; Total Commission Rs. 17,680 (13,600 + 4,080); Final Remittance Rs. 66,720.

Note : Discount on bill Rs. 200 is debited to consignment account and stock is valued at the lower of cost price or the market price.

(35) Santosh of Bangalore consigned 100 cases of biscuits to Yogesh of Gulbarga. The cost of each case is Rs. 30. Santosh incurred the following expenses :

Packing Rs. 40, Carriage Rs. 20 and Railway Freight Rs. 40.

Some of the cases were damaged in transit and Yogesh took delivery of 90 cases only. He paid Rs. 18 for cartage and Rs. 32 for godown rent and sold the whole of consignment at Rs. 45 per case.

Yogesh remitted the balance after deducting his expenses and commission at 5% on gross sales to Santosh.

Santosh received Rs. 180 from the insurance company in full settlement of the claim.

Prepare (a) Consignment A/c (b) Yogesh's A/c and (c) Abnormal Loss A/c in the books of Santosh and Santosh's A/c in the books of Yogesh.

(*Gulbarga, April, 1996*)

Ans. : Profit on Consignment Rs. 1,009; Abnormal Loss Rs. 312 (300 + 12); Balance remitted by Yogesh Rs. 3,797.

Note : After crediting the claim amount to Abnormal Loss A/c, the balance of Rs. 132 is transferred to P & L A/c being irrecoverable.

(36) Mallikarjun of Ilkal consigned 100 sarees to Mohan of Bijapur at an invoice price of Rs. 30,000 which was 20% above the cost. Mohan is entitled to 10% commission on the invoice price of the goods sold and 20% on any excess price realised above the invoice price.

Mohan sold 75 sarees realising Rs. 31,250 for which he spent Rs. 1,000 as non-recurring and Rs. 2,000 as selling and other expenses. He sent a bank draft of Rs. 25,000.

Mallikarjun spent Rs. 1,000 for despatching and other expenses. Give the necessary accounts in the books of both the parties.

(*Karnatak, April, 1997*)

Ans. : Profit on Consignment Rs. 5,000; Value of Closing Stock Rs. 8,000; Total Commission Rs. 4,000 (2,250 + 1,750); Loading on Goods Sent Rs. 5,000; Loading on Closing Stock Rs. 1,250 and Final Remittance Rs. 24,250.

(37) Chandan of Bijapur sends goods on consignment to Pawan to Hubli. The terms are that Pawan will receive 5% commission (including *del credere*) on the invoice price (which is cost plus 25%) of goods sold and 10% of any excess price realised over invoice price. Consignee is also allowed 5% of the net profit as extra commission, after charging such commission.

Chandan sent goods for Rs. 90,000 at invoice price and spent Rs. 6,740 on freight and insurance. Pawan accepted a bill for two months for Rs. 36,000 immediately on receiving consignment. His expenses were Rs. 1,200 as rent and Rs. 150 as advertisement. Pawan sold 3/4th of goods for Rs. 87,750. One customer failed to pay Rs. 1,800 and this amount could not be realised. Pawan remitted the amount due to Chandan.

Give : (a) Consignment Account, (b) Pawan's Account and (c) Goods Sent on Consignment Account.

Also write Chandan's Account in the books of Pawan.

(*Karnatak, April, 1998*)

Ans. : Profit on Consignment Rs. 20,900; Value of Closing Stock Rs. 24,185 (22,500 + 1,685); Total Commission Rs. 5,400 (3,375 + 2,025); Loading on Goods Sent Rs. 18,000; Loading on Closing Stock Rs. 4,500; Consignee's Share of Profit Rs. 1,045 (21,945 × 5/105) and Final Remittance Rs. 43,955.

Hints : (i) Profit before consignee's commission is Rs. 21,945.

(ii) Bad debt of Rs. 1,800 will not appear in the books as the *del credere* commission is allowed to consignee. Hence, it is borne by the consignee.

4

JOINT VENTURE ACCOUNTS

Meaning and Definition

A joint venture is temporary partnership without use of a firm name between two or more persons to undertake a particular business or venture and to share the profits or losses of that business in an agreed proportion. It is also called joint adventure, restricted or temporary partnership, or joint trade. The members of joint venture are called as co-venturers or co-adventurers. The joint venture or the temporary partnership comes to an end as soon as the particular venture or business is over.

Whenever a businessman finds shortage of either funds or business skills or whenever he wants to spread the risks involved in the business, he may associate with other businessmen. Such an association of persons for a short period is called as joint venture. The liability of co-venturers is limited for the adventure concerned. The co-adventurers enter into contract with each other. They agree to contribute the capital required for the business and share the profits or losses thereof in the agreed ratio. In the absence of any agreement between them, the profits or losses are to be shared equally.

Joint venture may be for construction of buildings, purchase and sale of goods, joint consignment of goods, undertaking of shares or debentures, speculation of shares or selling of a specific property etc.

A Dictionary for Accountants by Eric L. Kohler defines Joint Venture as under :

"A commercial undertaking by two or more persons, differing from a partnership in that it relates to the disposition of a single lot of goods or the completion of a single project. Its duration is limited to the period in which the goods are sold or the project is carried on."

Distinction between Joint-Venture and Partnership

Joint Venture	Partnership
(1) It does not use a firm name.	(1) It uses a firm name.
(2) It undertakes only a particular business.	(2) It undertakes its own independent business.
(3) It is for a shorter duration.	(3) It is for a longer duration.
(4) Members of joint venture are called 'co-venturers'.	(4) Members of partnership are called 'partners'.
(5) In a joint venture, the books of accounts are maintained jointly or separately.	(5) In a partnership, the books of accounts are to be maintained jointly.

Distinction between Joint Venture and Consignment

Joint Venture	Consignment
(1) In a joint venture, there is partnership.	(1) In a consignment, there is no partnership.
(2) In a joint venture, the relation between co-venturers is that of owners.	(2) In a consignment, the relation between consignor and consignee is that of principal and an agent.
(3) In a joint venture, all the co-venturers contribute capital.	(3) In a consignment, the finance is contributed only by the consignor.
(4) In a joint venture, the co-venturer acts on behalf of joint venture business.	(4) In a consignment, the consignee acts on behalf of consignor and at consignor's risk.
(5) In a joint venture, all the partners share profits or losses arising out of business.	(5) In a consignment, the entire profits or losses go to the consignor.
(6) In a joint venture, no account sale is sent by one co-venturer to another.	(6) In a consignment, an account sale is sent by the consignee to the consignor.

Methods of Recording Joint Venture Transactions

The following are the methods of maintaining the accounts of a joint venture :

I. When one of the co-venturers is appointed to manage the joint venture.

II. When a separate set of books is kept for joint venture.

III. When a separate set of books is not maintained or when all co-venturers keep the accounts :

(1) when each co-venturer keeps the accounts where all the joint venture transactions are recorded.

(2) when each co-venturer keeps the accounts where only his own transactions of joint venture are recorded. This is popularly known as 'Memorandum Method'.

Now, we shall discuss each of the above methods in detail.

I. When One of the Co-venturers is Appointed to Manage the Joint Venture

Under this method one co-venturer is appointed to manage the business and all other co-venturers are only contributing their share of investment to that co-venturer for managing the business. The managing co-venturer will be paid a commission for his service as agreed between the co-venturers. The following main accounts are maintained by the managing co-venturer :

(i) Joint Venture Account and

(ii) Personal accounts of all other co-venturers.

Joint venture account is a nominal account. It is similar to an ordinary P & L A/c. It is prepared to ascertain the amount of profit or loss made on joint venture. The balance of this account is either a profit or a loss.

Personal accounts of all other co-venturers are maintained to ascertain the amount due to or due from the other co-venturers.

The transactions relation to joint venture are recorded by the co-venturer so appointed in his books as below :

(1) When he receives cash from other co-venturers as their share of investment :

Cash or Bank A/c Dr.		With their respective share amount
To Other Co-venturers A/c		

(2) When he purchases goods :

Joint Venture A/c Dr.		With the cost of goods purchased
To Cash A/c		
(*If goods are purchased for cash*)		
OR To Suppliers' A/c or Creditors A/c		
(*If goods are purchased on credit*)		

(3) If, he supplies goods out of his stock :

Joint Venture A/c Dr.		With the cost of goods supplied
To Purchases or Goods A/c		

(4) When other co-venturers supply goods to the managing co-venturer:

Joint Venture A/c	Dr.	With the cost of goods supplied by other co-venturers
To Other Co-venturers A/c		

(5) When he incurs expenses on joint venture :

Joint Venture A/c	Dr.	With the amount of expenses incurred by the co-venturer
To Cash or Bank A/c		

(6) When he sells goods :

Cash or Bank A/c (*If goods are sold for cash*)	Dr.	With the amount of sale proceeds
OR Purchasers' or Debtors' A/c (*If goods are sold on credit*)	Dr.	
To Joint Venture A/c		

(7) When he gets commission :

Joint Venture A/c	Dr.	With the amount of commission
To Commission A/c		

(8) When he takes over (unsold stock) goods :

Purchases or Goods A/c	Dr.	With the value of goods taken over by him
To Joint Venture A/c		

(9) When other co-venturers take over (unsold) goods :

Other Co-venturers' A/c	Dr.	With the value of goods taken over by the other co-venturers
To Joint Venture A/c		

(10) When the joint venture account is closed by transferring the balance of profit or loss to P & L A/c (For managing or working venturer's share of profit or loss) and Other Co-venturers' Accounts (For their share of profit or loss)

(i) In case of profit :

Joint Venture A/c	Dr.	With total amount of profit
To Profit & Loss A/c		With his share of profit
To Other Co-venturers' A/c		With co-venturers' share of profit

(ii) In case of loss :

Profit & Loss A/c	Dr.	With the share of loss
Other Co-venturers' A/c	Dr.	With Co-venturers' share of loss
To Joint Venture A/c		With total amount of loss

(11) When the joint venture is completed and the amount due to the other co-venturers is paid :

Other Co-venturers' A/c Dr.		With the amount of cash
To Cash or Bills Payable A/c		paid or bills accepted

(12) When the joint venture is over and the amount due from the other co-venturers is received :

Cash or Bills Receivable A/c Dr.		With the amount of cash or
To Other Co-venturers' A/c		bills received

Proforma

Dr. **Joint Venture Account** Cr.

		Rs.			Rs.
To Cash/Suppliers or Creditors A/c (Goods purchased)		xxx	By Cash/Purchases or Debtors (Goods sold)		xxx
To Purchases or Goods A/c (Goods supplied)		xxx	By Purchases or Goods A/c (Unsold goods taken over)		xxx
To Other Co-venturers' A/c (Goods supplied & expenses incurred by other co-venturers)		xxx	By Other Co-venturers' A/c (Unsold goods taken over by other co-venturers)		xxx
To Cash A/c (Expenses)		xxx	By Loss on Joint Venture		
To Commission A/c		xxx	Profit and Loss A/c (Managing Co-venturer's share of profit)	xx	
To Profit on Joint Venture :			Other Co-venturers' A/c (Other Co-venturers' share of profit)	xx	xxx
Profit and Loss A/c (Managing Co-venturer's share of profit)	xx				
Other Co-venturers' A/c (Other Co-venturers' share of profit)	xx	xxx			
		xxx			xxx

Dr. **Other Co-venturers' Account** Cr.

	Rs.		Rs.
To Joint Venture A/c (Unsold goods taken over)	xxx	By Cash A/c (Share of investment)	xxx
To Joint Venture A/c (Loss)	xxx	By Joint Venture A/c (Goods supplied)	xxx
To Cash or Bills Payable A/c (Cash paid or Bills accepted)	xxx	By Joint Venture A/c (Profit)	xxx
		By Cash or Bills Receivable A/c (Cash or bills received)	xxx
	xxx		xxx

Illustration 1

A, B and C enter into a joint venture to purchase and sell goods and to share the profits or losses in the ratio of 2 : 1 : 1. A contributed Rs. 6.000, B Rs. 5,000 and C Rs. 2,000. A purchased goods worth Rs. 18,000 and supplied goods amounted to Rs. 2,000 out of his stock. C also supplied goods worth Rs. 2,100 from his stock and incurred expenses Rs. 100 in connection with the supplying of goods on account of joint venture. On behalf of the joint venture A sold the goods for Rs. 19,000. A paid Rs. 300 for expenses in connection with joint venture. A was entitled to a commission of 8% on sales. Unsold goods worth Rs. 900 were taken over by B. A settled the accounts of B and C by cheque.

Pass the journal entries and also prepare Joint Venture Account. B's and C's Account in the books of A.

Solution :

In the Books of A

Journal Entries

Sl. No.	Particulars		Debit Rs.	Credit Rs.
1.	Cash Account	Dr.	7,000	
	To B's A/c			5,000
	To C's A/c			2,000
	(Being amount of contribution received from B and C for joint venture)			
2.	Joint Venture A/c	Dr.	18,000	
	To Cash Account			18,000
	(Being goods purchased for joint venture)			
3.	Joint Venture A/c	Dr.	2,000	
	To Purchases or Goods A/c			2,000
	(Being goods supplied out of stock for J.V.)			
4.	Joint Venture A/c	Dr.	2,100	
	To C's A/c			2,100
	(Being goods worth Rs. 2,000 supplied for J.V. and expenses Rs. 100 incurred by C.)			
5.	Joint Venture A/c	Dr.	300	
	To Cash A/c			300
	(Being expenses incurred in connection with J.V.)			

(Contd.)

Journal Entries (*Contd.*)

Sl. No.	Particulars		Debit Rs.	Credit Rs.
6.	Cash A/c	Dr.	19,000	
	To Joint Venture A/c			19,000
	(Being goods sold on account of J.V.)			
7.	Joint Venture A/c	Dr.	1,520	
	To Commission A/c			1,520
	(Being commission due at 8% on sales)			
8.	B's A/c	Dr.	900	
	To Joint Venture A/c			900
	(Being unsold goods taken over by B)			
9.	Profit and Loss A/c	Dr.	1,608	
	B's A/c	Dr.	1,608	
	C's A/c	Dr.	804	
	To Joint Venture A/c			4,020
	(Being loss on Joint Venture transferred)			
10.	B's A/c	Dr.	2,492	
	C's A/c	Dr.	3,296	
	To Bank A/c			5,788
	(Being cheque remitted for settlement of their accounts)			

Dr. **Joint Venture Account** Cr.

	Rs.			Rs.
To Cash A/c (Goods purchased)	18,000	By Cash A/c		19,000
To Purchases or Goods A/c	2,000	(Sale proceeds)		
(Goods supplied)		By B's A/c		900
To C's A/c	2,100	(Unsold stock taken over)		
(Goods supplied and expenses incurred by C)		By Loss on Joint Venture transferred to :		
To Cash A/c (Expenses)	300	P & L A/c	1,608	
To Commission A/c	1,520	B' A/c	1,608	
		C' A/c	804	4,020
	23,920			23,920

Dr. **B's Account** Cr.

	Rs.		Rs.
To Joint Venture A/c	900	By Cash A/c	5,000
To Joint Venture A/c (Loss)	1,608		
To Bank A/c	2,492		
	5,000		5,000

Dr. **C's Account** Cr.

	Rs.		Rs.
To Joint Venture A/c (Loss)	804	By Cash A/c	2,000
To Bank A/c	3,296	By Joint Venture A/c	2,100
	4,100		4,100

Illustration 2

A and B enter into a joint speculation and purchase an old house with extensive grounds for Rs. 5,000 each contributing Rs. 2,500. For an agreed fee of Rs. 200 A is to manage the disposal of the property. Sale of internal fittings, windows etc., amounted to Rs. 1,500. A pays Rs. 200 for demolishing the house material of which realises Rs. 190. Sundry expenses paid by A were Rs. 80 and the whole of the land is eventually sold for Rs. 7,000. A and B share the net profits equally. A paying B his share by Bank draft.

Show the Joint Venture A/c and B's A/c in the A's Ledger.

(B.Com., Nagpur and Panjab)

Solution :

Dr. **Joint Venture Account** Cr.

		Rs.		Rs.
To Cash A/c (Purchase of old house)		5,000	By Cash A/c (Sale of internal fitting, window etc.)	1,500
To Cash A/c (Demolishing exps.)		200	By Cash A/c (Sale of house material)	190
To Cash A/c (Sundry exps.)		80	By Cash A/c (Sale of land)	7,000
To Commission (Fee) A/c		200		
To Profit on Joint Venture transferred to				
P & L A/c	1,605			
B's A/c	1,605	3,210		
		8,690		8,690

Dr. **B' Account** Cr.

	Rs.		Rs.
To Bank A/c (Final Remittance)	4,105	By Cash A/c	2,500
		By Joint Venture A/c (Profit)	1,605
	4,105		4,105

II. When a Separate Set of Books is Kept for Joint Venture

When the joint venture transactions are numerous, a separate set of books is maintained for recording all the joint venture transactions. When a separate set of books is maintained, it becomes necessary to maintain joint venture account, joint bank account and personal account of each venturer.

Joint Venture Account

It is just like a trading and profit and loss account. It is prepared for ascertaining the profits or losses arising from the joint venture transactions. The cost of goods purchased and all the expenses incurred on the joint venture should be debited and the sale proceeds of goods should be credited to the joint venture account. Finally joint venture account will be balanced. The balance of this account represents either profit or loss which will be transferred to the personal account of the co-venturers in the agreed profit sharing ratio.

Joint Bank Account

This account is opened separately in the name of joint venture or in the names of all co-venturers. It is also called 'Joint Account'. It is prepared for recording all cash transactions. All amounts contributed by the co-venturers and the sale proceeds of goods etc., are to be debited and all payments made for purchase of goods and for expenses of the venture are to be credited to the Joint Bank Account. Finally settlement of co-venturers is made through the Joint Bank Account.

Co-venturers' Account

The personal account of each co-venturer is also opened. This account is also called Co-venturers' Capital Account. It is prepared to ascertain the balance due to or due from each venturer. The amount contributed or goods brought by the concerned venturer is to be debited to this account. The respective share of profit or loss of the venture is also transferred to this account. The account is finally balanced. The balanced of this account represents either amount due to or due from each co-venturer.

In this method, the following journal entries are to be passed in the separate set of books or common books :

(1) When the co-venturers contribute or introduce or invest cash :

Joint Bank A/c	Dr.	With the amount of capital brought in
To Co-venturers' A/c		

(2) When goods are purchased :

Joint Venture A/c	Dr.	With the cost of goods purchased
To Joint Bank A/c		
(*If goods are purchased for cash*)		
To Suppliers' or Creditors' A/c		
(*If goods are purchased on credit*)		

(3) When payment is made to suppliers or creditors :

Suppliers' or Creditors' A/c	Dr.	With the amount of cash paid
To Joint Bank A/c		

(4) When expenses are paid out of joint bank account :

Joint Venture A/c	Dr.	With the amount of expenses paid
To Joint Bank A/c		

(5) When any co-venturer incurs expenses on joint venture :

Joint Venture A/c	Dr.	With the amount of expenses incurred
To Concerned Co-venturers' A/c		

(6) When any co-venturer supplies or purchases goods for joint venture :

Joint Venture A/c	Dr.	With the cost of goods supplied or purchased
To Concerned Co-venturer's A/c		

(7) When goods are sold :

Joint Bank A/c	Dr.	With the amount of sale proceeds
(*If goods are sold for cash*)		
Purchasers' or Debtors' A/c	Dr.	
(*If the goods are sold on credit*)		
To Joint Venture A/c		

(8) When bills receivable received from debtor is discounted :

Joint Bank A/c	Dr.	With the amount of cash received
Discount A/c	Dr.	With the amount of discount
To Bills Receivable		With the amount of bill

(9) When cash is received from purchasers or debtors :

Joint Bank A/c	Dr.	With the amount of cash received
To Purchasers or Debtors A/c		

(10) When bills payable are met on due date :

Bills Payable A/c	Dr.	With the amount of bills payable
To Joint Bank A/c		

(11) When discount on bill is charged to joint venture :

Joint Venture A/c	Dr.	With the amount of discount charged
To Discount A/c		

(12) When any co-venturer takes over the goods :

Concerned Co-venturer's A/c	Dr.	With the cost of goods
To Joint Venture A/c		taken over

(13) When commission is payable to any co-venturer :

Joint Venture A/c	Dr.	With the amount of
To Concerned Co-venturer's A/c		commission due

(14) When there is a profit on joint venture :

Joint Venture A/c	Dr.	With total amount of profit
To Each Co-venturer's A/c		With each co-venturer share

(15) When there is a loss on joint venture :

Each Co-venturer's A/c	Dr.	With each co-venturer share
To Joint Venture A/c		With total amount of loss

(16) When the final balance is paid to the co-venturers :

Each Co-venturer's A/c	Dr.	With the amount of cash paid to each co-venturer
To Joint Bank Account		With total amount of cash paid

(17) When the final balance is received from the co-venturers :

Joint Bank A/c	Dr.	With total amount paid
To Each Co-venturer's A/c		With the amount of cash received from each co-venturer

Proforma

Dr. **Joint Venture Account** Cr.

	Rs.		Rs.
To Joint Bank A/c (Goods purchased for cash)	xxx	By Joint Bank A/c (Goods sold for cash)	xxx
To Suppliers' or Creditors' A/c (Goods purchased on credit)	xxx	By Purchasers' or Debtors' A/c (Goods sold on credit)	xxx
To Joint Bank A/c (Exps.)	xxx	By Concerned Co-venturer's A/c (Unsold goods taken over by co-venturers)	xxx
To Concerned Co-venturer's A/c (Exps. met by co-venturers)	xxx		
To Concerned Co-venturer's A/c (Goods supplied or purchased by co-venturers)	xxx	By Loss on Joint Venture transferred to : Each Co-venturer's A/c	xxx
To Concerned Co-venturer's A/c (Commission payable)	xxx		
To Discount A/c	xxx		
To Profit on Joint Venture transferred to : Each Co-venturer's A/c	xxx		
	xxxx		xxxx

Dr. **Joint Venture Account** Cr.

	Rs.		Rs.
To Co-venturers' A/c (Capital contribution)	xxx	By Joint Venture A/c (Goods purchased)	xxx
To Joint Venture A/c (Sale proceeds)	xxx	By Suppliers' or Creditors' A/c (Cash paid)	xxx
To Purchasers' or Debtors' A/c (Cash received)	xxx	By Joint Venture A/c (Exps.)	xxx
To Bills Receivable A/c (Bills discounted)	xxx	By Bills Payable A/c (Bill is met on due date)	
To Each Co-venturer's A/c (Final balance received)	xxx	By Each Co-venturer's A/c (Final balance paid)	xxx
	xxxx		xxxx

Dr. **Co-Venturer's Account** Cr.

	Rs.		Rs.
To Joint Venture A/c (Goods taken over)	xxx	By Joint Bank A/c (Capital contribution)	xxx
To Joint Venture A/c (Share of loss)	xxx	By Joint Venture A/c (Expenses/goods)	xxx
To Joint Bank A/c (Final balance paid)	xxx	By Joint Venture A/c (Commission)	xxx
		By Joint Venture A/c (Share of profit)	xxx
		By Joint Bank A/c (Final balance received)	xxx
	xxxx		xxxx

Illustration 3

A and B entered into joint venture involving the buying and selling of goods. The profit or loss was to be shared equally. A and B agreed to contribute Rs. 29,000 each and deposited the same in a joint banking account. They purchased goods worth Rs. 55,000 from 'C' by paying Rs. 50,000 and accepting a bill drawn by 'C' for the balance. They paid Rs. 300 for freight, Rs. 400 for travelling expenses and Rs. 120 for sundry expenses. All the goods were sold for Rs. 75,000. They honoured the bill on the maturity date.

Pass the journal entries and show the necessary ledger accounts in the common books maintained, assuming that the final settlement between the co-venturers was made.

Solution :

Journal Entries

Sl. No.	Particulars		L.F.	Debit Rs.	Credit Rs.
1.	Joint Bank Account	Dr.		58,000	
	To A's Account				29,000
	To B's Account				29,000
	(Being amount contributed by A and B)				
2.	Joint Venture Account	Dr.		55,000	
	To C's Account				55,000
	(Being goods purchased from 'C' on account of joint venture)				
3.	C's Account	Dr.		55,000	
	To Joint Bank Account				50,000
	To Bills Payable Account				5,000
	(Being payment made to C)				
4.	Joint Venture Account	Dr.		820	
	To Joint Bank Account				820
	(Being expenses incurred on account of J.V.)				
5.	Joint Bank Account	Dr.		75,000	
	To Joint Venture Account				75,000
	(Being sales on account of joint venture)				
6.	Bills Payable Account	Dr.		5,000	
	To Joint Bank Account				5,000
	(Being bills payable met on maturity date)				
7.	Joint Venture Account	Dr.		19,180	
	To A's Account				9,590
	To B's Account				9,590
	(Being profit on joint venture transferred to A and B)				
8.	A's Account	Dr.		38,590	
	B's Account	Dr.		38,590	
	To Joint Bank Account				77,180
	(Being payment made to co-venturers)				

Joint Venture Account

Dr.		Rs.		Cr. Rs.
To C's A/c (Cost of goods purchased)		55,000	By Joint Bank A/c (Sale proceeds)	75,000
To Joint Bank A/c :				
Freight	300			
Travelling exps.	400			
Sundry exps.	120	820		
To Profit on Joint Venture transferred to :				
A (1/2)	9,590			
B (1/2)	9,590	19,180		
		75,000		75,000

Joint Bank Account

Dr.	Rs.		Cr. Rs.
To A's Account (Amount contributed)	29,000	By C's Account (Payment made in cash)	50,000
To B's Account (Amount contributed)	29,000	By Joint Venture Account (Expenses paid)	820
To Joint Venture Account (Sale proceeds)	75,000	By Bills Payable Account (Paid on maturity date)	5,000
		By A's Account (Payment made)	38,590
		By B's Account (Payment made)	38,590
	1,33,000		1,33,000

Co-Venturers' Account

Dr.	A Rs.	B Rs.		A Rs.	Cr. B Rs.
To Joint Bank Account (Final balance paid)	38,590	38,590	By Joint Bank A/c	29,000	29,000
			By Joint Venture A/c (Share of profit)	9,590	9,590
	38,590	38,590		38,590	38,590

Illustration 4

Das and Krishnan entered into a joint venture sharing profits and losses as 3 : 2. They opened a Bank Account by depositing Rs. 40,000 each.

Das purchased 800 Kgs an item at Rs. 60 and his expenses were Rs. 13,000. Krishnan purchased a second item of 10,000 Kgs at Rs. 2.10 p. and his expenses were Rs.11,000. Expenses were met from private sources and purchases were paid for from Bank Account.

Krishnan sold 600 Kgs of the first item at Rs. 100 and his selling expenses were Rs. 5,500. Das sold 8,000 Kgs the second item at Rs. 5.00 p. and his selling expenses were Rs. 6,000. All the sale proceeds were deposited in the Bank Account and expenses were met from private sources.

Write necessary accounts in the books of the venture. Also prepare a Balance Sheet of the venture.

(B.Com., Nagpur and I.C.W.A. Inter)

Solution :

In the Books of Venture

Dr. **Joint Venture Account** Cr.

		Rs.		Rs.
To Joint Bank A/c (Purchases 800 Kgs at Rs. 60 each)		48,000	By Joint Bank Account (Sale proceeds 600 Kgs at Rs. 100 each 60,000 8,000 Kgs at Rs. 5 each 40,000)	1,00,000
To Das's A/c (Expenses of purchases and sales Rs. 13,000 + Rs. 6,000)		19,000	By Unsold Stock (Rs. 48,000 + Rs. 13,000 × $\frac{200}{800}$ Cost + Expences = Rs. 15,250 Rs. 21,000 + Rs. 11,000 × $\frac{200}{1,000}$ Cost + Expenses = Rs. 6,400)	21,650
To Joint Bank Account (Purchases 10,000 kgs at Rs. 2.10 each)		21,000		
To Krishnan's A/c (Expenses of purchases and sales sales Rs. 11,000 + Rs. 5,500)		16,500		
To Profit on Joint Venture transferred to :				
Das 3/5	10,290			
Krishnan 2/5	6,860	17,150		
		1,21,650		1,21,650

Dr. **Joint Bank Account** Cr.

	Rs.		Rs.
To Das's A/c	40,000	By Joint Venture A/c (Purchases Rs. 48,000 + Rs. 21,000)	69,000
To Krishnan's A/c	40,000		
To Joint Venture A/c (Sales proceeds)	1,00,000	By Balance c/d	1,11,000
	1,80,000		1,80,000

Dr. **Co-Venturers' Account** Cr.

	Das Rs.	Krishnan Rs.		Das Rs.	Krishnan Rs.
To Balance c/d	69,290	63,360	By Joint Bank A/c	40,000	40,000
			By Joint Venture A/c (Expenses)	19,000	16,500
			By Joint Venture A/c (Share of profit)	10,290	6,860
	69,290	63,360		69,290	63,360

Balance Sheet

Liabilities		Rs.	Assets	Rs.
Capital Accounts :			Cash at Bank	1,11,000
Das	69,290		Closing Stock	21,650
Krishnan	63,360	1,32,650		
		1,32,650		1,32,650

Illustration 5

Harish, Iqbal and Joseph jointly undertook to construct a building for Prabhu and Co., at a price of Rs. 2,50,000. The price was to be paid as follows:

Rs. 2,00,000 in cash and the balance in preference shares of the company. The profit was agreed to be divided in the ratio of 2:2:1. The participants contributed cash as follows :

Harish Rs. 30,000; Iqbal Rs. 25,000 and Joseph Rs. 20,000.

These amounts were credited to a joint bank account. Iqbal was to be paid a remuneration of Rs. 1,500 for managing the business.

Harish prepared the plans and paid Rs. 3,500 for them. Iqbal brought a concrete mixer for Rs. 12,000 and Joseph brought a truck for Rs. 25,000. They brought plant for Rs. 15,000, material worth Rs. 1,20,000 and paid wages Rs. 1,05,000.

When the contract was completed, Harish took over unused materials for Rs. 10,000; Iqbal took back the concrete mixer for Rs. 11,000 and Joseph agreed to take back the truck for Rs. 18,000. The plant was sold as scrap for Rs. 6,000.

When the contract price was received, Harish agreed to take over the preference shares for Rs. 40,000. All the accounts were closed.

Show the accounts, assuming that the accounts are finally settled among the partners.

(*B.Com., Mysore and Madurai*)

Solution :

Dr. **Joint Venture Account** Cr.

		Rs.		Rs.
To Harish's A/c (Cost of plans paid)		3,500	By Joint Bank A/c (Sale proceeds of plant)	6,000
To Iqbal's A/c (Cost of concrete mixer brought)		12,000	By Joint Bank Account (Contract price received in cash)	2,00,000
To Joseph's A/c (Cost of truck brought)		25,000	By Preference Shares A/c (Contract price received in cash)	50,000
To Joint Bank A/c :			By Harish's A/c (Unsold materials taken over)	10,000
Plant	15,000			
Materials	1,20,000		By Iqbal's A/c (Concrete mixer taken over)	11,000
Wages	1,05,000	2,40,000		
To Iqbal's A/c (Remuneration)		1,500	By Joseph's A/c (Truck taken over)	18,000
To Preference Shares A/c (Loss on Pref. Shares)		10,000		
To Profit on Joint Venture transferred to :				
Harish	1,200			
Iqbal	1,200			
Joseph	600	3,000		
		2,95,000		2,95,000

Dr. **Joint Bank Account** Cr.

	Rs.			Rs.
To Harish's A/c (Cash contributed)	30,000	By Joint Venture A/c :		
		Plant	15,000	
To Iqbal's A/c (Cash contributed)	25,000	Materials	1,20,000	
		Wages	1,05,000	2,40,000
To Joseph's A/c (Cash contributed)	20,000	By Iqbal A/c (Final balance paid)		28,700
To Joint Venture A/c (Contract price received)	2,00,000	By Joseph's A/c (Final balance paid)		27,600
To Joint Venture A/c (Sale of plant)	6,000			
To Harsh's A/c (Final balance received)	15,300			
	2,96,300			2,96,300

Preference Shares Account

Dr.	Rs.		Cr. Rs.
To Joint Venture A/c (Contract price received in shares)	50,000	By Harish's A/c (Shares taken over)	40,000
		By Joint Venture A/c (Loss on Shares)	10,000
	50,000		50,000

Co-Ventures Accounts

Dr.	Harish Rs.	Iqbal Rs.	Joseph Rs.	Cr.	Harish Rs.	Iqbal Rs.	Joseph Rs.
To Joint Venture A/c (Unused material, concrete mixer and truck taken over)	10,000	11,000	18,000	By Joint Bank A/c (Cash contributed)	30,000	25,000	20,000
				By Joint Venture A/c (Cost of plans paid)	3,500	—	—
To Preference Shares A/c (Shares taken over)	40.000	—	—	By Joint Venture A/c (Concrete mixer brought)	—	12.000	—
To Joint Bank A/c (Final balance paid)	—	28,700	27,600	By Joint Venture A/c (Truck brought)	—	—	25.000
				By Joint Venture (Remuneration)	—	1,500	—
				By Joint venture A/c (Profit)	1,200	1,200	600
				By Joint Bank A/c (Final balance brought in)	15,300	—	—
	50,000	39,700	45,600		50,000	39,700	45,600

Illustration 6

Vikas and Vishal entered into a joint venture of underwriting 1,00,000 shares of Rs. 10 each at par issued by a joint stock company. The consideration for underwriting the shares was 2,500, other shares of Rs. 10 each fully paid to be issued to them.

The public took up 90,000 shares and the remaining 10,000 shares of the guaranteed issued were taken up by Vikas and Vishal who provide cash equally for the purchase of remaining shares. The entire share holding of the joint venture was sold through other brokers : 50% at a price of Rs. 10 less brokerage 50 paise per share, 20% at Rs. 9.50 less brokerage 50 paise per share and the balance were taken up by Vikas and Vishal equally at Rs. 9 per share. Expenses on account of joint venture were : advertisement Rs. 750 and other expenses Rs. 250.

You are required to prepare : (1) Joint Venture Account, (2) Joint Bank Account and (3) Account of Vikas and Vishal.

(C.A.I.I.B. Part I and B.Com., Shivaji)

Solution :

Joint Venture Account

Dr.			Rs.		Cr. Rs.
To Joint Bank A/c (Purchase of 10,000 shares at Rs. 10 each)			1,00,000	By Joint Bank Account (6,250 Shares of Rs. 9.50 each *i.e.*, Rs. 10.50)	59,375
To Joint Bank Account (Expenses Rs. 750 + 250)			1,000	By Joint Bank A/c (2,500 Shares of Rs. 9 each *i.e.*, Rs. 9.50 – 50 p.)	22,500
To Profit on Joint Venture transferred to :				By Vikas's A/c (1,875 Shares taken over at Rs. 9 each)	16,875
Vikas	7,312.50				
Vishal	7,312.50		14,625	By Vishal's A/c (1,875 Shares taken over at Rs. 9 each)	16,875
			1,15,625		1,15,625

Joint Bank Account

Dr.	Rs.		Cr. Rs
To Vikas 's A/c	50,000	By Joint Venture A/c (Purchase of Shares)	1,00,000.00
To Vishal 's A/c	50,000		
To Joint Venture A/c (Sale of Shares)	59,375	By Joint Venture A/c (Expenses)	1,000.00
To Joint Venture A/c (Sale of Shares)	22,500	By Vikas's A/c	40,437.50
		By Vishal's A/c	40,437.50
	1,81,875		1,81,875.00

Co-venturers' Account

Dr.	Vikas Rs.	Vishal Rs.	Cr.	Vikas Rs.	Vishal Rs.
To Joint Venture A/c (Shares taken)	16,875.00	16,875.00	By Joint Bank A/c (Cash contributed)	50,000.00	50,000.00
To Joint Bank A/c	40,437.50	40,437.50	By Joint Venture A/c	7,312.50	7,312.50
	57,312.50	57,312.50		57,312.50	57,312.50

Notes : (i) Cash Contributed by Co-venturers :

	Rs.
Total number of shares underwritten	1,00,000
Less : Number of shares taken over by public	90,000
No. of shares purchased by co-venturers	10,000

Amount required to purchase 10,000 shares (10,000 × Rs. 10) — Rs. 1,00,000

So, Rs. 1,00,000 is to be contributed by the co-venturers equally *i.e.*, Vikas Rs. 50,000 and Vishal Rs. 50,000

(ii) Number of Shares sold and taken up by Co-venturers :

Number of shares purchased	10,000
No. of shares received as consideration for underwriting shares	2,500
Total number of shares to be sold	12,500

Number of shares sold at Rs. 9.50 each = 6,250 (*i.e.*, 50% of 12,500)

No. of shares sold at Rs. 9 each = 2,500 (*i.e.*, 20% of 12,500)

Remaining shares 3,750 (*i.e.*, 12,500 – 6,250 = 6,250– 2,500) taken up by co-venturers equally *i.e.*, Vikas 1,875 shares and Vishal 1,875 shares.

III. When a Separate set of Books is not Maintained or when all Co-venturers keep the Accounts

In this method, there are two methods of keeping the books of accounts :

(1) When each co-venturer keeps the accounts where all the joint venture transactions are recorded.

(2) When each co-venturer keeps the accounts where only his own transactions of joint venture are recorded. This is popularly known as "Memorandum Method".

(1) When each co-venturer keeps the accounts where all the joint venture transactions are recorded

Under this method, each co-venturer records all the joint venture transactions made by himself as well as the joint venture transactions made by his co-venturers in his book. In this case, each co-venturer opens a Joint Venture Account to ascertain the profits or losses on the joint venture, and also personal account or accounts of the other co-venturer or venturers to ascertain the balance due to or due from the other co-venturer or venturers.

Under this method, the following journal entries are to be passed in the books of each co-venturer :

(i) When he purchases goods for joint venture :

Joint Venture A/c Dr.		With the cost of goods purchased
To Cash or Bank A/c		
(*If the goods are purchased for cash*)		
OR To Suppliers' or Creditors' A/c		
(*If the goods are purchased on credit*)		

(ii) When he incurs expenses on joint venture :

Joint Venture A/c	Dr.	With the amount of
To Cash or Bank A/c		expenses paid by him

(iii) When he supplies goods from his own stock for joint venture :

Joint Venture A/c	Dr.	With the cost of goods
To Purchases A/c		supplied

(iv) When co-venturer supplies goods for joint venture :

Joint Venture A/c	Dr.	With the cost of goods
To Co-venturer's A/c		supplied by the co-venturer

(v) When the co-venturer incurs expenses on joint venture :

Joint Venture A/c	Dr.	With the amount of expenses
To Co-venturer's A/c		incurred by the co-venturer

(vi) When he sells goods on joint venture :

Cash or Bank A/c	Dr.	
(*If the goods are sold for cash*)		With the amount
OR Purchasers' or Debtors' A/c	Dr.	of sale proceeds
(*If the goods are sold on credit*)		
To Joint Venture A/c		

(vii) When co-venturer sells the goods for cash or credit :

Co-venturer's A/c	Dr.	With the amount of
To Joint Venture A/c		sale proceeds

(viii) When he accepts bill drawn by co-venturer :

Co-venturer's A/c	Dr.	With the amount of
To Bills Payable A/c		bill accepted

(ix) When the bill is drawn by him on the co-venturer :

Bills Receivable A/c	Dr.	With the amount of
To Co-venturer's A/c		bill drawn

(x) When he discounts the above bill :

Cash or Bank A/c	Dr.	With actual cash received
Discount A/c	Dr.	With the amount of discount
To Bills Receivable A/c		With full amount of bill

(xi) When the above discount is charged to joint venture :

Joint Venture A/c	Dr.	With the amount
To Discount A/c		discounting charges

(xii) When co-venturer incurs discounting charges :

Joint Venture A/c	Dr.	With the amount of
To Co-venturer's A/c		discounting charges.

(xiii) When he takes over the (unsold) goods :

Purchases A/c	Dr.	With the value of goods
To Joint Venture A/c		taken over by him.

(xiv) When co-venturer takes over the (unsold) goods :

Co-venturer's A/c	Dr.	With the value of goods
To Joint Venture A/c		taken over by co-venturer

(xv) When he is entitled to get a commission :

Joint Venture A/c	Dr.	With the amount of
To Commission A/c		commission

(xvi) When commission is due to the co-venturer :

Joint Venture A/c	Dr.	With the amount of
To Co-venturer's A/c		commission

(xvii) When the Joint Venture A/c is balanced and the profit or loss on joint venture is shared between the co-venturers :

(a) *In case of profit :*

Joint Venture A/c	Dr.	With the total amount of profit
To P & L A/c		With his own share of profit
To Co-venturer's A/c		With co-venturer's share of profit

(b) *In case of loss :*

P & L A/c	Dr.	With his own share of loss
Co-venturer's A/c	Dr.	With the co-venturer's share of loss
To Joint Venture A/c		With total amount of profit

(xviii) When he gives the final balance in cash or bill to the co-venturer :

Co-venturer's A/c	Dr.	With the amount of cash
To Cash or Bank or B/P A/c		paid or bill accepted

(xix) When he receives the final balance in cash or bill from the co-venturer :

Cash or Bank or B/R A/c	Dr.	With the amount of cash
To Co-venturer's A/c		or bill received

Illustration 7

Anu and Manu were partners in a joint venture sharing profits and losses in the ratio of 3 : 2. Anu supplied goods of the value of Rs. 10,000 and spent Rs. 500 for carriage etc. Manu also supplied goods worth Rs. 8,000 and he spent Rs. 600 for advertisement etc. Anu sold the goods for Rs. 20,000. The balance of goods worth Rs. 1,500 was taken over by Manu. Anu is entitled to a commission of 5% on sales.

Give the journal entries and also the necessary ledger accounts in the books of Anu and Manu, where all the transactions of the joint venture are recorded.

Solution :

In the books of Anu

Journal Entries

Sl. No.	Particulars		L.F.	Debit Rs.	Credit Rs.
1.	Joint Venture A/c	Dr.		10,000	
	To Purchases A/c				10,000
	(Being cost of goods supplied for venture)				
2.	Joint Venture A/c	Dr.		500	
	To Cash or Bank A/c				500
	(Being paid for carriage etc. on goods)				
3.	Joint Venture A/c	Dr.		8,600	
	To Manu's A/c				8,600
	(Being goods supplied and expenses incurred by Manu)				
4.	Joint Venture A/c	Dr.		1,000	
	To Commission A/c				1,000
	(Being commission due on sales)				
5.	Cash or Bank A/c	Dr.		20,000	
	To Joint Venture A/c				20,000
	(Being the sale proceeds of goods)				
6.	Manu's A/c	Dr.		1,500	
	To Joint Venture A/c				1,500
	(Being unsold goods taken over by Manu)				
7.	Joint Venture A/c	Dr.		1,400	
	To Profit & Loss A/c				840
	To Manu's A/c				560
	(Being profit on joint venture transferred to P & L A/c and Manu's A/c in the agreed ratio)				
8.	Manu's A/c	Dr.		7,660	
	To Cash or Bank A/c				7,660
	(Being final Balance paid)				

Dr. **Joint Venture Account** Cr.

	Rs.		Rs.
To Purchases	10,000	By Cash or Bank (Sale proceeds)	20,000
To Cash or Bank (Expenses)	500		
To Commission	1,000	By Manu (Goods taken over)	1,500
To Manu (Goods supplied and expenses incurred)	8,600		
To Profit on Joint Venture transferred to : P & L A/c 3/5 840; Manu 2/5 560	1,400		
	21,500		21,500

Dr. **Manu's Account** Cr.

	Rs.		Rs.
To Joint Venture A/c	1,500	By Joint Venture A/c	8,600
To Bank (Balance paid)	7,660	By Joint Venture A/c (Profit)	560
	9,160		9,160

In the books of Manu
Journal Entries

Sl. No.	Particulars	L.F.	Debit Rs.	Credit Rs.
1.	Joint Venture A/c Dr.		8,600	
	To Purchases A/c			8,000
	To Cash or Bank A/c			600
	(Being cost of goods supplied and expenses paid)			
2.	Joint Venture A/c Dr.		10,500	
	To Anu's A/c			10,500
	(Being goods supplied and expenses paid by Anu)			
3.	Joint Venture A/c Dr.		1,000	
	To Anu's A/c			1,000
	(Being commission payable to Anu)			
4.	Anu's A/c Dr.		20,000	
	To Joint Venture A/c			20,000
	(Being sale proceeds of goods)			

Contd.

Sl. No.	Particulars		L.F.	Debit Rs.	Credit Rs.
5.	Purchases A/c	Dr.		1,500	
	To Joint Venture A/c				1,500
	(Being goods taken over)				
6.	Joint Venture A/c	Dr.		1,400	
	To P & L A/c				560
	To Anu's A/c				840
	(Being profit on joint venture transferred to P & L A/c and Anu's A/c in the agreed ratio)				
7.	Cash or Bank A/c	Dr.		7,660	
	To Anu's A/c				7,660
	(Being the final balance received)				

Joint Venture Account

Dr.		Rs.		Cr. Rs.
To Purchases		8,000	By Anu (Sale proceeds)	20,000
To Cash or Bank (Expenses)		600	By Purchases (Goods taken over)	1,500
To Anu (Goods supplied and expenses incurred)		10,500		
To Anu (Commission)		1,000		
To Profit on Joint Venture transferred to :				
P & L A/c	560			
Anu	840	1,400		
		21,500		21,500

Anu's Account

Dr.	Rs.		Cr. Rs.
To Joint Venture A/c (Sale proceeds)	20,000	By Joint Venture A/c (Cost of goods and expenses)	10,500
		By Joint Venture A/c (Commission)	1,000
		By Joint Venture A/c (Share of profit)	840
		By Bank or Cash A/c (Final balance received)	7,660
	20,000		20,000

Illustration 8

A of Ahmedabad and B of Mumbai enter into a joint venture to consign 100 bales of cloth to C of Kolkata to be sold on their joint risk which is in proportion of 3/5and 2/5 respectively. A sends 60 bales at Rs. 1,200 each, paying for freight and other charges Rs. 1,800. B sends 40 bales at Rs. 1,100 each paying for freight and other charges Rs. 1,000. All the bales are sold by C for Rs. 1,40,000 out of which C deducts Rs. 1,600 for his expenses and his commission at 3%. C remits B/R for Rs. 70,000 to A and B/R for the balance to B.

Prepare the Joint Venture Account and Co-adventurer's Account in the ledgers of both the Co-adventurers.

(B.Com., Madurai and Tirupati)

Solution :

In the Books of A

Dr. **Joint Venture Account** Cr.

	Rs.		Rs.
To Purchases (60 × 1,200)	72,000	By C's A/c (Sale proceeds)	1,40,000
To Cash or Bank (Freight and other charges)	1,800		
To B's A/c (Cost of goods sent 44,000 and freight and other charges Rs. 1,000)	45,000		
To C's A/c (Expenses Rs. 1,600 and commission Rs. 4,200)	5,800		
To Profit on Joint Venture transferred to : P & L A/c 3/5 9,240; B 2/5 6,160	15,400		
	1,40,000		1,40,000

Dr. **B's Account** Cr.

	Rs.		Rs.
To C' s A/c (Amount from 'C')	64,200	By Joint Venture A/c (Cost of goods and expenses)	45,000
		By Joint Venture A/c (Share of profit)	6,160
		By Bank (Balance received)	13,040
	64,200		64,200

In the books of B

Joint Venture Account

Dr.		Rs.		Cr. Rs.
To Purchases (40 × 1,100)		44,000	By C's A/c (Sale proceeds)	1,40,000
To Cash or Bank (Freight and other charges)		1,000		
To A's A/c (Cost of goods sent Rs. 72,000 + freight and other expenses Rs. 1,800)		73,800		
To C's A/c (Expenses Rs. 1,600 and commission Rs. 4,200)		5,800		
To Profit on Joint Venture transferred to :				
P & L A/c 2/5	6,160			
A 3/5	9,240	15,400		
		1,40,000		1,40,000

A's Account

Dr.	Rs.		Cr. Rs.
To C's A/c (B/R)	70,000	By Joint Venture A/c (Cost of goods sent and expenses)	73,800
To Bank (Balance paid)	13,040	By Joint Venture A/c (Share of profit)	9,240
	83,040		83,040

Illustration 9

A and B enter into a joint venture sharing profits and losses equally. A purchased goods for Rs. 5,000 and B spent Rs. 1,000 for freight on 1st January, 1991. On the same day B brought goods worth Rs. 10,000 on credit. Further expenses were incurred as follows :

On 1-2-1991 Rs. 1,500 by B

On 1-3-1991 Rs. 500 by A

Sales were made against cash as follows :

15-1-1991 Rs. 3,000 by A

31-1-1991 Rs. 6,000 by B

15-2-1991 Rs. 3,000 by A

1-3-1991 Rs. 4,000 by B

Creditors for goods were paid as follows :

1-2-1991 Rs. 5,000 by A

1-3-1991 Rs. 5,000 by B

On 31st March, 1991 the balance of stock was taken over by B at Rs. 9,000. The accounts between the venturers were settled by cash payment on this date. The venturers are entitled to interest at 12% per annum.

Prepare necessary ledger accounts in the books of venturers.

(*C.A. Inter*)

Solution :

In the Ledger of 'A'

Joint Venture Account

Dr. Cr.

Date		Rs.	Date		Rs.
1991			1991		
Jan. 1	To Bank (Purchases)	5,000	Jan. 15	By Bank (Sale proceeds)	3,000
Jan. 1	To B (Freight)	1,000	Jan. 31	By B (Sale proceeds)	6,000
Jan. 1	To Suppliers or Creditors (Credit purchases)	10,000	Feb. 15	By Bank (Sales)	3,000
Feb. 1	To B (Expenses)	1,500	Mar. 1	By B (Sale proceeds)	4,000
Mar. 1	To Bank (Expenses)	500	Mar. 31	By B (Goods taken over)	9,000
Mar. 31	To Interest	135	Mar. 31	By Interest	50
Mar. 31	To Profit on Joint Venture transferred to : P & L A/c 3,457; B 3,458	6,915			
		25,050			25,050

B's Account

Dr. Cr.

Date		Rs.	Date		Rs.
1991			1991		
Jan. 31	To Joint Venture A/c (Sales)	6,000	Jan. 1	By Joint Venture A/c (Freight)	1,000
Mar. 1	To Joint Venture A/c (Sales)	4,000	Feb. 1	By Joint Venture A/c (Exp.)	1,500
Mar. 31	To Joint Venture A/c (Goods taken over)	9,000	Mar. 1	By Supplier's A/c	5,000
Mar. 31	To Joint Venture A/c (Interest)	50		By Joint Venture A/c (Share of profit)	3,458
				By Bank A/c (Final balance received)	8,092
		19,050			19,050

Dr. **Supplier's Account** Cr.

Date		Rs.	Date		Rs.
1991			1991		
Feb. 1	To Bank A/c (Sales)	5,000	Jan. 1	By Joint Venture A/c (Purchases)	10,000
Mar. 1	To B	5,000			
		10,000			10,000

In the Ledger of 'B'

Dr. **Joint Venture Account** Cr.

Date		Rs.	Date		Rs.
1991			1991		
Jan. 1	To Supplier's or Creditor's (Credit purchases)	10,000	Jan. 15	By A (Sales)	3,000
			Jan. 31	By Bank (Sales)	6,000
Jan. 1	To A (Purchases)	5,000	Feb. 15	By A (Sales)	3,000
Jan. 1	To Bank (Freight)	1,000	Mar. 1	By Bank (Sales)	4,000
Feb. 1	To Bank (Expenses)	1,500	Mar. 31	By Goods A/c (Balance of stock taken over)	9,000
Mar. 1	To A (Expenses)	500			
Mar. 31	To A (interest)	135			
Mar. 31	To Profit on Joint Venture transferred to :		Mar. 31	By Interest	50
	P & L A/c	3,458			
	A	3,457			
		25,050			25,050

Dr. **Supplier's Account** Cr.

Date		Rs.	Date		Rs.
1991			1991		
Feb. 1	To A (Purchases)	5,000	Jan. 1	By Joint Venture A/c (Purchases)	10,000
Mar. 1	To Bank A/c	5,000			
		10,000			10,000

Dr. **A's Account** Cr.

Date		Rs.	Date		Rs.
1991			1991		
Jan. 15	To Joint Venture A/c (Sales)	3,000	Jan. 1	By Joint Venture A/c (Purchases)	5,000
Feb. 15	To Joint Venture A/c (Sales)	3,000	Feb. 1	By Supplier's A/c	5,000
			Mar. 1	By Joint Venture A/c (Expenses)	500
Mar. 31	To Bank A/c (Final balance paid)	8,092	Mar. 31	By Joint Venture A/c (Interest)	135
			Mar. 31	By Joint Venture A/c (Share of profit)	3,457
		14,092			14,092

Notes : Calculation of Interest :

(1) Payments made by A

Date	Amount	Month up to 31st March	Interest up to 31st March at 1% per month	
1-1-1991	Rs. 5,000	3	Rs. 150	
1-2-1991	Rs. 5,000	2	Rs. 100	
1-3-1991	Rs. 500	1	Rs. 5	Rs. 255
Less : Amounts received by A				
15-1-1991	Rs. 3,000	2½	Rs. 75	
15-2-1991	Rs. 3,000	1½	Rs. 45	Rs. 120
		Net interest due to A		Rs. 135

(2) Payments made by B

Date	Amount	Month	Interest	
1-1-1991	Rs. 1,000	3	Rs. 30	
1-2-1991	Rs. 1,500	2	Rs. 30	
1-3-1991	Rs. 5,000	1	Rs. 50	Rs. 110
Less : Amounts received by B				
31-1-1991	Rs. 6,000	2	Rs. 120	
1-3-1991	Rs. 4,000	1	Rs. 40	Rs. 160
			Net interest due from B	Rs. 50

(2) When each co-venturer keeps the accounts where only his own transactions of joint venture are recorded. This is popularly known as "Memorandum Method or Memorandum Joint Venture Method"

Under this method, each co-venturer records only his own transactions of joint venture in his books. The salient features of this method are as follows :

(i) Each co-venturer opens only ONE account in his books. This is known as **"Joint Venture Account with Other Co-venturer".** This account is a personal account in which the transactions effected by him are recorded. It does not show the profits or losses on joint venture, because the transactions effected by other co-venturers relating to joint venturers are not recorded in this account. If there are more than two co-venturers, only one personal account is to be opened in each party's book. For example, if X, Y and Z are partners in the Joint Venture, X opens one personal account of Y and Z in his books. Similarly Y opens a joint account of X and Z and Z keeps a joint account of X and Y and not a separate account for each party.

(ii) At the end of period, each co-venturer sends to the other co-venturers a copy of "Joint Venture Account With Other Co-venturers". On the receipt of this account each co-venturer prepares "Memorandum Joint Venture Account" outside his books by combining all the transactions to find out the results of the joint venture. Memorandum Joint Venture Account is prepared on the lines of a Trading and Profit and Loss Account. It is prepared on a separate sheet of paper outside the books of account. Therefore, it is called Memorandum Joint Venture Account. It is merely combination of personal accounts. Debit side of personal accounts is posted on the debit side of Memorandum Joint Venture Account and credit side of personal accounts is posted on the credit side of Memorandum Joint Venture Account. The profit or loss of this account will be transferred to the "Joint Venture Account with Other Venturers". Finally, "Joint Venture Account with Other Venturers" is balanced. The balance of this account will show the amount due to or due from the other co-venturers.

The following journal entries are to be passed in the books of each venturer where his own transactions are recorded.

(i) When he supplies goods for joint venture :

Joint Venture A/c with	Dr.	With cost of goods supplied
To Purchases A/c		

(ii) When he purchases goods for joint venture :

Joint Venture A/c with	Dr.	With the cost of goods purchased
To Cash or Bank A/c		
(If goods are sold for cash)		
OR To Supplier's or Creditor's A/c		
(If goods are sold on credit)		

(iii) When he incurs expenses on joint venture :

Joint Venture A/c with	Dr	With the amount of expenses
To Cash or Bank A/c		

(iv) When he sells goods :

Cash or Bank A/c	Dr.	With the amount of of sale proceeds
(If goods are sold for cash)		
OR Purchasers' or Debtors' A/c	Dr.	
To Joint Venture A/c with		

(v) When he is entitled to commission :

Joint Venture A/c with	Dr.	With the amount of commission
To Commission A/c		

(vi) When he accepts a bill drawn by other co-venturer :

Joint Venture A/c with	Dr.	With the amount of bill accepted
To Bills Payable A/c		

(vii) When he draws a bill on the co-venturer :

Bills Receivable A/c	Dr.	With the amount of bill drawn
To Joint Venture A/c with		

(viii) When he discounts the bills receivable :

Cash or Bank A/c	Dr.	With the amount of cash
Discount on B/R A/c	Dr.	With the amount of discount
To Bills Receivable A/c		With full amount of bill

(ix) When the above discount is charged to joint venture :

Joint Venture A/c with	Dr.	With the amount of discount charged
To Discount A/c		

(x) When he takes over the (unsold) goods :

Purchases A/c	Dr.	With value of goods taken over
To Joint Venture A/c with		

(xi) When Memorandum Joint Venture Account is balanced and profits or losses of this account are distributed among the partners or co-venturers :

(a) *In case of profits* :

Joint Venture A/c with	Dr.	With his share of
To Profit and Loss A/c		profits

(b) *In case of losses :*

Profit and Loss A/c	Dr.	With share of losses
To Joint Venture A/c with		

(xii) When he pays the final balance to other co-venturers :

Joint Venture A/c with	Dr.	With the amount of cash
To Cash or Bank or B/P A/c		paid or bill accepted

(xiii) When he receives the final balance from other co-venturers :

Cash or Bank or B/R A/c	Dr.	With the amount of
To Joint Venture A/c with		cash or bill received

Illustration 10

A and B decided to work in partnership agreeing to share the profits or losses in the ratio of 3 : 1. They guaranteed the subscription at par of 10,00,000 shares of Re. 1 each in C Ltd. and to pay all expenses up to allotment in consideration of C Ltd. issuing to them 50,000 other shares of Re. 1 each fully paid.

A and B introduced cash as follows :

A –	Stamp charges etc.	Rs. 4,000
	Advertising charges	Rs. 3,000
	Printing charges etc.	Rs. 2,000
B –	Rent	Rs. 2,000
	Solicitor's charges	Rs. 3,000

Applications fell short by 3,000 shares and B introduced Rs. 30,000 for the purchase of those shares.

The guarantee having been fulfilled, 'C' Ltd. handed over to the co-venturers 50,000 shares. All their holdings were subsequently sold by co-venturers, B receiving Rs. 18,000 and A Rs. 50,000.

Show the journal entries and ledger accounts in the books of both the co-venturers where each venturer records only his own transactions in his books.

(*C.A.I.I.B. Part-I, May, 1993*)

Solution :

In the books of 'A'
Journal Entries

Sl. No.	Particulars	L.F.	Debit Rs.	Credit Rs.
1.	Joint Venture Account with B Dr. To Bank Account (Being expenses incurred on joint venture)		10,000	10,000
2.	Bank Account Dr. To Joint Venture Account with B (Being sale proceeds of shares received)		50,000	50,000
3.	Joint Venture Account with B Dr. To Profit and Loss Account (Being 3/4 share of profit on joint venture transferred)		17,250	17,250
4.	Joint Venture Account with B Dr. To Bank Account (Being final balance paid)		22,750	22,750

Dr. **Memorandum Joint Venture Account** Cr.

		Rs.			Rs.
To Purchase of Shares			By Sales of Shares		
B		30,000	A	18,000	
To Expenses:			B	50,000	68,000
A (4,000+3,000+3,000)	10,000				
B (2,000 + 3,000)	5,000	15,000			
To Profit to :					
A	17,250				
B	5,750	23,000			
		68,000			68,000

Dr. **Joint Venture Account with B** Cr.

	Rs.		Rs.
To Bank A/c (Expenses)	10,000	By Bank A/c (Sale of Shares)	50,000
To P & L A/c (3/4 Share of Profit)	17,250		
To Bank A/c (Final Balance paid)	22,750		
	50,000		50,000

In the Books of 'B'

Journal Entries

Sl. No.	Particulars	L.F.	Debit Rs.	Credit Rs.
1.	Joint Venture Account with A Dr.		30,000	
	To Bank Account			30,000
	(Being shares purchased)			
2.	Joint Venture Account with A Dr.		5,000	
	To Bank Account			5,000
	(Being expenses incurred)			
3.	Bank Account Dr.		18,000	
	To Joint Venture Account with A			18,000
	(Being sale proceeds of shares received)			
4.	Joint Venture Account with A Dr.		5,750	
	To Profit and Loss Account			5,750
	(Being ¼ share of profit transferred)			
5.	Bank Account Dr.		22,750	
	To Joint Venture Account with A			22,750
	(Being the final balance received)			

Memorandum Joint Venture Account

Dr. Cr.

		Rs.			Rs.
To Purchases of Shares			By Sale of Shares		
B		30,000	A	18,000	
To Expenses :			B	50,000	68,000
A		10,000			
B		5,000			
To Profit to :					
A	17,250				
B	5,750	23,000			
		68,000			68,000

Joint Venture Account with A

Dr. Cr.

	Rs.		Rs.
To Bank A/c (Purchase of shares)	30,000	By Bank A/c (Sale of shares)	18,000
To Bank A/c (Expenses)	5,000	By Bank A/c (Final balance received)	22,750
To Profit and Loss A/c (1/4 share of profit)	5,750		
	40,750		40,750

Illustration 11

Ravi and Suresh entered into a joint venture for goods purchase and sale of electronic goods, sharing profit and loss in the ratio of 3 : 2. They agreed to receive 5% commission on their individual sales and the following information was extracted from the records :

July 1, 1993 : Ravi purchased goods worth Rs. 1,90,000 financed to the extent of 90% out of his funds and balance by loan from his uncle Shyam.

August 1, 1993 : Ravi sent goods costing Rs. 1,70,000 to Suresh and paid Rs. 1,410 as freight. Suresh paid Rs. 13,410 to Ravi.

October 1, 1993 : Suresh sold all the goods sent to him. Ravi repaid the loan taken from his uncle, including interest of Rs. 350.

All sales, by either party, were made at an uniform profit of 40% above cost. On November 30, 1993, they decided to close the venture by transferring the balance of goods unsold, lying with Ravi at cost of Rs. 9,000 to a whole sale dealer.

You are required to prepare the Memorandum Joint Account, personal accounts of partners as they would appear in the books of Ravi and of Suresh. They further disclosed that goods worth Rs. 4,000 were taken personally by Ravi at an agreed price of Rs. 5,000.

(*B.Com., Poona and I.C.W.A. Inter*)

Solution :

Dr. **Memorandum Joint Venture Account** Cr.

		Rs.		Rs.
To Purchases : Ravi		1,90,000	By Sales : Suresh	2,38,000
To Expenses : Ravi			Ravi	9,800
Freight	1,410		By Stock taken :	
Interest	350		Ravi	5,000
Commission	490	2,250	By Stock sent to	
(5% on 9,800)			wholesale dealer	9,000
To Commission : Suresh		11,900		
(5% on 2,38,000)				
To Profit to :				
Ravi	34,590			
Suresh	23,060	57,650		
		2,61,800		2,61,800

In the Books of Ravi

Dr. Joint Venture Account with Suresh Cr.

	Rs.		Rs.
To Bank (Purchases)	1,90,000	By Bank (Suresh)	13,410
To Suresh (Freight)	1,410	By Bank (Sales)	9,800
To Interest	350	By Stock taken	5,000
To Commission	490	By Bank	9,000
To Profit and Loss A/c (3/4 share of profit)	34,590	(Stock sent to whole sale dealer)	
		By Bank (Balance received)	1,89,630
	2,26,840		2,26,840

In the Books of Suresh

Dr. Joint Venture Account with Ravi Cr.

	Rs.		Rs.
To Bank (Ravi)	13,410	By Bank (Sales)	2,38,000
To Commission	11,900		
To Profit and Loss A/c (2/5 share of profit)	23,060		
To Bank (Balance paid)	1,89,630		
	2,38,000		2,38,000

Notes : 1. Sales by Ravi :

		Rs.
	Purchases	1,90,000
Less :	Goods sent Suresh	1,70,000
		20,000
Less :	Transferred to wholesale dealer	9,000
		11,000
Less :	Stock taken over by himself	4,000
		7,000
Add :	40% profit	2,800
	Sales made by Ravi	9,800

2. Sales by Suresh :

		Rs.
	Cost of goods received from Ravi	1,70,000
Add :	40% profit	68,000
	Sales made by Suresh	2,38,000

Illustration 12

Sakti and Sadhan agree to enter into a joint venture to buy and sell television sets. Profits and losses were to be shared equally.

On 5th May, 1993 Sakti purchased three television sets for Rs. 3,000, Rs. 3,500 and Rs. 4,000 respectively. He bought a special cabinet costing Rs. 750, which he fixed for one of the sets. On 31st May, 1993 he sold two of the sets for Rs. 4,000 each paying the proceeds into his private Bank Account.

On 15th June, 1993 he sold the other set for Rs. 4,500 which amount he paid over to Sadhan who paid it into his Bank Account.

On 6th May, 1993 Sadhan purchased a T.V. set for Rs. 3,000 having incurred expenditure of Rs. 200 on repairing, sold it on 14th May, 1993 for Rs. 3,800, paying the proceeds into his own bank account. This set developed mechanical trouble and on 26th May, 1993, Sadhan agreed to take the set back at price of Rs. 2,800 which he paid out of his bank account. The set was still unsold at 30th June, 1993 and it was agreed that Sadhan should take it over for his personal use at a valuation of Rs. 2,600.

Sakti incurred Rs. 300 as showroom charges and Sadhan incurred Rs. 225 as travelling and postage.

You are required to prepare : (a) Joint Venture Account with Sakti as it would appear in the books of Sadhan and (b) Memorandum Joint Venture Account showing the net profit.

(*B.Com., Nagpur and C.A. Inter*)

Solution :

Dr. **Memorandum Joint Venture A/c** Cr.

Date			Rs.	Date		Rs.
1993				1993		
May 5	To Purchases : Sakti		10,500	May 14	By Sales : Sadhan	3,800
May 5	To Expenses : Sakti (750 + 300)		1,050	May 31	By Sales : Sakti (2 × 4,000)	8,000
May 6	To Purchases : Sadhan		3,000	June 15	By Sales : Sadhan	4,500
May 6	Expenses : Sadhan (200 + 225)		425	June 30	By Set taken over : Sadhan	2,600
May 26	To Sales Return : Sadhan		2,800			
May 31	To Profit to :					
	Sakti	562.50				
	Sadhan	562.50	1,125			
			18,900			18,900

In the Books of Sadhan

Joint Venture Account with Sakti

Dr. Cr.

Date		Rs.	Date		Rs.
1993			1993		
May 6	To Bank (T.V. set purchased)	3,000.00	May 14	By Bank (Sale proceeds)	3,800.00
May 6	To Bank (Exps.) (Repairs Rs. 200 + Travelling and postage Rs. 225)	425.00	June 15	By Bank (Sale proceeds)	4,500.00
			June 30	T.V. set taken over	2,600.00
May 26	To Sales Return	2,800.00			
May 31	To Profit and Loss A/c (Share of profit)	562.50			
July 1	To Bank (Balance paid)	4,112.50			
		10,900.00			10,900.00

Conversion of Consignment into Joint Venture

Illustration 13

Pande of Patna, a manufacturer of 'Mini-Grinder' sent 100 Nos. of such machines to Shinde of Simla on lst August, 1994, to be sold on consignment basis at a commission of 15%, such commission to cover his expenses but not freight to Simla. The cost of each machine is Rs. 230, but is invoiced at Rs. 250. Expenses incurred by Pande were Rs. 400. A case containing 10 machines was lost for which Pande received Rs. 1,800 from Railway authorities as compensation on 31st December, 1994.

Shinde paid Rs. 1,800 as freight and Rs. 500 for salesmen's commission etc. Shinde also accepted a bill of exchange drawn by Pande for three months (dated 1st August, 1994) for Rs. 10,000. Pande got it discounted at 6% per annum. On 31st December, 1994 Shinde reported that he had sold 75 machines at Rs. 320 per machine remitted the balance due from him.

After making up the accounts on 31st December, 1994, it was decided that the relationship between Pande and Shinde should be one of joint venture, the cost of each machine being taken as Rs. 250, Shinde being entitled to 8% commission on sales and Pande being entitled to interest at 6% per annum on his outlay.

Prepare the accounts relating to the consignment in the books of Pande and give the adjusting entries required on conversion of the consignment to joint venture.

(Osmania and Madurai : Uni., Sept., 1987)

Solution :

In the Books of Pande

Dr. **Consignment to Simla Account** Cr.

Date		Rs.	Date		Rs.
1994			1994		
Aug. 1	To Goods Sent on Consignment (100 × Rs. 25)	25,000	Dec. 31	By Shinde : Sales	24,000
Aug. 1	To Bank : Expenses	400	Dec. 31	By Abnormal	2,340
Dec. 31	To Shinde : Freight	1,800	Dec. 31	By Consignment Stock (Closing stock)	4,110
Dec. 31	To Shinde : Commission (15% on 24,000)	3,600	Dec. 31	By Goods Sent on Consignment (Loading on goods sent 100 × Rs. 20)	2,000
Dec. 31	To Stock Reserve (Loading on closing stock 15 × Rs. 20)	300			
Dec. 31	To Profit and Loss A/c (Profit transferred)	1,350			
		32,450			32,450

Dr. **Goods Sent on Consignment** Cr.

Date		Rs.	Date		Rs.
1994			1994		
Dec. 31	To Consignment to Simla	2,000	Aug. 1	By Consignment to Simla	25,000
Dec. 31	To Trading A/c (Transfer)	23,000			
		25,000			25,000

Dr. **Abnormal Loss Account** Cr.

Date		Rs.	Date		Rs.
1994			1994		
Dec. 31	To Consignment to Simla	2,340	Dec. 31	By Bank (Railway Co.)	1,800
			Dec. 31	By Profit & Loss A/c (Net loss transferred)	540
		2,340			2,340

Dr. **Shinde's Account (Consignee A/c)** Cr.

Date		Rs.	Date		Rs.
1994			1994		
Dec. 31	To Consignment to Simla	24,000	Aug. 31	By Bills Receivable	10,000
			Dec. 31	By Consignment to Simla : Freight 1,800 Commission 3,600	5,400
			Dec. 31	By Bank (Balance received)	8,600
		24,000			24,000

On Conversion to Joint Venture

Dr. **Memorandum Joint Venture Account** Cr.

Date		Rs.	Date		Rs.
1994			1994		
Aug. 1	To Goods Supplied : Pande	25,000	Dec. 31	By Sales : Shinde	24,000
Aug. 1	To Expenses : Pande	400		By Claim of Railway Company	1,800
Dec. 31	To Expenses : Shinde	500	Dec. 31	By Closing stock	4,110
Dec. 31	To Freight : Shinde	1,800		By Loss to :	
Dec. 31	To Discount : Pande	150		Pande 274	
Dec. 31	To Commission : Shinde (8% on Rs. 24,000)	1,920		Shinde 274	548
Dec. 31	To Interest : Pande	388			
Dec. 31	To Stock Reserve	300			
		30,458			30,458

Adjustment Entry

Date	Particulars		L.F.	Debit Rs.	Credit Rs.
1994	Profit and Loss A/c	Dr.		1,084	
Dec.31	Shande's Account	Dr.		1,454	
	To Trading A/c				2,000
	To Discount A/c				150
	To Interest A/c				388
	(Being adjustment of accounts on conversion of consignment to joint venture)				

Working Notes

(i) **Calculation of Abnormal Loss**

	Rs.
Cost price of 10 damaged machines of Rs. 230 each	2,300
Add : Proportionate NRE upto the stage of damage *i.e.,* $\frac{400 \times 10}{100}$	40
Value of Abnormal Loss	2,340

(ii) **Calculation of Closing Stock**

		Rs.
Invoice price of 15 (*i.e.,* 100 – 10 = 90 – 75) machines (15 × 250)		3,750
Add : Proportionate NRE of consignor $\left(\frac{15 \times 400}{100}\right)$	Rs. 60	
Proportionate NRE of consignee $\left(\frac{15 \times 1{,}800}{90}\right)$	Rs. 300	360
Value of Closing Stock		4,110

(iii) **Calculation of Interest**

Interest is calculated at 6% on 15,550 (i.e., 25,000 + 400 – 9,850 i.e., 10,000 – 150 discount) for 5 months

$$\frac{15{,}550 \times 6 \times 5}{100 \times 12} = \text{Rs. 388 Aproximately}$$

(iv) **Calculation of Discount**

Discount is calculated at 6% on 10,000 for 3 months

$$\frac{10{,}000 \times 6 \times 3}{100 \times 12} \text{ Rs. 150}$$

(v) Under the new agreement of joint venture Shinde is to be debited Rs. 1,646 (*i.e.*, Rs. 1,920 commission less Rs. 274 share of loss on joint venture). But previously he received Rs. 3,100 *i.e.*, commission less expenses borne by him (Rs. 3,600 – 500). Therefore, he is to be debited with Rs. 1,454 (*i.e.*, Rs. 3,100 – 1,646).

(vi) Pande will now credit Trading Account by Rs. 2,000 extra because machines are to be valued at Rs. 250 instead of Rs. 230.

(vii) In case of consignment Pande's profit was Rs. 1,350 less Rs. 540 abnormal loss or Rs. 810. Now under the new agreement there is loss of Rs. 274. Therefore, the Profit and Loss Account should be debited by Rs. 1,084.

EXAMINATION QUESTIONS

(A) Answer the following questions not exceeding 4 lines each :

(Each Carries two Marks)

(1) What is a Joint Venture? *(Kar., April, 1995 & 1998)*

(2) Define Joint Venture.

(3) What is Joint Bank Account? *(Kar., April, 1996)*

(4) What is Joint Venture Account?

(5) Who are Co-venturers?

(6) Mention the two methods of recording the Joint Ventures dealings.

(7) Mention the two differences between joint venture and partnership. *(B'lore, Oct., 1993)*

(8) Why is co-venturer's account maintained? *(M.K.U., April, 1991)*

(9) Mention any two differences between Joint Venture and Consignment. *(Madras, Oct., 1992)*

(10) What is a Memorandum Joint Venture Account? *(Kar., Oct., 1996)*

(11) Explain the different methods of maintaining the accounts under joint venture. *(Kar., April, 1997)*

(B) Answer the following questions/problems :

(Each Carries eight Marks)

(1) What do you mean by Joint Venture? Explain its salient features.

(2) Bring out the distinction between :

(a) Joint Venture and Partnership;
(b) Joint Venture and Consignment.

(3) What do you mean by Joint Bank Account? Why is it opened?

(4) What is Memorandum Joint Venture Account? How it is prepared?

(5) Give journal entries when each co-venturer records all the joint venture transactions made by himself as well as his co-venturers.

(6) Give journal entries when co-venturer records only his own transactions of joint venture in his books.

(7) A and B entered into a joint venture sharing profits and losses in the ratio of 3 : 2. A contributed Rs. 30,000 and B Rs. 40,000. The amounts contributed by them were deposited into a joint bank account. They bought goods for cash Rs. 50,000 and from 'A' Rs. 20,000. They paid for carriage Rs. 3,500; godown rent Rs. 1,000; insurance Rs. 1,500 and other expenses Rs. 2,000. All the goods were sold for Rs. 90,000.

Pass the necessary journal entries. *(Agra, Oct., 1989)*

Hints : Profit on Joint Venture Rs. 12,000 (7,200 + 4,800)
Joint Bank A/c Total Rs. 1,60,000
Final Remittance to 'A' Rs. 57,200 and 'B' Rs. 44,800.

(8) X, Y and Z entered into a joint venture. X bought goods for Rs. 15,000 and supplied from his stock goods valued at Rs. 5,000. He received Rs. 5,000 from 'Y' and Rs. 7,000 from 'Z' as their contribution. He paid expenses of Rs. 1,300. All the goods were sold for Rs. 25,000. X is entitled to a commission of 4% on sales. X settled the accounts with Y and Z.

Open the necessary accounts in the books of X.

(Bangalore, Oct., 1992)

Ans. : Profit on Joint Venture Rs. 2,700 (900 + 900 + 900)
Final Balance paid : Y Rs. 5,900 and 'Z' Rs. 7,900.

(9) A, B and C enter into a Joint Venture to share profits and losses as 5 : 3 : 3. No separate set of books are maintained. Amounts contributed and received by different venturers are as follows :

	A	B	C
Cost of Material	40,000	20,000	10,000
Expenses	6,000	4,000	2,000
Sales proceeds received	17,000	34,000	68,000
Stock taken over	3,000	6,000	9,000

Prepare Memorandum Joint Venture Account.

(M.K.U., Oct., 1994)

Ans. : Profit on Joint Venture Rs. 55,000 (25,000 + 15,000 + 15,000)
Memorandum Joint Venture A/c Total Rs. 1,37,000.

(10) M/s A and B are in a joint venture sharing profits equally. B brought goods costing Rs. 6,000 and sent the same to 'A' incurring expenses of Rs. 200. 'A' provided goods valued at Rs. 4,000 from his stock and sold the entire goods for Rs. 15,000. A is entitled to a commission at 5% on sales. The accounts were duly settled.

Prepare Joint Venture Account and B's A/c in the books of 'A'.

(Kar., Oct., 1995)

Ans. : Profit on Joint Venture Rs. 4,050 (2,025 + 2,025)
Final Remittance to 'B' Rs. 8,225.

(11) Mahesh and Umesh undertake a work of construction a building jointly. The construction price of Rs. 2,50,000 payable as Rs. 2,00,000 in cash and Rs. 50,000 fully paid shares. A joint bank account is opened, Mahesh deposited Rs. 75,000 and Umesh Rs. 40,000 in connection with the joint venture. They share the profit and losses in the ratio of 2 : 1. The transactions of joint venture are as follows :

		Rs.
(a)	Wages paid	45,000
(b)	Material bought	1,70,000
(c)	Material supplied by Mahesh	10,000
(d)	Material supplied by Umesh	7,000
(e)	Architect's fees paid by Umesh	3,000

The building was completed and contract price duly received. Mahesh takes up shares at Rs. 45,000 and Umesh takes up closing stock at Rs. 9,000. Prepare Joint Venture Account.

(*Karnatak, April, 1997*)

Ans. : Profit on joint venture Rs. 19,000 (12,667 + 6,333); Loss on shares debited to Joint Venture A/c Rs. 5,000; Joint Venture A/c total Rs. 2,59,000.

(12) Ajay and Vijay entered into a joint venture in timber. Vijay is allowed a commission on sales at 10% and profits are to be shared in the ratio of Ajay 2/3 and Vijay 1/3. Ajay provides timber from stock for Rs. 10,000 and incurs expenses amounting to Rs. 1,000. Vijay pays Rs. 1,000 for unloading and other non-recurring expenses. Ajay drew upon Vijay for Rs. 6,000. The draft was accepted and Ajay got it discounted for Rs. 5,760. Vijay sold 90% of the timber for Rs. 15,000 and took over the remaining timber at cost plus 20%.

Vijay settles his account by bank draft. Write Joint Venture Account in the books of Ajay. Also show valuation of stock taken by Vijay.

(*Karnatak, April, 1998*)

Ans. : Profit on consignment transferred to : P & L A/c Rs. 1,800 and Vijay A/c Rs. 900; Value of goods taken over by Vijay Rs. 1,440, *i.e.*, 1/10th of cost, 1/10 of Ajay's expenses and 1/10 of Vijay's expenses Rs. 1,000 +100 + 100 = 1,200 + 240 *i.e.*, 20% of Rs. 1,200) and Joint Venture A/c total Rs. 16,440.

(C) Solve the Following Problems :

(*Each Carries 16 Marks*)

(1) C of Kolkata entered into a joint venture with 'A' of Amritsar and M of Mirzapur on the following arrangements :

(a) A would purchase blankets and M would purchase carpets both of whom would sent goods to C for sale.

(b) C would sell the goods at the best possible price and would send the remittance to A and M in accordance with their respective dues.

(c) Profit would be shared equally between the parties. A purchased 500 blankets at Rs. 50 each and sent Rs. 600 for freight etc. M purchased 100 carpets at Rs. 350 each spent Rs. 800 for freight etc.

C sold all the blankets and carpets at Rs. 75,000 and his expenses amounted to Rs. 1,600.

Show the Joint Venture Account and Co-venturer's Accounts in the books of C.

(*I.C.W.A. Inter*)

Ans. : Profit on Joint Venture Rs. 12,000 (C – Rs. 4,000, A – Rs. 4,000 and M – Rs. 4,000) (*i.e.*, Cr. 75,000; Dr. 25,000 + 600 + 35,000 + 800 + 1,600) Final Remittance to A – Rs. 29,600 (*i.e.*, 25,000 + 600 + 4,000); Final Remittance to M Rs. 39,800 (*i.e.*, 35,000 + 800 + 4,000).

(2) Dimple and Simple entered into a Joint Venture. They agreed to share profit and losses in the proportion of their initial contribution to the joint venture. They opened a joint bank account and deposited Rs. 60,000 and Rs. 40,000 respectively as initial contribution.

They made cash purchases of Rs. 70,000. They also paid Rs. 4,500 for insurance and freight and Rs. 1,750 for sundry expenses.

At the end of venture, the sales amounted to Rs. 1,10,000, There was unsold stock of goods worth Rs. 5,000. Simple took over the unsold stock. The Joint Venture was closed.

You are asked to prepare Joint Venture Account, Joint Bank Account and Co-adventurer's Accounts.

(*C.A.I.I.B. Part-I, Nov., 1983*)

Ans. : Profit on Joint venture Rs. 38,750 (Dimple Rs. 23,250 and Simple Rs. 15,500) (*i.e.*, Cr. 1,10,000 + 5,000; Dr. 70,000 + 4,500 +1,750); Joint Bank Account Total Rs. 2,10,000. Final Balance paid; Dimple Rs. 83,250 and Simple Rs. 50,500.

(3) Gopal and Ahmad undertook jointly to construct a building for contract price of Rs. 3,00,000. A joint banking account was opened by them in their joint names. Gopal paid into it Rs. 1,00,000 and Ahmed Rs. 50,000. Profit or loss is to be distributed in ratio of 2 : 1. The details of transactions made are given below : Wages Rs. 80,000, Materials purchased Rs. 1,60,000, Material supplied by Gopal Rs. 10,000, Material supplied by Ahmed Rs. 8,000. Gopal paid the Architect's fee Rs. 4,000.

After the completion of contract, the price was duly received. There was stock of unused materials which were valued at Rs. 10,000 and this was taken over by Ahmad. Prepare Joint Venture Account and Joint Bank Account.

(C.A.I.I.B. Part-I, May, 1982)

Ans. : Profit on Joint Venture Rs. 48,000 (Gopal Rs. 32,000 and Ahmad Rs. 16,000 (*i.e.,*Cr. 3,00,000 + 10,000; Dr. 2,40,000 + 14,000 + 8,000); Joint Bank Accounttotal Rs. 4,50,000; Final Balance paid : Gopal Rs. 1,46,000 and Ahmad Rs. 64,000.

(4) Jones, Strong and Black enter into a Joint Venture to divide profits equally. They bought goods from Smart and Co. for Rs. 12,500 and from Jones for Rs. 2,500. Jones contributed Rs. 3,000, Strong Rs. 4,000 and Black Rs. 9,000 which amounts were banked in a joint account. They settled their account with Smart and Company by cheque and paid for carriage and other expenses Rs. 750. They sold, goods for cash Rs. 6,500 and to Smith and Son on credit for Rs. 14,000 who accepted a draft for the amount. The acceptance was cashed and realised Rs. 13,700. Jones was allowed 5% commission on sales for effecting the transactions.

Pass journal entries and open the necessary accounts, assuming that final settlement between the parties was made by cheques.

(Mysore, B.Com., Oct., 1970)

Ans. : Profit on Joint Venture Rs. 3,425 (*i.e.*, Cr. 6,500 + 14,000; Dr. 12,500 + 2,500 + 750 + 300 + 1,025); Joint Bank Account Total Rs. 36,200; Final Balance paid : Jone Rs. 7,666.67, Strong Rs. 5,141.67 and Black Rs. 10,141.66.

(5) On 1st April, 1980, Ashok and Kapoor entered into a joint account venture to produce a publicity film for Sahyadri Co. Ltd. The contract price of the film was Rs. 1,50,000. On the same day, they opened a Joint Banking Account towards which Ashok contributed Rs. 50,000 and Kapoor contributed Rs. 25,000, Sahyadri Co. Ltd., made an advance payment of Rs. 25,000 in cash, of which Rs. 13,000 were deposited in the Joint Banking Account and the balance was taken by Ashok for purchase of raw films. The expenses of the Joint Venture were as under :

		Rs.
(a)	Purchase of raw films (of which Rs. 15,000 were paid by Ashok)	60,000
(b)	Remuneration to Artists (of which Rs. 5,000 were paid by Kapoor)	25,000
(c)	Remuneration to technical staff	18,000
(d)	Other production expenses	12,000

The film was completed on 30th September, 1980, and delivered to Sahyadri Co. Ltd., on the same day. The stock of unused raw film was valued at Rs. 10,000 and was taken over by Ashok.

The company was not satisfied with the film and asked the producers to reduce the price. The venturers agreed to accept 20 percent less than the contract price. On 31st October, 1980, the company paid their dues. On 5th November, 1980, the Joint Bank Account was closed and Ashok and Kapoor were paid the balance standing to the credit of their accounts. They agreed to share profits and losses in proportion to their initial contribution.

Show Ledger Accounts recording all the above transactions in the books of Joint Venture.

(*Mysore, B.Com., April, 1974*)

Ans. : Profit on Joint Venture Rs. 15,000 (Ashok Rs. 10,000 and Kapoor Rs. 5,000) (*i.e.*, Cr.10,000 + 1,20,000; Dr.45,000 + 15,000 + 20,000 + 5,000 +18,000 +12,000); Joint Bank A/c total Rs. 1,83,000; Final Balance paid : Ashok Rs. 53,000 and Kapoor Rs. 35,000.

Note : Contract price is calculated below :

Original Contract price is	Rs. 1,50,000
Less : 20% reduction in contract price	Rs. 30,000 = Rs. 1,20,000.

(6) A, B and C undertake construction of an office building of a company at a contract price of Rs. 10,00,000. The contract price is to be received by cheque Rs. 6,00,000 and Rs. 4,00,000 in equity shares of the contractee company. They decided to share profits and losses equally. They open a Joint Bank A/c and contributes the following amounts :

A – Rs. 3,00,000; B – Rs. 3,00,000; C – Rs. 2,00,000. A pays towards fees of Architects Rs. 10,000. B brings in Mixer worth Rs. 25,000 and C brings in Motor Lorry worth Rs. 55,000.

The following transactions were made from the Joint Bank A/c : Purchase of materials Rs. 4,50,000. Purchase of plants Rs. 30,000, Freight and Wages Rs. 1,50,000.

At the close of venture, A took over the unused materials worth Rs. 8,000, B took back the mixer at Rs. 15,000 and C took back motor lorry at Rs. 35,000. Scrap value of plants realised Rs. 6,000. Contract price was received in full and B took over the shares at an agreed value of Rs. 4,10,000.

Prepare (i) Joint Venture A/c (ii) Joint Bank A/c (iii) Co-ventures A/c.

(C.A.I.I.B. Part-I, May, 1987)

Ans. : Profit on Joint Venture Rs. 3,54,000, (*i.e.*, Cr. 6,00,000 + 4,00,000 + 8,000 + 35,000 + 15,000 + 6,000 + 10,000. Dr. 6,30,000 + 10,000 + 25,000 + 55,000); Joint Bank A/c Total Rs. 14,06,000; Final Balance paid : A – Rs. 4,20,000, B – Rs. 18,000 and C – Rs. 3,38,000.

Note : Profit on sale of shares Rs. 10,000 (*i.e.*, 4,10,000 – 4,00,000).

(7) Dilip and Raj are doing business separately as engineering contractors. They undertake jointly to build and instal new machinery for a company for a contract price of Rs. 1,34,000 – Rs. 84,000 payable in instalments in cash and the balance as fully paid shares in the new company. A bank account is opened in Joint, Dilip paying Rs. 45,000 and Raj Rs. 20,000. They are to share profits and losses in the proportion of 3/5 and 2/5 respectively. Their transactions were as follows :

	Rs.
Amount advanced to supply of materials	52,000
Value of materials supplied by suppliers	89,000
Balance amount paid to suppliers in full and final settlement	35,500
Paid wages	36,000
Materials purchased in cash	2,500
Material supplied by Dilip from stock	9,250
Engineering consultant fees paid	3,250
Value of stock lost by fire and not covered by insurance	3,500

The contract was completed and price duly received.

Dilip took all the shares at the agreed value of Rs. 47,000 and Raj took the balance of stock of materials worth Rs. 3,500 at an agreed value of Rs. 2,750.

Prepare the joint venture account, showing the resultant profit or loss and the accounts of Dilip and Raj and also the Bank a/c.

Ans. : Loss on Joint Venture Rs. 4,750 (Dilip Rs. 2,850 and Raj Rs. 1,900) (*i.e.*, Cr. 1,500 + 84,000 + 50,000 + 2,750. Dr. 89,000 + 36,000 + 2,500 + 3,250 + 9,250 + 3,000); Joint Bank Account Total Rs. 1,49,000; Final Balance paid : Dilip Rs. 4,400 and Raj Rs. 15,350.

(8) Mr. K in Madras purchases cotton goods and sends them to Mr. B in Delhi for sale on joint venture basis, profits and losses to be divided equally.

On 1st July, 1980, K purchased goods worth Rs. 10,000 and sent them to B in Delhi, the freight paid Rs.1,000 by K.

K drew upon B a bill of Rs. 8,000 payable after 6 months. B accepted the same. K got it discounted for Rs. 7,800. On 31st December, 1980 'B' informed K that he had incurred expenses amounting to Rs. 1,200 and that the entire lot had been sold for Rs. 18,000. B remitted the requisite sum to K.

You are required to show :

(a) Joint Venture A/c (b) Other Party's A/cs as it would appear to the books of K and B.

(C.A.I.I.B. Part-I, May, 1987)

Ans. : Profit on Joint Venture Rs. 5,600 (*i.e.*, Cr. 18,000. Dr. 10,000 + 1,000 + 200 + 1,200); Final Balance Remitted by 'B' to 'K' Rs. 6,000.

(9) X of Mumbai sent goods worth Rs. 7,500 to Y of Chennai to be sold by the latter on profit sharing basis. The profit sharing ratio being 3 : 2 after charging all expenses and commission.

X paid Rs. 550 for freight and insurance and drew a bill for Rs. 3,000 on Y. The bill was discounted by X for Rs. 2,900. Y paid Rs. 300 for clearing and storage. The goods were sold for Rs. 12,500. Y also paid selling expenses of Rs. 250 and forwarded a sight draft for the balance due to X after charging commission on sales at 5% on the gross proceeds.

Write up necessary Ledger A/c's in the books of both the parties.

Ans. : Profit on Joint Venture Rs. 3,175 (X Rs. 1,905 and Y Rs. 1,270) (*i.e.*, Cr. 12,500; Dr. 8,050 + 100 + 550 + 625); Final Balance Remitted by Y to X Rs. 7,055.

Note : Commission 5% on 12,500 = Rs. 650.

(10) X and Y entered into a Joint Venture of underwriting the subscription at par of the entire share capital of Copper Mines Limited consisting of 10,000 shares of Rs. 10 each and to pay all expenses up to allotment. They were to share profits in the ratio of 3 : 2 respectively. The consideration in return for the guarantee was 1,200, other shares of Rs. 10 each fully paid to be issued to them.

X provided the funds for registration fees Rs. 1,200, advertising Rs. 1,100 and printing and stationery Rs. 950. Y contributed towards payment of office rent Rs. 300; legal charges Rs. 1,550 and staff salaries Rs. 900.

The prospects was issued and the applications fell short of the full issue by 1,500 shares, X took these over on joint account and paid for the same in full. They received the 1,200 fully paid shares as underwriting commission. They sold their entire holding at Rs. 12 per share. The proceeds were received by X for 1,500 shares and by Y for 1,200 shares.

Write up the necessary accounts in the books of both the parties showing the final adjustment.

(*B.Com., Shivaji*)

Ans. : Profit on Joint Venture Rs. 11,400 (X Rs. 6,840 and Y Rs. 4,560) (*i.e.*, Cr.14,400 +18,000. Dr.1,200 +1,100 + 950 +300 +1,550 + 900 + 15,000); Final Balance Remitted by Y to X Rs. 7,090.

(11) Shaji of Cochin and Arun of Mumbai enter into a Joint Venture to consign handicrafts to McDonald of Germany. Shaji sends goods to the value of Rs. 25,000 and pays Rs. 2,500 as expenses.

Arun ships goods worth Rs. 16,000. Expenses incurred by him amounted to Rs. 1,800.

McDonald sold all the goods for Rs. 63,700. After deducting his expenses and commission of Rs. 5,700, the balance is forwarded to Shaji. He then settled the account with Arun of Mumbai, by bank draft.

Show the Memorandum Joint Venture Account and Joint Venture Account with Arun in the books of Shaji and Joint Venture A/c with Shaji in the books of Arun.

(*Institute of Banker's Part Nov., 1985*)

Ans. : Profit on Joint Venture Rs. 12,700 (Shaji Rs. 6,350 and Arun Rs. 6,350) (*i.e.*, Cr. 63,700; Dr.25,000 + 16,000 + 2,500 + 1,800 + 5,700); Memorandum Joint Venture A/c Total Rs. 63,700; Final Balance Remitted by Arun to Shaji Rs. 24,150.

(12) X and Y decided to work as a Joint Venture for the sale of electric motors on 21st May, 1982, X purchased 200 electric motors at Rs. 175 each and dispatched 150 motors to Y incurring Rs. 1,000 as freight and insurance charges. 10 electric motors were damaged in transit. On 1st Feb., 1983, Rs. 500 were received by X from the insurance company in full settlement of his claim. On 15th March, 1983, X sold 50 electric motors at Rs. 225 each. He received Rs. 15,000 from Y on 1st April, 1983.

On 15th May, 1982, Y took delivery of electric motors and incurred the following expenses :

	Rs.
Clearing charges	170
Repair Charges to electric motors damaged in transit	300
Godown Rent for 3 months	600

He sold the electric motors as below :

1-2-1983	10 damaged motors at Rs. 170 each
	40 motors at Rs. 200 each
15-3-1983	20 motors at Rs. 315 each
1-4-1983	80 motors as Rs. 250 each.

It is agreed that they are entitled to commission of 10% on the respective sales effected by them and that the profits and losses shall be shared between X and Y in the ratio of 2 : 1.

Y remits X the balance of monies due on 30th April, 1983.

You are required to show the Memorandum Joint Venture Account only.

(*C.A. Adapted*)

Ans. : Profit on Joint Venture Rs. 5,955 (X Rs. 3,970 and Y Rs. 1,985) (*i.e.*, Cr.11,250 + 36,000 + 500; Dr. 35,000 + 1,000 + 1,070 + 1,125 + 3,600); Memorandum Joint Venture A/c total Rs. 47,750.

Note : X – commission 10% on 11,250 = Rs. 1,125; Y – commission 10% on 36,000 = Rs. 3,600, X – insurance claim is credited to Memorandum Joint Venture Account.

(13) A and B entered into a Joint Venture for plucking and selling apples. They bought all fruits in the 1979 season in the high orchard at Manali, paying Rs. 30,000 to the owner on August 1, 1979. Labour was engaged to Pluck and Pack the fruit for which a sum of Rs. 5,000 was paid, spread over a period of a month. A paid for the fruit as well as labour expenses.

The fruit was despatched to B in Mumbai who sold it for Rs. 60,000. The sale proceeds were collected over the period of two months. At the end of the season some fruits were sold locally by A for Rs. 2,000. Settlement of account was made on October 31, 1979.

After reckoning (a) interest at 12% p.a. for moneys invested as well as received, (b) allowing 5% commission to B on sales made by him and (c) salary of Rs. 1,000 p.m. to A for the season, the balance was to be divided equally.

Prepare Memorandum Joint Venture A/c and Joint A/c with B in the books of A and Joint A/c with A in the books for 'B'.

(*I.C.W.A., June, 1985*)

Ans. : Profit on Joint Venture Rs. 22,220 (*i.e.*, Cr. 61,200 + 2,000; Dr. 30,000 + 5,000 + 2,000 + 980 + 3,000); Memorandum Joint Venture A/c Total Rs. 63,200; Final Balance Remitted by A to B Rs. 47,090.

(14) Sri Memon sent goods to Sri Gupta to be sold on consignment basis at 5% commission. Goods costing Rs. 4,00,000 were sent and Rs. 40,000 expenses were incurred. Sri Gupta had to incur Rs. 10,000 expenses for loading and 75% of the goods were sold out for Rs. 4,80,000. Sri Gupta sent the amount due from him with the Account sale, but wanted to return the balance of goods as he was not agreeable to carry on as a commission agent. He was however, persuaded to continue on Joint Venture basis for one-third profit for Rs. 2,00,000 worth of goods was further despatched by Sri Memon. All the goods (except Rs. 20,000 which were taken over by Sri Gupta for the same amount) were sold out for Rs. 5,00,000. Sri Memon incurred Rs. 20,000 expenses and expenses of Sri Gupta amounted to Rs. 17,000.

Show the necessary accounts in the books of both the parties.

(*I.C.W.A. Inter*)

Ans. : Profit on consignment Rs. 1,18,500; Value of closing stock Rs. 1,12,500; Final remittance as per consignment Rs. 4,46,000; Profit on Joint Venture Rs. 1,70,500 (Memon Rs. 1,13,667 and Gupta Rs. 56,833); Final Remittance as per Joint Venturer Rs. 4,46,167.

(15) Pandit and Bhat entered into a joint venture to undertake a contract for construction of a building for Rs. 4,00,000. They agreed to share the profit or loss in the ratio of 3 : 2. Pandit contributed Rs. 1,00,000 and Bhat Rs. 1,50,000 and deposited the same by opening a Joint Bank Account. The payments were made as under :

	Rs.
Materials purchased	1,20,000
Wood supplied by Pandit	60,000
Wages paid	1,40,000
Architect's fees paid by Bhat	30,000

The contract was completed and the full price was received. The unused materials valued at Rs. 10,000 were taken up by Pandit.

Prepare necessary ledger accounts in a separate set of books maintained for the joint venture.

(*Karnatak, April, 1996*)

Ans. : Profit on Joint Venture Rs. 60,000 (*i.e.*, Pandit Rs. 36,000, Bhat Rs. 24,000); Joint Bank Account Total Rs. 6,50,000. Final Balance paid : Pandit Rs. 1,86,000 and Bhat Rs. 2,04,000.

5

CONVERSION OF A PARTNERSHIP FIRM INTO A LIMITED COMPANY

(Sale of a Partnership Firm to a Limited Company)

Meaning

Sometimes a partnership firm may decide to convert itself into a limited company or may sell its business to an existing (or a new) company. Conversion of partnership means changing or converting the structure or constitution of partnership firm into a new company. It is just like sale of partnership business to an existing or newly formed company. Sale of partnership business to a limited company is nothing but a form of dissolution. The partners who are interested to dissolve their partnership firm, can sell their partnership business to a company, or the partners can form a new joint stock company for taking over the business of a partnership firm. When a partnership firm is converted into a limited company, an agreed amount is to be paid as a purchase price by the purchasing company to the partnership firm. The purchasing company generally pays the purchase price partly in cash and partly in its own shares and debentures. When the shares or debentures are allotted to partners for taking over their business of partnership, the partners will become the shareholders or debentureholders of a company. When the conversion is taken place, the necessary entries should be passed to close the books of partnership firm and opening entries should be passed in the limited company.

Purposes

The main objects of such conversion are as follows :

(1) Limiting the liability of members or partners to the value of shares held by them.

(2) Expansion of business by collecting more funds from the new members.

(3) Getting the more tax facilities and less rate of income-tax than a partnership firm.

(4) Getting a separate entity different from its members.

Purchase Consideration

Meaning

The amount or price paid by the purchasing company to the partnership firm for taking over the various assets and liabilities is called purchase consideration. Purchase consideration may be paid to the partnership firm in the form of cash, shares and debentures. The purchasing company may take over the entire business or only assets or all assets and a few liabilities or a few assets and all liabilities of partnership firm. The value of such assets and liabilities may be ascertained in different methods depending upon the agreement between the purchasing company and partnership firm.

Methods

The following are the different methods of calculating the purchase consideration.

(1) Net Payment Method : Under this method a lump sum is given as a purchase consideration by purchasing company to the partnership firm for taking over the assets and liabilities. This lump sum is paid in the form of cash or shares or debentures or partly in cash and partly in shares and debentures of the company.

(2) Net Assets Method : Under this method purchase consideration is calculated as below :

(i) When all assets and liabilities are taken over by the purchasing company, the remaining balance after deducting the agreed value of liabilities in the agreed value of assets will be treated as purchase consideration (*i.e.*, Purchase consideration = Total agreed value of assets taken over – Total agreed value of liabilities taken over).

(ii) When only assets are taken over by the purchasing company, the total agreed values of all assets taken over will be treated as purchase consideration.

(iii) When a few of assets and a few of liabilities or a few of assets and all liabilities or all assets and a few of liabilities are taken over by the purchasing company, the remaining balance after deducting the total agreed value of liabilities taken over in the total agreed value of assets taken over will be treated as purchase consideration.

The student should note that the cash at bank or cash in hand of partnership firm should also be transferred to the purchasing company unless it is specifically mentioned in the problem that the same is not taken over by the company.

Accounting Procedure

Entries in the Books of the Firm

When partnership firm is converted into limited company, its assets are realised and liabilities are settled. For this purpose a Realisation Account is opened, the profit or loss of Realisation Account is transferred to Partners Capital Account in their profit sharing ratio. The following are the entries to be passed in the books of selling firm :

(a) For transfer of assets to Realisation Account :

Realisation Account	Dr.	With book value
To Assets Account		of assets

(b) For transfer of liabilities to Realisation Account :

Liabilities Account	Dr.	With book value
To Realisation Account		of liabilities

(c) For the assets not taken over by the purchasing company :

(i) *When the assets sold for cash :*

Bank or Cash Account	Dr.	With total amount
To Assets Account		received

(ii) *When assets are taken by any partner :*

Concerned Partners' Capital A/c	Dr.	With the amount
To Relative Asset or Assets A/c		as agreed

Note : Any loss on such assets should be debited and any profit on such assets should be credited to Realisation Account and the corresponding credit or debit must be given to the relative asset or assets account.

(d) For the liabilities not taken over by the purchasing company :

(i) *When liabilities paid :*

Liabilities A/c	Dr.	With total amount
To Bank or Cash A/c		paid

(ii) *When liabilities taken over by any partner :*

Relative Liability or Liabilities A/c	Dr.	With the amount
To Concerned Partners' Capital A/c		as agreed

Note : Any profit on payment of such liabilities should be credited and any loss on payment of such liabilities should be debited to Realisation Account and the corresponding debit or credit must be given to the relative liability or liabilities account.

(e) For recording the purchase consideration :

(*i.e.*, for purchase consideration to be received)

Purchasing Company Account	Dr.	With the amount of
To Realisation Account		purchase Consideration

(f) For receiving the purchase consideration :

Cash or Bank Account	Dr.	As the case may be at agreed values
Shares in Purchasing Company A/c	Dr.	
Debentures in Purchasing Company A/c	Dr.	
To Purchasing Company Account		

(g) For payment of realisation expenses :

Realisation Account	Dr.	With the amount of expenses
To Cash or Bank Account		

(h) For transfer of realisation profit :

Realisation Account	Dr.	Profit transferred in profit sharing ratio
To Partners' Capital A/c		

Note : If there is a loss, the above entry is to be reversed.

(i) For transfer of Reserve or P & L A/c (Cr.) balance :

Reserve or P & L A/c	Dr.	With amount of reserve or profit in profit sharing ratio.
To Partners' Capital A/c		

Note : If P & L A/c showed debit balance, partners capital accounts should be debited and P & L A/c should be credited in profit sharing ratio.

(j) For payment of partners loan, if any :

Partners' Loan A/c	Dr.	With the amount of loan repaid
To Cash or Bank A/c		

Note : If the partners capital accounts show the debit balances, the partners' loan account should be debited and capital accounts should be credited.

(k) For repayment of partners capitals :

Partners' Capital A/c	Dr.	With balance amount paid
To Bank or Cash A/c		

Note : If the partners capital accounts show the debit balances they should bring required cash. In such case the above entry will be reversed.

(l) For distribution of shares and debentures among partners :

Partners' Capital A/c	Dr.	As the case may be in agreed proportion
To Shares in Purchasing Company A/c		
To Debentures in Purchasing Company A/c		

Note : If there is no agreed ratio as to how the shares or debentures are to be distributed among partners, the same should be distributed among the partners in their final claim ratio *i.e.*, in the ratio of capitals standing to their credit after making all the other adjustments to their capital accounts. The shares and debentures should be distributed in full unit and not in fraction.

Entries in the Books of a Limited Company

(a) For assets and liabilities taken over from the partnership firm and for the purchase price payable to the partnership firm :

Assets A/c	Dr.	With the amount of assets and liabilities of firm and purchase consideration
To Liabilities A/c		
To Firms A/c (Purchase price)		

Note : When the purchase price is given in lump sum and it is not ascertained on the basis of value of assets taken minus value of liabilities taken; there may result of a Goodwill or Capital Reserve. It is calculated as below :

Purchase Price minus Value of Net Assets = Goodwill

Value of Net Assets minus Purchase Price = Capital Reserve

(b) For payment of cash and issue of shares or debentures in settlement of purchase consideration :

Partnership Firm A/c	Dr.	With the amount of purchase consideration in form of cash, shares and debentures
Discount on Issue of Debentures A/c (If issued at discount)	Dr.	
To Equity or Pref. Share Capital A/c		
To Equity or Pref. Share Premium A/c (If issued at premium)		
To Debentures A/c (Face value)		
To Cash or Bank A/c		

Illustration 1

Ravi Company Ltd. was formed to take over the business of Siri and Giri who were carrying on business in partnership sharing profits and losses in the ratio of 3 : 2. The Balance Sheet of the firm was as follows :

Liabilities		Rs.	Assets	Rs.
Creditors		50,000	Buildings	35,000
Bills Payable		5,000	Machinery	20,000
Profit & Loss A/c		25,000	Furniture	5,000
Capitals :			Stock	22,000
Siri	30,000		Debtors	15,000
Giri	20,000	50,000	Bills Receivable	14,000
			Investments	15,000
			Cash	4,000
		1,30,000		1,30,000

The company took over all the assets and liabilities, except investments, at book values and the purchase consideration of Rs. 90,000 payable is as follows :

5,000 Equity Shares of Rs. 10 each, 300 Debentures at Rs. 100 each and balance in cash.

The investments were taken over by Siri at book value. The shares in Ravi Company Ltd. have been distributed between Siri and Giri in the ratio of 3:2 and the final settlement is being made in the form of debentures and cash.

Show the necessary ledger accounts to close the books of the firm.

Solution :

Realisation Account

Dr.		Rs.		Rs. Cr.
To Buildings		35,000	By Creditors	50,000
To Machinery		20,000	By Bills Payable	5,000
To Furniture		5,000	By Siri's Capital (Investments taken)	15,000
To Stock		22,000		
To Debtors		15,000	By Ravi Co. Ltd. (Purchase Consideration)	90,000
To Bills Receivable		14,000		
To Investments		15,000		
To Cash		4,000		
To Capital Accounts : (Profit transferred)				
Siri	18,000			
Giri	12,000	30,000		
		1,60,000		1,60,000

Ravi Co. Ltd. Account

Dr.	Rs.		Rs. Cr.
To Realisation (Purchase Consideration)	90,000	By Shares in Ravi Co. Ltd.	50,000
		By Debentures in Ravi Co. Ltd.	30,000
		By Bank	10,000
	90,000		90,000

Shares in Ravi Co. Ltd. Account

Dr.	Rs.		Rs. Cr.
To Ravi Co. Ltd.	50,000	By Siri's Capital	30,000
		By Giri's Capital	20,000
	50,000		50,000

Dr. **Debentures in Ravi Co. Ltd. Account** Cr.

	Rs.		Rs.
To Ravi Co. Ltd.	30,000	By Siri's Capital	13,500
		By Giri's Capital	16,500
	30,000		30,000

Dr. **Cash Account** Cr.

	Rs.		Rs.
To Ravi Co. Ltd.	10,000	By Siri's Capital	4,500
		By Giri's Capital	5,500
	10,000		10,000

Dr. **Partners' Capital Account** Cr.

	Siri Rs.	Giri Rs.		Siri Rs.	Giri Rs.
To Realisation (Investments)	15,000	—	By Balance b/d	30,000	20,000
			By P & L A/c	15,000	10,000
To Shares in Ravi Co. Ltd. (3:2)	30,000	20,000	By Revaluation Profit	18,000	12,000
To Deb. in Ravi Co. Ltd. (18:22)	13,500	16,500			
To Cash (Balance paid in 18 : 22 ratio)	4,500	5,500			
	63,000	42,000		63,000	42,000

Note : (i) Allotment of Purchase Consideration :

	Rs.
Total purchase consideration	90,000
Less : Shares (5,000 × 10)	50,000
	40,000
Less : Debentures (300 × 100)	30,000
Balance in Cash	10,000

(ii) Debentures and cash are distributed in the ratio of final balances on capitals *i.e.*, 18,000 (*i.e.*, 63,000 – 45,000) and 22,000 (*i.e.*, 42,000 – 20,000) *i.e.*, 18 : 22.

Illustration 2

Black and White were the partners, in a firm sharing profits and losses equally, decided to convert their business into a Limited Company, named Black White Ltd. on 31st March, 1992, when their Balance Sheet was :

Balance Sheet

Liabilities		Rs.	Assets	Rs.
Creditors		30,000	Buildings	40,000
Bills Payable		10,000	Plant	12,000
Capitals :			Furniture	6,600
Black	40,300		Debtors	20,000
White	30,300	70,600	Stock	22,000
			Cash	10,000
		1,10,600		1,10,600

Black White agreed to take over all the assets and liabilities at the values stated below :

Buildings Rs. 44,600; Plant Rs. 10,000; Furniture Rs. 5,500; Stock Rs. 20,000; Debtors subject to provision for doubtful debts at 5% and Creditors at discount of 3%.

The company issued 5,500 equity shares of Rs. 10 each at 12 per share and the balance of purchase price is paid in cash.

The company issued for cash 4,000 equity shares at Rs. 12 each for cash to the public. All these shares were taken up and paid for.

Give journal entries and Ledger Accounts in the books of the firm and also journal entries and a Balance Sheet in the books of Black White Ltd.

Solution :

In the Books of the Firm

Journal Entries

Sl. No.	Particulars		L.F.	Dr. Rs.	Cr. Rs.
1.	Realisation A/c	Dr.		1,10,600	
	To Buildings A/c				40,000
	To Plant A/c				12,000
	To Furniture A/c				6,600
	To Debtors A/c				20,000
	To Stock A/c				22,000
	To Bank A/c				10,000
	(Being assets transferred at book value)				
2.	Creditors A/c	Dr.		30,000	
	Bills Payable A/c	Dr.		10,000	
	To Realisation A/c				40,000
	(Being liabilities transferred at book value)				

(Contd.)

Journal Entries (*Contd.*)

Sl. No.	Particulars	L.F.	Dr. Rs.	Cr. Rs.
3.	Black White Ltd.'s A/c Dr.		70,000	
	To Realisation A/c			70,000
	(Being purchase consideration due from Black White Ltd.)			
4.	Black's Capital A/c Dr.		300	
	White's Capital A/c Dr.		300	
	To Realisation A/c			600
	(Being realisation loss transferred to Capital A/cs)			
5.	Equity Shares in Black White Ltd. A/c Dr.		66,000	
	Bank A/c Dr.		4,000	
	To Black White Ltd. A/c			70,000
	(Being 5,500 shares of Rs. 10 each at Rs. 12 per share, and Rs. 4,000 in cash received settlement of purchase consideration)			
6.	Black's Capital A/c Dr.		37,714	
	White's Capital A/c Dr.		28,286	
	To Equity Shares in Black White Ltd. A/c			66,000
	(Being shares received from Black White Ltd. issued to Black and White in their Capital Ratio *i.e.*, 4 : 3)			
7.	Black's Capital A/c Dr.		2,286	
	White's Capital A/c Dr.		1,714	
	To Bank A/c			4,000
	(Being balance on Capital A/cs paid in cash)			

Dr. **Realisation Account** Cr.

	Rs.			Rs.
To Buildings	40,000	By Creditors		30,000
To Plant	12,000	By Bills Payable		10,000
To Furniture	6,600	By Black White Ltd. (Purchase price)		70,000
To Debtors	20,000	By Capital Accounts : (Loss transferred)		
To Stock	22,000	Black	300	
To Bank	10,000	White	300	600
	1,10,600			1,10,600

Dr. **Black White Ltd. Account** Cr.

	Rs.		Rs.
To Realisation (Purchasing price)	70,000	By Equity Shares	66,000
		By Bank	4,000
	70,000		70,000

Dr. **Partners' Capital Account** Cr.

	Black	White		Black	White
To Realisation Loss	300	300	By Balance b/d	40,300	30,300
To Equity Shares	37,714	28,286			
To Bank	2,286	1,714			
	40,300	30,300		40,300	30,300

In the Books of Black White Ltd.
Journal Entries

Sl.No.	Particulars	L.F.	Dr. Rs.	Cr. Rs.
1.	Building A/c Dr.		44,600	
	Plant A/c Dr.		10,000	
	Furniture A/c Dr.		5,500	
	Stock A/c Dr.		20,000	
	Debtors A/c Dr.		20,000	
	Bank A/c Dr.		10,000	
	Reserve for Discount on Creditors A/c Dr.		900	
	To Creditors A/c			30,000
	To Bills Payable A/c			10,000
	To R.D.D. A/c			1,000
	To Black White Ltd. A/c			70,000
	(Being assets & liabilities taken over from Black and White and the purchase price payable to them)			
2.	Bank A/c Dr.		48,000	
	To Equity Shares Capital A/c			40,000
	To Equity Share Premium A/c			8,000
	(Being cash received on the shares subscribed by the public)			

Contd.

Journal Entries (*Contd.*)

Sl.No.	Particulars	L.F.	Dr. Rs.	Cr. Rs.
3.	Black White Ltd. A/c Dr.		70,000	
	To Equity Share Capital A/c			55,000
	To Equity Share Premium A/c			11,000
	To Bank A/c			4,000
	(Being 5,500 shares of Rs. 10 each issued at a premium of Rs. 2 per share as fully paid and paid Rs. 4,000 in cash to Black and White in payment of purchase consideration)			

Black White Company Ltd.
Balance Sheet as on 1-4-1992

Liabilities		Rs.	Assets	Rs.
Share Capital :			Fixed Assets :	
9,500 Equity Shares of Rs. 10 each of which 5,500 shares issued to vendors without receiving cash		95,000	Building	44,600
			Plant	10,000
			Furniture	5,500
Reserve & Surplus :			Current Assets :	
Share Premium (11,000 + 8,000)		19,000	Stock	20,000
Current Liabilities :			Debtors	19,000
Creditors	29,100		Bank	54,000
Bills Payable	10,000	39,100		
		1,53,100		1,53,100

Notes : (i) Shares are distributed in the ratio of final balances on capitals i.e. Rs. 40,000 : Rs. 30,000 (after deducting realisation loss from Rs. 40,300 and Rs. 30,300).

(ii) Purchase Consideration is calculated as below :

Value of assets taken over :	Rs.	Rs.
Buildings		44,600
Plant		10,000
Furniture		5,500
Stock		20,000
Debtors	20,000	
Less : R.D.D.	1,000	19,000
Cash		10,000
		1,09,100

Balance c/d		1,09,100
Less : Liabilities taken over :		
Creditors	30,000	
Less : Reserve for Discount	900	
	29,100	
Bills Payable	10,000	39,100
Purchase Consideration		70,000

(iii) Bank Balance is calculated as below :

Amount taken from the firm (Rs. 10,000 + 48,000 received on issue of shares)	58,000
Less : Paid to the firm	4,000
Bank Balance	54,000

Illustration 3

X, Y and Z carry business in partnership sharing profits and losses in the ratio of 3 : 2 : 1 on 31st March, 1992 they agreed to sell their business to a Limited Company. Their position on that date was as follows :

	Rs.		Rs.
Creditors	10,000	Freehold Property	30,000
Loan on Mortgage	5,000	Machinery	15,000
X's Capital	39,400	Furniture	8,000
Y's Capital	29,600	Bills Receivable	10,000
Z's Capital	19,800	Book Debts	22,000
		Stock	15,000
		Cash	3,800
	1,03,800		1,03,800

The Company took the following assets at the valuation shown below :

	Rs.		Rs.
Freehold Property	28,000	Machinery	13,000
Furniture	7,000	Bills Receivable	9,500
Book Debts	21,500	Stock	14,000
Goodwill	8,000		

The company also agreed to pay the creditors which were agreed at Rs. 9,000. The company paid Rs. 72,000 in fully paid shares of Rs. 10 each and the balance in cash. The realisation expenses amounted to Rs. 800.

Prepare Ledger Accounts in the books of the firm and give a Ltd. Company's Balance Sheet.

Solution :

In the Books of Firm

Realisation Account

Dr.		Rs.		Rs. Cr.
To Sundry Assets (30,000 + 15,000 + 8,000 + 10,000 + 22,000 + 15,000)		1,00,000	By Sundry Creditors	10,000
			By Loan on Mortgage	5,000
			By Ltd. Company (Purchase Consideration)	92,000
To Bank :				
Loan Paid	5,000			
Realisation Exp.	800	5,800		
To Capital Accounts : (Profit transferred)				
X	600			
Y	400			
Z	200	1,200		
		1,07,000		1,07,000

Partners' Capital Account

Dr.	X	Y	Z	Cr.	X	Y	Z
To Shares in a Ltd. Company	32,000	24,000	16,000	By Balance b/d	39,400	29,600	19,800
To Bank	8,000	6,000	4,000	By Realisation Profit	600	400	200
	40,000	30,000	20,000		40,000	30,000	20,000

Limited Company's Account

Dr.	Rs.	Cr.	Rs.
To Realisation (Purchase price)	92,000	By Equity Shares	72,000
		By Bank	20,000
	92,000		92,000

Cash Account

Dr.	Rs.	Cr.	Rs.
To Balance b/d	3,800	By Realisation A/c (Loan & Expenses paid)	5,800
To Ltd. Company's A/c	20,000	By X's Capital A/c	8,000
		By Y's Capital A/c	6,000
		By Z's Capital A/c	4,000
	23,800		23,800

In the Books of the Company
Balance Sheet of a Limited Company as on 1-4-1992

Liabilities	Rs.	Assets	Rs.
Share Capital :		Fixed Assets :	
7,200 shares of Rs. 10 each		Goodwill	8,000
issued to vendors as fully paid	72,000	Freehold Property	28,000
Unsecured Loan :		Machinery	13,000
Bank Overdraft	20,000	Furniture	7,000
Current Liabilities :		Current Assets :	
Creditors	9,000	Books Debts	21,500
		Bills Receivable	9,500
		Stock	14,000
	1,01,000		1,01,000

Notes : (i) Shares are distributed in the ratio of final capital balances *i.e.*, 4:3:2.

(ii) Cash balance is not taken over by the company.

(iii) Loan on mortgage is not taken over by the company. Therefore, it should be paid by the firm itself.

(iv) It is presumed that the creditors are not yet paid.

(v) Purchase Consideration is calculated as below :

	Rs.
Agreed value of assets taken over	1,01,000
(28,000 + 13,000 + 7,000 + 9,500 + 21,500 + 14,000 + 8,000)	
Less : Agreed value of liabilities taken over (Creditors Rs. 9,000)	9,000
Purchase Consideration	92,000

(vi) Payment of cash Rs. 20,000 to vendors is treated as overdraft from Bank. Hence it is taken on the liability side.

Illustration 4

JK Co. Ltd. was formed to take over the business of A and B who were sharing profits and losses in the ratio of 3 : 1. The balance sheet of the firm was as under :

Liabilities		Rs.	Assets		Rs.
Creditors		25,000	Goodwill		20,000
Bills Payable		5,000	Building		50,000
Bank Overdraft		25,000	Plant		25,000
Loan from Mrs. B		1,000	Investments		15,000
Capital Accounts :			Stock		22,000
Mr. A	69,250		Debtors	22,000	
Mr. B	29,750	99,000	*Less :* Provision	2,000	20,000
			Cash		3,000
		1,55,000			1,55,000

The company agreed to take over the assets including cash at book value except the building and debtors which were taken over at Rs. 55,000 and Rs. 17,000 respectively. But investments were retained by the firm and were sold by them for Rs. 14,000. The firm also discharges a loan of Mrs. B. The company took over the remaining liabilities including the bank overdraft at book value. The value of goodwill was fixed at Rs. 20,000 only.

Purchase Consideration was paid by the issue of 9,000 equity shares of Rs. 10 each at Rs. 8 per share and the balance in cash.

Show the necessary ledger accounts in the books of the firm.

Solution :

Dr. **Realisation Account** Cr.

		Rs.		Rs.
To Goodwill		20,000	By R.D.D.	2,000
To Buildings		50,000	By Creditors	25,000
To Plant		25,000	By Bills Payable	5,000
To Investments		15,000	By Bank Over Draft	25,000
To Stock		22,000	By Cash	14,000
To Debtors		22,000	(Investments sold)	
To Cash		3,000	By JK Co. Ltd.	87,000
To Capital Accounts :			(Purchase Consideration)	
(Profit transferred)				
A	750			
B	250	1,000		
		1,58,000		1,58,000

Dr. **JK Co. Ltd. Account** Cr.

	Rs.		Rs.
To Realisation	87,000	By Equity Shares in	
(Purchase Consideration)		JK Co. Ltd.	72,000
		By Cash	15,000
	87,000		87,000

Dr. **Shares in JK Co. Ltd. Account** Cr.

	Rs.		Rs.
To JK Co. Ltd.	72,000	By Mr. A's Capital	50,400
		By Mr. B's Capital	21,600
	72,000		72,000

Cash Account

Dr.	Rs.		Cr. Rs.
To Realisation (Investments sold)	14,000	By Mrs. B's Loan	1,000
		By A's Capital	19,600
To JK Co. Ltd.	15,000	By B's Capital	8,400
	29,000		29,000

Partners' Capital Accounts

Dr.	A Rs.	B Rs.	Cr.	A Rs.	B Rs.
To Equity Shares	50,400	21,600	By Balance b/d	69,250	29,750
To Cash	19,600	8,400	By Realisation Profit	750	250
	70,000	30,000		70,000	30,000

Notes : (i) Purchase Consideration is calculated as below :

	Rs.
Agreed value of assets taken over (*i.e.*, Goodwill Rs. 20,000 + Building Rs. 55,000 + Plant Rs. 25,000 + Stock Rs. 22,000 + Debtors Rs. 17,000 + Cash Rs. 3,000)	1,42,000
Less : Agreed amount of liabilities taken over (Creditors Rs. 25,000 + B/P Rs. 5,000 + Bank O/D Rs. 25,000)	55,000
Purchase Consideration	87,000

(ii) Calculation of capital ratio is as under :

	A Rs.	B Rs.
Capital balance as per balance sheet	69,250	29,750
Add : Realisation Profit	750	250
The ratio is 70,000 : 30,000 or 7 : 3	70,000	30,000

Illustration 5

Raju and Viju were in partnership sharing profits and losses in the ratio of 2 : 1. The following was the balance sheet of the firm as on 31-12-1992 :

Liabilities		Rs.	Assets	Rs.
Creditors		23,000	Fixed Assets	30,000
Loan from Raju		8,000	Stock	15,000
Capital Accounts :			Debtors	10,000
Raju	25,000		Work-in-progress	8,000
Viju	22,000	47,000	Cash at Bank	18,000
Current Account :			Current Account :	
Raju		4,000	Viju	1,000
		82,000		82,000

The Kumar Ltd. agreed to take over Work-in-progress, Stock and Fixed Assets excluding the value of Motor Van Rs. 6,000 for a consideration of Rs. 55,000 which is to be satisfied :

(a) by payment of cash Rs. 15,000

(b) by the allotment of 200 preference shares of Rs. 100 each valued at Rs. 80 per share and

(c) by allotment of 2,000 equity shares of the face value of Rs. 10 each for the remaining balance.

The debtors realised Rs. 9,000 and the creditors were paid Rs. 22,000 in full settlement.

It was agreed between the partners as follows :

(i) Viju is to take over the Motor Van at an agreed value of Rs. 7,000.

(ii) Equity shares are to be allotted in their profit sharing ratio.

(iii) The preference shares are to allotted to Raju to the value of his loan amount and the remaining preference shares are to be allotted to the partners equally.

(iv) The remaining balance is to be paid in cash.

Prepare the necessary Ledger Accounts in the books of the firm.

Solution :

In the Books of the Firm

Realisation Account

Dr. Cr.

		Rs.		Rs.
To Fixed Assets		30,000	By Creditors	23,000
To Stock		15,000	By Viju's Capital	7,000
To Debtors		10,000	(Motor Van taken over)	
To Work-in-progress		8,000	By Bank	9,000
To Bank (Creditors paid)		22,000	(Debtors realised)	
To Capital Accounts :			By Kumar Ltd.	55,000
(Profit transferred)			(Purchase consideration)	
Raju	6,000			
Viju	3,000	9,000		
		94,000		94,000

Kumar Ltd. Account

Dr. Cr.

	Rs.		Rs.
To Realisation	55,000	By Preference Shares	16,000
(Purchase consideration)		By Equity Shares	24,000
		By Bank	15,000
	55,000		55,000

Preference Shares Account

Dr.	Rs.		Cr. Rs.
To Kumar Ltd.	16,000	By Raju's Loan	8,000
		By Raju's Capital	4,000
		By Viju's Capital	4,000
	16,000		16,000

Equity Shares Account

Dr.	Rs.		Cr. Rs.
To Kumar Ltd.	24,000	By Raju's Capital	16,000
		By Viju's Capital	8,000
	24,000		24,000

Bank Account

Dr.	Rs.		Cr. Rs.
To Balance b/d	18,000	By Realisation	22,000
To Realisation	9,000	By Raju's Capital	15,000
To Kumar Ltd.	15,000	By Viju's Capital	5,000
	42,000		42,000

Raju's Loan Account

Dr.	Rs.		Cr. Rs.
To Preference Shares	8,000	By Balance b/d	8,000
	8,000		8,000

Partner's Capital Account

Dr.	Raju Rs.	Viju Rs.		Raju Rs.	Viju Rs. Cr.
To Current A/c	—	1,000	By Balance b/d	25,000	22,000
To Realisation (Motor Van)	—	7,000	By Current A/c	4,000	—
			By Realisation Profit	6,000	3,000
To Preference Shares (Equal ratio)	4,000	4,000			
To Equity Shares (2 : 1 ratio)	16,000	8,000			
To Bank (3 : 1) (Balance paid)	15,000	5,000			
	35,000	25,000		35,000	25,000

Notes : (i) The value of each share is Rs. 12.

(ii) Capital ratio is 15,000 : 5000 or 3 : 1.

Illustration 6

A, B and C carrying on business in partnership (profit and loss sharing ratio being 1/2, 1/3 and 1/6 respectively) decided to form a private limited company, ABC Co. (Private) Ltd., with an authorised capital of Rs. 1,20,000 divided into 90,000 equity shares of Re. 1 each and 30,000, 6% preference shares of Re. 1 each. The company is incorporated on 31-3-1991 and taken over the business, goodwill and some of the assets of the firm as on 31-3-1991, on which date the Balance Sheet of the firm is given here as under:

	Rs.		Rs.
Creditors	5,600	Cash at Bank	17,200
A's Loan	8,000	Debtors	10,400
Current Accounts :		Current Account :	
A	5,850	B	4,200
C	4,150	Stock-in-trade	36,000
Capitals Accounts :		Furniture & Fixtures	1,200
A	30,000	Scooters	3,600
B	20,000	Machinery	13,000
C	12,000		
	85,600		85,600

'A' who retires, is presented with a scooter, book value being Rs. 1,200. The company takes over the remaining scooter for Rs. 2,000. 'A' takes over all the debtors and agrees to pay off creditors. He also received certain furniture for which he is charged Rs. 300. The company agrees to discharge A's loan by issue to him 6,000 preference shares of Re. 1 each fully paid and the balance in cash. 'C' is the owner of the premises from where the business of the firm is carried on. 'C' agrees to sell the above premises to the company for Rs. 20,000 in consideration whereof he agrees to receive 20,000 preference shares of Re. 1 each fully paid.

The company takes over the remaining Furniture at Rs. 600, Stock at Rs. 33,200, Cash at Bank and Machinery at book value. The Goodwill is valued at Rs. 8,000 for the purpose of taking over.

The purchase consideration is to be discharged by the issue to the partner at par 60,000 equity shares of Re. 1 each in proportion to final balance of their combined capital and Current Account and the balance is to be paid in cash.

Preliminary expenses amounting to Rs. 800 are paid by the company.

Prepare — (i) Realisation Account, (ii) Combined Capital and Current Accounts of Partners, (iii) Opening Balance Sheet of the Limited Company.

(Poona, B.Com.; B.U., B.Com. & C.A. Inter)

Solution :

Realisation Account

Dr.		Rs.		Cr. Rs.
To Cash at Bank		17,200	By Creditors	5,600
To Debtors		10,400	By B's Capital	800
To Stock-in-trade		36,000	(Scooter presented to	
To Furniture & Fixtures		1,200	'A' : 2/3 × 1,200)	
To Scooters		3,600	By C's Capital	400
To Machinery		13,000	(Scooter presented to	
To A's Capital		5,600	'A' : 1/3 × 1,200)	
(Creditors taken over)			By A's Capital	10,700
To Capital Accounts :			(Debtors and Furniture taken	
(Profit transferred)			over *i.e.,* 10,400+300 = 10,700)	
A	2,250		By ABC Co. (Private) Ltd.	74,000
B	1,500		(Purchase consideration)	
C	750	4,500		
		91,500		91,500

Combined Capital and Current Accounts

Dr.	A Rs.	B Rs.	C Rs.	Cr.	A Rs.	B Rs.	C Rs.
To Current A/c	—	4,200	—	By Balance b/d	30,000	20,000	12,000
To Realisation	—	800	400	By Current A/cs	5,850	—	4,150
(Scooter presented to 'A')				By Realisation (Creditors taken over)	5,600	—	—
To Realisation (Debtors & Furniture taken over)	10,700	—	—	By Realisation Profit	2,250	1,500	750
To Balance c/d	33,000	16,500	16,500				
	43,700	21,500	16,900		43,700	21,500	16,900
To Equity Shares	30,000	15,000	15,000	By Balance b/d	33,000	16,500	16,500
To Cash (Balance paid)	3,000	1,500	1,500				
	33,000	16,500	16,500		33,000	16,500	16,500

Balance Sheet of ABC Co. (Private) Ltd. as on 1-4-1991

Liabilities	Rs.	Assets		Rs.
Authorised Capital :		Goodwill		8,000
90,000 Equity shares of		Premises		20,000
Re. 1 each	90,000	Machinery		13,000
30,000, 6% Preference		Scooter		2,000
shares of Re. 1 each	30,000	Furniture		600
		Stock		33,200
	1,20,000	Cash at Bank :		
Issued and Paid up Capital :		Taken over	17,200	
26,000, 6% Preference		*Less* : Paid to the firm	8,000	
shares of Re. 1 each	26,000		9,200	
(6,000 issued to A,		*Less* : Paid for		
20,000 issued to C)		preliminary expenses	800	8,400
60,000 Equity shares of		Preliminary Expenses		800
Re. 1 each	60,000			
	86,000			86,000

Notes : (i) Purchase consideration is calculated as below :

	Rs.
Value of assets taken over :	
Scooter	2,000
Furniture	600
Stock	33,200
Cash at Bank	17,200
Machinery	13,000
Goodwill	8,000
Purchase consideration	74,000
Paid in preference shares (6,000 × 1)	6,000
	68,000
Paid in Equity Shares (60,000 × 1)	60,000
Balance paid in cash	8,000

(ii) Out of cash Rs. 8,000, Rs. 2,000 is paid to 'A' to discharge his loan. The remaining cash of Rs. 6,000 is distributed among the partners.

(iii) Scooter presented to 'A' has been debited to 'B' and 'C' in their profit sharing ratio of 1/3 : 1/6 or 2 : 1.

(iv) Equity shares have been divided amongst partners in proportion to their final amount due *i.e.,* 33,000 : 16,500 : 16,500.

EXAMINATION QUESTIONS

(A) Answer the following questions in not exceeding 4 lines each :

(Each Carrying two Marks)

(1) What do you mean by conversion of partnership?

(2) Give two reasons for conversion of partnership.

(3) What is purchase consideration?

(B'lore, Nov., 1981; Kar., Oct., 1996 and B'lore, April, 1998)

(4) Why partners decide to convert their firm into a limited company?

(B'lore, Nov., 1983)

(5) What are the methods of discharging purchase consideration?

(B'lore, April, 1992)

(6) Mention the two methods of finding out the purchase consideration.

(B'lore, May, 1981)

(7) State which reasons as to which ratio should the shares (received as purchase price) be distributed among the partners of the firm.

(B'lore, Nov., 1982)

(8) Give the journal entry for the distribution of shares and debentures among partners.

(9) How do you ascertain the purchase consideration?

(B'lore, May, 1991)

(10) Mention the journal entry for receiving the purchase consideration in shares and debentures.

(M.K.U., Oct., 1994)

(B) Answer the following questions/problems :

(Each Carries 8 Marks)

(1) What is purchase consideration? How is it ascertained ?

(Gulbarga, Oct., 1989)

(2) What are the methods of finding out the purchase consideration?

(B'lore, Oct., 1993)

(3) What are the objectives of conversion of a partnership firm into a limited company?

(4) How do you treat the following in the books of the purchasing company :

(a) the excess of purchase price over the net assets take over, and

(b) the excess of the net assets acquired over the purchase price?

(B'lore, Oct., 1992)

(5) Give the proforma journal entries to be passed in the books of the purchasing company.

(*Shivaji, April, 1991*)

(6) How do you treat the following :

(a) Assets and liabilities not taken over by the company.

(b) Distribution of shares among partners.

(*Poona, Oct., 1987*)

(7) A Co. Ltd., took over the following assets at an agreed value :

Building Rs. 45,000; Machinery Rs. 20,600; Stock Rs. 20,000; Debtors Rs. 29,000; Cash at Bank Rs. 9,600 and Goodwill Rs. 28,600.

The company also agreed to pay the creditors and Bank overdraft at Rs. 8,000 and Rs. 20,800 respectively.

Calculate the purchase consideration.

Ans. : Purchase consideration Rs. 1,24,000 (1,52,800 – 28,800).

(8) The partners of 'XY' firm agreed to sell their entire business including cash at Bank of Rs. 7,000 to ABC Ltd. The assets were valued as follows :

Plant Rs. 20,000; Debtors Rs. 35,000; Stock Rs. 22,000 and Goodwill Rs. 12,000.

The company agreed to take over the bills payable at Rs. 4,000 and the creditors at Rs. 30,000. The purchase consideration was paid by the issue of 3,000 shares of Rs. 10 each fully paid and the remaining amount in cash.

Ascertain the purchase consideration payable to 'XY' firm.

Ans. :		
	Purchase consideration	62,000
	Paid in shares (*i.e.*, 3,000 × 10)	30,000
	Balance paid in Cash	32,000

(9) A firm sells its business to a limited company. The company does not take over the debtors and creditors of the firm but agrees to collect and pay them as the firms agent at a commission of 5% on all receipts and payments. The firm's debtors are of Rs. 30,000 and the creditors are of Rs. 10,000.

The company collects Rs. 28,000 from the firm's debtors and pays Rs. 9,000 to firm's creditors in full satisfaction of their claims. After charging its commission it remits the balance of amount to the firm.

Pass the journal entries in the books of the firm.

(*Madurai, April, 1981*)

Ans. : Total loss and commission Rs. 2,850 (1,000 + 1,850).

(C) Solve the Following Problems :

(Each Carries 16 Marks)

(1) X Ltd., was formed to take over the business of M/s X and Y who are carrying on business in partnership. The balance sheet of the firm as on 31-12-1985 was as follows :

Liabilities	Rs.	Assets	Rs.
Sundry Creditors	65,000	Plant and Machinery	2,60,000
Bills Payable	22,000	Land and Buildings	69,000
Profit and Loss Account	43,000	Stock	1,30,000
Partners' Capital :		Investments	52,000
X	2,00,000	Sundry Debtors	1,38,000
Y	3,19,000		
	6,49,000		6,49,000

The company took over all the assets and liabilities except the investments at book values and the purchase consideration of Rs. 5,50,000 was satisfied by the issue of Rs. 2,00,000, 7% debentures of X Ltd., and the balance in fully paid equity shares of Rs. 100 each in X Ltd. The investments were taken over by 'Y' at book value. The shares in the X Ltd. have been taken over by X and Y in the ratio of 3 : 2 and the final settlement is being made in the form of the debentures.

Pass the journal entries to close the books of the firm.

(Karnatak, April, 1976 New)

Ans. : Realisation Profit : X Rs. 20,000; Y Rs. 20,000
Shares Distributed : X Rs. 2,10,000; Y Rs. 1,40,000
Debentures Distributed : X Rs. 31,500; Y Rs. 1,68,500.

(2) A, B and C carry on business in partnership sharing profits and losses in proportion of 1/2, 3/8 and 1/8 respectively. On 31-12-1982, they agreed to sell their business to a limited company. Their position on that date was as follows :

Liabilities	Rs.	Assets	Rs.
A's Capital	2,00,000	Freehold Property	1,80,000
B's Capital	1,50,000	Machinery	1,20,000
C's Capital	1,30,000	Book Debts	1,50,000
Loan	40,000	Stock	1,30,000
Sundry Creditors	80,000	Cash	20,000
	6,00,000		6,00,000

The company took over the following assets at the valuation of :

Freehold Property	2,20,000
Machinery	1,10,000
Book debts	1,40,000
Stock	1,20,000
Goodwill	40,000

The company also agreed to pay the creditors which were agreed at Rs. 77,000. The company paid Rs. 3,36,000 in fully paid shares of Rs. 10 each and the balance in cash. The expenses amounted to Rs. 5,000.

Prepare the ledger accounts in the books of the firm.

(Gulbarga, Oct., 1983 Mod.)

Ans. : Realisation profit : 'A' Rs. 24,000; 'B' Rs. 18,000 and 'C' Rs. 6,000.
Purchase consideration Rs. 5,53,000 (6,30,000 – 77,000)
Shares Distributed in profit sharing ratio of 4 : 3 : 1 = 'A' Rs. 1,68,000; 'B' Rs. 1,26,000 and 'C' Rs. 42,000.
Balance paid in cash : 'A' Rs. 56,000; 'B' Rs. 42,000 and 'C' Rs. 94,000.

Note : Shares may also be distributed in capital ratio of 28 : 2 : 17 and the balance in cash.

(3) Jek & Co. Ltd. was formed to take over the partnership business of M and N who share profits and losses in the ration of 2 : 1. The balance sheet of the firm was as under :

Liabilities	Rs.	Assets	Rs.
Bank Overdraft	8,000	Buildings	40,000
Creditors	20,800	Machinery	20,600
Loan from Mrs. M	3,200	Stock	24,000
Capital Accounts :		Debtors	29,000
Mr. M	61,000	Investments	4,800
Mr. N	43,000	Cash at Bank	9,600
		Goodwill	8,000
	1,36,000		1,36,000

The company agreed to take over the assets at book values except the Buildings and Stock which are to be taken over at Rs. 45,000 and Rs. 20,000 respectively. The investments are maintained by the firm M and N and are sold by them for Rs. 4,200. They also discharged the loan of Mrs. M. The company takes over the remaining liabilities including the Bank Overdraft. The value of Goodwill is fixed at Rs. 28,600.

The purchase consideration is discharged by the issue of 10,000 equity shares of Rs. 10 each as fully paid and the balance in cash.

Prepare the necessary ledger accounts in the books of the firm.

(*Mysore, Oct., 1975 & Kar., Oct., 1984 Mod.*)

Ans. : Realisation Profit : 'M' Rs. 14,000 and 'N' Rs. 7,000
Purchase Consideration Rs. 1,24,000 (1,52,800 – 28,800)
Shares Distributed : 'M' Rs. 60,000 and 'N' Rs. 40,000
Balance paid in cash : 'M' Rs. 15,000 and 'N' Rs. 10,000.

Notes : (i) Shares are distributed in capital ratio of 3 : 2.
(ii) The company has taken over the Cash at Bank also.

(4) Pai and Kamath who were in hotel business for a number of years, decide to convert their business into a limited company on 31st Dec., 1983. Their balance sheet on that date was as follows :

Liabilities		Rs.	Assets	Rs.
Capital :			Cash Balance	66,000
Pai	3,00,000		Customers Accounts	40,000
Kamath	3,86,000	6,86,000	Stores and Utensils	1,80,000
Suppliers of Stores		70,000	Furniture	1,00,000
Expenses due		30,000	Buildings	4,00,000
		7,86,000		7,86,000

The firm was sold to a newly formed company, known as Dream Flowers Ltd., on the following terms :

(i) The company is to take over all assets except the cash balance and the customers' accounts for an agreed sum of Rs. 8,00,000 to be discharged by the issue of :
(a) Fully paid 6,000 equities of Rs. 100 each and
(b) Fully paid 2,000 debentures of Rs. 100 each.

(ii) The firm realised from the customers 90% of the sums due in final settlement and paid all outstanding liabilities. A 10% discount was obtained from the suppliers at final settlement.

(iii) The expense of the formation of the company amounted to Rs. 9,000 and this expense was born by the partnership.

(iv) The debentures were taken over by Kamath at face value. The equities were shared equally by the partners.

(v) Mutual settlement was made by partners by cash payments.

(vi) Pai and Kamath shared profits and losses in the ratio 3 : 2.

Close the ledger accounts of the firm.

(*Adapted from My. U., B.Com.*)

Ans. : Realisation profit—Pai Rs. 68,400 and Kamath Rs. 4,56,000
Purchase consideration Rs. 8,00,000 (6,00,000 + 2,00,000)
Cash brought in by Kamath Rs. 68,400
Final payment made to 'Pai' Rs. 68,400
Shares distributed : Pai Rs. 3,00,000 and Kamath Rs. 3,00,000;
Debentures given to Kamath Rs. 2,00,000.

(5) Radhey and Sita are in Partnership sharing profits and losses as to two-third and one-third respectively. Their Balance Sheet at December 31, 1981 on which date they have agreed to convert their business into a private limited company was as follows :

Liabilities		Rs.	Assets	Rs.
Sundry Creditors		30,000	Cash	7,000
Mortgage on Freehold			Sundry Debtors	26,000
Premises		10,000	Stock-in-trade	16,000
Capitals :			Plant and Machinery	5,000
Radhey	20,000		Freehold Premises	16,000
Sita	10,000	30,000		
		70,000		70,000

The company takes over all the assets and liabilities with the exception of the mortgage on freehold premises, the purchase price being Rs. 60,000 payable as to Rs. 12,000 in cash, Rs. 24,000 in debentures and the balance in equity shares of the company.

Close the books of the firm after the above transactions have been carried out including the payment of mortgage. The partners agree to share the debentures and shares in proportion of their capitals.

(B'lore, Oct., 1990 & April, 1993 & Karnatak, April, 1994)

Ans. : Realisation profit : Radhey Rs. 13,333 and Sita Rs. 6,667.
Final payments in debentures : Radhey Rs. 16,000 and Sita Rs. 8,000; Shares : Radhey Rs. 16,000 and Sita Rs. 8,000, Cash : Radhey Rs. 1,333 and Sita Rs. 667.

(6) G and S were partners sharing profits and losses in the ratio of 3 : 2 on 1-7-1987 and their balance sheet was as under :

Liabilities	Rs.	Assets		Rs.
Creditors	20,000	Plant		50,000
Reserve	15,000	Stock		20,000
Capitals :		Debtors	18,000	
G	40,000	*Less* : Provision	900	17,100
S	30,000	Cash at Bank		17,900
	1,05,000			1,05,000

The partners sold the business including cash at bank to P Ltd. The valuation put on the various assets was :

Goodwill	30,000
Plant	45,000
Stock	18,000
Debtors	17,500

It was found that the liabilities contained Rs. 1,600 which was not to be paid. The company issued 8,250 shares of Rs. 10 each fully paid and paid the remaining amount in cash.

Close the books of the firm by preparing the necessary ledger accounts.

(Karnatak, April, 1978 Non-sem)

Ans. : Realisation Profit : 'G' Rs. 15,000 and 'S' Rs. 10,000
Purchase Consideration Rs. 1,10,000 (1,28,400 – 18,400)
Shares Distributed : 'G' Rs. 49,500 and 'S' Rs. 33,000
Balance paid in Cash : 'G' Rs. 14,500 and 'S' Rs. 13,000.

Note : The shares are distributed in profit sharing ratio.

(7) Black, White and Green are in partnership. Their profit sharing ratio is 1/2, 1/8 and 1/6 respectively. They decide to convert their firm into a Private Limited Company as B.W.G. Private Ltd., on 31st March, 1988. Their balance sheet as at that date was as follows :

Liabilities	Rs.	Assets		Rs.
Creditors	8,000	Land and Buildings		11,400
Capitals :		Stock		10,000
Black	17,400	Debtors	10,000	
Green	8,000	*Less :* Provision	1,000	9,000
White	6,000	Cash		6,000
		Profit and Loss		3,000
	39,400			39,400

B.W.G. Private Ltd. was incorporated on March 31, 1988 with an authorised capital of Rs. 50,000 (500 shares of Rs. 100 each) for the purpose of purchasing and continuing the partnership business of Black, Green and White. Rs. 32,900 was the purchase price, which was paid by allotment of 180 shares (full paid) in B.W.G. Private Ltd., and the balance in cash. The company then issued the remaining shares to Brown and Blue in equal proportion, who paid for them in full. Pass the journal entries necessary to close the books.

(B.Com., Marathwada Uni., 1989 & Andhra Uni., 1985, B'lore, April, 1992)

Ans. : Profit on realisation Rs. 4,500
Payment in Shares : Black Rs. 9,000; Green Rs. 3,000; White Rs. 6,000
Payment in Cash : Black Rs. 9,150; Green Rs. 5,250; White Rs. 500.

Hint : Unless otherwise agreed upon it is fairest to distribute shares in profit sharing ratio and then pay in cash the balance remaining unpaid.

(8) A, B and C carry business in partnership sharing profits and losses 1/2, 3/8 and 1/8 respectively. On 31st March, 1980 they agreed to sell their business to a limited company. Their position on that date was as follows :

Liabilities	Rs.	Assets	Rs.
A's Capital	20,000	Freehold Property	18,000
B's Capital	15,000	Machinery	12,000
C's Capital	13,000	Book Debts	15,000
Loan on Mortgage	4,000	Stock	13,000
Sundry Creditors	8,000	Cash	2,000
	60,000		60,000

The company took the following assets at the valuation shown below :

Freehold Property	Rs. 22,000	Machinery	Rs. 11,000
Book Debts	Rs. 14,000	Stock	Rs. 12,000
Goodwill	Rs. 4,000		

The company also agreed to pay the creditors which were agreed to Rs. 77,000. The company paid Rs. 33,500 in fully paid shares of Rs. 10 each and the balance in cash. The expenses amounted to Rs. 500.

Prepare Ledger Accounts in the books of the firm and give a Ltd., Company's Balance Sheet.

(*S.U., Oct., 1983 & C.A. Inter*)

Ans. : Realisation profit : 'A' Rs. 2,400; 'B' Rs. 1,800 and 'C' Rs. 600.
Purchase consideration Rs. 55,300.
Final payment in shares : 'A' Rs. 14,210; 'B' Rs. 10,660; and 'C' Rs. 8,630.
Final payment in cash : 'A' Rs. 8,190 ; 'B' Rs. 6,140 and 'C' Rs. 4,970.
Capital Ratio : 28 : 21 : 17; Balance Sheet Total Rs. 63,000.

(9) Bomi and Homi were partners sharing profits and losses in the ratio of 3:2. The following was the balance sheet of the firm as at 31-12-1988.

Liabilities		Rs.	Assets	Rs.
Capital Accounts :			Machinery	72,000
Bomi	75,160		Motor Cars (Two)	12,000
Homi	44,080	1,19,240	Investments	32,000
Loans :			Stock	40,000
Bomi	30,000		Debtors	35,000
Homi	800	30,800		
Creditors		25,000		
Bank Overdraft		15,960		
		1,91,000		1,91,000

(a) The partners desired to dissolve the firm and accept the offer of Merwanjee Ltd. to purchase their business. The company agreed on the following terms :

(i) to take over machinery and stock and

(ii) that the purchase consideration of Rs. 2,00,000 was to be satisfied by cash payment of Rs. 1,10,000 and the balance by allotment of 9,000 shares of Rs. 10 each.

(b) Homi took over one motor car at a valuation of Rs. 8,500 and Bomi the other Car at Rs. 3,500.

(c) Cash realised on sale of investments amounted to Rs. 31,000. The debtors realised Rs. 30,000 and the creditors were settled for Rs. 24,000.

(d) The cost incurred on realisation were Rs. 1,500.

(e) The partners agreed to divide the shares in proportion to their profit sharing ratio.

Prepare the Realisation Account, Bank Account and Partners' Capital Accounts.

(Bombay & Karnatak, April, 1969)

Ans. : Realisation profit : Bomi Rs. 48,900 and Homi Rs. 32,600

Shares Distributed : Bomi Rs. 54,000 and Homi Rs. 36,000

Final Settlement : Bomi Rs. 96,560 and Homi Rs. 32,980.

Note : Shares are distributed in profit sharing ratio.

(10) The Bombay Company Ltd., was formed to acquire the business of A and B who share profit 2/3 and 1/3 respectively. The Balance Sheet of A and B was as under on 31st December, 1983.

Balance Sheet as on 31-12-1993

		Rs.			Rs.
Bills Payable		7,200	Land and Building		40,000
Sundry Creditors		21,600	Machinery		20,000
Mrs. A's Loan		3,200	Stock		24,000
Capitals :			Sundry Debtors	30,000	
A	64,000		*Less* : R.D.D.	1,400	28,600
B	40,000	1,04,000	Investments		4,800
			Cash at Bank		10,600
			Goodwill		8,000
		1,36,000			1,36,000

It was agreed by the company to take over the assets at book values with the exception of Land and Buildings and Stock which were taken over at Rs. 45,000 and Rs. 20,000 respectively. The investments are retained by the firm and sold by them for Rs. 4,000. They also discharged the loan of Mrs. A. The company takes over the remaining liabilities.

The purchase consideration is fixed at Rs. 1,24,200 payable as follows :

Rs. 45,000 in 5% Debentures at Rs. 90 ; 4,000 Equity shares of Rs. 15 each at a premium of Re. 1 and the balance in cash.

Close the books of the firm by showing Ledger Accounts only. Give Journal entries and a Balance Sheet in the books of Bombay Co. Ltd.

(*B.Com., Gorakhpur, Patna, Sagar & Berhampur*)

Ans. : Realisation Profit : 'A' Rs. 14,000 and 'B' Rs. 7,000

Final payment in Debentures 'A' Rs. 28,080 and 'B' Rs. 16,920

Final payment in Shares 'A' Rs. 39,936 and 'B' Rs. 24,064

Final payment in Cash 'A' Rs. 9,984 and 'B' Rs. 6,016

Balance Sheet Total Rs. 47,400 ; Capital Ratio = 78:47

Goodwill Rs. 28,800 (purchase price Rs. 1,53,000 – 1,24,200 Assets)

Bank Overdraft Rs. 4,600 (15,200 – 10,600)

Number of debentures to be issued = 500 (45,000/90).

(11) Santosh and Prakash were in partnership sharing profits and losses in the ratio of 3 : 1. The following is the balance sheet of the firm as on 31-12-1989 :

Liabilities		Rs.	Assets	Rs.
Capital Accounts :			Fixed Assets	31,500
Santosh	36,000		Stock	16,800
Prakash	12,000	48,000	Debtors	29,400
Current Accounts :			Cash at Bank	5,580
Santosh	6,300			
Prakash	3,000	9,300		
Loan from Prakash		4,500		
Creditors		21,480		
		83,280		83,280

The Prakash Ltd., agreed to take over Stock and Fixed Assets excluding the value of Motor Car Rs. 6,150, for a consideration of Rs. 72,000 which is to be satisfied :

(i) by the payment of cash Rs. 24,000

(ii) by allotment of 240 preference shares of Rs. 100 each valued at Rs. 75 per share, and

(iii) the balance by allotment of 2,400 equity shares of the face value of Rs. 10 each.

The debtors realised Rs. 28,800 and the creditors were settled for Rs. 21,000.

It was agreed between the partners as follows :

(a) Equity shares be allotted in their fixed capital ratio.

(b) Santosh to take over the motor car at an agreed value of Rs. 6,300.

(c) The preference shares be allotted to Prakash to the value of loan amount and the remaining preference shares be allotted to partners equally.

(d) The balance remaining be paid in cash.

Prepare the Realisation Account, Partners' Capital Accounts and Bank Account in the books of the firm and also the statement showing the distribution of shares between the partners.

(K.U.D., Non-Sem., April, 1981)

Ans. : Realisation Profit Rs. 29,880 (*i.e.*, 22,410 + 7,470);
Capital Ratio = 3 : 1.

(12) Amit and Asit were in partnership sharing profits losses : Amit 2/3rd : Asit 1/3rd. The summarised partnership Balance Sheet as on March 31, 1989 was as follows :

Liabilities		Rs.	Assets		Rs.
Fixed Capital :			Fixed Assets		70,000
Amit	50,000		Current Assets :		
Asit	40,000	90,000	Stock	35,000	
Current Accounts :			Debtors	65,000	
Amit	20,000		Balance at Bank	15,000	1,15,000
Less : Asit	10,000	10,000			
Loan—Asit		30,000			
Creditors		55,000			
		1,85,000			1,85,000

The fixed assets included two Motor Cars having book value of Rs. 8,000 and Rs. 6,000 respectively.

The partners desiring to retire from business accepted the offer of Western India Limited to acquire the stock and fixed assets, other than the Motor Cars, at an agreed purchase price of Rs. 1,60,000.

The purchase consideration was to be satisfied by a cash payment of Rs. 56,000, the allotment by the company to the partners of 900 equity shares of Rs. 100 each and the balance by the allotment of 400, 5% preference shares of Rs. 100 each.

The partners agreed that the following should be the basis of distribution on dissolution of the partnership :

(1) Amit to take over one Car at a valuation of Rs. 12,000 and Asit the other at Rs. 8,000.

(2) Asit to be allotted preference shares to the value of his loan the remainder to be allotted to Amit.

(3) The equity shares to be allotted in proportion of fixed capitals.

(4) Both the preference and equity shares to be valued at Rs. 80 per share.

(5) The balance to be settled in cash. You are required to prepare :

(a) the Realisation Account ;

(b) the Bank Account ; and

(c) Partners' Capital Accounts showing the final settlement between them.

(*C.A. Inter*)

Ans. : Realisation Profit : Amit Rs. 50,000 and Asit Rs. 25,000
Purchase consideration Rs. 1,60,000
Final payment : Preference Shares—Amit Rs. 2,000 and Asit Rs. 30,000
Equity Shares—Amit Rs. 40,000 and Asit Rs. 32,000
Bank—Amit Rs. 66,000 and Asit Rs. 15,000.

(13) Teju, Rashmi and Pratibha were in partnership sharing profits and losses in the ratio of 3 : 2 : 1. They decided to convert it into a limited company on the basis of the following Balance Sheet as on 30-6-1988.

Liabilities	Rs.	Assets	Rs.
Capital :		Machinery	8,000
Teju	12,000	Building	13,000
Rashmi	6,000	Furniture	2,000
Pratibha	3,000	Investments	2,500
Loan from Mr. Rashmi	6,000	Debtors	8,500
Bills Payable	5,000	Stock	8,000
Creditors	7,000	Bank	3,000
Profit and Loss Account	6,000		
	45,000		45,000

It was agreed that Rashmi to pay her husband's loan. The company agreed to issue 2,500 equity shares of Rs. 10 each at 20% premium, Rs. 600 in 6% debentures and Rs. 3,000 in cash.

The expenses of dissolution amounted to Rs. 1,500 and were paid by the firm.

The shares and debentures are shared by the partners in the profit sharing ratio and the final settlement was done in cash.

Prepare the necessary accounts to close the books of the firm.

(*Karnatak, April, 1989*)

Ans. : Realisation of profit Rs. 4,500 (2,250 + 1,500 + 750);
Purchased Consideration Rs. 39,000 (30,000 + 6,000 + 3,000);
Shares distributed : Taju—Rs. 15,000, Rashmi—Rs. 10,000 and Pratibha—Rs. 5,000;
Debentures : Taju—Rs. 3,000, Rashmi—Rs. 2,000 and Pratibha—Rs. 1,000;
Cash received from Taju—Rs. 750 and Pratibha—Rs. 1,250;
Cash paid to Rashmi—Rs. 3,500 and Cash Account Total Rs. 5,000.

(14) Ram and Co. Ltd. was formed to take over the running business of M/s Ram and Shyam who shared the profit in the ratio of 3 : 2.

Liabilities		Rs.	Assets	Rs.
Creditors		20,000	Buildings	42,000
Bills Payable		10,000	Machinery	20,000
Mrs. Ram's Loan		4,000	Stock	22,000
Capital Accounts :			Debtors	28,000
Ram	60,000		Investments	5,000
Shyam	40,000	1,00,000	Goodwill	15,000
			Bank	2,000
		1,34,000		1,34,000

The company agreed to take over the assets as under :

Machinery Rs. 15,000 ; Building Rs. 60,000 ; Stock Rs. 20,000 ; Debtors Rs. 25,000 ; Goodwill Rs. 20,000.

The company also agreed to take over the creditors and bills payable at book values.

The firm retained investments and sold them for Rs. 6,000 and paid Mrs. Ram's loan.

The purchase consideration was settled by the issue of 10,000 equity shares of Rs. 10 each and the balance in cash.

Prepare the necessary ledger accounts to close the books of the firm.

(Karnatak, April, 1991)

Ans. : Realisation profit : 14,000 (8,400 + 5,600);
Purchase consideration Rs. 1,10,000 (1,00,000 + 10,000);
Shares distributed : Ram Rs. 60,000 and Shyam Rs. 40,000;
Cash paid to Ram Rs. 8,400 and Shyam Rs. 5,600;
Bank Account Total Rs. 18,000.

Note : Shares are distributed in the profit sharing ratio. They may be distributed in the capital ratio also.

(15) A business known as Kartik Enterprises was sold to Hima Co. Ltd. when their balance sheet appeared as under. The partners Kartik and Ishwar were sharing profits and losses in the ratio of 3 : 2.

Liabilities		Rs.	Assets	Rs.
Capital Accounts :			Cash in Hand	18,000
Kartik	3,00,000		Closing Stock	1,48,000
Ishwar	2,00,000	5,00,000	Plant and Machinery	3,40,000
Sundry Creditors		2,00,000	Investments	82,000
Bank Overdraft		20,000	Sundry Debtors	1,60,000
Reserve Fund		28,000		
		7,48,000		7,48,000

The business was sold on the following conditions :

(1) The company was to take over the whole concern except cash and investments at 10% less than the book value.
(2) The creditors were taken over at book value.
(3) Ishwar agreed to pay bank overdraft with an interest of Rs. 600.
(4) The Hima Co. Ltd. agreed to pay Rs. 20,000 towards Goodwill.
(5) The purchase price was paid half in cash and the remaining half in fully paid Rs. 10 shares of the company.

The firm sold its own investments and the shares at 5% less. The realisation expenses amounted to Rs. 2,000.

Prepare the necessary ledger accounts in the books of the firm.

(Gulbarga, Oct., 1988 & Mysore, 1992)

Ans. : Realisation loss Rs. 61,580 (36,948 + 24,632); Purchased consideration : 4,03,200 (Shares—2,01,600 + Cash—2,01,600) (6,48,000 – 64,800 = 5,83,200 + 20,000 – 2,00,000); Cash Paid to Kartik Rs. 2,79,852 and Ishwar Rs. 2,07,168; Cash Account Total : 4,89,020.

(16) Anand and Bushan carrying on business in partnership resolve to dissolve the firm and sell off the business to 'C' Co. Ltd. on 31st December, 1990, when the position was as under :

Liabilities	Rs.	Assets	Rs.
Capitals :		Land	40,000
Anand	34,000	Furniture	3,320
Bushan	17,000	Stock	15,380
Sundry Creditors	21,250	Debtors	8,430
		Cash	5,120
	72,250		72,250

The arrangement with the company was as follows :

(a) Land purchased at Rs. 50,000.
(b) Furniture and stock are taken at 10% below the book value.
(c) Goodwill of the firm is valued at Rs. 7,500.
(d) Debtors are taken at Rs. 8,000. But the creditors at the balance sheet figure.
(e) The purchase consideration is to be discharged by the company in fully paid equity shares of Rs. 10 each.

Show the Realisation Account and Capital Accounts of the firm assuming that the shares are duly received from the company and paid off to the partners.

(Bangalore, April, 1991)

Ans. : Realisation Profit : Anand Rs. 7,600 and Bushan Rs. 7,600; Purchase consideration Rs. 61,080 (Assets Rs. 82,330 – Liabilities Rs. 21,250);
Final Payment : In Shares : Anand Rs. 38,380 and Bushan Rs. 22,700
In Cash : Anand Rs. 3,220 & Bushan Rs. 1,900.

Hints : (i) Cash is not taken over by the company. Hence, it is not included in the purchase consideration.
(ii) Shares are distributed in the capital ratio *i.e.*, 416 : 246 or 208:123.

(17) Madhav and Govind are partners sharing profits in the ratio 2 : 1 and their Balance Sheet on 31-12-1988 was as follows :

Liabilities	Rs.	Assets		Rs.
Creditors	20,000	Cash in Hand		150
Bills Payable	5,000	Bills Receivable		2,500
Madhav's Loan	10,000	Debtors	30,000	
Govind's Capital	10,000	*Less* : Reserve	1,500	28,500
Madhav's Capital	15,000	Stock		21,850
Reserve Fund	3,000	Machinery		10,000
	63,000			63,000

They agreed to sell the business to a Ltd. Co., and the Co. to take over the assets and liabilities as follows :

Machinery at Rs. 8,000 ; Stock at Rs. 17,500 ; Debtors at Rs. 25,350 ; Bills Receivable at Rs. 2,500 and Goodwill at Rs. 3,000. The company agreed to take over creditors at Rs. 19,500. The expenses of realisation amounted to Rs. 150. The firm received Rs. 20,000 of the purchase price in Rs. 10 fully paid equity shares and the balance in cash.

Prepare necessary ledger accounts in the books of the firm.

(*Bangalore, May, 1992*)

Ans. : Realisation loss : Madhav Rs. 4,100 and Govind Rs. 2,050; Purchase consideration Rs. 32,000 (Cash Rs. 20,000 and Shares Rs. 12,000) ;
Final payments : In Shares : Madhav Rs. 12,370 and Govind Rs. 7,630 ;
In Cash : Madhav Rs. 530 and Govind Rs. 1,320.

Notes : (i) It is assumed that cash and bills payable are taken over by the purchasing company.
(ii) Shares are distributed among the partners in the capital ratio *i.e.*, 12,900 : 8,950 or 86 : 53.

(18) The Balance Sheet of A, B and C stood as follows, as on 31st December, 1988 :

Liabilities		Rs.	Assets		Rs.
Creditors		20,000	Cash at Bank		9,000
Bills Payable		5,000	Debtors	25,000	
Capital Accounts :			*Less* : R.D.D.	2,000	23,000
A	24,000		Stock		26,000
B	24,000		Machinery		19,000
C	14,000	62,000	Furniture		10,000
		87,000			87,000

It was decided to sell the business to PQR Co. Ltd. agreeing to allot 7,500 fully paid shares of Rs. 10 each and Rs. 1,800 in cash in full satisfaction of the purchase consideration. The company assumed the liabilities except the bills payable and took over all the assets except the bank balance. The expenses amounted to Rs. 800 which were paid by the firm itself. The partners shared profits and losses in 1/2, 1/3rd and 1/6th ratio respectively. 1/4th of the shares were sold at Rs. 8 per share and 1/3rd of the remaining shares were taken by B at Rs. 9 per share.

Pass the necessary journal entries to close the books of the firm.

Also prepare the necessary accounts showing the final settlement among the partners.

(*Bangalore, November, 1993*)

Ans. : Realisation profit : A Rs. 9,000 ; B Rs. 6,000 and C Rs. 3,000
Purchase consideration Rs. 76,800 (shares Rs. 75,000 + cash Rs. 1,800)
Loss on 1/4 shares at Rs. 2 per share : Rs. 3,750 (1,875 × 2)
Loss on 1/3rd of the remaining shares at Re. 1 per share : Rs. 1,875 (1,875 × 1)
Loss on sale of shares in the capital ratio : A—Rs. 2,320; B—Rs. 2,109; C—Rs. 1,196
Final payment : In Shares : A—Rs. 15,470 ; B—Rs. 14,060 and C—Rs. 7,970.
In Cash : A—Rs. 15,210 and C—Rs. 7,834.

Hints : (i) 3,750 shares of Rs. 10 each are distributed in the capital ratio of 33 : 30 : 17.

(ii) Cash brought in by B—Rs. 3,044 and shares in PQR Co. Ltd., A/c Total—Rs. 75,000.

(19) Ram, Rahim and Robert were in partnership sharing profit and losses in the ratio of 4 : 3 : 1 respectively. On 31st March, 1993, they agreed to sell their business to a Limited company. Their position on that date was as follows :

Liabilities	Rs.	Assets	Rs.
Capital Accounts :		Freehold Property	36,000
Ram	40,000	Machinery	24,000
Rahim	30,000	Book Debts	30,000
Robert	26,000	Stock	26,000
Loan from Bank	8,000	Cash	4,000
Sundry Creditors	16,000		
	1,20,000		1,20,000

The company took the following assets at the valuation shown :

Freehold property Rs. 44,000; Machinery Rs. 22,000; Book Debts Rs. 28,000; Stock Rs. 24,000 and Goodwill Rs. 8,000. The company also agreed to pay the creditors, which was agreed at Rs. 15,400. The company paid Rs. 3,300 shares of Rs. 10 each fully paid and the balance in cash. The expenses amounted to Rs. 1,000.

Prepare Realisation A/c, Cash A/c and Capital Accounts in the books of the firm.

Also pass the journal entries in the books of Purchasing Co. and prepare the Balance Sheet as on that date of purchase of business.

(Bangalore, April, 1994)

Ans. : Realisation Profit : Ram Rs. 4,800; Rahim Rs. 3,600 and Robert Rs. 1,200

Purchase consideration under net assets method Rs. 1,10,600

Final Payment : In Shares : Ram Rs. 14,000; Rahim Rs. 10,500 and Robert Rs. 8,500

In Cash : Ram Rs. 30,800; Rahim Rs. 23,100 and Robert Rs. 18,700

Capital Ratio : 28 : 21 : 17; Bank overdraft Rs. 77,600 and Balance Sheet Total : Rs. 1,26,000.

Notes : (i) Shares are distributed in the final capital claim ratio.

(ii) As the other details are not available, whatever cash is paid to the vendor firm is assumed to be 'Bank Overdraft'.

(20) David and Eshwar sharing profits and losses equally decided to convert their business into Limited Company on 31st Dec., 1990. When their balance sheet stood as follows :

Liabilities	Rs.	Assets	Rs.
Sundry Creditors	24,000	Cash	33,000
Loan Creditors	20,000	Debtors	7,000
Bank Overdraft	8,000	Bills Receivable	5,000
Reserve Fund	3,000	Stock	8,000
Capitals :		Patents	4,000
David	20,000	Machinery	8,000
Eshwar	20,000	Land and Buildings	30,000
	95,000		95,000

The company has agreed to base the purchase consideration on the following :

(i) The goodwill of the firm will be valued at two years' purchase of the average profits of the previous three years. Profit in 1987—Rs. 18,000; in 1988—Rs. 21,000 and in 1989—Rs. 21,000.

(ii) The company will take over the loan creditors by offering 9% preference shares; the company will not take over the sundry creditors and the overdraft.

(iii) Land and buildings will be valued at Rs. 50,000 and machinery at Rs. 12,000 and all other assets taken (except cash) valued at their book values.

(iv) The vendor to be allotted ordinary shares of Rs. 10 each to the amount equivalent to the purchase consideration. You are required to show the Realisation Account and Capital Accounts of partners in the books of the firm.

Also show the Journal Entries in the books of the purchasing company and prepare the Opening Balance Sheet.

(*Bangalore, Oct., 1991 & April, 1995*)

Ans. : Realisation Profit : David—Rs. 32,000 and Eshwar—Rs. 32,000; Purchase consideration : Rs. 1,06,000 and Goodwill Rs. 40,000; Final Payments : In Shares : David Rs. 53,000 and Eshwar Rs. 53,000 In Cash : Devid Rs. 500 and Eshwar Rs. 500; Share Capital : Rs. 1,26,000 (Equity Rs. 1,06,000 + Preference Rs. 20,000) and Balance Sheet Total Rs. 1,26,000.

Hints : (i) Cash, Sundry Creditors and Bank Overdraft are not taken over by the purchasing company. Hence, Sundry Creditors and Bank Overdraft are paid out of cash available.

(ii) Loan creditors are discharged by the issue of company's 9% preference shares.

(21) Ram Kumar and Prem Kumar are partners sharing profits and losses in the ratio of 2 : 1 and their Balance Sheet as on 31-12-1997 was as follows :

Liabilities	Rs.	Assets		Rs.
Creditors	40,000	Cash in Hand		300
Bills Payable	10,000	Bills Receivable		5,000
Ram Kumar's Loan	20,000	Debtors	60,000	
Ram Kumar's Capital	30,000	*Less* : Reserve	3,000	57,000
Prem Kumar's Capital	20,000	Stock		43,700
Reserve Fund	6,000	Machinery		20,000
	1,26,000			1,26,000

They agreed to sell the business to a Limited company and the company to take over the assets and liabilities as follows :

Machinery at Rs. 16,000, Stock at Rs. 35,000, Debtors at Rs. 50,700, B/R at Rs. 5,000 and Goodwill at Rs. 6,000. The Company agreed to take over Creditors at Rs. 38,000 and B/P at Rs. 10,000. The expenses of realisation amounted to Rs. 300. The firm received Rs. 40,000 of the purchase price in Rs. 10 fully paid equity shares and balance in cash. Distribute the shares as per original capital ratio. Prepare the necessary ledger accounts in the books of the firm.

(*Bangalore, April, 1998*)

Ans. : Realisation Loss : Ram Kumar Rs. 7,533 and Prem Kumar Rs. 3,767

Purchase consideration Rs. 64,700 (Cash Rs. 24,700 + Shares Rs. 40,000)

Final Payments : In Shares : R. Kumar Rs. 24,000 and P. Kumar Rs. 16,000

In Cash : R. Kumar Rs. 22,467 and P. Kumar Rs. 2,233

Notes : (i) Shares are distributed among the partners in the capital ratio of 3 : 2.

(ii) Realisation A/c Total Rs. 1,29,000 and Cash A/c Total Rs. 25,000.

6

AMALGAMATION OF FIRMS

Meaning

When the two or more existing business units which are carrying on similar type of business may combine themselves to form a new firm, it is called amalgamation. Two or more firms working separately may decide to carry on their business jointly as one firm. In such cases, the books of accounts of old firm are closed and the new set of books of accounts are opened for recording all assets and liabilities under agreed valuations of each firm.

Purposes

The main objects of amalgamation are :

(i) to have more capital and skill.

(ii) to have internal and external economies of large scale production.

(iii) to avoid cut-throat competition.

(iv) to eliminate unnecessary expenditure in the nature of fixed charges.

(v) to expand business and get more profit.

Accounting Procedure

Following is the accounting procedure to be followed on amalgamation :

(A) Accounting Treatment in the Books of Amalgamating Firms (*i.e.*, old firms)

Following entries are to be passed to close the books of old firms :

(1) Revaluation of assets and liabilities : As per the agreement the assets and liabilities of the old firms will be revalued. Any increase in the value of assets and decrease in the value of liabilities is credited to the revaluation account and any decrease and increase in the value is debited to the revaluation account. The profit or loss shown by revaluation account is transferred to the capital accounts of the partners of that firm in their old profit sharing ratio.

(i) Entry for increase in the value of assets and decrease in the value of liabilities :

Assets Account	Dr.	With the amount of increase.
Liabilities Account	Dr.	With the amount of decrease.
To Revaluation Account		With the amount of above two debit items.

(ii) Entry for decrease in the value of assets and increase in the value of liabilities :

Revaluation Account	Dr.	With the total amount of below two credit items.
To Assets Account		With the amount of increase.
To Liabilities Account		With the amount of decrease.

(iii) Entry for transfer of profit on revaluation :

Revaluation Account	Dr.	With the amount of
To Partners' Capital A/cs		net profit.

Note : If there is a loss (*i.e.*, debit balance) a reverse entry is to be passed.

(2) Any asset not taken over by the new firm : If any asset is not taken over by the new firm, its agreed value is transferred to the capital accounts of partners. If any asset is taken over by only one partner it should be transferred to his capital account only.

Entry for assets not taken over by the new firm :

Partners' Capital Accounts	Dr.	With an agreed value
To Assets Account		of assets.

(3) Any liability not taken over by the new firm : If any liability is not taken over by the new firm, its agreed value is either paid or transferred to the capital accounts of partners. The entry in this case is :

(i) If the value of liability is paid in cash :

Liabilities Accounts	Dr.	With the amount of
To Cash or Bank Account		actually paid.

(ii) If the value of liability is transferred to partners :

Liabilities Accounts	Dr.	With agreed value of
To Partners' Capital Accounts		liabilities.

(4) Assets and liabilities taken over by the new firm : When assets and liabilities are taken over by the new firm, the agreed value of assets and liabilities are to be transferred to the new firm. The journal entry in this case is :

New Firm Account	Dr.	Balancing figure amount.
Each Liability (taken over) A/c	Dr.	Revalued amount of liability.
To Each Asset (taken over) A/c		Revalued amount of assets.

Note : Balancing figure represents Assets minus Liabilities taken over.

(5) Reserve and undistributed profits : If there are reserve fund accumulated profit etc., in the Balance Sheet of the firms, they are to be transferred to the capital accounts of the partners. The journal entry in this case is :

Reserve Fund Account	Dr.	With the amount
Profit and Loss Account	Dr.	reserve/profit.
To Partners' Capital A/cs		

Note : If there is loss, a reversed entry is to be passed.

(6) Goodwill : The value of goodwill of each firm will be ascertained and the amount of goodwill will be transferred to their respective partners' capital accounts in their old profit sharing proportion. The journal entry in this case is :

Goodwill Account	Dr.	With the amount of
To Partners' Capital Accounts		goodwill.

Note : If the amount of goodwill is given in the balance sheet, only increased amount of goodwill should be taken. If there is decrease in the amount of goodwill, a reverse entry is to be passed for the above entry.

(7) Transfer of partners' capitals : Finally capital accounts will be closed. The balances remaining in the capital accounts after making above adjustments are to be transferred to the new firms account. The journal entry for this will be :

Partners' Capital Accounts	Dr.	With the final balance
To New Firm Account		of capitals.

(B) Accounting Treatment in the Books of New Firm

When the new firm takes over the assets and liabilities, the opening entries are required to be passed. They are as follows :

(1) For incorporating the assets and liabilities :

Assets (taken over) Accounts	Dr.	With revalued amount.
To Liabilities (taken over) Accounts		With revalued amount.
To Partners' Capital Accounts		With amount of capital balances.

(2) For writing off goodwill, if required :

Partners' Capital Accounts	Dr.	With the amount of
To Goodwill Account		goodwill.
(In the new profit sharing ratio)		

Note : In this case, goodwill account will not appear in the amalgamated Balance Sheet.

(3) For Adjustment Capital, if required :

(i) For further contribution of capital by the partners in case of deficiency :

Bank or Cash Account	Dr.	With the amount of
To Partners' Capital Accounts		brought in.

(ii) For excess capital withdrawn by the partners :

Partners' Capital Accounts	Dr.	With the amount
To Bank or Cash Account		paid out.

(iii) For excess capital of partners transferred to their current accounts:

Partners' Capital Accounts	Dr.	With the amount
To Partners' Current Accounts		transferred.

(iv) For deficiency transferred to the partners' current accounts :

Partners' Current Accounts	Dr.	With the amount
To Partners' Capital Accounts		transferred.

After passing the above opening entries, amalgamated balance sheet or opening balance sheet of the new firm will be prepared.

Illustration 1

The following are the Balance Sheets of M/s Reena and Radha who shared profits and losses in the ratio of 3 : 2 and M/s Asha and Chaya who shared in the ratio of 2 : 1.

Liabilities	Reena & Radha Rs.	Asha & Chaya Rs.	Assets	Reena & Radha Rs.	Asha & Chaya Rs.
Creditors	10,000	15,000	Buildings	50,000	40,000
Bills Payable	6,000	4,000	Machinery	12,000	8,000
Bank Loan	4,000	—	Furniture	6,000	5,000
Reserves	5,000	3,000	Investments	10,000	2,000
Capitals :			Stock	12,000	4,000
Reena	50,000	—	Debtors	9,000	7,000
Radha	40,000	—	Bills Receivable	13,000	—
Asha	—	30,000	Cash in Hand	3,000	1,000
Chaya	—	15,000			
	1,15,000	67,000		1,15,000	67,000

Both the firms decided to amalgamate their business on 1-1-1992. The terms of amalgamation were as follows :

(i) The new firm was to take over all assets and liabilities of both the firms.

(ii) The assets of Reena and Radha were valued as under :
Buildings Rs. 60,000; Machinery Rs. 10,000; Furniture Rs. 5,000; Investments and Stock at book values; Debtors Rs. 8,000; Bills Receivable Rs. 12,000 and Goodwill Rs. 10,000.

(iii) The assets of Asha and Chaya were valued as under :
Buildings Rs. 50,000; Machinery Rs. 7,000; Furniture and Investments at book values; Stock Rs. 3,000; Debtors Rs. 6,500 and Goodwill Rs. 7,500.

(iv) The new profit sharing ratio of Reena, Radha, Asha and Chaya was 3 : 3 : 2 : 2.

Pass the journal entries and show the necessary accounts in the books of both the firms and also pass the opening entries in the books of the firm and prepare the amalgamated balance sheet.

Solution :

In the Books of M/s Reena and Radha
Journal Entries

Sl. No.	Particulars		Debit Rs.	Credit Rs.
1.	Reserves Account	Dr.	5,000	
	To Reena's Capital A/c			3,000
	To Radha's Capital A/c			2,000
	(Being transfer of reserves)			
2.	Goodwill Account	Dr.	10,000	
	To Reena's Capital A/c			6,000
	To Radha's Capital A/c			4,000
	(Being goodwill raised in the books)			
3.	Revaluation Account	Dr.	5,000	
	To Machinery			2,000
	To Furniture			1,000
	To Debtors			1,000
	To Bills Receivable			1,000
	(Being decrease in the value of assets)			

Contd.

Sl. No.	Particulars	Debit Rs.	Credit Rs.
4.	Buildings Account Dr.	10,000	
	To Revaluation A/c		10,000
	(Being increase in the value of buildings)		
5.	Revaluation Account Dr.	5,000	
	To Reena's Capital A/c		3,000
	To Radha's Capital A/c		2,000
	(Being profit transferred to partners' capital accounts)		
6.	New Firm Account Dr.	1,30,000	
	To Buildings		60,000
	To Machinery		10,000
	To Furniture		5,000
	To Investments		10,000
	To Stock		12,000
	To Debtors		8,000
	To Bills Receivable		12,000
	To Cash in Hand		3,000
	To Goodwill		10,000
	(Being assets transferred at new values)		
7.	Creditors Dr.	10,000	
	Bills Payable Dr.	6,000	
	Bank Loan Dr.	4,000	
	To New Firm A/c		20,000
	(Being liabilities transferred)		
8.	Reena's Capital Account Dr.	62,000	
	Radha's Capital Account Dr.	48,000	
	To New Firm A/c		1,10,000
	(Being capital balance transferred)		

Dr. **Revaluation Account** Cr.

		Rs.		Rs.
To Machinery		2,000	By Buildings	10,000
To Furniture		1,000		
To Debtors		1,000		
To Bills Receivable		1,000		
To Capital Accounts :				
(Profit transferred)				
Reena	3,000			
Radha	2,000	5,000		
		10,000		10,000

Dr. **Partners' Capital Account** Cr.

Particulars	Reena Rs.	Radha Rs.	Particulars	Reena Rs.	Radha Rs.
To New Firm	62,000	48,000	By Balance b/d	50,000	40,000
(Balance transferred)			By Reserves	3,000	2,000
			By Goodwill	6,000	4,000
			By Revaluation Profit	3,000	2,000
	62,000	48,000		62,000	48,000

Dr. **New Firm's Account** Cr.

	Rs.		Rs.
To Buildings	60,000	By Creditors	10,000
To Machinery	10,000	By Bills Payable	6,000
To Furniture	5,000	By Bank Loan	4,000
To Investments	10,000	By Reena's Capital	62,000
To Stock	12,000	By Radha's Capital	48,000
To Debtors	8,000		
To Bills Receivable	12,000		
To Cash in Hand	3,000		
To Goodwill	10,000		
	1,30,000		1,30,000

In the books of M/s Asha and Chaya
Journal Entries

Sl. No.	Particulars	Debit Rs.	Credit Rs.
1.	Reserves Account Dr.	3,000	
	To Asha's Capital A/c		2,000
	To Chaya's Capital A/c		1,000
	(Being transfer of reserves)		
2.	Goodwill Account Dr.	7,500	
	To Asha's Capital A/c		5,000
	To Chaya's Capital A/c		2,500
	(Being goodwill raised in the books of partners)		
3.	Building Account Dr.	10,000	
	To Revaluation Account		10,000
	(Being increase in the value of buildings)		
4.	Revaluation Account Dr.	2,500	
	To Machinery		1,000
	To Stock		1,000
	To Debtors		500
	(Being decrease in the value of assets)		
5.	Revaluation Account Dr.	7,500	
	To Asha's Capital Account		5,000
	To Chaya's Capital Account		2,500
	(Being revaluation profit transferred)		
6.	New Firm Account Dr.	82,000	
	To Buildings		50,000
	To Machinery		7,000
	To Furniture		5,000
	To Investments		2,000
	To Stock		3,000
	To Debtors		6,500
	To Cash in Hand		1,000
	To Goodwill		7,500
	(Being assets transferred at new values)		

Contd.

7.	Creditors' Account Dr.	15,000	
	Bills Payable Account Dr.	4,000	
	To New Firm Account		19,000
	(Being liabilities transferred)		
8.	Asha's Capital Account Dr.	42,000	
	Chaya's Capital Account Dr.	21,000	
	To New Firm A/c		63,000
	(Being capitals transferred)		

Revaluation Account

Dr. Cr.

		Rs.		Rs.
To Machinery		1,000	By Buildings	10,000
To Stock		1,000		
To Debtors		500		
To Capital Accounts : (Profit transferred)				
Asha	5,000			
Chaya	2,500	7,500		
		10,000		10,000

Partners' Capital Accounts

Dr. Cr.

Particulars	Asha Rs.	Chaya Rs.	Particulars	Asha Rs.	Chaya Rs.
To New Firm (Balance transferred)	42,000	21,000	By Balance b/d	30,000	15,000
			By Reserves	2,000	1,000
			By Goodwill	5,000	2,500
			By Revaluation Profit	5,000	2,500
	42,000	21,000		42,000	21,000

New Firm's Account

Dr. Cr.

	Rs.		Rs.
To Buildings	50,000	By Creditors	15,000
To Machinery	7,000	By Bills Payable	4,000
To Furniture	5,000	By Asha's Capital	42,000
To Investments	2,000	By Chaya's Capital	21,000
To Stock	3,000		
To Debtors	6,500		
To Cash in Hand	1,000		
To Goodwill	7,500		
	82,000		82,000

In the books of New Firm
Opening Entries

Sl. No.	Particulars		Debit Rs.	Credit Rs.
1.	Building Account	Dr.	60,000	
	Machinery Account	Dr.	10,000	
	Furniture Account	Dr.	5,000	
	Investments Account	Dr.	10,000	
	Stock Account	Dr.	12,000	
	Debtors Account	Dr.	8,000	
	Bills Receivable Account	Dr.	12,000	
	Cash in Hand Account	Dr.	3,000	
	Goodwill Account	Dr.	10,000	
	To Creditors Account			10,000
	To Bills Payable Account			6,000
	To Bank Loan Account			4,000
	To Reena's Capital Account			62,000
	To Radha's Capital Account			48,000
	(Being the incorporation of assets and liabilities taken over from M/s Reena and Radha)			
2.	Building Account	Dr.	50,000	
	Machinery Account	Dr.	7,000	
	Furniture Account	Dr.	5,000	
	Investments Account	Dr.	2,000	
	Stock Account	Dr.	3,000	
	Debtors Account	Dr.	6,500	
	Cash in Hand Account	Dr.	1,000	
	Goodwill Account	Dr.	7,500	
	To Creditors Account			15,000
	To Bills Payable Account			4,000
	To Asha's Capital Account			42,000
	To Chaya's Capital Account			21,000
	(Being incorporation of assets and liabilities taken over from M/s Asha and Chaya)			

Amalgamated Balance Sheet of New Firm as on 1-1-1992

Liabilities		Rs.	Assets	Rs.
Capitals :			Goodwill (10,000 + 7,500)	17,500
Reena	62,000		Buildings (60,000 + 50,000)	1,10,000
Radha	48,000		Machinery (10,000 + 7,000)	17,000
Asha	42,000		Furniture (5,000 + 5,000)	10,000
Chaya	21,000	1,73,000	Investments (10,000 + 2,000)	12,000
Creditors (10,000 + 15,000)		25,000	Stock (12,000 + 3,000)	15,000
Bills Payable (6,000 + 4,000)		10,000	Bills Receivable	12,000
Bank Loan		4,000	Debtors (8,000 + 6,500)	14,500
			Cash in Hand (3,000 + 1,000)	4,000
		2,12,000		2,12,000

Illustration 2

M/s A & B and M/s C & D agreed to amalgamate their business. Their position as on 31-12-1992 was as follows :

Balance Sheet of M/s A & B as on 31-12-1992

Liabilities		Rs.	Assets	Rs.
Creditors		8,000	Machinery	10,000
Reserves		4,000	Furniture	4,000
A's Loan		2,000	Debtors	6,000
Capitals :			Stock	15,000
A	15,000		Cash	9,000
B	15,000	30,000		
		44,000		44,000

Balance Sheet of M/s C & D as on 31-12-1992

Liabilities		Rs.	Assets		Rs.
Creditors		10,000	Buildings		15,000
Bills Payable		5,000	Furniture		4,000
Outstanding Expenses		1,000	Stock		8,000
Capitals :			Debtors	3,000	
C	18,000		*Less* : Provision	100	2,900
D	12,000	30,000	Bills Receivable		13,000
			Cash		3,100
		46,000			46,000

The terms of amalgamation are as follows :

(i) The goodwill of A & B is valued at Rs. 8,000 and that of C & D at Rs. 12,000.

(ii) The stock and furniture of both the firms were to be reduced by 10%.

(iii) The machinery of A & B is not to be taken over by the new firm.

(iv) The building of C & D is to be valued at Rs. 18,000.

(v) The provision of doubtful debts is to be made at 5% on the debtors of both the firms.

(vi) The loan of 'A' and the outstanding expenses are to be paid off by the respective firms and are not to be brought into the new firm.

(vii) A and B shared profits equally and C and D in the ratio of 3 : 2 in their respective old firms. But in the new firm they should be shared equally.

(viii) The capital of new firm is to be Rs. 68,000 to be contributed by the partners equally and any difference in capital is to be brought in or withdrawn in cash.

Close the books of old firms and prepare the balance sheet of the new firm.

Solution :

In the Books of M/s A & B

Revaluation Account

Dr. Cr.

	Rs.			Rs.
To Stock	1,500	By Capital Accounts :		
To Furniture	400	(Loss transferred)		
To Reserve for Doubtful Debts	300	A	1,100	
		B	1,100	2,200
	2,200			2,200

Partners' Capital Account

Dr. Cr.

Particulars	A Rs.	B Rs.	Particulars	A Rs.	B Rs.
To Revaluation Loss	1,100	1,100	By Balance b/d	15,000	15,000
To Machinery	5,000	5,000	By Goodwill	4,000	4,000
To New Firm (balance transferred)	17,000	17,000	By Reserves	2,000	2,000
			By Bank	2,100	2,100
	23,100	23,100		23,100	23,100

In the Books of M/s C & D

Revaluation Account

Dr.	Rs.	Rs.		Cr. Rs.
To Stock		800	By Buildings	3,000
To Furniture		400		
To Reserve for Doubtful Debts (Increase of bed debts)		50		
To Capital Accounts : (Profit transferred)				
C	1,050			
D	700	1,750		
		3,000		3,000

Partners' Capital Accounts

Dr. Particulars	C Rs.	D Rs.	Particulars	C Rs.	D Rs. (Cr.)
To Bank	9,250	500	By Balance b/d	18,000	12,000
To New Firm (Balance transferred)	17,000	17,000	By Goodwill	7,200	4,800
			By Revaluation Profit	1,050	700
	26,250	17,500		26,250	17,500

Cash Account

Dr.	Rs.		Cr. Rs.
To Balance b/d (3,100 + 9,000)	12,100	By A's Loan	2,000
		By Outstanding Expenses	1,000
To A's Capital A/c	2,100	By C's Capital A/c	9,250
To B's Capital A/c	2,100	By D's Capital A/c	500
		By Balance c/d	3,550
	16,300		16,300

Balance Sheet of New Firm

Liabilities		Rs.	Assets		Rs.
Creditors		18,000	Goodwill		20,000
Bills Payable		5,000	Buildings		18,000
Capitals :			Furniture		7,200
A	17,000		Stock		20,700
B	17,000		Bills Receivable		13,000
C	17,000		Debtors	9,000	
D	17,000	68,000	*Less* : Provision	450	8,550
			Cash		3,550
		91,000			91,000

Illustration 3

Two firms P & Q and R & S carrying on a similar business, agreed on an amalgamation as from 1-1-1992 on which date their respective balance sheets were as follows :

Balance Sheet of M/s P & Q as on 1-1-1992

Liabilities		Rs.	Assets	Rs.
Creditors		26,000	Bank	11,200
Bills Payable		10,000	Stock	40,800
Mr. P's Loan		10,000	Debtors	30,000
Capital Accounts :			Furniture	1,000
P	80,000		Bills Receivable	3,000
Q	40,000	1,20,000	Premises	80,000
		1,66,000		1,66,000

Balance Sheet of M/s R & S as on 1-1-1992

Liabilities		Rs.	Assets	Rs.
Creditors		29,000	Bank	13,400
Bank Loan		15,000	Stock	36,600
Capital Accounts :			Debtors	40,000
R	48,000		Furniture	2,000
S	32,000	80,000	Bills Receivable	2,000
			Investments	30,000
		1,24,000		1,24,000

It was mutually agreed that Mrs. P's loan be repaid and that the investments of M/s R & S not to be taken over by the new firm. Premises were revalued at Rs. 1,00,000 but the stock of M/s P & Q was found under valued by Rs. 8,000. The stock of M/s R & S was over valued by Rs. 4,000.

Goodwill of M/s P & Q was fixed at Rs. 16,000 and that of M/s R & S at Rs. 20,000. A reserve of 5% was created for bad debts of both the firms.

The total capital of the new firm was to be Rs. 1,60,000 and the capital of each partner was to be in his profit sharing ratio which was to be 3 : 2 : 3 : 2. Goodwill Account in the new firm was to be written off.

Show the revaluation account and capital accounts in the books of the old firms and the balance sheet of the new firm.

Solution :

In the Books of M/s P & Q

Revaluation Account

Dr.		Rs.		Cr. Rs.
To Stock		8,000	By Premises	20,000
To Reserve for Doubtful Debts		1,500		
To Capital Accounts : (Profit transferred)				
P	5,250			
Q	5,250	10,500		
		20,000		20,000

Partners' Capital Accounts

Dr. Particulars	P Rs.	Q Rs.	Particulars	P Rs.	Q Rs. Cr.
To New Firm (Balance transferred)	93,250	53,250	By Balance b/d	80,000	40,000
			By Goodwill	8,000	8,000
			By Revaluation Profit	5,250	5,250
	93,250	53,250		93,250	53,250

In the Books of M/s R & S

Revaluation Account

Dr.		Rs.		Cr. Rs.
To Reserve for Doubtful Debts		2,000	By Stock	4,000
To Capital Accounts : (Profit transferred)				
R	1,000			
S	1,000	2,000		
		4,000		4,000

Partners' Capital Accounts

Dr. Particulars	R Rs.	S Rs..	Particulars	R Rs.	S Rs. Cr.
To Investments	15,000	15,000	By Balance b/d	48,000	32,000
To New Firm (Balance transferred)	44,000	28,000	By Goodwill	10,000	10,000
			By Revaluation Profit	1,000	1,000
	59,000	43,000		59,000	43,000

Balance Sheet of New Firm

Liabilities		Rs.	Assets		Rs.
Creditors		55,000	Bank (11,200 +13,400–10,000)		14,600
Bills Payable		10,000	Premises (80,000 + 20,000)		1,00,000
Bank Loan		15,000	Furniture (1,000 + 2,000)		3,000
Capital Accounts :			Stock (32,000 + 40,600)		73,400
P	48,000		Debtors	70,000	
Q	32,000		*Less:* R.D.D.	3,500	66,500
R	48,000		Bills Receivable (3,000+2,000)		5,000
S	32,000	1,60,000	Current Accounts :		
Current Accounts :			R	14,800	
P	34,450		S	11,200	26,000
Q	14,050	48,500			
		2,88,500			2,88,500

Dr. **Partners' Capital Accounts** Cr.

Particulars	P Rs.	Q Rs.	R Rs.	S Rs.	Particulars	P Rs.	Q Rs.	R Rs.	S Rs.
To Goodwill	10,800	7,200	10,800	7,200	By Balance b/d	93,250	53,250	44,000	28,000
To Current A/c	34,450	14,050	—	—	By Current A/c	—	—	14,800	11,200
To Balance c/d	48,000	32,000	48,000	32,000					
	93,250	53,250	58,800	39,200		93,250	53,250	58,800	39,200

Illustration 4

The following were the balance sheets of the firms M/s Kumar and Radha and M/s Sunil and Sudha on 31-12-1983, when they decided to amalgamate their business :

Liabilities	Kumar & Radha Rs.	Sunil & Sudha Rs.	Assets		Kumar & Radha Rs.	Sunil & Sudha Rs.
Creditors	24,000	54,000	Cash at Bank		12,000	10,000
Bills Payable	12,000	—	Bills Receivable		—	10,000
Reserves	18,000	—	Debtors	56,000		
Capitals :			*Less*: Provision	4,000	52,000	40,000
Kumar	50,000	—	Stock		30,000	40,000
Radha	40,000	—	Premises		50,000	—
Sunil	—	60,000	Furniture		—	12,000
Sudha	—	40,000	Motor Vans		—	24,000
			Goodwill		—	18,000
	1,44,000	1,54,000			1,44,000	1,54,000

(a) The new firm was to take over the assets and liabilities of both the firms subject to Kumar and Radha meeting their bills payable out of their bank balance.

(b) Kumar and Radha's assets were valued as : Debtors Rs. 50,000; Stock Rs. 26,000; Premises Rs. 60,000 and Goodwill Rs. 20,000.

(c) Sunil and Sudha's assets were valued as : Debtors Rs. 36,000; Stock Rs. 36,000; Furniture Rs. 10,000 and Goodwill Rs. 16,000.

(d) Sunil took the motor vans at an agreed value of Rs. 20,000.

(e) Sunil and Sudha to be credited with Rs. 10,000 being the value of patent rights which were not included in their balance sheet.

(f) The capital of the partners in the new firm were fixed at Rs. 40,000 each. Any excess or deficiency was to be transferred to the current accounts of partners.

(g) It was decided that the new firm should not maintain goodwill balance in the books.

(h) Kumar and Radha shared profits equally, and Sunil and Sudha in the ratio of 3 : 2 in their old firms. But in the new firm they shared in their capital ratio.

Show the necessary accounts in the books of M/s Kumar and Radha and M/s Sunil and Sudha and the balance sheet of the new firm.

(Bombay, B.Com. and Gulbarga, B.Com., Oct., 1983)

In the Books of M/s Kumar and Radha

Dr. **Revaluation Account** Cr.

		Rs.		Rs.
To Debtors		6,000	By Premises	10,000
To Stock		4,000	By Provision for Bad Debts	4,000
To Capital Accounts : (Profit transferred)				
Kumar	2,000			
Radha	2,000	4,000		
		14,000		14,000

Dr. **Partners' Capital Accounts** Cr.

Particulars	Kumar Rs.	Radha Rs.	Particulars	Kumar Rs.	Radha Rs.
To New Firm (Balance transferred)	71,000	61,000	By Balance b/d	50,000	40,000
			By Reserves	9,000	9,000
			By Goodwill	10,000	10,000
			By Revaluation Profit	2,000	2,000
	71,000	61,000		71,000	61,000

Dr. **New Firm's Account** Cr.

	Rs.		Rs.
To Debtors	50,000	By Creditors	24,000
To Stock	26,000	By Kumar's Capital	71,000
To Premises	60,000	By Radha's Capital	61,000
To Goodwill	20,000		
	1,56,000		1,56,000

In the Books of M/s Sunil and Sudha

Dr. **Revaluation Account** Cr.

	Rs.			Rs.
To Debtors	4,000	By Patent Rights		10,000
To Furniture	2,000	By Capital Accounts :		
To Stock	4,000	(Loss transferred)		
To Motor Vans	4,000	Sunil	2,400	
		Sudha	1,600	4,000
	14,000			14,000

Dr. **Partners' Capital Accounts** Cr.

	Sunil Rs.	Sudha Rs.		Sunil Rs.	Sudha Rs.
To Goodwill	1,200	800	By Balance b/d	60,000	40,000
To Motor Vans	20,000	—			
To Revaluation Loss	2,400	1,600			
To New Firm (Balance transferred)	36,400	37,600			
	60,000	40,000		60,000	40,000

New Firms's Account

Dr.	Rs.		Cr. Rs.
To Bank	10,000	By Creditors	54,000
To Bills Receivable	10,000	By Sunil's Capital	36,400
To Debtors	36,000	By Sudha's Capital	37,600
To Stock	36,000		
To Furniture	10,000		
To Patent Rights	10,000		
To Goodwill	16,000		
	1,28,000		1,28,000

Balance Sheet of New Firm

Liabilities		Rs.	Assets		Rs.
Capital Accounts :			Premises		60,000
Kumar	40,000		Furniture		10,000
Radha	40,000		Patent Rights		10,000
Sunil	40,000		Stock		62,000
Sudha	40,000	1,60,000	Debtors		86,000
Creditors		78,000	Bills Receivable		10,000
Current Accounts :			Cash at Bank		10,000
Kumar	22,000		Current Accounts :		
Radha	12,000	34,000	Sunil	12,600	
			Sudha	11,400	24,000
		2,72,000			2,72,000

Partners' Capital Accounts

Dr. Cr.

Particulars	Kumar Rs.	Radha Rs.	Sunil Rs.	Sudha Rs.	Particulars	Kumar Rs	Radha Rs.	Sunil Rs.	Sudha Rs.
To Goodwill	9,000	9,000	9,000	9,000	By Sundries	71,000	61,000	36,400	37,600
To Current A/c	22,000	12,000	—	—	By Current A/c	—	—	12,600	11,400
To Balance c/d	40,000	40,000	40,000	40,000	(transfer)				
	71,000	61,000	49,000	49,000		71,000	61,000	49,000	49,000

Illustration 5

A and B carry on independent business and their positions as at 30th September, 1977 are reflected in provisions the Balance Sheet given below :

	A	B
	Rs.	Rs.
Stock-in-trade	1,70,000	98,000
Sundry Debtors	89,000	37,000
Cash at Bank	13,000	7,500
Cash in Hand	987	234
Furniture and Fixtures	2,750	1,766
Investments	513	–
	2,76,250	1,44,500
Represented by Sundry Creditors for :		
Purchases	1,10,000	47,000
Expenses	750	2,000
Bills Payable	12,500	–
Capital Account	1,53,000	95,500
	2,76,250	1,44,500

Both of them want to form a partnership firm from 1st October, 1977 on the following understandings :

(a) The capital of the partnership would be Rs. 3 lakhs which would be contributed by them in the ratio 2 : 1.

(b) The firm is not to assume any creditors other than the dues on account of purchase made.

(c) The assets of the individual business would be evaluated by 'C' at which values, the firm will take them over and the value would be adjusted against the contribution due by A and B.

(d) 'C' gave his valuation report as follows : Business of A : Stock-in-trade to be written down by 15% and a portion of sundry debtors amounting to Rs. 9,000 estimated unrealisable not to be assumed by the firm; furniture and fixtures to be valued at Rs. 2,000 and investments to be taken at market value of Rs. 1,000.

(e) A's Bills payable for Rs. 12,500 are not on account of credit purchases.

(f) Assets of B : Stocks to be written up by 10% and sundry debtors to be admitted at 85% of their value. Other assets to be taken at book value.

Prepare the Opening Balance Sheet of the firm showing necessary working of Partners' Capital Accounts.

(Shivaji, B.Com., Nov., 1982 and C.A. Inter)

Solution :

Balance Sheet of M/s A and B as on 1st Oct., 1977

Liabilities		Rs.	Assets	Rs.
Creditors for Purchases		1,57,000	Cash at Bank	88,484
Capital Accounts :			Stock	2,52,300
A	2,00,000		Debtors	1,11,450
B	1,00,000	3,00,000	Investments	1,000
			Furniture	3,766
		4,57,000		4,57,000

Working Notes :

(i) Capital balances transferred to the partnership firm are ascertained as below :

			A Rs.		B Rs.
Capitals as per Balance Sheets			1,53,000		95,500
Add : Appreciation in assets :					
Investments			487	Stock	9,800
			1,53,487		1,05,300
Less : Depreciation in assets :					
	Stock	25,500		Debtors	5,550
	Debtors	9,000			
	Furniture	750	35,250		
Capital balances transferred			1,18,237		99,750

(ii) Cash brought in the partnership firm by the partners is calculated as below:

	A Rs.	B Rs.
Capital required in the firm	2,00,000	1,00,000
Less : Capital Accounts balances	1,18,237	99,750
Cash brought in by the partners	81,763	250

(iii) Cash at Bank is calculated as below :

	A	B
Cash and Bank balances	13,987	7,734
Less : Expenses and Bills Payable paid	13,250	2,000
Balance taken over by the firm	737	5,734
Add : Cash brought in by A and B	81,763	250
	82,500	5,984

EXAMINATION QUESTIONS

(A) Answer the following questions in not exceeding 4 lines each :

(*Each Carrying two Marks*)

(1) What is amalgamation of firms ? (*Kar., April, 1996*)

(2) Why amalgamation is needed ?

(3) Give three objects of amalgamation of partnership firms. (*Kar., Oct., 1996*)

(4) Why is revaluation account opened in the books of the amalgamating firms ?

(5) How do you treat an asset or liability of old firm not taken over by the new firm on amalgamation ? (*B'lore, April, 1991*)

(6) How does the amalgamated firm treat goodwill raised for the purpose of amalgamation ?

(7) Mention two important reasons for amalgamation of firms. (*Sagar, April, 1989*)

(8) Give the entry to take over the assets and liabilities by the new firm in amalgamation. (*B'lore, Oct., 1981*)

(9) Give the entry to close the capital accounts of partners in the books of old firm for the purpose of amalgamation.

(10) What are the reasons for amalgamation of firms ? (*B'lore, Nov., 1994*)

(11) Specify any two objectives of amalgamation of partnership firm. (*B'lore, April, 1995*)

(12) Give the meaning of amalgamation of partnership firm. (*B'lore, April, 1998*)

(B) Answer the following questions/problems :

(*Each Carries 8 Marks*)

(1) What do you mean by amalgamation ? Mention the objectives of amalgamation? (*B'lore, May, 1981*)

(2) Give the reasons for amalgamation of partnership firms. (*B'lore, April, 1983*)

(3) What are the objectives of amalgamation of partnership firms? (*B'lore, April, 1984*)

(4) Give the opening entries in the books of the amalgamated firm.

(5) Pass the necessary adjusting entries in the amalgamation of firm :

(a) When one partner has more capital than what he should bring into new firm, and

(b) What another partner of the same partnership has less capital than what he has. *(Agra, Oct., 1979)*

(6) State the closing entries in the books of old firm in the event of amalgamation.

(7) Give the journal entries that are to be passed in the books of firms to be amalgamated.

(8) Pass the journal entries that are to be passed in the books of new firm in the event of amalgamation.

(9) What accounting treatment would you give to assets and liabilities not taken over by the new firm at the time of amalgamation ? *(B'lore, April, 1995)*

(C) Solve the following problems :

(Each Carries 16 Marks)

(1) The following are the balance sheets of M/s Ramdas and Narayan who shared profits and losses equally and M/s Kamat and Pai who shared in the ratio of 3 : 2.

Balance Sheet of M/s Ramdas and Narayan as on 31-12-1982

Liabilities	Rs.	Assets	Rs.
Sundry Creditors	3,000	Cash in Hand	1,000
Capitals :		Stock-in-trade	2,000
Ramdas	3,000	Sundry Debtors	2,000
Narayan	2,000	Furniture	1,000
		Plant	2,000
	8,000		8,000

Balance Sheet of M/s Kamat and Pai as on 31-12-1982

Liabilities	Rs.	Assets	Rs.
Sundry Creditors	1,800	Cash in Hand	1,000
Capitals :		Stock-in-trade	2,400
Kamat	2,000	Debtors	1,400
Pai	3,000	Investments	2,000
Reserve Fund	5,000	Furniture	1,600
		Patents	3,400
	11,800		11,800

Both the firms decided to amalgamate themselves with effect from 1-1-1983. They agreed to revalue their assets and liabilities as follows :

M/s Ramdas and Narayan : Plant Rs. 1,600; Stock Rs. 1,800; Debtors Rs. 1,680; Furniture at book value and Goodwill Rs. 1,200.

M/s Kamat and Pai : Furniture Rs. 1,400; Debtors Rs. 1,200; Stock Rs. 2,200; Goodwill Rs. 1,000 and Patents Rs. 3,000.

New profit sharing ratio was 3 : 3 : 2 : 2 respectively for Ramdas, Narayan, Kamat and Pai.

You are required to give :

1. Revaluation and Capital Accounts of M/s Ramdas and Narayan.
2. Revaluation and Capital Accounts of M/s Kamat and Pal.
3. Opening balance sheet of the new firm.

(*Gulbarga, April, 1988*)

Ans. : Revaluation Loss : Ramdas Rs. 460; Narayan Rs. 460; Kamat Rs. 600, and Pai Rs. 400.

Capital Account Balance Transferred : Ramdas Rs. 3,140; Narayan Rs. 2,140; Kamat Rs. 5,000 and Pai Rs. 5,000.

New Firm Balance Sheet Total Rs. 20,080.

(2) The following were the balance sheets of the firms M/s A and B and M/s C & D on 31-12-1984 when they decided to amalgamate their business.

Balance Sheet of M/s A and B

Liabilities		Rs.	Assets		Rs.
Creditors		12,000	Cash at Bank		6,000
Bills Payable		6,000	Debtors	28,000	
Reserves		9,000	*Less* : Provision	2,000	26,000
Capitals :			Stock		15,000
A	25,000		Buildings		25,000
B	20,000	45,000			
		72,000			72,000

Balance Sheet of M/s C and D

Liabilities		Rs.	Assets	Rs.
Creditors		27,000	Cash at Bank	5,000
Capitals :			Bills Receivable	5,000
C	30,000		Debtors	20,000
D	20,000	50,000	Stock	20,000
			Furniture	6,000
			Motor Van	12,000
			Goodwill	9,000
		77,000		77,000

The terms of amalgamation were as follows :

(a) The new firm was to take over the assets and liabilities of both the firms subject to M/s A and B meeting their bills payable out to their banks balance.

(b) A and B's assets were valued as :

Debtors Rs. 25,000; Stock Rs. 13,000; Buildings Rs. 30,000 and Goodwill Rs. 7,000.

(c) C and D's assets were valued as :

Debtors Rs. 18,000; Stock Rs. 18,000, Furniture Rs. 5,000 and Goodwill Rs. 8,000.

(d) 'C' took over the Motor Van at an agreed value of Rs. 10,000. Show the necessary accounts in the books of both the old firms and the new firm.

(*Karnatak, April, 1996 and Gulbarga, Oct., 1995*)

Ans. : Revaluation Profit 'A' Rs. 1,000 and 'B' Rs. 1,000.
Revaluation Loss 'C' Rs. 3,500 and 'D' Rs. 3,500.
Capital Account balance transferred : 'A' Rs. 34,000; 'B' Rs. 29,000; 'C' Rs. 16,000 and 'D' Rs. 16,000.
New Firm Balance Sheet Total : Rs. 1,34,000.

Note : Decreased value of Goodwill Rs. 1,000 is adjusted to Capital A/cs.

(3) Black and White and Red and Blue are the two partnership firms carrying on a similar type of business. They agreed to amalgamate their business as on 1-1-1988 under the name and style of Blue Button and Co., Black and White share profit in the ratio of 3 : 2 and Red and Blue in the ratio of 2 : 3.

The respective Balance Sheets as on 31-12-1977

Liabilities	Black & White Rs.	Red & Blue Rs.	Assets		Black & White Rs.	Red & Blue Rs.
Bills Payable	1,500	7,200	Cash at Bank		13,000	11,500
Creditors	14,000	28,000	Bills Receivable		7,500	6,000
Mrs. White's Loan	10,000	—	Debtors		20,000	—
Outstanding Expenses	—	2,800	Debtors	40,000		
Reserve Fund	—	12,000	*Less* : Provision	1,500	—	38,500
Capitals :			Furniture		6,000	11,500
Black	30,000	—	Buildings		—	35,000
White	15,000	—	Stock		24,000	22,500
Red	—	45,000				
Blue	—	30,000				
	70,500	1,25,000			70,500	1,25,000

The terms of amalgamation agreed upon are as follows :

(1) The goodwill of Black and White is to be taken at Rs. 6,000 and that of Red and Blue at Rs. 20,000.

(2) Profits in the new firm are to be shared in the proportion of 2/10 to Black, 1/10 to White, 4/10 to Red and 3/10 to Blue.

(3) The capital of the new firm is to be Rs. 1,50,000 to be provided by the partners in their profit sharing ratios and adjustments to be made in cash.

(4) The stock of Black and White is to be valued at Rs. 22,000 and that of Red and Blue at Rs. 24,000.

(5) Furniture of Black and White is not to be brought into the new firm.

(6) The new business is to be carried in the buildings of Red and Blue which is valued at Rs. 42,000.

(7) A provision for bad and doubtful debts is to be maintained at 5% on the book debts of both the firms.

(8) Loan of Mrs. White and the outstanding liabilities for expenses are to be paid off and not to be brought into the new firm. You are required to :–

(a) Pass the journal entries to close the books of the old firms, and

(b) Prepare the amalgamated balance sheet of the new firm.

(B.Com., Mysore and Kar., 1978, Semester)

Ans. : Revaluation Loss : Black Rs. 1,800 and White Rs. 1,200; Revaluation Profit : Red Rs. 3,200 and Blue Rs. 4,800; Capital Account balance transferred : Black Rs. 28,200, White Rs. 13,800; Red Rs. 61,000 and Blue Rs. 54,000; Cash Brought: Black Rs. 1,800 and White Rs. 1,200; Cash paid : Red Rs. 1,000 and Blue Rs. 9,000: New Firm Balance Sheet total : Rs. 2,00,700.

Note : Furniture is debited to Capital Accounts in profit sharing ratio.

(4) The following were the balance sheets of M/s Murthy and Mehta and M/s Sastry and Sundar as on 31-12-1984.

Liabilities	Murthy & Mehta Rs.	Sastry & Sundar Rs.	Assets	Murthy & Mehta Rs.	Sastry & Sundar Rs.
Bills Payable	36,000	30,000	Buildings	60,000	—
Creditors	24,000	60,000	Machinery	30,000	60,000
Capitals Accounts :			Furniture	15,000	6,000
Murthy	1,50,000	—	Stock	1,50,000	2,25,000
Mehta	1,50,000	—	Investments	6,000	—
Sastry	—	1,80,000	Debtors	90,000	1,35,000
Sundar	—	1,80,000	Cash at Bank	9,000	24,000
	3,60,000	4,50,000		3,60,000	4,50,000

Murthy and Mehta shared profits in the ratio of 3 : 2 and Sastry and Sundar in the ratio of 7 : 3. They decide to amalgamate their business on 1-1-1985.

The following adjustments are to be made in the balance sheet of Murthy and Mehta :

(a) Stock to be depreciated by 10%.
(b) Debtors amounting to Rs. 3,000 were bad.
(c) Buildings were to be revalued at Rs. 60,000.
(d) Machinery was to be appreciated by Rs. 6,000.
(e) The investments were not to be taken over by new firm.

The following adjustments were to be made in the balance sheet of Sastry and Sundar :

(a) Stock to be depreciated by Rs. 7,500.
(b) 5% provision for doubtful debts was to be made on debtors.
(c) Furniture is not to be taken by the new firm.

Further, the goodwill of Murthy and Mehta was valued at Rs. 15,000 and that of Sastry and Sundar at Rs. 24,000. Goodwill should not be shown in the books of the new firm. All the partners share profits and losses in the new firm equally. The capital of the new firm was fixed at Rs. 6,00,000.

Pass the journal entries to close the books of both the old firms and prepare the amalgamated balance sheet of the new firm.

(Gulbarga, April, 1985)

Ans. : Revaluation Loss : Murthy Rs. 7,200; Mehta Rs. 4,800; Shastry Rs. 9,975 and Sundar Rs. 4,275.
Capital Account balance transferred : Murthy Rs. 1,49,200; Mehta Rs. 1,47,800; Sastry Rs. 1,82,625 and Sundar Rs. 1,81,125.
Current A/c balance : Murthy (Cr.) Rs. 22,875; Mehta (Cr.) Rs. 21,375; Shastry (Dr.) Rs. 11,550 and Sundar (Dr.) Rs. 10,950.
New Firm Balance Sheet Total : Rs. 7,94,250.

Note : Investments and Furniture are transferred to Capital Account in Profit Sharing Ratio.

(5) The following were the Balance Sheets as at 31st December, 1985 of two firms of M/s P and Q and M/s R and S.

Balance Sheet of P and Q as at 31st Dec., 1985

Liabilities	Rs.	Assets	Rs.
Sundry Creditors	20,000	Cash at Bank	5,600
Mrs. P's Loan	5,000	Stock	20,400
Capitals :		Debtors	15,000
P	40,000	Furniture	4,000
Q	20,000	Premises	40,000
	85,000		85,000

Balance Sheet of 'R' and 'S' as at 31st Dec., 1985

Liabilities	Rs.	Assets	Rs.
Sundry Creditors	25,000	Cash	6,700
Capitals :		Stock	18,300
R	24,000	Debtors	20,000
S	16,000	Furniture	5,000
		Investments	15,000
	65,000		65,000

The two firms decided to amalgamate their business as from 1st January, 1986 under the name and style of Bharat Traders. For this purpose, it was agreed that Mrs. P's Loan should be repaid and the investments of M/s 'R' and 'S' be not taken over by the new firm.

Goodwill of 'P' and 'Q' was fixed at Rs. 8,000 and that of 'R' and 'S' at Rs. 10,000. Premises were revalued at Rs. 50,000; but the Stock of 'P' and 'Q' was found over valued by Rs. 4,000. The stock of R and S was undervalued by Rs. 2,000. A reserve of 5% on Debtors was created for bad debts of both firms.

The total capital of the Bharat Traders was to be Rs. 80,000 and the capital of 'P', 'Q', 'R' and 'S' was to be in their profit sharing ratio which was to be 3 : 2 : 3 : 2 respectively. Goodwill account in the new firm to be written off.

Close the books of 'P' and 'Q' and pass opening entries in the books of Bharat Traders.

Give the Balance Sheet of the new firm.

(B.Com., Agra and Mangalore, April, 1993 Mod.)

Ans. : Balance Sheet— Rs. 1,49,250.

(6) The following are the balance sheets of the firms M/s A and B and X and Y as on 31-12-1988.

Liabilities	A & B Rs.	X & Y Rs.	Assets	A & B Rs.	X & Y Rs.
Creditors	16,000	23,000	Buildings	—	50,000
Reserve	10,000	—	Machinery	20,000	30,000
Capitals :			Patents	10,000	5,000
A	40,000	—	Stock	25,000	20,000
B	10,000	—	Debtors	10,000	16,000
X	—	50,000	Investments	5,000	—
Y	—	50,000	Cash	6,000	2,000
	76,000	1,23,000		76,000	1,23,000

A and B shared profits and losses in the ratio of 3 : 2 and X and Y shared equally. The firms decided to amalgamate on the following terms :

(a) Investments of A and B were not to be taken over by the new firm. A and B to take them in their profit sharing ratio.

(b) Goodwill of A and B was Rs. 20,000 and that of X and Y Rs. 40,000. Goodwill was not to remain in the new firm.

(c) Patents of A and B were valued at Rs. 15,000 and Stock at Rs. 30,000. A provision of 8% was to be created on debtors.

(d) Machinery of X and Y was to be written down to Rs. 25,000. Stock of X and Y was found over valued by Rs. 2,000 and book debts of Rs. 1,000 was bad and had to be written off. Patents of X and Y were to be valued at Rs. 8,000.

(e) The new profit sharing proportion was to be : A 2/10, B 2/10, X 3/10 and Y 3/10.

(f) The total capital of the new firm was to be Rs. 2,00,000 to be contributed by the partners in proportion to their new profit sharing ratio and the partners to bring in or to withdraw cash.

Show the necessary ledger accounts to close the books of the old firms and pass the opening entries in the books of the new firm and prepare the opening balance sheet of the new firm.

(*Kar., April, 1987 and B'lore, April, 1998*)

Ans. : Revaluation Profit : 'A' Rs. 5,520 and 'B' Rs. 3,680, Revaluation Loss : X Rs. 2,500 and Y Rs. 2,500; Capital A/cs balance transferred: 'A' Rs. 60,520; 'B' Rs. 23,680; X Rs. 67,500 and 'Y' Rs. 67,500; Cash Brought : 'B' Rs. 28,320; X Rs. 10,500 and 'Y' Rs. 10,500; Cash paid : A Rs. 8,520; New Firm Balance Sheet Total Rs. 2,39,000.

(7) M/s Auto Industries and M/s Chandra Industries decided to amalgamate their businesses of Auto Spares on 1st January, 1984. Their Balance Sheets as at 31st December, 1983 were as follows :

M/s Auto Industries

Balance Sheet as at 31-12-1983

Liabilities		Rs.	Assets	Rs.
Capital of Partners :			Premises	1,00,000
Shashikant	1,20,000		Machinery	70,000
Harshal	1,10,000	2,30,000	Furniture	30,000
Bills Payable		10,000	Stock	1,20,000
Sundry Creditors		1,30,000	Bank Balance	50,000
		3,70,000		3,70,000

M/s Chandra Industries
Balance Sheet as at 31-12-1983

Liabilities		Rs.	Assets	Rs.
Capital of Partners :			Building	1,20,000
Chandra	2,00,000		Furniture	40,000
Ratnakar	1,00,000	3,00,000	Equipments	80,000
Bank Loan		1,00,000	Sundry Debtors	60,000
Sundry Creditors		30,000	Stock	90,000
			Cash at Bank	40,000
		4,30,000		4,30,000

The terms of amalgamation and valuation of their Assets and Liabilities were agreed for the take over by the new firm namely M/s Chandra Auto as follows :

		M/s Auto Rs.	M/s Chandra Rs.
(1)	Premises	1,20,000	—
(2)	Building	—	1,30,000
(3)	Machinery	50,000	—
(4)	Equipments	—	60,000
(5)	Furniture	20,000	20,000
(6)	Stock	1,30,000	1,00,000
(7)	Debtors	—	50,000
(8)	Goodwill	40,000	30,000

(9) Mr. Shashikant and Harshal were equal partners whereas Chandru and Ratnakar were sharing profits in the ratio of 2 : 1.

(10) In the new firm their profit sharing ratios were agreed to be equal for which the partners agreed to maintain their capitals equally at Rs. 1,50,000 each.

(11) They also agreed to introduce fresh capitals if necessary in the new firm.

(12) The goodwill was to continue in the new firm.

You are required to close the books of the firm and prepare Balance Sheet of the new firm M/s Auto Chandra as at 1-1-1984.

(B.U. & S.U., April, 1984)

Ans. : New firm Balance Sheet Total Rs. 8,70,000; Cash at Bank Rs. 1,20,000.

(8) 'A' and 'B' are partners sharing profits and losses equally in a business similar to that carried on by 'C'. In order to avoid competition they decide to amalgamate the two businesses by taking over the assets and liabilities of 'C' and admitting him into partnership with them as from January 1st, 1985. The Balance Sheets as at 31st December, 1984 of each business were as follows :

A and B

Liabilities		Rs.	Assets		Rs.
Capital Accounts :			Cash		300
A	20,000		Debtors	35,000	
B	15,000	35,000	*Less:* Reserve for		
Sundry Creditors		15,000	Bad Debts	1,500	33,500
Bank Overdraft		5,000	Stock		21,200
		55,000			55,000

C

Liabilities	Rs.	Assets	Rs.
Sundry Creditors	37,500	Cash in Hand	700
Bills Payable	3,000	Sundry Debtors	25,000
Bank Overdraft	32,000	Stock	26,300
Loan	10,500	Investments	27,000
		C's Capital Overdrawn	4,000
	83,000		83,000

The new partnership is to be carried on as A, B and C and it was agreed among all the partners that the Book-Debts of both the businesses should be provided with Bad Debts Reserve at 10% and the Stock is to be reduced by 5% for the purpose of amalgamation and that the Investments of 'C' should be valued at Rs. 35,000 and that 'C' was to be credited with a sum of Rs. 5,000 for Goodwill. It was further agreed that in order to raise the total capital of the firm to Rs. 60,000 each. Partner shall introduce such sum as would make his capital in the new business equal to one-third of the total capital.

Give Journal Entries in the books of the new firm and show the amalgamated Balance Sheet as at 1st January, 1985.

(*Bangalore, Nov., 1991*)

Ans. : Capital brought in by each partner : 'A' Rs. 1,530; 'B' Rs. 6,530 and 'C' Rs. 14,815; New Firm Balance Sheet Total Rs. 1,63,000.

(9) Following were the Balance Sheets as on 31st December, 1989 of the two firms M/s 'A' and 'B' and M/s 'C' and 'D' :

Balance Sheets

Liabilities	A & B Rs.	C &D Rs.	Assets		A & B Rs.	C & D Rs.
Sundry Creditors	20,000	10,000	Cash at Bank		15,000	8,000
Bills Payable	5,000	—	Investments (cost)			
Bank Overdraft	2,000	10,000	(A & B)		10,000	8,000
A's Loan	6,000	—	Debtors	10,000		
Capital A/cs :			*Less :* Provision	1,000	9,000	8,000
A	35,000	—	Furniture		12,000	6,000
B	22,000	—	Premises		30,000	—
C	—	36,000	Land		—	50,000
D	—	20,000	Machinery		15,000	—
General Reserve	8,000	—	Goodwill		9,000	—
Investment Fluctuation Fund	2,000	4,000				
	1,00,000	80,000			1,00,000	80,000

The two firms decided to amalgamate on 1st January, 1990. The two firms agreed :

(1) The new firm shall not take over furniture of both the firms.

(2) The new firm shall take over :
Investment at 10% depreciation, Land at Rs. 80,000, Premises at Rs. 45,000, Machinery at Rs. 9,000. Debtors of 'A' and 'B' Rs. 9,000 and those of 'C' and 'D' at Rs. 8,000.
Goodwill of both the firms was valued at Rs. 12,000 each.

(3) Unrecorded typewriter with 'C' and 'D', valued at Rs. 800 was not taken over by the new firm.

(4) The capital of the new firm was agreed at Rs. 1,60,000 and this will be contributed by A, B, C and D, in the proportion 30% A, 20% B, 30% C and 20% D. Any credit balance or debit balance shall be adjusted to their Current A/cs respectively.

(5) It was agreed that the assets which are not taken over by the new firm shall be adjusted to the concerned Partners' Capital A/cs equally.

Prepare Opening Balance Sheet of A, B, C and D after amalgamation.

(*B.U. and S.U., April, 1981*)

Ans. : Profit : 'A' Rs. 4,500; 'B' Rs. 4,500; 'C' Rs. 20,000 and 'D' Rs. 20,000; Capital : 'A' Rs. 39,500; 'B' Rs. 26,500; 'C' Rs. 56,000 and 'D' Rs. 40,000; Balance Sheet Total : A and B Rs. 93,000 and C and D Rs. 1,16,000.

(10) Shankar and Sundar and Rustum and Davar agreed to amalgamate their business. Their position as on 31-12-1989 was as follows :

Balance Sheet of Shankar and Sundar as on 31-12-1989

Liabilities	Rs.	Assets	Rs.
Capitals :		Cash at Bank	1,56,000
Shankar	1,82,000	Stock-in-trade	42,000
Sundar	1,30,000	Furniture	10,000
Reserve Fund	20,000	Building	78,000
Creditors	84,000	Debtors	1,30,000
	4,16,000		4,16,000

Balance Sheet of Rostum and Davar as on 31-12-1989

Liabilities	Rs.	Assets	Rs.
Capitals :		Cash at Bank	65,000
Rustum	91,000	Stock-in-trade	26,000
Davar	65,000	Furniture	13,000
Creditors	52,000	Debtors	1,00,000
		Profit and Loss A/c	4,000
	2,08,000		2,08,000

The new firm "Shankar, Sundar and Rustum, Davar" did not take over Creditors and Debtors. Building was retained by Shankar and Sundar. But the new firm agreed to pay monthly rent of Rs. 400. The cash required for working of the new firm was estimated at Rs. 1,30,000 to be provided by the partners in their new profit sharing ratios as under :

Shankar 3/10, Sundar 3/10, Rustum 2/10, and Davar 2/10.

(i) Write up the accounts in the books of Shankar and Sundar and Rustum and Davar.

(ii) Give the opening balance sheet of the new firm.

(iii) State your assumptions if any.

(*Gulbarga, April, 1984 and B.Com., Madras, 1971*)

Ans. : Capital : Shankar Rs. 69,334 (30,334 + 39,000); Sundar Rs. 60,666 (21,666 + 39,000); Rustam Rs. 48,750 (22,750 + 26,000); Davar Rs. 42,250 (16,250 + 26,000); Balance Sheet Total Rs. 2,21,000.

(11) The following are the balance sheets of the firm of M/s A and B and X and Y on the date they decided to amalgamate :

Liabilities	A & B Rs.	X & Y Rs.	Assets		A & B Rs.	X & Y Rs.
Creditors	7,000	14,000	Cash		5,000	4,000
Bills Payable	750	3,600	Bills Receivable		6,000	5,000
Reserves	—	6,000	Debtors	10,000		
Mrs. B's Loan	5,000	—	*Less* : Provision	5,000	9,500	20,000
Expenses Due	—	1,400	Furniture		4,500	7,500
Capitals :			Building		—	28,500
A	15,000	—	Stock		12,750	10,000
B	10,000	—				
X	—	30,000				
Y	—	20,000				
	37,750	75,000			37,750	75,000

M/s A and B share the profits or losses in their capital ratio and M/s X and Y equally.

The terms of amalgamation were :

(1) Goodwill of M/s A and B was valued at Rs. 6,000 and that of X and Y Rs. 15,000.

(2) Stock of both the firms be appreciated in the value by 10%.

(3) Provision for doubtful debts at 4% on debtors was thought necessary.

(4) Building was valued at Rs. 25,000.

(5) Mrs. B's Loan and expenses unpaid by M/s X and Y are to be paid out of cash by the respective firms.

(6) Furniture of M/s A and B was not taken over by the new firm.

(7) The capital of the new firm is agreed to be Rs. 1,00,000 contributed equally, the adjustments to be made in cash.

Prepare the necessary accounts in the books of the old firms and the balance sheet of the new firm.

(*Karnatak, Oct., 1989*)

Ans. : Revaluation Profit : A and B Rs. 1,375 (*i.e.*, 1,275 + 100); Revaluation Loss : X and Y Rs. 3,300 (*i.e.*, 800 + 3,500 – 1,000); Capital account balances transferred : A Rs. 16,725, B Rs. 11,150; X Rs. 38,850 and Y Rs. 28,850; New firm balance sheet total Rs. 1,25,350; Cash paid : X Rs. 13,850 and Y Rs. 3,850; Cash brought : A Rs. 8,275 and B Rs. 13,850; Cash balance Rs. 7,025 and Cash A/c total Rs. 24,725.

Note : Furniture is debited to pártners' capital accounts in their profit sharing ratio.

(12) The following were the Balance Sheets of the firms. M/s Anil and Akbar and M/s Singh and Dev on 31-12-1992 when they decided to amalgamate their business.

Liabilities	Anil & Akbar Rs.	Singh & Dev Rs.	Assets	Anil & Akbar Rs.	Singh & Dev Rs.
Creditors	42,000	54,000	Cash at Bank	24,000	12,000
Bills Payable	18,000	—	Debtors	33,000	36,000
Reserves	24,000	—	Stock	27,000	37,500
Capitals :			Furniture	—	25,500
Anil	16,500	—	Motor Vans	—	15,000
Akbar	19,500	—	Premises	36,000	—
Singh	—	60,000	Goodwill	—	24,000
Dev	—	36,000			
	1,20,000	1,50,000		1,20,000	1,50,000

The terms of amalgamation were as follows :

(a) The new firm was to take over the assets and liabilities of both the firms subject to M/s Anil and Akbar meeting their bills payable out of their bank balance.

(b) The assets of Anil and Akbar were valued as follows :

Debtors	Rs. 30,000	Premises	Rs. 54,000
Stock	Rs. 18,000	Goodwill	Rs. 15,000

(c) The assets of Singh and Dev were valued as follows :

Debtors	Rs. 30,000	Furniture	Rs. 18,000
Stock	Rs. 28,500	Goodwill	Rs. 9,000

(d) Singh took over the motor vans at an agreed value of Rs. 12,000.

(e) M/s Singh and Dev to be credited with Rs. 10,500 being the value of patent rights which were not shown in the balance sheet.

(f) Anil and Akbar shared profits equally and Singh and Dev in the ratio of 3 : 2 in their respective firms. But in the new firm they should share in their capital ratio.

(g) It was decided that the new firm should not maintain goodwill balance in the books.

(h) The capital of the partners in the new firm was fixed at Rs. 30,000 each. Any excess or deficiency was to be transferred to the current accounts of the partners.

Show the necessary accounts in the books of the old firms and the balance sheet of the new firm and also the capital accounts of the partners.

(Gulbarga, April, 1994)

Ans. : Realisation Profit : Anil and Akbar Rs. 6,000 (3,000 + 3,000)
Realisation Loss : Singh and Dev Rs. 15,000 (9,000 + 6,000)
Capital accounts balances transferred : Anil Rs. 39,000; Akbar Rs. 42,000; Singh Rs. 30,000 and Dev Rs. 24,000
Current account balances : Anil Rs. 3,000 (Cr.), Akbar Rs. 6,000 (Cr.), Singh Rs. 6,000 (Dr.) and Dev Rs. 12,000 (Dr.); New firm Balance Sheet total Rs. 2,25,000; Cash at Bank Rs. 18,000.

(13) The following are the Balance Sheets of M/s A and B who shared profits and losses equally and M/s C and D who shared in the ratio of 3 : 2.

Balance Sheet of M/s A and B as on 31-12-1995

Liabilities	Rs.	Assets	Rs.
Sundry Creditors	6,000	Cash in Hand	2,000
Capital Accounts :		Stock	4,000
A	6,000	Sundry Debtors	4,000
B	4,000	Machinery	6,000
	16,000		16,000

Balance Sheet of M/s C and D as on 31-12-1995

Liabilities	Rs.	Assets	Rs.
Sundry Creditors	3,600	Cash in Hand	2,000
Reserve Fund	10,000	Stock	4,800
Capital Accounts :		Sundry Debtors	2,800
C	4,000	Investments	4,000
D	6,000	Machinery	10,000
	23,600		23,600

Both the firms decided to amalgamate themselves on 31-12-1995. They agreed to revalue their assets as follows :

	A & B	C & D
	Rs.	Rs.
Machinery	5,200	8,800
Stock	3,600	4,400
Debtors	3,360	2,400
Goodwill	2,400	2,000

Show the necessary accounts in the books of the old firms and the balance sheet of the new firm.

(Gulbarga, April, 1996)

Ans. : Revaluation Loss : A & B Rs. 1,840 (920 + 920); C & D Rs. 2,000 (1,200 + 800).

Capital balances transferred : A Rs. 6,280; B Rs. 4,280; C Rs. 10,000 and D Rs. 10,000; Total Goodwill Rs. 4,400; New Firm Balance Sheet Total : Rs. 40,160.

Note : The share of goodwill is directly credited to the partners' capital accounts of the old firms.

(14) The Balance Sheet of Amir and Sudhir as on 1-1-1990 was as follows :

Liabilities	Amir Rs.	Sudhir Rs.	Asset	Amir Rs.	Sudhir Rs.
Creditors	10,000	8,000	Machinery	7,500	10,000
Bank Loan	5,000	—	Stock	10,000	5,000
Capital	15,000	20,000	Debtors	12,500	11,000
			Bank	—	2,000
	30,000	28,000		30,000	28,000

They decided to amalgamate their business. The following revaluations were agreed :

(a) Machinery to be reduced by 10%.

(b) Stock of Amir to be reduced by 20% and that of Sudhir by 10%.

(c) A provision of 5% is to be made against debtors of both.

(d) Each partner is to be credited with goodwill of Rs. 5,000.

(e) Bank Loan of Amir is to be paid by him.

Prepare : (1) Revaluation A/c in the books of Amir and Sudhir and Amir's and Sudhir's Capital A/c.

(2) Pass the opening entries in the books of the New Firm.

(3) Amalgamated Balance sheet as on 1-1-90 in the books of the New Firm.

(*Bangalore, April, 1992*)

Ans. : Revaluation Loss : Amir Rs. 3,375 and Sudhir Rs. 2,050. Capital A/cs balances transferred : Amir Rs. 21,625 and Sudhir Rs. 22,950; New Firm Balance Sheet Total Rs. 62,575.

(15) The respective balance sheets of A and B and C and D on the date of amalgamation are as follows :

A and B

Liabilities		Rs.	Assets	Rs.
Sundry Creditors		21,500	Cash at Bank	3,000
Capitals :			Sundry Debtors	20,000
A	25,000		Stock	30,000
B	15,000	40,000	Investments	8,000
			Office Furniture	500
		61,500		61,500

C and D

Liabilities		Rs.	Assets		Rs.
Sundry Creditors		21,000	Cash at Bank		1,000
Reserve Fund		11,500	Book Debts	25,000	
Capitals :			*Less* : Reserve	500	24,500
C	19,000		Stock		20,000
D	11,000	30,000	Trade Fixtures		1,000
			Leasehold Premises		12,000
			Goodwill		4,000
		62,500			62,500

It was agreed that the balance sheet of A and B should be adjusted as follows before amalgamation :

(a) That Rs. 400 be reserved for doubtful debts.

(b) That the stock and fixtures be depreciated by 10 per cent.

(c) That investments be taken over at Rs. 10,000.

(d) That Rs. 300 be reserved for discount on creditors.

The following adjustments were agreed upon in C and D's balance sheet :

(a) That book debts, stock and trade fixtures be taken over at book figures.

(b) That the leasehold premises and goodwill be valued at Rs. 18,000 and Rs. 30,000 respectively.

The goodwill was to be shown at Rs. 10,000 in the book of the new firm. The total capitals of the new firm were fixed at Rs. 90,000 to be contributed by all the partners according to new profit sharing ratio.

Pass journal entries in the books of A and B. Prepare also the Balance Sheet of the amalgamated firm.

(*Bangalore, Oct., 1993*)

Ans. : Revaluation profit : A—Rs. 575; B—Rs. 575; C—Rs. 16,000 and D—Rs. 16,000; Capital A/cs balances transferred : A—Rs. 24,425; B—Rs. 14,425; C—Rs. 40,750 and D—Rs. 32,750; Current A/cs balances : A—Rs. 3,075 (Dr.) (27,500 – 24,425); B—Rs. 13,075 (Dr.) (27,500 – 14,425); C—Rs. 13,250 (Cr.) (40,750 – 27,500) and D—Rs. 5,250 (Cr.) (32,750 – 27,500).

New Firm Balance Sheet Total : Rs. 1,50,700.

(16) Following were the Balance Sheets as at 31st December, 1990 of two firms M/s A and B and M/s C and D.

Liabilities	A & B	C & D	Assets	A & B	C & D
	Rs.	Rs.		Rs.	Rs.
Creditors	3,000	25,000	Stock	50,000	75,000
Bills Payable	6,000	—	Debtors	30,000	45,000
Bank Overdraft	—	10,300	Premises	20,000	—
Capitals :			Plant and Machinery	5,000	20,000
A	50,000	—	Bank	1,500	—
B	50,000	—	Furniture	500	300
C	—	52,500	Defence Bonds	2,000	—
D		52,500			
	1,09,000	1,40,300		1,09,000	1,40,300

The two firms decided to amalgamate their business from 1st January, 1991. For this purpose it was agreed that premises and plant and machinery belonging to A & B should be taken over by the new firm at Rs. 25,000 and Rs. 10,000 respectively. C & D were to be credited with Rs. 5,000 at the value of certain patent rights they possessed which became the property of the partnership and which were not included in their balance sheet. All the other assets were taken over at book values except the defence bonds belonging to A and B which was not taken over. Both the firms undertook to discharge their own liabilities, and it was agreed that A & B should introduce cash, to make their capital equal to that of C and D.

Pass incorporating entries in the books of the new firm and prepare also the balance sheet of the new firm.

(Bangalore, Oct., 1991, 1994 and 1995)

Ans. : Revaluation profit : A—Rs. 5,000; B—Rs. 5,000; C—Rs. 2,500 and D—Rs. 2,500; Capital A/cs balances transferred : A—Rs. 58,500; B—Rs. 58,500; C—Rs. 72,650 and D—Rs. 72,650;

New Firm A/c Total : A and B Rs. 1,17,000 and C and D Rs. 1,45,300; New Firm Balance Sheet Total : Rs. 2,90,600;

Cash Brought : A—Rs. 14,500 and B—Rs. 14,500; Cash at Bank: Rs. 29,800 (1,500 + 14,500 + 14,500).

(17) The following are the Balance Sheets of A & B and C & D as on 1-1-1992 when they decided to amalgamate their business :

Balance Sheets of A & B and C & D as on 1-1-1992

Liabilities	A & B Rs.	C &D Rs.	Assets	A & B Rs.	C & D Rs.
Creditors	5,000	3,000	Machinery	25,000	15,000
Bills Payable	—	1,500	Building	—	20,000
Capitals :	—	—	Stock	10,500	21,200
A	30,000	—	Debtors	18,000	12,000
B	20,000	—	Cash in Hand	1,500	3,300
C	—	35,000			
D	—	32,000			
	55,000	71,500		55,000	71,500

A & B were sharing the profits in the ratio of 2 : 1; C and D, equally.

The terms of the amalgamations were as follows :

(a) The new firm was to take over all assets and liabilities of the both firms.

(b) The assets of A and B were valued as follows :

Machinery Rs. 22,500; Stock Rs. 10,300 and Provision to be made on Debtors at 5% for doubtful debt.

(c) The assets of C and D valued as follows :

Building be appreciated by 10%, Machinery be depreciated by 20%; Stock at Rs. 19,400; and Provision for doubtful debt is to be made on debtors at 5%.

Prepare necessary accounts in the books of A & B, C & D and also draft amalgamated Balance Sheet in the books of new firm.

(Karnatak, April, 1997)

Ans. : Revaluation Loss : A—Rs. 2,400; B—Rs. 1,200; C—Rs. 1,700 and D—Rs. 1,700; Capital A/cs balances transferred :

A—Rs. 27,600; B—Rs. 18,800; C—Rs. 33,300 and D—Rs. 30,300;

New Firm A/c Total A & B Rs. 52,300 and C & D Rs. 68,700;

New Firm Balance Sheet Total Rs. 1,19,500.

7

JOINT LIFE POLICY

When a partner dies or retires, the amount due to him by the partnership firm is required to be paid to his legal representatives. In order to provide the funds to the legal representatives of the deceased or retired partner, usually joint life policy is taken by the partnership firm. If no such provision is made for the payment of dues, the firm will find shortage of funds and face the financial difficulties. Hence, joint life policy is taken on the joint lives of partners. Joint life policy means 'it is a contract between the firm and Life Insurance Corporation under which the latter (LIC) undertake to pay the amount of policy either on death of anyone of the partners or on maturity of policy whichever is earlier. When joint life policy is taken out by the firm, the firm has to pay insurance premium regularly to the LIC. The policy amount will received by the partnership firm on death (or on retirement) of the partner or on maturity whichever is earlier.

The main object of taking a life policy on the lives of its partners is to provide the necessary funds due to the deceased partner or retiring partner without straining the financial arrangement of the business. Life policy either it may be joint policy on the lives of partners or it may be separate (individual) policies on the life of each partner. If there is a joint policy, the amount of the policy is received by the firm on death of anyone partner. In case of the several (separate) policies, the amount of only deceased partner's policy is received by the firm. For example, if a firm took out a joint life policy for Rs. 75,000 on the lives of A, B and C partners, the amount of Rs. 75,000 is received on death of either 'A' or 'B' or 'C', but if separate policies are taken as for 'A' Rs. 30,000, 'B' Rs. 25,000 and 'C' Rs. 20,000 and if 'B' dies, the amount of 'B' policy only (*i.e.*, Rs. 25,000) is received from the Life Insurance Corporation.

Surrender Values

A firm may surrender its policy to the Life Insurance Company if it finds it impossible to continue to pay premiums. Surrender value is the present value of the policy paid to the firm by the insurance company when the firm wishes to surrender the policy before maturity. When the premiums have been paid on a policy for at least three years, it acquires a surrender value.

Accounting Procedure

(A) Joint Life Policy : The following are the main methods of recording the transactions in connection with the Joint Life Policy.

(1) *When Joint Life Policy Account is not maintained* : Under this method payment of premium is treated as a revenue expenditure and it is transferred to the Profit and Loss Account at the end of every year. On receipt of cash from the insurance company either on death of a partner or on maturity of the policy, it is treated as a gain and transferred to the capital account of all partners' accounts in their profit sharing ratio. Joint Life Policy Account will not appear in the Balance Sheet under this method. In this method, the following journal entries will be passed :

(i) When premium is paid :

Insurance Premium A/c	Dr.	With the amount of premium paid
To Cash or Bank A/c		

(ii) When premium is transferred to P & L A/c :

Profit and Loss Account	Dr.	With the amount of premium transferred
To Insurance Premium Account		

(iii) When policy amount is received on death of a partner :

Cash or Bank A/c	Dr.	With realised policy amount
To Joint Life Policy A/c		

(iv) When policy amount distributed among the partners in their profit sharing ratio :

Joint Life Policy A/c	Dr.	With realised policy amount transferred
To Partners' Capital A/c		

Under this method, the payment of premium is treated as revenue expenditure. This cannot be said to be correct method. The amount of policy is definitely recovered by the firm from the insurance company either on death of a partner or on maturity of the policy. Therefore, the premium amount is in the nature of investment with the Life Insurance Corporation and not a revenue expenditure.

This method is advantageous in case the partners withdraw their share in profits in cash because the financial burden to the extent of premium is reduced as the profit is reduced by the amount of premium charged.

(2) *When Joint Life Policy Account is maintained at its surrender value without creating reserve* : In order to remove the drawback of the first method, the payment of premium is treated as an investment. The premium amount is debited to the Joint Life Policy Account and is shown as an asset in the Balance Sheet. The surrender value of the policy is treated as the value of the policy

and is carried forward to the next period. At the end of every year the difference of the two sides of the policy account is transferred to the P & L A/c except the last year during which any partner dies. The amount realised from the policy on the maturity date is credited to the Joint Life Policy Account and the final balance is distributed among the partners in the their profit sharing ratio. Under this method, the following journal entries are passed :

(i) When insurance premium paid :

Joint Life Policy A/c Dr.		With the amount of premium
To Cash or Bank A/c		paid

(ii) When balance of policy account is brought down to its surrender value by charging excess amount over surrender value to P & L A/c :

Profit and Loss A/c Dr.		With the amount of difference
To Joint Life Policy A/c		between premium paid and surrender value

(iii) When policy amount is received on its surrender, maturity or on death of partner :

Cash or Bank A/c Dr.		With the amount of policy
To Joint Life Policy A/c		realised

(iv) When balance of Policy Account is transferred to the partners in their profit sharing ratio :

Joint Life Policy A/c Dr.		With the balance amount of
To All Partners' Capital A/c		policy account

Under this method, the accumulated amount of premium is treated as an asset. Therefore, it fails to show the true value of the policy on the date of Balance Sheet. But as a matter of fact if the Balance Sheet has to give 'true and fair' view, the surrender value of the insurance policy as on the date of Balance Sheet is required to be shown.

(3) *When Joint Life Policy Account is maintained with creating reserve* : Under this method Joint Life Policy Account and Joint Life Policy Reserve (Fund) Account are maintained to remove the defects of all other methods. There are two systems in maintaining the Joint Life Policy Account together with Joint Life Policy Reserve Account. They are as follows :

(a) *Joint Life Policy Account and Joint Life Policy Reserve Account are maintained at surrender value :*

In this method the premium paid is debited to Joint Life Policy Account and credited to Bank Account. At the end of each year except the last year, the amount equal to the premium is charged to P & L Appropriation Account and credited to Joint Life Policy Reserve Account. Under this method the balance of the Joint Life Policy Account is reduced to the surrender value by charging excess amount over surrender value to Joint Life Policy Reserve Account. Therefore, at the end of every year the debit balance of Joint Life Policy Account and credit balance of Joint Life Policy Reserve Account show the same balance. In the last year no adjustments are made in the Joint Life Policy Reserve Account but the balance of Joint Life Policy Reserve Account is transferred either to the Joint Life Policy Account or to the capital accounts of the partners. This method resembles to sinking fund method. The following journal entries are passed :

(i) When insurance premium paid :

Joint Life Policy Account	Dr.	With the amount of
To Bank or Cash Account		premium paid

(ii) When reserve (fund) created :

Profit & Loss Appropriation t A/c	Dr.	With the amount equal
To Joint Life Policy Reserve A/c		to premium

(iii) When excess amount over surrender value adjusted :

Joint Life Policy Reserve A/c	Dr.	With excess amount over
To Joint Life Policy A/c		surrender value.

(iv) When balance of reserve account transferred :

Joint Life Policy Reserve A/c	Dr.	With the amount of
To Joint Life Policy A/c		balance

(v) When policy amount received on maturity or on death of a partner :

Bank or Cash A/c	Dr.	With the amount of
To Joint Life Policy A/c		policy

(vi) When balance of policy account transferred to the capital accounts of partners :

Joint Life Policy A/c	Dr.	With the balance of
To Partners' Capital Accounts		policy account

(b). *Joint Life Policy Account is maintained at its full value and Joint Life Policy Reserve Account is maintained at difference between the Policy Account and surrender value :*

In this method, Joint Life Policy Reserve is created in the same way as in the above system. But amount equal to the yearly premium is not charged to the Profit and Loss Appropriation Account. Such amount charged (kept) is equal to a difference between premium paid and the surrender value. Under this method, the balance of Joint Life Policy Account is not reduced to the surrender value, because, Joint Life Policy Account is maintained at its full value in the books. Therefore, Joint Life Policy Account remains unaffected. The following journal entries are passed :

(i) When insurance premium paid :

Joint Life Policy A/c	Dr.	With the amount of
To Bank or Cash A/c		premium paid

(ii) When reserve created :

P & L Appropriation A/c	Dr.	With total premium paid
To Joint Life Policy Reserve A/c		(Value of opening balance of J.L.P.R. A/c + Present surrender value)

(iii) When balance of reserve account transferred :

Joint Life Policy Reserve A/c	Dr.	With the amount of
To Joint Life Policy A/c		balance in reserve

(iv) When policy amount received on maturity or on death of a partner :

Bank or Cash A/c	Dr.	With the amount of
To Joint Life Policy A/c		policy

(v) When balance of policy account transferred to the capital accounts of partners :

Joint Life Policy A/c	Dr.	With the balance of
To Partners' Capital A/c		policy account

(B) Several (Individual) Policies : Sometimes the firm may be taken individual or separate policy on the lives of each partner. The premium of such individual policies are charged to P & L A/c of the firm. In this case if a partner dies, only the deceased partner's policy amount is received from the Life Insurance Corporation and the policies of other remaining partners will be continued. Under this method, the deceased partner gets his share in the total value of his policy and his share in the surrender value of policies of other partners. This will clear from illustration No. 7. The accounting treatment is similar to that of a joint life policy.

Illustration 1

A, B and C are the partners in a firm sharing profits and losses in the ratio of 2 : 2: 1. In order to provide funds for the settlement of an account of the deceased or a retired partner, a Joint Life Policy is taken on 1-1-1990 for Rs. 50,000. The annual premium is Rs. 5,000. The surrender value of the policy is as follows :

1990, Nil; 1991 Rs. 1,000 and 1992 Rs. 1,800.

'B' died on 2-12-1992 and the policy amount is realised on 31-12-1992. The accounts are closed on 31st December every year.

Prepare Ledger Accounts under the following methods :

(i) When Joint Life Policy Account is not maintained.

(ii) When Joint Life Policy Account is maintained at its surrender value without creating reserve.

(iii) When Joint Life Policy Account and Reserve Account are maintained at surrender value.

(iv) When Joint Life Policy Account is maintained at full value along with a Reserve Account.

Solution :

I. ***Method***

Dr. **Insurance Premium Account** Cr.

Date		Rs.	Date		Rs.
1-1-1990	To Bank A/c	5,000	31-12-90	By P & L A/c	5,000
		5,000			5,000
1-1-1991	To Bank A/c	5,000	31-12-91	By P & L A/c	5,000
		5,000			5,000
1-1-1992	To Bank A/c	5,000	31-12-92	By P & L A/c	5,000
		5,000			5,000

Dr. **Joint Life Policy Account** Cr.

Date		Rs.	Date		Rs.
31-12-92	To Capital A/cs :		31-12-92	By Bank A/c	50,000
	A—2/5	20,000		(Policy amount	
	B—2/5	20,000		realized)	
	C—1/5	10,000			
		50,000			50,000

Dr. **Profit and Loss Account** Cr.

		Rs.			Rs.
31-12-90	To Insurance Premium	5,000			
31-12-91	To Insurance Premium	5,000			
31-12-92	To Insurance Premium	5,000			

II. ***Method***

Dr. **Joint Life Policy Account** Cr.

Date		Rs.	Date		Rs.
1-1-1990	To Bank A/c (Premium paid)	5,000	31-12-90	By P & L A/c (5000 – Nil)	5,000
			31-12-90	By Balance c/d (Surrender value)	Nil
		5,000			5,000
1-1-1991	To Balance b/d	Nil	31-12-91	By P & L A/c (5,000 – 1,000)	4,000
1-1-1991	To Bank A/c (Premium paid)	5,000	31-12-91	By Balance c/d (Surrender value)	1,000
		5,000			5,000
1-1-1992	To Balance b/d	1,000	31-12-92	By Bank A/c (Policy amount realised)	50,000
1-1-1992	To Bank A/c	5,000			
31-12-92	To Capital A/cs : Profit transferred : A— 2/5 17,600 B— 2/5 17,600 C— 1/5 8,800	44,000			
		50,000			50,000

Dr. **Profit and Loss Account** Cr.

		Rs.			Rs.
31-12-90	To Joint Life Policy	5,000			
31-12-91	To Joint Life Policy	4,000			

III. ***Method***

Dr. **Joint Life Policy Account** Cr.

Date		Rs.	Date		Rs.
1-1-90	To Bank A/c (Premium paid)	5,000	31-12-90	By Joint Life Policy Reserve A/c (5,000 – Nil)	5,000
			31-12-90	By Balance c/d (Surrender value)	Nil
		5,000			5,000
1-1-91	To Balance b/d	Nil	31-12-91	By Joint Life Policy Reserve A/c (5,000 – 1,000)	4,000
1-1-91	To Bank A/c (Premium paid)	5,000	31-12-91	By Balance c/d (Surrender value)	1,000
		5,000			5,000
1-1-92	To Balance b/d	1,000	31-12-92	By Bank A/c (Policy amount realized)	50,000
1-1-92	To Bank A/c (Premium paid)	5,000			
31-12-92	To Capital A/cs : A— 2/5 18,000; B— 2/5 18,000; C— 1/5 9,000	45,000	31-12-92	By Joint Life Policy Reserve A/c (Transferred from)	1,000
		51,000			51,000

Dr. **Joint Life Policy Reserve Account** Cr.

Date		Rs.	Date		Rs.
31-12-90	To Joint Life Policy A/c	5,000	31-12-90	By P & L Appropriation A/c (Amount provided)	5,000
	To Balance c/d (Surrender value)	Nil			
		5,000			5,000
31-12-91	To Joint Life Policy A/c	4,000	1-1-91	By Balance b/d	Nil
31-12-91	To Balance c/d (Surrender value)	1,000	31-12-91	By P & L Appropriation A/c	5,000
		5,000			5,000
31-12-92	To Joint Life Policy A/c (Transferred to)	1,000	1-1-92	By Balance b/d	1,000
		1,000			1,000

Dr. **Profit and Loss Appropriation Account** Cr.

		Rs.			Rs.
31-12-1990	To Joint Life Policy Reserve	5,000			
31-12-1991	To Joint Life Policy Reserve	5,000			

IV. *Method*

Joint Life Policy Account

Dr. Date		Rs.	Date		Cr. Rs.
1-1-90	To Bank A/c	5,000	31-12-90	By Balance c/d	5,000
		5,000			5,000
1-1-91	To Balance b/d	5,000	31-12-91	By Balance c/d	10,000
1-1-91	To Bank A/c	5,000			
		10,000			10,000
1-1-92	To Balance b/d	10,000	31-12-92	By Bank A/c	50,000
1-1-92	To Bank A/c	5,000		(Policy amount realised)	
31-12-92	To Capital A/cs :			By Joint Life Policy	
	Profit transferred			Reserve A/c	9,000
	A—2/5 17,600			(Transferred from)	
	B—2/5 17,600				
	C—1/5 8,800	44,000			
		59,000			59,000

Joint Life Policy Reserve Account

Dr. Date		Rs.	Date		Cr. Rs.
31-12-90	To Balance c/d	5,000	31-12-90	By P & L Appr. A/c	5,000
		5,000			5,000
31-12-91	To Balance c/d	9,000	1-1-91	By Balance b/d	5,000
			31-12-91	By P & L Appr. A/c* [10,000 – 6,000 (5,000 + 1,000)]	4,000
		9,000			9,000
31-12-92	To Joint Life Policy A/c (Transferred to)	9,000	1-1-92	By Balance b/d	9,000
		9,000			9,000

*Total premium paid — (Opening Balance of Reserve A/c + Present Surrender Value).

Profit and Loss Appropriation Account

Dr. Date		Rs.	Date		Cr. Rs.
31-12-90	To Joint Life Policy Reserve	5,000			
31-12-91	To Joint Life Policy Reserve	4,000			

Note : The Surrender Value for the year 1992 should not be considered since the policy is realized in that year.

Illustration 2

Kamala, Vimala and Sumala were partners in a firm sharing profits and losses in the ratio of 2 : 2 : 1. They took out a Joint Life Policy for Rs. 75,000 for which the annual premium of Rs. 3,500 was being paid on every 15th May, 1990. The surrender value of the policy on 31st December of different years was as follows :

1990	Rs. Nil
1991	Rs. 750
1992	Rs. 1,500
1993	Rs. 3,000

Vimala died on 10th April, 1994. Prepare Ledger Accounts assuming that the Joint Life Policy Account is maintained on Surrender Value basis.

Solution :

Dr. **Joint Life Policy Account** Cr.

Date		Rs.	Date		Rs.
15-5-90	To Bank A/c (Premium paid)	3,500	31-12-90	By P & L A/c	3,500
		3,500			3,500
15-5-91	To Bank A/c (Premium paid)	3,500	31-12-91	By P & L A/c	2,750
			31-12-91	By Balance c/d (Surrender value)	750
		3,500			3,500
1-1-92	To Balance b/d	750	31-12-92	By P & L A/c	2,750
15-5-92	To Bank A/c (Premium paid)	3,500	31-12-92	By Balance c/d (Surrender value)	1,500
		4,250			4,250
1-1-93	To Balance b/d	1,500	31-12-93	By P & L A/c	2,000
15-5-93	To Bank A/c (Premium paid)	3,500	31-12-93	By Balance c/d (Surrender value)	3,000
		5,000			5,000
1-1-94	To Balance b/d	3,000	10-4-94	By Bank A/c (Policy amount realised)	75,000
10-4-94	To Capital A/cs : Kamala 28,800; Vimala 28,800; Sumala 14,400	72,000			
		75,000			75,000

Illustration 3

From the following details prepare Joint Life Policy Account and Joint Life Policy Reserve Account in the books of Anju, Manju and Sunju and show how these two accounts would appear in the Balance Sheet :

(i) Profit sharing ratio of partners 5 : 3 : 2.

(ii) Period of Joint Life Policy 16 years.

(iii) Date of policy taken 1-1-1990.

(iv) Annual premium of policy Rs. 2,500.

(v) Amount of Joint Life Policy Rs. 40,000.

(vi) Surrender values were : year ending 1990 Rs. Nil, year ending 1991 Rs. 500, year ending 1990 Rs. 1,000 and year ending 1993 Rs. 1,500.

(vii) Sunju died on 8th March, 1993.

(viii) Claim received from the insurance corporation on 30th April, 1993.

Solution :

Dr. **Joint Life Policy Account** Cr.

Date		Rs.	Date		Rs.
1-1-90	To Bank A/c (Premium paid)	2,500	31-12-90	By Joint Life Policy Reserve A/c	2,500
		2,500			2,500
1-1-91	To Bank A/c (Premium paid)	2,500	31-12-91	By J. L.P.R. A/c	2,000
				By Balance c/d (Surrender value)	500
		2,500			2,500
1-1-92	To Balance b/d	500	31-12-92	By J. L.P.R. A/c	2,000
1-1-92	To Bank A/c (Premium paid)	2,500	31-12-92	By Balance c/d (Surrender value)	1,000
		3,000			3,000
1-1-93	To Balance b/d	1,000	30-4-93	By J. L.P.R. A/c	1,000
1-1-93	To Bank A/c (Premium paid)	2,500	30-4-93	By Bank A/c (Policy amount realized)	40,000
30-4-93	To Capital A/cs : Anju 18,750; Manju 11,250; Sanju 7,500	37,500			
		41,000			41,000

Dr. **Joint Life Policy Reserve Account** Cr.

Date		Rs.	Date		Rs.
31-12-90	To Joint Life Policy A/c	2,500	31-12-90	By P & L Appr. A/c	2,500
		2,500			2,500
31-12-91	To J.L.P. A/c	2,000	31-12-91	By P & L Appr. A/c	2,500
31-12-91	To Balance c/d (Surrender value)	500			
		2,500			2,500
31-12-92	To J.L.P. A/c	2,000	1-1-92	By Balance b/d	500
31-12-92	To Balance c/d (Surrender value)	1,000	31-12-92	By P & L Appr. A/c	2,500
		3,000			3,000
30-4-93	To J.L.P. A/c	1,000	1-1-93	By Balance b/d	1,000
		1,000			1,000

Balance Sheet as on 31-12-91

Liabilities	Rs.	Assets	Rs.
Joint Life Policy Reserve	500	Joint Life Policy	500

Balance Sheet as on 31-12-92

Liabilities	Rs.	Assets	Rs.
Joint Life Policy Reserve	1,000	Joint Life Policy	1,000

Note : There are no balance in the Joint Life Policy Account and Joint Life Policy Reserve Account in the year 1990 and 1993. Therefore, they do not appear in the Balance sheet.

Illustration 4

Sundar, Shashidar and Shivadar are partners in a firm sharing profits and losses in the proportion of $^2/_4$, ¼ and ¼ respectively. As a provision for repayment of capital and goodwill in the event of any of them a Joint Life Policy of the face value of Rs. 50,000 was taken on 20-2-1990. Annual premium payable was Rs. 4,000. The surrender value of the policy was as follows :

On payment of first premium Nil

On payment of second premium 15%
On payment of third premium 25%
On payment of fourth premium 30%
On payment of fifth premium 45%
On payment of sixth premium 55%

} Of the total premium paid excluding the first premium amount.

Shivadar died on 25-10-1994 and the policy amount was immediately realised. The firm closes the books of account on 31st December every year.

Show the Joint Life Policy Account and Joint Life Policy Reserve Account.

Solution :

Dr. **Joint Life Policy Account** Cr.

Date		Rs.	Date		Rs.
20-2-90	To Bank A/c (Premium paid)	4,000	31-12-90	By J.L.P.R. A/c (Transfer of Rs. 4,000 — Surrender value Nil)	4,000
		4,000			4,000
20-2-91	To Bank A/c (Premium paid)	4,000	31-12-91	By J. L.P.R. A/c (Tr. of Rs. 4,000– 600)	3,400
			31-12-91	By Balance c/d (Surrender value)	600
		4,000			4,000
1-1-92	To Balance b/d	600	31-12-92	By J.L.P.R. A/c (Tr. of Rs. 4,600 – 2,000)	2,600
20-2-92	To Bank A/c (Premium paid)	4,000	31-12-92	By Balance c/d (Surrender value)	2,000
		4,600			4,600
1-1-93	To Balance b/d	2,000	31-12-93	By J.L.P.R. A/c (Tr. of Rs. 6000– 3600)	2,400
20-2-93	To Bank A/c (Premium paid)	4,000	31-12-93	By Balance c/d (Surrender value)	3,600
		6,000			6,000
1-1-94	To Balance b/d	3,600	25-10-94	By Bank A/c (Policy amount realised)	50,000
20-2-94	To Bank A/c (Premium paid)	4,000			
25-10-94	To Capital A/cs : Sundar 23,000; Shashidar 11,500; Shivadar 11,500	46,000	25-10-94	By J.L.P.R. A/c (Transferred from)	3,600
		53,600			53,600

Dr. **Joint Life Policy Reserve Account** Cr.

Date		Rs.	Date		Rs.
31-12-90	To Joint Life Policy A/c	4,000	31-12-90	By P & L Appr. A/c	4,000
		4,000			4,000
31-12-91	To Joint Life Policy A/c (4,000 – 600)	3,400	31-12-91	By P & L Appr. A/c	4,000
31-12-91	To Balance c/d (Surrender value)	600			
		4,000			4,000
31-12-92	To Joint Life Policy A/c (4,600 – 2,000)	2,600	1-1-92	By Balance b/d	600
			31-12-92	By P & L Appr. A/c	4,000
31-12-92	To Balance c/d (Surrender value)	2,000			
		4,600			4,600
31-12-93	To Joint Life Policy A/c (6,000 – 3,600)	2,400	1-1-93	By Balance b/d	2,000
			31-12-93	By P & L Appr. A/c	4,000
31-12-93	To Balance c/d (Surrender value)	3,600			
		6,000			6,000
25-10-94	To Joint Life Policy A/c (Transferred to)	3,600	1-1-94	By Balance b/d	3,600
		3,600			3,600

Notes : (i) Calculation of surrender value :

	Rs.
1990 : Nil	Nil
1991 : 15% of Rs. 4,000 (*i.e.*, 8,000 – 4,000 first premium)	600
1992 : 25% of Rs. 8,000 (*i.e.*, 12,000 – 4,000 first premium)	2,000
1993 : 30% of Rs. 12,000 (*i.e.*, 16,000 – 4,000 first premium)	3,600

(ii) Surrender values of remaining years are not required.

Illustration 5

Mala and Neela were partners in a partnership firm sharing profits and losses in the proportion of 3/5 and 2/5 respectively. The partnership deed provided for interest on capital at 9% p.a. and for valuation of goodwill on death of a partner at two years purchases of the average profits for the last three completed years.

An assurance policy for Rs. 50,000 was taken out on their joint lives of two partners.

Neela died on 30th Sept., 1990 when the surrender value of the policy appearing in the last Balance sheet was Rs. 20,000. The net profits for the last three years were Rs. 20,000, Rs. 25,000 and Rs. 30,000 respectively.

On 1st Jan., 1990 Neela's capital was Rs. 30,000 and her drawings from 1-1-1990 to 30-9-1990 were Rs. 10,000, Neela's share of profit was to be ascertained on the basis of profits of the last year. Balance on the General Reserve was Rs. 7,000.

Prepare Neela's Capital Account, showing the amount due to her executors.

Solution :

Dr. **Neela's Capital Account** Cr.

Date		Rs.	Date		Rs.
30-9-90	To Drawings	10,000	1-1-90	By Balance b/d	30,000
30-9-90	To Neela's Executors			By Interest on Capital (for 9 months)	2,025
	To Loan A/c	70,025		By General Reserve	7,000
				By Goodwill	20,000
				By P & L Suspense A/c	9,000
				By Joint Life Policy A/c	12,000
		80,025			80,025

Notes : (i) Interest on Capital : $\frac{30{,}000 \times 9 \times 9}{100 \times 12}$ = Rs. 2,025

(ii) Goodwill : Average profit = $\frac{20{,}000 + 25{,}000 + 30{,}000}{3}$ = Rs. 25,000

Total goodwill = Twice the average profit

Rs. 50,000 = 25,000 × 2

Neela's share of goodwill Rs. 20,000 (*i.e.*, 50,000 × 2/5)

(iii) Neela's share of profit up to death is Rs. 9,000 $\left(i.e., \frac{30{,}000 \times 9 \times 2}{12 \times 5}\right)$

(iv) Neela's share in the policy Amount :

	Rs.
Joint Life Policy Amount	50,000
Less : Surrender value	20,000
	30,000

Neela's share of policy Rs. 12,000 $\left(i.e., \frac{30{,}000 \times 2}{5}\right)$

Illustration 6

Surya, Chandra and Nakshatra were partners sharing profits and losses in the ratio of 2 : 2 : 1. Their Balance Sheet on 31st Dec., 1990 was as follows:

		Rs.		Rs.
Sundry Creditors		3,000	Cash	8,000
Capital :			Freehold Premises	40,000
Surya	32,000		Debtors	10,000
Chandra	30,000		Loan of Nakshatra	15,000
Nakshatra	20,000	82,000	Furniture	5,000
			Stock-in-trade	7,000
		85,000		85,000

The firm had taken insurance policy for Rs. 25,000 on the joint lives of partners. Nakshatra died on 1st January, 1991. The amount of policy was realised on 1st January, 1991. The partnership deed provides that the goodwill was to be calculated at three years purchases of the average profits of four completed years preceding the death or retirement of a partner. The deceased partner's share in goodwill, capital etc. was paid out in cash on 1st March, 1991, the available cash being supplemented by a loan from the firm's banker on the security of the freehold property. The profit of the years 1987 Rs. 15,000, 1988 Rs. 18,000, 1989 Rs. 20,000 and 1990 Rs. 25,000.

You are required to prepare the ledger accounts of the partners and balance sheet of Surya and Chandra as it would appear after Nakshatra's share is paid off, assuming that no goodwill account is retained in the books of Surya and Chandra.

Solution :

Dr. **Capital Account of Partners** Cr.

	S Rs.	C Rs.	N Rs.		S Rs.	C Rs.	N Rs.
To Goodwill	23,400	23,400	—	By Balance b/d	32,000	30,000	20,000
To Nakshatra's Loan	—	—	15,000	By Goodwill	—	—	11,700
				By Joint Life Policy	10,000	10,000	5,000
To Nakshatra's Executors Loan	—	—	21,700				
To Balance c/d	18,600	16,600	—				
	42,000	40,000	36,700		42,000	40,000	36,700
				By Balance b/d	18,600	16,600	—

Dr. Nakshatra's Executor's Loan Account Cr.

Date		Rs.	Date		Rs.
1-3-91	To Bank	21,700	1-1-91	By Nakshatra's Capital	21,700
		21,700			21,700

Balance Sheet of Surya and Chandra as on 1-3-1991

Liabilities		Rs.	Assets	Rs.
Sundry creditors		3,000	Freehold Property	40,000
Bank Loan		23,800	Debtors	10,000
(Secured by freehold property			Furniture	5,000
i.e., Balancing figure)			Stock-in-trade	7,000
Capital :				
Surya	18,600			
Chandra	16,600	35,200		
		62,000		62,000

Note : Goodwill is calculated as below : Rs.

Average profit = $\frac{15{,}000 + 18{,}000 + 20{,}000 + 25{,}000}{4}$ = 19,500

Total goodwill = Thrice the average profit

Rs. 58,500 = 19,500 × 3

	Rs.
Surya's share of goodwill	23,400
Chandra's share of goodwill	23,400
Nakshatra's share of goodwill	11,700

Illustration 7

Prabha, Chandra and Sharada carried on a business in partnership sharing profit and losses in the ratio of 2 : 1 : 1. Their capital on 1st Jan., 1990 were : Prabha Rs. 25,000, Chandra Rs. 15,000 and Sharada Rs. 12,000. The partnership agreement provides that in the event of death of retirement of a partner his legal representatives would receive : (i) her capital as at the date, (ii) her share of goodwill as calculated on the basis of 2½ years purchase of the average profits of the last four years, (iii) her share of profits from the date of last accounting to the date of retirement or death on the basis of profits of the previous year and (iv) interest on capital at 9% p.a.

Chandra died on 30th June, 1990. Her drawings to the date of death were Rs. 3,000. The annual profits of the firm were : 1986 Rs. 15,000, 1987 Rs. 18,000, 1988 Rs. 20,000 and 1989 Rs. 22,000. The firm had insured the partner's lives severally (individually and not jointly), Prabha for Rs. 25,000,

Chandra for Rs. 20,000 and Sharada for Rs. 15,000. The premiums were charged to P & L A/c. The surrender values of these policies in 1990 were 30% of the face value.

Show the amount payable to Chandra.

Solution :

Dr. **Chandra's Capital Account** Cr.

Date		Rs.	Date		Rs.
30-6-90	To Drawings	3,000	1-1-90	By Balance b/d	12,000
30-6-90	To Chandra's Executors Loan (Amount payable)	32,009	30-6-90	By Interest on Capital (For 6 months)	540
			30-6-90	By P & L A/c $\left(\frac{22,000 \times 1 \times 6}{4 \times 12}\right)$	2,750
			30-6-90	By Goodwill	11,719
				By Life Policy	8,000
		35,009			35,009

Notes : (i) Calculation of Goodwill :

$$\text{Average profit} = \frac{15,000 + 18,000 + 20,000 + 22,000}{4} = \text{Rs. } 18,750$$

Total Goodwill = Rs. 46,875 (*i.e.*, 18,750 × 2½)

Chandra's share of Goodwill = Rs. 11,719 (*i.e.*, 46,875 ×1/4)

(ii) Calculation of life policy credited to Chandra's Account :

30% of face value of policies of Prabha and Sharada (*i.e.*, 30% of 25,000 and 15,000)	Rs. 12,000
Plus policy amount of Chandra's policy	Rs. 20,000
	Rs. 32,000

Hence, Chandra's 1/4th share in Rs. 32,000 = Rs. 8,000.

EXAMINATION QUESTIONS

(A) Answer the following questions in not exceeding 4 lines each :

(*Each Carries 2 Marks*)

(1) What do you mean by joint life policy?

(2) What is the object of taking joint life policy?

(3) What is surrender value? (*M.K.U., April, 1981*)

(4) What is the advantage of not maintaining the joint life policy account?

(5) What is the defect of maintaining the joint life policy account at its surrender value without creating reserve?

(6) What are the two systems of maintaining the joint life policy account together with joint life policy reserve account?

(7) What do you understand by individual policy?

(8) What is use of taking individual policy?

(9) What are the methods of treatment of joint life policy transactions?

(*Bangalore, April, 1991*)

(B) Answer the following questions/problems :

(*Each Carries 8 Marks*)

(1) What is joint life policy? What is the need of taking such policy?

(2) What are the different methods of treatment of a joint life policy?

(3) How the arrangement regarding 'joint life policy' on the lives of the partners is recorded in the accounts of a partnership firm?

(4) A, B and C are partners in a firm sharing profits and losses in the ratio of 3 : 2 : 1. They have taken a joint life policy for Rs. 1,80,000 on 1-1-1993. The annual premium is Rs. 15,000. Mr. 'A' died on 25-12-1995 and the policy amount is received from the Life Insurance Corporation on 31-12-1995. The premium has charged to P & L A/c every year on 31st December.

Pass the necessary journal entries. Premium is adjusted through P & L Account.

(*Shivaji, April, 1995*)

Ans. : Policy transferred to partners' capital accounts : 'A' Rs. 90,000; 'B' Rs. 60,000 and 'C' Rs. 30,000.

(5) 'A' and 'B' who shared profits in the ratio of 3 : 2 took a joint life policy on May 1, 1994 for Rs. 30,000. The annual premium was Rs. 1,300. The surrender value of the policy was :

1994 – Nil, 1995 – Rs. 400; 1996 – Rs. 900 and 1997 – Rs. 1,450. B died on September 15, 1997 and the amount of the policy was received on Dec. 31, 1997. The books are closed on December 31 each year.

Show joint life policy account assuming that premiums are written off through joint life policy reserve account.

(*C.A. Inter, 1996*)

Ans. : Balance of policy accounts transferred to partners' capital accounts : A – Rs. 17,220 and 'B' – Rs. 11,480.

(6) 'A', 'B' and 'C' are partners in a business sharing profit and losses in the ratio of 3 : 2 : 1. The firm has taken a joint life insurance policy on the lives of partners for a joint life with effect from 1 January, 1986. The annual premium is Rs. 2,000. On 31 December, 1988, 'C' dies and full money is received from the Life Insurance Corporation. The firm has charged the premium to profit and loss account each year on 31 December. You are required to make the necessary journal entries.

(*Osmania, Oct., 1989*)

Ans. : Policy amount transferred to partners : 'A' Rs. 15,000; 'B' Rs. 10,000 and 'C' Rs. 5,000.

(7) X, Y and Z sharing profit and losses in the ratio of 5 : 3 : 2 took out a joint policy for Rs. 15,000 paying an annual premium of Rs. 600, starting from 10th April, 1985. The surrender value of the policy was as follows :

	Rs.
1985	Nil
1986	200
1987	500
1988	850
1989	1,500

'Y' died on 6th October, 1989 and the insurance company paid Rs. 15,000 on 30th November, 1989.

The books of the firm were closed on 31st December each year. Show the account relating to joint life policy, when surrender value is to be treated as an asset.

(*Madras, April, 1990*)

Ans. : Balance of policy account transferred to partners : 'X' Rs. 6,775; 'Y' Rs. 4,065 and 'Z' Rs. 2,710.

(C) Solve the following problems :

(Each Carries 16 Marks)

(1) A, B and C sharing profit and losses, in the ratio of 5 : 3 : 2 took out a joint life policy for Rs. 30,000 paying an annual premium of Rs. 1,500 starting from 15th May, 1990.

The surrender value of the policy was as follows :

	Rs.
1990	Nil
1991	300
1992	500
1993	900
1994	1,460

B died in November 1994 and the Life Insurance Corporation paid the policy amount on 15th December, 1994. Prepare ledger accounts.

(B.Com., Mysore, Karnatak and Bombay)

Ans. : (i) When premium is charged to P & L A/c (*i.e.*, I method) : Policy A/c balance transferred to capital accounts of partners: 'A' Rs. 15,000; 'B' Rs. 9,000 and 'C' Rs. 6,000.

(ii) When premium is charged to Policy A/c and surrender value treated as asset without creating reserve (*i.e.*, II method) : Policy A/c balance transferred to capital accounts of partners: 'A' Rs. 13,800; 'B' Rs. 8,280 and 'C' Rs. 5,520.

(iii) When premium is charged to Policy Account and Reserve Account maintained at surrender value (*i.e.*, III method) : Policy A/c balance transferred to capital accounts of partners: 'A' Rs. 14,250; 'B' Rs. 8,550 and 'C' Rs. 5,700.

(iv) When Policy Account maintained at its full value with Reserve Account (*i.e.*, IV method) : Policy Account balance transferred to capital accounts of partners : 'A' Rs. 13,800; 'B' Rs. 8,280 and 'C' Rs. 5,520.

(2) Pai, Bhat and Hegde shared Profits and Losses in the ratio of 5 : 3 : 2. They took out a joint life policy in 1980 for Rs. 1,00,000 for which the annual premium of Rs. 6,000 was being paid on every 10th June.

The surrender value of the policy on 31st December of different years was as follows :

	Rs.
1980	Nil
1981	1,800
1982	4,000
1983	7,200

Hegde died on 15th April, 1984.

(Gulbarga, April, 1986, 1990, 1993 & 1994)

Ans. : Balance of Policy Account transferred to partners' capital accounts—Pai Rs. 46,400; Bhat Rs. 27,840 and Hegde Rs. 18,500.

(3) P, Q and R were partners sharing profits and losses in the ratio of 3 : 2 : 1. On 1-5-1982 the firm took a joint life policy for Rs. 50,000 on an annual premium of Rs. 2,000. The surrender value of the policy was as under:

	Rs.
1982	Nil
1983	800
1984	2,000
1985	2,500

R died on 15-4-1985 and the policy amount is received on 30-4-1985.

Prepare the Joint Life Policy Account and Joint Life Policy Reserve Account assuming that the firm closes its accounts on 31st December every year.

(*Karnataka, B.Com., Oct., 1986 and 1994*)

Ans. : Balance of Policy Account transferred to 'P' Rs. 25,000; 'Q' Rs. 16,667 and 'R' Rs. 8,333. On 30-4-1985 Rs. 2,000 being credit balance in reserve transferred to Policy Account.

Note : Premium is not payable in 1985 since 'R' dies before the due date.

(4) P, Q and R were the partners sharing profits and losses in the ratio of 2 : 1 : 1. They took a joint life policy for Rs. 80,000 on 1-4-1980. The annual premium payable was Rs. 4,000. The first premium was paid on 1-4-1980 itself.

The surrender value of the policy was as under :

Year	Rs.
1980	Nil
1981	800
1982	2,000
1983	3,600
1984	6,000

Mr. R died on 15-3-1984 and the policy amount was received on 31-3-1984.

The books are closed on 31st December every year. Prepare Joint Life Policy Account and Joint Life Policy Reserve Account as maintained at surrender value.

(*Gulbarga, B.Com., April, 1988*)

Ans. : Balance of Policy Account transferred to 'P' Rs. 40,000, 'Q' Rs. 20,000 and 'R' Rs. 20,000. Rs. 3,600 being credit balance in Reserve Account transferred to Policy Account.

(5) From the following details prepare, (i) Joint Life Policy Account and (ii) Joint Life Policy Reserve Account in the books of A and B and show how these two accounts should be represented in the Balance Sheets of the year ending 1990, 1991, 1992, 1993 :

(i)	Profit sharing ratio	3 : 2
(ii)	Date of taking out the Joint Life Policy	1-1-1990
(iii)	Period of policy	20 Years
(iv)	Annual premium	Rs. 1,000
(v)	Amount of policy	Rs. 20,000
(vi)	Surrender values were : Year ending 1990 Rs. Nil, Year ending 1991 Rs. 200, Year ending 1992 Rs. 550, Year ending 1993 Rs. 970.	
(vii)	B died on 8th March, 1993.	
(viii)	Claim received on 30th April, 1993.	

(*Shivaji, B.Com., April, 1981*)

Ans. : Rs. 550 credit balance in Reserve Account transferred to Policy Account. Balance of Policy Account transferred to A—Rs. 11,400 and B—Rs. 7,600.

(6) Ramesh, Satish and Prakash are carrying on business in partnership sharing profits and losses in the ratio of 5 : 3 : 2. On 15-1-1990 they took out a Joint Life Policy for Rs. 30,000 paying an annual premium of Rs. 1,500. The surrender value of the policy is as under:

On payment of first premium	Nil	
On payment of second premium	20%	Of the total premium paid except first one.
On payment of third premium	30%	
On payment of fourth premium	40%	
On payment of fifth premium	50%	
On payment of sixth premium	60%	

On 29-9-1994 Ramesh died and the policy amount was immediately realised.

Show the Joint Life Policy Account and the Joint Life Policy Reserve Account.

(*Karnataka, B.Com., April, 1975 & Gulbarga, 1990*)

Ans. : Rs. 1,800 being credit balance in Reserve Account transferred to Policy Account. Balance Policy Account transferred to Ramesh—Rs. 14,250, Satish—Rs. 8,550 and Prakash—Rs. 5,700.

(7) Anil, Prakash and Ramesh were partners sharing profits and losses in the proportion of 2/5, 2/5 and 1/5 respectively. On 1-1-1988 they took a Joint Life Policy for Rs. 30,000 for which they pay an annual premium of Rs. 1,000. The premium is debited to profit and loss account every year. According to partnership deed, whenever any partners dies, the goodwill of the firm is to be valued at twice the average profits of the last three years. Interest on capital is to be allowed at 5% per annum. The share of profit from the date of the last Balance Sheet to the date of death is to be calculated on the basis of the previous year's profit. Prakash died on 1-4-1991 and his capital on 1-1-1991 was Rs. 25,000 and he had withdrawn from the firm Rs. 2,000 for his private expenses.

The profits for the previous three years were : 1988— Rs. 7,500, 1989— Rs. 9,000 and 1990—Rs. 12,000.

Prepare Prakash's Capital Account and find out the amount due to his executors. (*Karnataka, B.Com., 1982 & Shivaji, B.Com., 1989*)

Ans. : Prakash's share of goodwill Rs. 7,600 (2/5 × 19,000); Prakash's share of Profit Rs. 1,200 (up to date of death). Amount due to executors of Prakash Rs. 43,100.

(8) Anu, Banu and Canu carried on business in partnership sharing as 3:2:1. Their capitals on 31-12-1990 were : Anu Rs. 10,400; Banu Rs. 5,000 and Canu Rs. 3,000.

On 28th February, 1991, Anu died, and you are instructed to prepare his Loan Account having regard to the following facts :

(i) The firm had insured the partners, lives severally (individually and not jointly), Anu for Rs. 9,000, Banu for Rs. 4,800 and Canu for Rs. 2,400. The premiums have been charged to Profit and Loss Account and the surrender value on 28th February, 1990 amounted in each case to one-fourth of the sum assured.

(ii) Capital carried interest at 5% p.a.

(iii) Anu's drawings from 1-1-1990 to the date of his death amounted to Rs. 1,200.

(iv) Anu's share of profits for the portion of the current financial year for which he lived was to be taken at the sum calculated on the average of the last three completed years and goodwill was to be raised on the basis of two years' purchase of the average profits of those three years.

The annual profits were Rs. 9,200; Rs. 7,400 and Rs. 8,600 respectively. Show Anu's Account.

(*B.Com., Bombay, April, 1988 and Madras, 1996*)

Ans. : Anu's share in profits : Rs. 700; Anu's share in goodwill Rs. 8,400; Anu's share in Joint Life Policy Rs. 5,400 and Amount due to executors of Anu Rs. 23,787.

8

DISSOLUTION OF A PARTNERSHIP FIRM

Meaning

Dissolution of a partnership firm means, it is a process by which the business of the firm is closed. Section 39 of the Partnership Act, 1932 provides that, "the dissolution of partnership between all the partners of the firm is called the dissolution of a firm". It implies the complete break down of the relation between all the partners. The process of dissolution involves the realisation of the assets, payment of liabilities and distribution of surplus if any, amongst the partners of the firm.

Dissolution of Partnership Vs. Dissolution of Firm

Indian Partnership Act recognises the difference between the dissolution of a partnership and the dissolution of a firm. Dissolution of partnership involves any change in the relation of the partners. On the other hand, the dissolution of firm involves the complete closure of the business. For example: A, B and C are partners in a partnership firm. If anyone of the partners dies or retires or becomes insolvent then the firm would come to an end. But if there is a partnership between A and B and a new partner C is admitted, the partnership between A and B comes to an end and a new partnership between A, B and C comes into existence. Therefore, the firm continues in a reconstituted form. Following are the main differences between dissolution of partnership and dissolution of firm.

Dissolution of Partnership	Dissolution of Firm
1. It merely involves a change in the relation of the partners.	1. It involves the complete break down of partnership relation.
2. In this case, the business of the firm continues for all practical purpose as before.	2. In this case, the business of the firm would be closed.
3. In this case, only some of the partners severs their connection with the firm.	3. In this case, all the partners terminate the connection with the firm.
4. It occurs in the event of a partner's death, retirement, insanity or insolvency.	4. It occurs in the event of death, insanity or insolvency of all partners and expiry of the term, mutual consent or court order.
5. It does not necessarily involves dissolution of firm.	5. It does involves dissolution of partnership.

Reasons for Dissolution*

The following are the main reasons for dissolution :

D – Death of a partner
I – Insanity or incapacity of a partner
S – Stipulated period of partnership completed
S – Serious misconduct of a partner
O – Object of the partnership firm completed
L – Lunacy of partner
U – Unavoidable continuous loss of the firm
T – Transfer of interest in the firm (sale of firm to a company)
I – Insolvency of a partner
O – Objectionable objects of the firm
N – Notice of dissolution by a partner.

Modes of Dissolution of a Firm

Sections 40 to 44 of the Partnership Act, 1932 deal with the various modes in which a firm may be dissolved. A partnership firm may be dissolved with or without the intervention of the court.

(A) Dissolution without the Intervention of the Court (Sections 40 to 43)

(1) Dissolution by mutual agreement between all the partners.
(2) Compulsory dissolution or dissolution by operation of law, when the business of the firm becomes unlawful.
(3) Dissolution on the happening of certain contingencies.
(4) Dissolution of partnership at will by notice.

(B) Dissolution by the Court (Section 44)

Dissolution by the court may take place under the following circumstances :

(1) When a partner has become permanently incapable of performing his duties as a partner.
(2) When a partner has become of unsound mind.
(3) When a partner has committed wilful breach of agreement regarding the conduct of the business.
(4) When a partner has transferred or sold his interest in the firm to the third party.
(5) When the business of the firm can be carried on only at a loss.
(6) When the court considers any other ground to be just and equitable for the dissolution of the firm.

---

* *Accountancy* by A.K. Aditya and B.B. Roy.

Settlement of Accounts on Dissolution

Section 48 of the Partnership Act deals with the mode of settlement of accounts between the partners after dissolution of the firm. Usually, the partnership deed contains the rules as to how the accounts of a firm should be settled on dissolution. In the absence of any agreement between the partners, the rules stated in Section 48 of the Partnership Act shall apply. The rules of Section 48 are as follows :

(A) The Losses of a Firm

The losses suffered by the firm including the deficiency of the capital should be made good :

(i) First, out of the profits of the firm.

(ii) Next, out of capitals of the partners.

(iii) Lastly if need arises, out of the contributions made by the partners from their private estates in their profit sharing ratio.

(B) The Assets of a Firm

The assets of a firm including the contribution made by the partners are to be distributed for settling the debts of the firm in the following order :

(i) First, in paying the debts due to third parties.

(ii) Secondly, in paying the partners rateably the loans due to them.

(iii) Thirdly, in paying the partners rateably the amount due to them on account of capital.

(iv) Lastly, if there is any surplus, it should be distributed among the partners in their profits sharing ratio.

Settlement of Firm's Debts and Private Debts of Partners

When there are debts of the firm (*i.e.*, debts due from the firm) and private debts of the partners (*i.e.*, debts due from the partners), they should be settled in the following manner.

(A) Assets of the firm should be used :

(i) First, in paying the debts of the firm

(ii) Then, the surplus, if any, should be paid to all the partners in their profit sharing ratio.

(B) The private assets of each partner should be utilised :

(i) First, in paying his private debt due to third party.

(ii) Then, the surplus, if any, should be brought to the firm so as to be used in paying the debts of the firm.

Accounting Procedure on Dissolution

When a partnership firm is dissolved, all its assets are sold away and liabilities paid off. Therefore, the following accounts are usually prepared in connection with the dissolution of a firm.

(A) Realisation Account

In order to find out any profit or loss on realisation of assets and making payment of liabilities, a new account called 'Realisation Account' is prepared, which is the nature of nominal account. It is called 'Realisation Account' because, it is prepared to realise assets and pay liabilities. The Realisation Account is closed by transferring the profit or loss to capital or current accounts of partners.

There are three methods of preparing the Realisation Account. They are as follows :

(1) Total of Assets and Liabilities Method : Under this method, all realisable assets appearing in the Balance Sheet, except cash and bank balance or any losses, are to be entered on the debit side of the 'Realisation Account' at their Book Value (Full Value). All the outsiders liabilities, such as creditor, loans (*i.e.*, other than partners' loan) etc. and provisions against assets, such as provisions for bad debts, discount on debtors, depreciation etc. appearing in the Balance Sheet are to be entered on the credit side of the Realisation Account. Any amount received on sale of assets is entered on the credit side of the Realisation Account and any assets taken over by a partner or the amount due from the partner, is entered on the credit side of the Realisation Account. Any liabilities paid to outsiders and any liabilities taken over by the partner or amount due to partner, is entered on the debit side of the Realisation Account. If any expense incurred in connection with dissolution of a firm is entered on the debit side of Realisation Account. After all the above entries are recorded in the Realisation Account, the Realisation Account is balanced. The balance in the Realisation Account represents either profit or loss which is transferred to the Capital Accounts (or current accounts if the capitals are fixed) of all the partners in their profit sharing ratio.

Under this method, the following journal entries are to be passed for preparing the Realisation Account :

(i) **For the transfer of all realisable assets to Realisation Account at their book values :**

Realisation Account	Dr.	With book value of various assets
To Various Assets Account		

Notes : (a) Cash and bank balances and also losses if any should not be transferred to Realisation Account.

(b) Unrecorded assets should not be transferred to Realisation Account, as they have no book values.

(ii) For the transfer of provisions against assets, such as provision for bad debts, discount on debtors, depreciation etc. to Realisation Account at their book values :

Provisions and Reserves A/c	Dr.	With book value of such Provisions and Reserve
(*i.e.,* Reserve for Bad Debts A/c		
Or Reserve for Discount on Debtors A/c		
Or Provisions for Depreciation A/c)		
To Realisation A/c		

(iii) For the transfer of all outside or external liabilities to Realisation Account at their book values :

Various Liabilities to Outsiders A/c	Dr.	With book value of various liabilities
To Realisation A/c		

Notes : (a) Unrecorded liabilities (i.e., liabilities which are not given in the Balance Sheet) should not be transferred to Realisation Account, as they have no book values.

(b) Partners' loans and capitals, reserves and accumulated profits should not be transferred to Realisation Account as they are not liabilities to outsiders.

(iv) For the realisation of the assets in cash at their realised values :

Cash or Bank A/c	Dr.	With total amount received
To Realisation A/c		

Note : Any amount received from the sale of unrecorded assets is also to be included in the above amount.

(v) For the assets taken over by the partners at their agreed values:

Partners' Capital A/cs	Dr.	With agreed value of assets
To Realisation A/c		

Note : If an agreed value of the assets (*i.e.*, recorded or unrecorded assets) taken over by a partner are not specially given, it is to be assumed that those assets are taken over by the partner at their book values.

(vi) For the payment of liabilities in cash :

Realisation A/c	Dr.	With the amount actually paid
To Cash or Bank A/c		

Note : The above amount not only include the recorded liabilities (*i.e.*, liabilities given in the Balance Sheet) but also the unrecorded liabilities, if any.

(vii) For the liabilities taken over by a partner or partners at their agreed values :

Realisation A/c	Dr.	With the agreed
To Partner or Partners' Capital A/cs.		amount

Note : The above amount may also include the unrecorded liabilities taken over by the partner or partners.

(viii) For the payment of realisation expenses :

(*a*) *If the realisation expenses paid by the firm :*

Realisation A/c	Dr.	With the amount
To Cash or Bank A/c		of expenses

(*b*) *If the realisation expenses are to be paid by a partner as agreed before :*

Realisation A/c	Dr.	With the agreed
To Partner's Capital A/cs		amount of expenses

(ix) For the transfer of profit or loss on realisation :

(*a*) *If the Realisation Account shows profit :*

Realisation A/c	Dr.	Profit transferred in
To Partner's Capital A/c		profit sharing ratio

(*b*) *If the Realisation Account shows loss :*

Partner's Capital A/c	Dr.	Loss transferred in
To Realisation Account		profit sharing ratio

After passing the above entries in the Realisation Account, Realisation account is now closed.

Limitations and Criticisms of Total of Assets and Liabilities Method

(i) When a partnership firm is dissolved, realisation of assets and payment (liquidation) of liabilities are recorded in the Realisation Account. But the title of Realisation Account is not so suitable. It should be called as 'Realisation and Liquidation Account'.

(ii) Under this method, all realisable assets and liabilities are closed before they are actually realised and paid. But this system is not quite correct. Assets and liabilities accounts are to be closed as and when they are realised and paid.

(iii) Preparation of Realisation Account under this method is somewhat laborious.

(iv) Even though this method having number of limitations and comments, this method is widely used.

(2) Total of Assets and Balance of Liabilities Method : Under this method, all the realisable assets given in the Balance Sheet are entered on the debit side of the Realisation Account their book values and provisions against assets (book values of provisions), amount received from the sale of assets and amount due from the partners for the assets taken over are entered on the credit side of the Realisation Account. But in case of liabilities, only the balance on liabilities accounts is entered into the Realisation Account. Balance on liabilities accounts means any profit or loss on the payment of any liability (*i.e.,* book value actual— amount paid). Profit on the settlement of the liabilities should be credited and loss on the settlement of liabilities should be debited to the Realisation Account. If there is any expense relating to realisation of assets and payment of liabilities, that should be debited to the Realisation Account. After all the above entries are made in the Realisation Account, the Realisation Account is balanced. The balance of Realisation Account represents either profit or loss, which is transferred to the capital or current accounts of all the partners in their profit sharing ratio.

Under this method, the following journal entries are to be passed for preparing the Realisation Account.

(i) For the transfer of all realisable assets given in the Balance Sheet to Realisation Account at their book values :

Realisation Account	Dr.	With book values of
To Various Assets A/cs		various assets

Notes : (a) Cash and bank balances and losses are not realisable assets. Hence, they should not be transferred to realisation account.

(b) Unrecorded assets should not be transferred to Realisation Account, as they have no book values.

(ii) For the transfer of Provisions and Reserves against assets, such as provision for depreciation, provision for discount on debtors, reserve for bad debts etc. given in Balance Sheet to Realisation Account at their book values :

Provisions and Reserves A/c	Dr.	With book values of
To Realisation A/c		such provisions and reserves

(iii) For the realisation of the assets in cash at their realised values :

Cash or Bank A/c	Dr.	With total amount
To Realisation A/c		received

Note : Any amount received from the sale of unrecorded assets is also to be included in the above amount.

(iv) For the assets taken over by the partners at their agreed values :

Partners' Capital A/cs	Dr.	With agreed value
To Realisation A/c		of assets

Note : If an agreed value of the assets (recorded or unrecorded assets) taken over by a partner are not specially given, it is to be assumed that those assets are taken over by the partner at their book values.

(v) For the payment of liabilities in cash :

(*a*) *For cash paid to all the liabilities* (*i.e., both the recorded and the unrecorded liabilities*) :

Concerned Liabilities A/c	Dr.	With the amount of each liability
To Cash or Bank A/c		

Note : When the liabilities of the firm are paid off in cash, concerned liabilities account should be debited and not the Realisation Account.

(*b*) *For profit on payment of any liability* (*i.e., if the actual amount paid is less than the book value of any liability*) :

Concerned Liabilities A/c	Dr.	With the amount of profit
To Realisation A/c		

(*c*) *For loss on payment of any liability* (*i.e., if the actual amount paid is more than the book value of any liability*) :

Realisation A/c	Dr.	With the amount of loss
To Concerned Liabilities A/c		

(vi) For the liabilities taken over by a partner or partners at their agreed values :

(*a*) *For any liability* (*whether recorded or unrecorded liabilities*) *taken over by any partner :*

Concerned Liabilities A/c	Dr.	With the amount of concerned liability
To Concerned Partner's Capital A/c		

Note : When any liability of the firm taken over by any partner, concerned liability account should be debited and not the Realisation Account.

(*b*) *For the profit on the liability taken over by a partner* (*i.e., if the agreed value is less than the book value of the liabilities taken over by a partner*) :

Concerned Liabilities A/c	Dr.	With the amount of profit
To Realisation A/c		

(*c*) *For loss on the liabilities taken over by a partner* (*i.e.. if the agreed value is more than the book value of the liabilities taken over by a partner*) :

Realisation A/c	Dr.	With the amount of loss
To Concerned Liabilities A/c		

(vii) For the payment of realisation expenses :

(*a*) *If realisation expenses are paid by the firm :*

Realisation A/c	Dr.	With the amount of expenses
To Cash or Bank A/c		

(*b*) *If realisation expenses are to be paid by a partner as agreed before :*

Realisation A/c	Dr.	With the agreed
To Partner's Capital A/c		amount of expenses

(*c*) *If realisation expenses are paid by the firm on behalf of partner :*

Partner's Capital A/c	Dr.	With amount paid
To Cash A/c		on behalf of partner

Note : If the realisation expenses is paid by the partner himself no entry is passed in the books of the firm.

(viii) For the transfer of profit or loss on realisation :

(*a*) *If Realisation Account shows profit :*

Realisation A/c	Dr.	Profit transferred in
To Partners' Capital A/c		profit sharing ratio

(*b*) *If Realisation Account shows loss :*

Partner's Capital A/c	Dr.	Loss transferred in
To Realisation A/c		profit sharing ratio

After passing the above entries in the Realisation Account, Realisation account is now closed.

Limitations and Advantages of Total of Assets and Balance of Liabilities Method :

(i) Under this method, assets accounts are closed before they are actually realised. Such procedure is not so correct, because in actual practice, all the realisable assets accounts are closed as and when they are completely realised.

(ii) Under this method, all the realisable assets and the amount realised from sale of assets are recorded in the Realisation Account. But so for as liabilities concerned, only the profit or loss made on their settlement is recorded in the Realisation Account. Therefore, the title of the account viz., the Realisation Account is quite correct.

(iii) Under this method, liabilities are paid directly and not through the realisation account. This procedure is correct. If the payment is made through realisation account, confusion may arise in ascertaining the correct result of realisation.

(iv) Under this method, liabilities are paid directly without transferring them to realisation account. Therefore, the preparation of realisation account is not as laborious as the first method.

Anyway this method is recommended by the some authors. But this method is not widely used by all the authors.

3. Balance of Assets and Balance of Liabilities Method : Under this method, the assets appearing on the Balance Sheet are not transferred to Realisation Account and realisation of assets or assets taken over by the partners are not recorded in the Realisation Account. But only the difference between the book values of assets and the realised values of assets are recorded in the Realisation Account. Profit on realisation of assets is credited and loss on realisation of assets is debited to Realisation Account. As regards the unrecorded assets, the entire realised amount of unrecorded assets should be taken as profit on realisation of assets and credited to Realisation Account. Similarly, the liabilities appearing in the Balance Sheet are not transferred to Realisation Account and actual amounts paid for liabilities or liabilities taken over by the partner are not recorded in the Realisation Account. But, only the profit or loss on the payment of liabilities (*i.e.*, the difference between the book values and actual amount paid in respect of liabilities) is recorded in the Realisation Account. The profit made on the payment of liabilities should be credited and loss incurred on the payment of liabilities is debited to Realisation Account. As regards the unrecorded liabilities, the entire payment made for the unrecorded liabilities should be treated as a loss and debited to Realisation Account. Realisation expenses, if any, are entered on the debit side of the Realisation Account. After all these entries are made in the Realisation Account, the Realisation Account is balanced. The balance of Realisation Account may represents either profit or loss, which is transferred to the capital or current accounts of all the partners in their profit-sharing ratio.

Under this method, the following journal entries are to be passed for preparing the realisation account :

(i) For the transfer of Provisions and Reserves against assets given in the Balance Sheet to Realisation Account at their book values :

Provisions and Reserves A/c	Dr.	With book values of such Provisions and Reserves
To Realisation A/c		

(ii) For the realisation of the assets in cash at their realised values :

(*a*) *If realised values of all the assets (i.e., both the recorded and unrecorded assets) :*

Cash or Bank A/c	Dr.	With the total amount received
To Concerned Assets A/c		

Note : When the cash received from the sales of assets, the concerned assets account should be credited and not the Realisation Account.

(*b*) *For profit on the realisation of any asset (i.e., if the realised value of any asset is more than its book value) :*

Concerned Assets A/c Dr. } With the amount
To Realisation A/c } of profit

(*c*) *For loss on the realisation of any asset* (*i.e., if the realised value of any asset is less than its book value*) *:*

Realisation A/c Dr. } With the amount
To Concerned Assets Account } of loss

(iii) For the assets (*i.e.*, recorded or unrecorded) taken over by the partners at their agreed values :

(*a*) *For assets taken over by the partners:*

Concerned Partner's Capital A/c Dr. } With agreed value of
To Concerned Assets A/c } assets

Note : When the assets taken over by the partner, concerned assets account should be credited but not Realisation Account.

(*b*) *For profit on any asset taken over by the partners :*

Concerned Assets A/c Dr. } With the amount of
To Realisation A/c } profit

(*c*) *For loss on any asset taken over by the partners :*

Realisation A/c Dr. } With the amount of
To Concerned Assets A/c } loss

(iv) For the payment of liabilities in cash :

(*a*) *For cash paid to all the liabilities* (*i.e., both the recorded and the unrecorded liabilities*) *:*

Concerned Liabilities A/c Dr. } With the amount of
To Cash or Bank A/c } each liability

Note : When the liabilities are paid off in cash, concerned liabilities account should be debited and not Realisation Account.

(*b*) *For profit on payment of any liability :*

Concerned Liability A/c Dr. } With the amount of
To Realisation A/c } profit

(*c*) *For loss on payment of any liability :*

Realisation Account Dr. } With the amount of
To Concerned Liability Account } loss

(v) For the liabilities (*i.e.*, recorded or unrecorded) taken over by a partner at their agreed values :

(*a*) *For any liabilities taken over by any partner :*

Concerned Liability A/c Dr. } With the amount of
To Concerned Partner's Capital A/c } concerned liability.

Note : When any liability taken over by any partner, concerned liability account should be debited and not Realisation Account.

(*b*) *For profit on the liabilities taken over by a partner :*

Concerned Liability A/c To Realisation A/c	Dr.	With the amount of profit

(*c*) *For loss on the liabilities taken over by a partner :*

Realisation A/c To Concerned Liability A/c	Dr.	With the amount of loss

(vi) For the payment of realisation expenses :

(*a*) *If the realisation expenses are paid by the firm :*

Realisation A/c To Cash or Bank A/c	Dr.	With the amount of expenses

(*b*) *If the realisation expenses are to be paid by the partner :*

Realisation A/c To Partner's Capital A/c	Dr.	With the agreed amount of expenses

(*c*) *If realisation expenses are paid by the firm on behalf of partner :*

Partner's Capital A/c To Cash or Bank A/c	Dr.	With the amount paid on behalf of partner

Note : If the realisation expenses are paid by the partner himself no entry is passed in the books of the firm.

(vii) For the transfer of profit or loss on realisation :

(*a*) *If Realisation Account shows profit :*

Realisation A/c To Partner's Capital A/c	Dr.	Profit transferred in profit sharing ratio

(*b*) *If Realisation Account shows loss :*

Partner's Capital A/c To Realisation A/c	Dr.	Loss transferred in profit sharing ratio

After passing above entries in the Realisation Account, Realisation Account will be closed.

Advantages of Balance of Assets and Balance of Liabilities Method

(i) Under this method preparation of Realisation Account is easier than the earlier two methods because, instead of transferring the assets and liabilities to Realisation Account at their book values. Only the profit or loss made on the realisation of assets and payment of liabilities is recorded in the Realisation Account.

(ii) Under this method, assets are closed as and when they are completely realised and liabilities accounts are also closed as and when they are settled. Therefore, this method is superior than the earlier two methods.

Though this method is easier and more superior than the earlier two methods, it is not recommended by the many authors and it is not widely used for the purpose of examination.

After knowing the above three methods of preparing the Realisation Account, the "Total of Assets and Total of Liabilities Method" (*i.e.*, 1 Method) is widely used in the examination for preparing the Realisation Account. Though the "Total of Assets and Total of Liabilities Method" is subject to the some limitations, most of the authors are recommended this method to the students for the examination purposes. Therefore, the students are advised to follow "Total of Assets and Total of Liabilities Method" in the examination, unless they are specifically asked to follow some other method.

Proforma of Realisation Account under the Total of Assets and Total of Liabilities Method is as follows :

Dr. **Realisation Account** Cr.

	Rs.		Rs.
To Sundry Assets (Book values of all assets except Cash, Bank and Loss)	xxx	By Sundry Liabilities (Book values of all liabilities except partners' loans)	xxx
To Bank or Cash (Liabilities paid)	xxx	By Bank or Cash (Amount realised from sale of assets)	xxx
To Bank or Cash (Realisation expenses paid)	xxx	By R.D.D., Dep. Fund etc. (Book values of provisions)	xxx
To Partners' Capital Accounts (Liabilities taken over by any partner)	xxx	By Partners' Capital Accounts (Assets taken over by any partner)	xxx
To Profit transferred to Capital A/cs (In profit sharing ratio)	xxx	By Loss transferred to Capital A/cs (If any, in profit sharing ratio)	xxx
	xxxx		xxxx

(B) Partners' Capital Accounts

To find out the amounts due to the partners, the partners' capital accounts are to be prepared. Partners' capital accounts show the settlement of the amounts due to the partners.

The following journal entries are to be passed for preparing the capital accounts of partners :

(i) **For the transfer of General Reserve, Other Accumulated Reserves and Profit and Loss Account credit balance given in the Balance Sheet to all the Partners' Capital Accounts :** To find the amounts due to the Partners' Reserves and Profits belonging to all the partners, they have to be transferred to the capital of all the partners in their profit sharing ratio. The entry will be :

General Reserve A/c	Dr.	With the amount of Reserves and Profits
Other Accumulated Reserves A/cs	Dr.	
Profit and Loss A/c	Dr.	
To All the Partners' Capital A/cs		

(ii) For the transfer of Profit and Loss A/c debit balance to all the Partners' Capital Accounts :

All the Partners' Capital A/cs	Dr.	With the amount of loss
To Profit and Loss A/c		

(iii) For the assets (*i.e.*, recorded or unrecorded assets) taken over by the partners :

Partners' Capital A/cs	Dr.	With the amount as agreed
To Realisation A/c		

(iv) For the liabilities (*i.e.*, recorded or unrecorded liabilities) taken over by the partners :

Realisation A/c	Dr.	With the amount as agreed
To Partners' Capital A/cs		

(v) For realisation expenses to be paid by a partner as agreed before :

Realisation A/c	Dr.	With the agreed amount of expenses
To Partner's Capital A/c		

(vi) For realisation expenses to be paid by the firm on behalf of partners:

Partners' Capital A/cs	Dr.	With the amount paid on behalf of partners
To Cash or Bank A/c		

(vii) For transfer of profit on realisation :

Realisation A/c	Dr.	Profit transferred in profit sharing ratio
To Partners' Capital A/cs		

(viii) For transfer of loss on realisation :

Partners' Capital A/cs	Dr.	Loss transferred in profit sharing ratio
To Realisation A/c		

(ix) For the amount paid to partners in settlement of their accounts :

Partners' Capital A/cs	Dr.	With the balance amount paid
To Cash or Bank A/c		

(x) For the amount brought by partners in settlement to their accounts:

Bank or Cash A/c	Dr.	With the required amount received
To Partners' Capital A/cs		

(C) Cash or Bank Account

As and when the partnership firm is dissolved, the assets are to be realised and liabilities are to be paid off. In order to record the receipts and payments of cash relating to dissolution of a firm, Cash or Bank Account is to be prepared.

The following journal entries are to be passed to record the transactions relating to dissolution of a firm in Cash Account.

(i) For cash realised on the sales of assets (i.e., both recorded or unrecorded assets) :

Cash or Bank A/c	Dr.	With the total amount
To Realisation A/c		of cash received

(ii) For the payment of liabilities (i.e., both recorded or unrecorded liabilities) in cash :

Realisation A/c	Dr.	With the amount
To Cash or Bank A/c		actually paid

Note : Under the balance of assets and liabilities method when the assets are realised in cash, cash account is debited and concerned Asset Account is credited, similarly when the liabilities are paid in cash, concerned Liability Account is debited and Cash Account is credited.

(iii) For payment of realisation expenses :

(*a*) *If paid by the firm :*

Realisation A/c	Dr.	With the amount of
To Cash or Bank A/c		expenses

(*b*) *If agreed amount of expenses is paid by the firm on behalf of partner :*

Partner's Capital A/c	Dr.	With the amount paid
To Cash or Bank A/c		on behalf of partner

(iv) For repayment of partner's loan:

Partner's Loan A/c	Dr.	With the amount of
To Cash or Bank A/c		loan repaid

(v) For repayment of partner's capitals :

Partner's Capital A/c	Dr.	With the balance
To Cash or Bank A/c		amount paid

(vi) For amount received from partner to make good the debit balance in his capital account :

Cash or Bank A/c	Dr.	With the required
To Partner's Capital A/c		amount received

Steps for Working Out the Problems on Dissolution

While working out the problems on dissolution, the student should remember the following steps :

First Step :

(1) Transfer all assets (except cash/bank balance) and all liabilities (except Partner's Loan A/c, Capital A/c or Current A/c, Reserve and Profits) appearing in the Balance Sheet to Realisation A/c.

(2) Transfer Capitals, Reserves, Profits etc. given in the Balance Sheet to Capital Accounts.

(3) Transfer cash or bank balance given in the Balance Sheet to Cash or Bank Account.

Second Step :

(1) Record the cash received on sale of all assets (including unrecorded assets) in the Realisation Account and transfer the assets taken over by the partners to Partners' Capital Accounts.

(2) Record the cash paid for realisation expenses and liabilities (including unrecorded liabilities) in the Realisation Account and transfer the liabilities taken over by the partners to Partners' Capital Accounts.

(3) Record the realisation profit or loss in the Partners' Capital Accounts.

Third Step : Payment of partner's loan, if any.

Fourth Step : Settlement of Partners' Capital Accounts.

Fifth Step : Closing of Current Accounts, if any.

Methods of Working Out the Problems on Dissolution

Problems on dissolution can be studied under the following heads :

(1) Simple dissolution

(2) Insolvency of partners

(3) Piece meal distribution

(4) Sale of a partnership firm to a company or conversion of partnership firm into a limited company.

*'**Simple Dissolution**' is studied in this chapter and other methods of working out the problems on dissolution can be studied in the subsequent chapters.*

Illustration 1

Neela, Mala and Sheela were partners in a firm sharing profits and losses in the ratio of 2 : 2 : 1. They dissolved the firm. Their Balance Sheet stood as follows on the date of dissolution :

Balance Sheet as on 31-12-1990

Liabilities		Rs.	Assets		Rs.
Capital Accounts :			Plant and Machinery		50,000
Neela	30,000		Stock		20,000
Mala	20,000		Joint Life Policy		5,000
Sheela	10,000	60,000	Debtors	25,000	
Reserve Fund		9,000	Less Provision	3,000	22,000
Bills Payable		5,000	Cash at Bank		12,000
Neela's Loan A/c		15,000			
Creditors		20,000			
		1,09,000			1,09,000

The firm was dissolved on 31st Dec., 1990. Plant and Machinery was sold for Rs. 45,000. Stock realised for Rs. 19,000. Joint Life Policy was taken over by Neela at Rs. 6,000. Debtors realised for Rs. 22,500. Liabilities were paid in full. In addition one bill for Rs. 900 under discount was dishonoured and had to be taken up by the firm. There were no expenses.

Prepare the following accounts :

(A) Realisation Account under different methods, (B) Partners' Capital Accounts, and (C) Bank Account.

Solution :

(A) Realisation Account under different methods

(1) Total of Assets and Total of Liabilities Method

Dr. **Realisation Account** Cr.

	Rs.			Rs.
To Plant and Machinery	50,000	By Provisions for Doubtful Debts		3,000
To Stock	20,000	By Sundry Creditors		20,000
To Joint Life Policy	5,000	By Bills Payable		5,000
To Debtors (Gross amount)	25,000	By Bank :		
To Bank : Bills Payable	5,000	Plant & Machinery	45,000	
Creditors	20,000	Stock	19,000	
To Bank : Liability on Dishonoured Discounted Bill	900	Debtors	22,500	86,500
		By Neela's Capital A/c (Joint Life Policy taken over)		6,000
		By Loss Transferred :		
		Neela	2,700	
		Mala	1,800	
		Sheela	900	5,400
	1,25,900			1,25,900

(2) Total of Assets and Balance of Liabilities Method

Dr.	Realisation Account			Cr.
	Rs.			Rs.
To Plant and Machinery	50,000	By Provisions for Doubtful Debts		3,000
To Stock	20,000	By Bank :		
To Joint Life Policy	5,000	Plant and Machinery	45,000	
To Debtors (Gross amount)	25,000	Stock	19,000	
To Liability on Dishonoured		Debtors	22,500	86,500
Discounted Bill	900	By A's Capital A/c		6,000
(Loss on payment of liability		(Joint Life Policy taken over)		
Rs. 25,000 – 25,900)		By Loss on Realisation transferred		
		to Partners' Capital A/cs :		
		Neela	2,700	
		Mala	1,800	
		Sheela	900	5,400
	1,00,900			1,00,900

(3) Balance of Assets and Balance of Liabilities Method

Dr.	Realisation Account			Cr.
	Rs.			Rs.
To Plant and Machinery	5,000	By Provisions for Doubtful Debts		3,000
(Loss on Realisation of		By Joint Life Policy		1,000
Plant & Machinery)		(Profit on Realisation of		
To Stock (Loss on Realisation	1,000	Joint Life Policy)		
of Stock)		By Loss on Realisation transferred		
To Debtors	2,500	to Partners' Capital A/cs :		
(Loss on Realisation of		Neela	2,700	
Debtors)		Mala	1,800	
To Liability on Dishonoured		Sheela	900	5,400
Discounted Bill	900			
(Loss on Payment of Liability)				
	9,400			9,400

(B) Dr. **Partners' Capital Accounts** Cr.

	Neela Rs.	Mala Rs.	Sheela Rs.		Neela Rs.	Mala Rs.	Sheela Rs.
To Realisation A/c	6,000	—	—	By Balance b/d	30,000	20,000	10,000
(Jt. Life Policy taken)				By Reserve Fund	4,500	3,000	1,500
To Realisation A/c	2,700	1,800	900				
(Realisation Loss)							
To Bank A/c	25,800	21,200	10,600				
(Final Payments)							
	34,500	23,000	11,500		34,500	23,000	11,500

(C)

Dr. **Bank Account** Cr.

		Rs.			Rs.
To Balance b/d		12,000	By Realisation A/c :		
To Realisation A/c :			Bills Payable	5,000	
Plant & Machinery	45,000		Sundry Creditors	20,000	
Stock	19,000		Liability on Bills		
Debtors	22,500	86,500	Discounted	900	25,900
			By Neela's Loan A/c		15,000
			By Neela's Capital A/c (Final Payments)		25,800
			By Mala's Capital A/c (Final Payments)		21,200
			By Sheela's Capital A/c (Final Payments)		10,600
		98,500			98,500

Illustration 2

Anand, Amar and Akbar were partners in the firm sharing profits and losses in the ratio of 2 : 1 : 1 and they decided to dissolve the partnership on 31-12-1990 on which day their Balance Sheet stood as follows :

Balance Sheet

Liabilities		Rs.	Assets		Rs.
Sundry Creditors		6,000	Bank		5,500
Bank Overdraft		2,000	Bills Receivable		3,000
Bills Payable		1,500	Stock		8,000
Reserve Fund		4,000	Debtors	6,500	
Capitals :			*Less* : R.D.D.	500	6,000
Anand	15,000		Motor Car		20,000
Amar	12,000		Furniture		3,000
Akbar	10,000	37,000	Goodwill		5,000
		50,500			50,500

Anand took over furniture at Rs. 2,000 and stock at a discount of 10 per cent. Amar took over goodwill at Rs. 6,000 and bills payable at book value. Akbar took over a motor car at a depreciation of 10 per cent. Debtors realised at Rs. 6,000 and all the bills receivable were fully realised. A liability for legal expenses of Rs. 1,000 had to be paid in addition to creditors. The bank loan was paid off including interest of Rs. 2,240.

Show the Realisation Account, Partners' Capital Accounts and Bank Account.

Solution :

Dr. **Realisation Account** Cr.

		Rs.			Rs.
To Bills Receivable		3,000	By Sundry Creditors		6,000
To Stock		8,000	By Bank Overdraft		2,000
To Debtors		6,500	By Bills Payable		1,500
To Motor Car		20,000	By R.D.D.		500
To Furniture		3,000	By Anand's Capital A/c :		
To Goodwill		5,000	Furniture	2,000	
To Amar's Capital A/c		1,500	Stock	7,200	9,200
(B/P taken over)			By Amar's Capital A/c		6,000
To Bank A/c :			(Goodwill taken over)		
Creditors	6,000		By Akbar's Capital A/c		18,000
Legal Exp.	1,000	7,000	(Motor Car taken over)		
To Bank A/c		2,240	By Bank A/c :		
(Bank overdraft including interest)			Debtors	6,000	
			Bills Receivable	3,000	9,000
			By Loss transferred to Partners' Capital A/cs :		
			Anand	2,020	
			Amar	1,010	
			Akbar	1,010	4,040
		56,240			56,240

Dr. **Partners' Capital Accounts** Cr.

	Anand Rs.	Amar Rs.	Akbar Rs.		Anand Rs.	Amar Rs.	Akbar Rs.
To Realisation A/c (Realisation Loss)	2,020	1,010	1,010	By Balance b/d	15,000	12,000	10,000
				By Reserve Fund	2,000	1,000	1,000
To Realisation A/c (Furniture & Stock taken over)	9,200	—	—	By Realisation A/c (B/P taken over)	—	1,500	—
To Realisation A/c (Goodwill taken over)	—	6,000	—	By Bank A/c (Cash brought)	—	—	8,010
To Realisation A/c (Motor Car taken over)	—	—	18,000				
To Bank A/c (Final settlements)	5,780	7,490	—				
	17,000	14,500	19,010		17,000	14,500	19,010

Dr. Bank Account Cr.

	Rs.			Rs.
To Balance b/d	5,500	By Realisation A/c :		
To Realisation A/c	9,000	Creditors	6,000	
(Sales of assets)		Legal Exp.	1,000	
To Akbar's Capital A/c	8,010	Bank Overdraft	2,240	9,240
		(Including interest)		
		By Anand's Capital A/c		5,780
		By Amar's Capital A/c		7,490
	22,510			22,510

Note : While Preparing the Realisation Account, the students are advised to follow "Total of Assets and Total of Liabilities Method" unless they are specifically asked to follow some other method.

Illustration 3

The following was the Balance Sheet of Deepa and Neepa sharing profits and losses in the ratio of 5 : 5 as on 31st Dec., 1990.

Balance Sheet

Liabilities		Rs.	Assets		Rs.
Creditors	20,000		Bank		7,000
Less: Reserve	500	19,500	Plant & Machinery		20,000
Deepa's Loan		12,500	Furniture		15,000
Mr. Neepa's Loan		12,000	Debtors	30,000	
Reserve Fund		18,000	*Less* : Provision	2,000	28,000
Capitals :			Stock		18,000
Deepa	28,000		Land and Building		22,000
Neepa	32,000	60,000	Investments		12,000
		1,22,000			1,22,000

The firm was dissolved on 31st December, 1990 and following was the result :

(a) Neepa took over investment at Rs. 14,000 and agreed to pay off the loan of her husband.

(b) The assets realised as follows :

Plant and Machinery Rs. 5,000 less. Furniture Rs. 400 more. Debtors Rs. 4,000 less. Stock Rs. 2,000 less. Land and Building Rs. 3,000 more.

(c) Creditors were paid off less 5 per cent discount.

(d) Bad debts Rs. 500 written off in the past were recovered.

(e) A bills receivable of Rs. 2,200 which was discounted was dishonoured.

(f) Expenses of realisation were Rs. 800.

Prepare the Realisation Account, Partners' Capital Accounts and Bank Account.

Solution :

Dr. **Realisation Accounts** Cr.

	Rs.			Rs.
To Plant and Machinery	20,000	By Creditors		20,000
To Furniture	15,000	By Provision		2,000
To Debtors	30,000	By Neepa's Capital A/c		14,000
To Stock	18,000	(Investment taken over)		
To Land and Building	22,000	By Bank A/c :		
To Investments	12,000	Plant & Machinery	15,000	
To Reserve for Discount on		Debtors	26,000	
Creditors	500	Stock	16,000	
To Bank A/c (Creditors)	19,000	Land & Building	25,000	
To Bank A/c	2,200	Furniture	15,400	97,400
(Discounted Bills Dishonoured)		By Bank A/c		500
To Bank A/c	800	(Bad Debts Recovered)		
(Dissolution Expenses)		By Loss transferred to		
		Partners' Capital A/cs :		
		Deepa	2,800	
		Neepa	2,800	5,600
	1,39,500			1,39,500

Dr. **Partners' Capital Accounts** Cr.

	Deepa Rs.	Neepa Rs.		Deepa Rs.	Neepa Rs.
To Realisation A/c (Loss)	2,800	2,800	By Balance b/d	28,000	32,000
To Realisation A/c	—	14,000	By Reserve Fund	9,000	9,000
(Investment Taken over)			By Mrs. Neepa's Loan	—	12,000
To Bank A/c	34,200	36,200			
(Final Payments)					
	37,000	53,000		37,000	53,000

Bank Account

Dr.	Rs.		Cr. Rs.
To Balance b/d	7,000	By Realisation A/c (Creditors)	19,000
To Realisation A/c (Sales of Assets)	97,400	By Realisation A/c (Dishonour of Bills Discounted)	2,200
To Realisation A/c (Bad Debts Recovered)	500	By Realisation A/c (Dissolution Expenses)	800
		By Deepa's Loan	12,500
		By Deepa's Capital A/c	34,200
		By Neepa's Capital A/c	36,200
	1,04,900		1,04,900

Illustration 4

Ravi and Mahesh were partners and decided to dissolve the firm on 31-12-1990. Their Balance Sheet was as follows :

Balance Sheet

Liabilities	Rs.	Assets	Rs.
Creditors	5,600	Bank	4,000
Bank Loan	5,000	Debtors	7,900
Capital A/cs :		Stock	13,300
Ravi	20,000	Furniture	3,500
Mahesh	20,000	Assets	20,000
Current A/c :		Profit and Loss A/c	3,000
Ravi	1,700	Current A/c :	
		Mahesh	600
	52,300		52,300

Debtors realised Rs. 7,500, Stock realised Rs. 12,600, Furniture Rs. 4,000 and Assets Rs. 16,000. A liability for legal charges Rs. 1,200 had to be paid in addition to cost of dissolution Rs. 1,800.

Write Journal Entries and show the necessary Ledger Accounts to close the books of the firm.

(Bombay, B.Com., Panjab, B.Com. and Kar. P.U. Board)

Solution :

Journal Entries

Sl. No.	Particulars		L.F.	Dr. Rs.	Cr. Rs.
1.	Realisation Account	Dr.		44,700	
	To Debtors A/c				7,900
	To Stock A/c				13,300
	To Furniture A/c				3,500
	To Assets A/c				20,000
	(Being transfer of above assets to Realisation Account)				
2.	Creditors A/c	Dr.		5,600	
	Bank Loan A/c	Dr.		5,000	
	To Realisation A/c				10,600
	(Being transfer of above liabilities to Realisation Account)				
3.	Bank A/c	Dr.		40,100	
	To Realisation A/c				40,100
	(Being realisation of assets such as Debtors Rs. 7,500, Stock Rs. 12,600, Assets Rs. 16,000 and Furniture Rs. 4,000)				
4.	Realisation A/c	Dr.		13,600	
	To Bank A/c				13,600
	(Being liabilities are paid : Creditors Rs. 5,600 Rs. 5,600, Bank loan Rs. 5,000, Legal charges Rs. 1,200 and Dissolution expenses Rs. 1,800)				
5.	Ravi 's Current A/c	Dr.		3,800	
	Mahesh's Current A/c	Dr.		3,800	
	To Realisation A/c				7,600
	(Being the realisation loss transferred to partners' current account in their profit sharing ratio)				
6.	Ravi's Current A/c	Dr.		1,500	
	Mahesh's Current A/c	Dr.		1,500	
	To Profit and Loss A/c				3,000
	(Being debit balance of P & L A/c transferred to partners' current account equally)				

Contd.

			Dr.	Cr.
7.	Ravi's Capital A/c	Dr.	3,600	
	Mahesh's Capital A/c	Dr.	5,900	
	To Ravi's Current A/c			3,600
	To Mahesh's Current A/c			5,900
	(Being the balances of Partners' Current A/c transferred to their capital accounts)			
8.	Ravi's Capital A/c	Dr.	16,400	
	Mahesh's Capital A/c	Dr.	14,100	
	To Bank A/c			30,500
	(Being the final balance paid)			

Dr. Realisation Account Cr.

		Rs.			Rs.
To Debtors		7,900	By Creditors		5,600
To Stock		13,300	By Bank Loan		5,000
To Furniture		3,500	By Bank A/c :		
To Assets		20,000	Debtors	7,500	
To Bank A/c :			Stock	12,600	
Creditors	5,600		Assets	16,000	
Bank Loan	5,000	10,600	Furniture	4,000	40,100
To Bank A/c (Legal charges)		1,200	By Loss transferred to Partners' Current A/cs :		
To Bank A/c (Dissolution expenses)		1,800	Ravi	3,800	
			Mahesh	3,800	7,600
		58,300			58,300

Dr. Partners' Current Accounts Cr.

	Ravi Rs.	Mahesh Rs.		Ravi Rs.	Mahesh Rs.
To Balance b/d	—	600	By Balance b/d	1,700	—
To Realisation A/c (Loss)	3,800	3,800	By Capital A/c (Transfer)	3,600	5,900
To P & L A/c	1,500	1,500			
	5,300	5,900		5,300	5,900

Dr. Partners' Capital Accounts Cr.

	Ravi Rs.	Mahesh Rs.		Ravi Rs.	Mahesh Rs.
To Current A/c (Transfer)	3,600	5,900	By Balance b/d	20,000	20,000
To Bank A/c (Final settlement)	16,400	14,100			
	20,000	20,000		20,000	20,000

Dr. **Bank Account** Cr.

	Rs.			Rs.
To Balance b/d	4,000	By Realisation A/c :		
To Realisation A/c (Sales of Assets)	40,100	Creditors	5,600	
		Bank Loan	5,000	10,600
		By Realisation A/c (Legal Charges)		1,200
		By Realisation A/c (Dissolution Expenses)		1,800
		By Partners' Current A/c :		
		Ravi	16,400	
		Mahesh	14,100	30,500
	44,100			44,100

Illustration 5

Kavita, Savita and Vanita who were carrying on business in partnership and sharing profits and losses equally, decided to dissolve on 31st December, 1990. Their Balance Sheet on that date was as under :

Balance Sheet

Liabilities		Rs.	Assets		Rs.
Sundry Creditors		12,000	Bank		6,500
Life Policy Fund		10,000	Furniture		3,500
Investment Fluctuation Fund		8,000	Machinery		25,000
Reserve Fund		6,000	Stock		8,000
Mrs. Savita's Loan		11,000	Debtors	10,000	
Capital A/cs :			*Less :* Provision	1,000	9,000
Kavita	25,000		Investments		18,000
Savita	30,000	55,000	Joint Life Policy		15,000
			Current A/c : Vanita		17,000
		1,02,000			1,02,000

Savita took over investment at Rs. 15,000 and agreed to pay off the loan of her husband. Kavita takes over machinery at Rs. 22,000 and debtors amounting to Rs. 7,000 at Rs. 5,000. The remaining debtors realise 75 per cent of book value. Stock sold for Rs. 10,000 and the life policy is surrendered for Rs. 13,000. The expenses of realisation were Rs. 900. It was found that an investment not recorded in the books is worth Rs. 2,000. The same is taken over by one of the creditors at this value. An outstanding liability of Rs. 500 not included in the Balance Sheet was paid off.

Show the ledger accounts.

Solution :

Dr. **Realisation Account** Cr.

		Rs.			Rs.
To Furniture		3,500	By Creditors		12,000
To Machinery		25,000	By Life Policy Fund		10,000
To Stock		8,000	By Investment Fluctuation Fund		8,000
To Debtors		10,000	By Provision		1,000
To Investment		18,000	By Savita's Capital A/c		15,000
To Joint Life Policy		15,000	(Investment taken over)		
To Bank A/c :		10,000	By Kavita's Capital A/c		27,000
(Crs. 12,000 – 2,000)			(Machinery and Debtors		
To Bank A/c :			taken over)		
O/S Liabilities	500		By Bank A/c :		
Dissolution Exps.	900	1,400	Stock	10,000	
To Profit transferred to			Joint Life Policy	13,000	
Partners' Capital A/cs :			Debtors	2,250	25,250
Kavita	2,450				
Savita	2,450				
Vanita	2,450	7,350			
		98,250			98,250

Dr. **Partners' Current Accounts** Cr.

	Kavita Rs.	Savita Rs.		Kavita Rs.	Savita Rs.
To Realisation A/c (Investment taken over)	—	15,000	By Balance b/d	25,000	30,000
To Realisation A/c (Machinery & Debtors taken over)	27,000	—	By Realisation A/c (Profit)	2,450	2,450
To Bank A/c (Final settlement)	2,450	30,450	By Reserve Fund	2,000	2,000
			By Mrs. Savita's Loan	—	11,000
	29,450	45,450		29,450	45,450

Dr. **Vanita's Current Account** Cr.

	Rs.		Rs.
To Balance b/d	17,000	By Realisation A/c (Profit)	2,450
		By Reserve Fund	2,000
		By Bank (Cash brought)	12,550
	17,000		17,000

Dr. **Bank Account** Cr.

	Rs.			Rs.
To Balance b/d	6,500	By Realisation A/c :		10,000
To Realisation A/c	25,250	(Creditors Paid)		
(Sales of Assets)		By Realisation A/c :		
To Vanita's Current A/c	12,550	O/S Liabilities	500	
		Dissolution Expenses	900	1,400
		By Partners' Current A/cs :		
		Kavita	2,450	
		Savita	30,450	32,900
	44,300			44,300

Notes : (i) Investment fluctuation fund is treated as a provision against the investment. Hence, it should be transferred to realisation account.

(ii) Life policy fund is considered as a provision against the life policy. Therefore, it should be transferred to realisation account.

(iii) In the absence of capital account of Vanita, only the Vanita's Current Account is prepared.

Illustration 6

A, B and C who were in partnership sharing profits and losses in the proportions of 2/5, 2/5 and 1/5 respectively, decided to dissolve partnership as on 31st Dec., 1990. At the date of the dissolution A's capital was Rs. 8,000, B's Rs. 9,000 and C's Rs. 8,500. The creditors of the firm amounted to Rs. 5,000 and bills payable to the extent of Rs. 3,000. The reserve accumulated so far amounted to Rs. 4,000. The cash balance was Rs. 35,000 after the payment of bills payable and payment of creditors at 3 per cent discount but before paying the realisation expenses amounted to Rs. 800.

Prepare the necessary accounts showing the final settlement between the partners.

Solution :

In this problem, the value of asset is not given. Therefore, we have to ascertain the value of assets. It can be ascertained by preparing the Balance Sheet of the firm as at the date of dissolution.

Balance Sheet

(To find out the book value of assets)

Liabilities		Rs.	Assets	Rs.
Creditors		5,000	Assets	37,500
Bills Payable		3,000	(Balancing Figure)	
Reserve Fund		4,000		
Capital A/cs :				
A	8,000			
B	9,000			
C	8,500	25,500		
		37,500		37,500

Dr. **Realisation Account** Cr.

		Rs.		Rs.
To Assets		37,500	By Creditors	5,000
To Bank A/c :			By Bills Payable	3,000
Creditors	4,850		By Bank A/c	42,850
Bills Payable	3,000	7,850	(Sale of Assets	
To Bank A/c		800	(35,000 + 4,850 + 3,000)	
(Dissolution Expenses)				
To Profit transferred to Partners' Capital A/cs :				
A	1,880			
B	1,880			
C	940	4,700		
		50,850		50,850

Dr. **Partners' Capital Accounts** Cr.

	A Rs.	B Rs.	C Rs.		A Rs.	B Rs.	C Rs.
To Bank A/c (Final Payments)	11,480	12,480	10,240	By Balance b/d	8,000	9,000	8,500
				By Realisation A/c (Profit)	1,880	1,880	940
				By Reserve Fund	1,600	1,600	800
	11,480	12,480	10,240		11,480	12,480	10,240

Dr. **Bank Account** Cr.

	Rs.			Rs.
To Realisation A/c	42,850	By Realisation A/c :		
(Sales of Assets)		Creditors	4,850	
		Bills Payable	3,000	7,850
		By Realisation A/c		800
		(Dissolution Exps.)		
		By Partners' Capital A/cs :		
		A	11,480	
		B	12,480	
		C	10,240	34,200
	42,850			42,850

Illustration 7

Muneer, Kumar and Shekar commenced business on 1st January, 1990 with capital of Rs. 30,000, Rs. 25,000 and Rs. 20,000 respectively. Profits and losses were shared in the ratio of 2:1:1. The Partnership Deed provides interest on capital at 10 per cent p.a. During the year 1990, they made a profit of Rs. 28,000 (before allowing interest on partners' capital). During the year their drawings were Muneer : Rs. 6,000, Kumar Rs. 5,500 and Shekar Rs. 3,500.

On 31st December, 1990, the firm was dissolved. Creditors on that date were Rs. 16,000. Expenses of realisation amounted to Rs. 1,200. The assets were realised at Rs. 96,000.

Give the necessary accounts to close the books of the firm.

Solution :

In this problem, the value of assets is not given. This can be ascertained by preparing the Balance Sheet. The total of the liability side will be treated as sundry assets of the firm.

Dr. **Profit and Loss Appropriation Account** Cr.

		Rs.		Rs.
To Interest on Capital :			By Net Profit	28,000
Muneer	3,000			
Kumar	2,500			
Shekar	2,000	7,500		
To Profit transferred to Partners' Capital A/cs :				
Muneer	10,250			
Kumar	5,125			
Shekar	5,125	20,500		
		28,000		28,000

Dr. **Partners' Capital Accounts** Cr.

	Muneer Rs.	Kumar Rs.	Shekar Rs.		Muneer Rs.	Kumar Rs.	Shekar Rs.
To Bank A/c (Drawings)	6,000	5,500	3,500	By Balance b/d	30,000	25,000	20,000
To Balance c/d	37,250	27,125	23,625	By Interest on Capital	3,000	2,500	2,000
				By Profit	10,250	5,125	5,125
	43,250	32,625	27,125		43,250	32,625	27,125
				By Balance b/d	37,250	27,125	23,625

Balance Sheet as on 31-12-1990

Liabilities		Rs.	Assets	Rs.
Creditors		16,000	Sundry Assets (Balancing figure)	1,04,000
Capital's A/cs :				
Muneer	37,250			
Kumar	27,125			
Shekar	23,625	88,000		
		1,04,000		1,04,000

Dr. **Realisation Account** Cr.

	Rs.			Rs.
To Sundry Assets	1,04,000	By Creditors A/c		16,000
To Bank A/c (Creditors Paid)	16,000	By Bank A/c (Assets Realised)		96,000
To Bank A/c (Realisation Expenses)	1,200	By Losses transferred to Partners' Capital A/cs :		
		Muneer	4,600	
		Kumar	2,300	
		Shekar	2,300	9,200
	1,21,200			1,21,200

Dr. **Partners' Capital Accounts** Cr.

	Muneer Rs.	Kumar Rs.	Shekar Rs.		Muneer Rs.	Kumar Rs.	Shekar Rs.
To Realisation A/c (Losses)	4,600	2,300	2,300	By Balance b/d	37,250	27,125	23,625
To Bank (Final Settlement)	32,650	24,825	21,325				
	37,250	27,125	23,625		37,250	27,125	23,625

Dr. **Bank Account** Cr.

	Rs.			Rs.
To Realisation A/c (Sales of Assets)	96,000	By Realisation A/c (Creditors Paid)		16,000
		By Realisation A/c (Realisation Exp. Paid)		1,200
		By Partners' Capital A/cs :		
		Muneer	32,650	
		Kumar	24,825	
		Shekar	21,325	78,800
	96,000			96,000

Illustration 8

Hiten and Nayan entered into partnership from January 1990. They commenced business with a capital of Rs. 60,000 and Rs. 40,000. Profits and losses were shared in the ratio of 3 : 2.

The business was carried on for 3 years, for which the results were as under :

Year ending 31st December, 1990 : Profit Rs. 60,000

Year ending 31st December, 1991 : Profit Rs. 44,400

Year ending 31st December, 1992 : Profit Rs. 10,760

As the business was no longer profitable, they agreed to dissolve the partnership on 31st Dec., 1992.

The partners drew Rs. 8,000 each per annum on the date of dissolution, creditors were Rs. 32,800. The assets of the partnership realised Rs. 1,50,000, the expenses being Rs. 1,100. Close the books of the firm.

(*B.Com., Agra and C.A.I.I.B.*)

Solution :

In this problem, the book values of the assets on the date of dissolution are not given. Therefore, they have to be found out by preparing the Balance Sheet of the firm on the date of dissolution. Similarly, capitals of the partners on the date of dissolution are not given. Therefore, they have to be found out by preparing the partners' capital accounts on the date of dissolution.

Dr. Partners' Capital Accounts Cr.

(To find out their capitals on the date of dissolution *i.e.*, on 31-12-92)

Date		Hiten Rs.	Nayan Rs.	Date		Hiten Rs.	Nayan Rs.
31-12-90	To Drawings	8,000	8,000	1-1-90	By Bank (Initial Capital)	60,000	40,000
	To Balance c/d	88,000	56,000	31-12-90	By P & L A/c (H=60,000 × 3/5) (N=60,000 × 2/5)	36,000	24,000
		96,000	64,000			96,000	64,000
31-12-91	To Drawings	8,000	8,000	1-1-91	By Balance b/d	88,000	56,000
31-12-91	To Balance c/d	1,06,640	65,760	31-12-91	By P&L A/c	26,640	17,760
		1,14,640	73,760			1,14,640	73,760
31-12-92	To Drawings	8,000	8,000	1-1-92	By Balance b/d	1,06,640	65,760
31-12-92	To Balance c/d	1,05,096	62,064	31-12-92	By P&L A/c	6,456	4,304
		1,13,096	70,064			1,13,096	70,064

Balance Sheet of Hiten and Nayan as on 31-12-1992

(To find out the book values of the assets on the date of dissolution)

Liabilities	Rs.	Assets	Rs.
Creditors	32,800	Sundry Assets (Balancing figure)	1,99,960
Capitals :			
Hiten	1,05,096		
Nayan	62,064		
	1,99,960		1,99,960

Dr. Realisation Account Cr.

	Rs.			Rs.
To Sundry Assets	1,99,960	By Creditors		32,800
To Bank A/c (Paid to Creditors)	32,800	By Bank A/c (Assets Realised)		1,50,000
To Bank A/c (Expenses Paid)	1,100	By Loss transferred to Partners' Capital A/cs :		
		Hiten	30,636	
		Nayan	20,424	51,060
	2,33,860			2,33,860

Dr. **Partners' Capital Accounts** Cr.

	Hiten Rs.	Nayan Rs.		Hiten Rs.	Nayan Rs.
To Realisation (Losses)	30,636	20,424	By Balance b/d	1,05,096	62,064
To Bank (Final Settlement)	74,460	41,640			
	1,05,096	62,064		1,05,096	62,064

Dr. **Bank Account** Cr.

	Rs.			Rs.
To Realisation A/c (Assets Realised)	1,50,000	By Realisation A/c (Paid to Creditors)		32,800
		By Realisation A/c (Expenses Paid)		1,100
		By Partners' Capital A/cs :		
		Hiten	74,460	
		Nayan	41,640	1,16,100
	1,50,000			1,50,000

Illustration 9

A, B and C decide to dissolve their partnership on 31st December, 1990. In terms of the Partnership Deed, Trading, profit and losses are to be divided in the ratio of 3 : 2 : 1 and the capital profits and losses in proportion to the respective capitals. The balance sheet as on that date showed the following position :

	Rs.		Rs.
Sundry Creditors	6,800	Cash at bank	5,000
Capitals :		Debtors	12,400
A	24,000	Stock-in-trade	7,400
B	18,000	Tools	1,600
C	12,000	Vehicles	2,400
		Machinery	12,000
		Building	20,000
	60,800		60,800

A and B decided to form a new partnership and agreed to take over the following assets from the old firm according to the value indicated below :

Stock-in-trade	8,000	Machinery	15,000
Tools	1,000	Building	18,000
Vehicles	5,000	Goodwill	12,000

Debtors realised Rs. 11,800 and discounts earned on payment to creditors Rs. 150.

Prepare the Realisation and Partners' Capital Accounts giving effect to the above and also the opening Balance Sheet of the new firm.

(Bombay, B.Com. & Mysore, B.Com.)

Solution :

Dr. **Realisation Account** Cr.

		Rs.			Rs.
To Debtors		12,400	By Sundry Creditors		6,800
To Stock		7,400	By Bank A/c (Debtors realised)		11,800
To Tools		1,600	By New Firm's A/c :		
To Vehicles		2,400	(A & B's Joint A/c)		
To Machinery		12,000	Stock	8,000	
To Buildings		20,000	Tools	1,000	
To Bank A/c (Creditors paid)		6,650	Vehicles	5,000	
(6,800–150)			Machinery	15,000	
To Profit transferred to			Building	18,000	
Partners' Capital A/cs :			Goodwill	12,000	59,000
A	6,742				
B	5,050				
C	3,358	15,150			
		77,600			77,600

Dr. **Partners' Capital Accounts** Cr.

	A Rs.	B Rs.	C Rs.		A Rs.	B Rs.	C Rs.
To Bank A/c (Part of capital paid)	—	—	10,150	By Balance b/d	24,000	18,000	12,000
To 'C' Loan A/c (Balance transferred to his Loan A/c)	—	—	5,208	By Realisation A/c (Profits)	6,742	5,050	3,358
To Net Firms A/c (Transfer)	30,742	23,050	—				
	30,742	23,050	15,358		30,742	23,050	15,358

Bank Account

Dr.	Rs.		Cr. Rs.
To Balance b/d	5,000	By Realisation A/c	6,650
To Realisation A/c	11,800	(Creditors paid)	
(Debtors realised)		By C's Capital A/c	10,150
		(Amount paid to 'C')	
	16,800		16,800

'C' Loan Account

Dr.	Rs.		Cr. Rs.
To B & C's Joint A/c	5,208	By C's Capital A/c	5,208
(Transfer)			
	5,208		5,208

New Firm's Account (A & B's Joint A/c)

Dr.		Rs.		Cr. Rs.
To Realisation A/c :			By A's Capital A/c	30,742
Stock	8,000		(Transfer)	
Tools	1,000		By B's Capital A/c	23,050
Vehicles	5,000		(Transfer)	
Machinery	15,000		By C's Loan A/c	5,208
Building	18,000		(Transfer)	
Goodwill	12,000	59,000		
		59,000		59,000

Note : Calculation of Profit Distributed among the Partners :

The total realisation profit of Rs.15,150 includes trading profit and capital profit.

Trading profit is Rs. 150 (*i.e.*, Realisation of Stock of Rs. 600 plus Payment of Creditors of Rs. 150 minus Realisation of Debtors of Rs. 600).

Capital profit is Rs. 15,000 (*i.e.*, Total Realisation Profit of Rs.15,150 minus Trading Profit of Rs. 150).

	A Rs.	B Rs.	C Rs.
The trading profit of Rs. 150 is distributed among the partners in the ratio of 3 : 2 : 1	75	50	25
The capital profit of Rs. 15,000 is distributed among the partners in their capital ratio *i.e.*, 4:3:2	6,667	5,000	3,333
Realisation Profit	6,742	5,050	3,358

Illustration 10

The following is the Balance Sheet at 31st March, 1990 of A, B & C carrying on business in partnership sharing profits and losses at 2 : 2 : 1.

Liabilities		Rs.	Assets	Rs.
Capital Accounts :			Fixed Assets	70,000
A	40,000		Sundry Debtors	30,000
B	25,000	65,000	Stock	10,000
Mortgage Loan		40,000	Cash	5,000
Reserve		6,000	Capital Account : 'C'	6,000
Sundry Creditors		10,000	(Dr. Balance)	
		1,21,000		1,21,000

They decided to dissolve the partnership and the following arrangements were agreed upon :

(1) Fixed assets included :

(i) Motor Car Rs. 5,500 taken over by 'B' at an agreed value of Rs. 9,000 after necessary repairing costs amounting to Rs. 2,000 to be borne by the firm.

(ii) Land and Building Rs. 50,000 subject to Mortgage loan, taken over by 'A' at an agreed value of Rs. 60,000 subject to Mortgage loan, taken over at Rs. 40,000.

(2) Other assets excluding cash and creditors are taken over by Eureka Limited in consideration of issue of 5,000 equity shares of Rs. 10 each fully paid. These shares are taken over at a total agreed value of Rs. 48,000 equally by A & B.

(3) 'A' Creditor for Rs. 2,500 not provided for in the books had to be paid.

Prepare the following Accounts, assuming that the final settlement was made by the partners bringing in the amounts due from them :

(1) Realisation A/c, (2) Partners' Capital A/cs, (3) Cash A/c.

(B.Com., Delhi, Bombay, Sagar and Panjab)

Solution :

Dr. **Realisation Account** Cr.

		Rs.		Rs.
To Fixed Assets		70,000	By Mortgage Loan	40,000
To Sundry Debtors		30,000	By Sundry Creditors	10,000
To Stock		10,000	By B's Capital A/c : (Motor car taken over)	9,000
To Bank (Creditors Paid)		2,500		
To Bank (Paid for repair of Car)		2,000	By A's Capital A/c (Land & Building taken over)	60,000
To A's Capital A/c (Mortgage loan)		40,000		
			By Shares in Eureka Ltd.	50,000
To Share in Eureka Ltd. (Loss)		2,000		
To Profit transferred to Partners' Capital A/cs :				
A	5,000			
B	5,000			
C	2,500	12,500		
		1,69,000		1,69,000

Dr. **Partners' Capital Accounts** Cr.

	A Rs.	B Rs.	C Rs.		A Rs.	B Rs.	C Rs.
To Balance b/d	—	—	6,000	By Balance b/d	40,000	25,000	—
To Realisation A/c (Land & Building)	60,000	—	—	By Reserve	2,400	2,400	1,200
				By Realisation A/c (Mortgage loan)	40,000	—	—
To Realisation A/c (Motor car)	—	9,000	—	By Realisation A/c (Profit)	5,000	5,000	2,500
To Shares in Eureka Ltd.	24,000	24,000	—				
To Bank (Final settlement)	3,400	—	—	By Bank (Cash brought)	—	600	2,300
	87,400	33,000	6,000		87,400	33,000	6,000

Dr. **Bank Account** Cr.

	Rs.		Rs.
To Balance b/d	5,000	By Realisation A/c (Car repairs)	2,000
To C's Capital A/c	2,300		
To B's Capital A/c	600	By Realisation A/c (Creditors)	2,500
		By A's Capital A/c	3,400
	7,900		7,900

EXAMINATION QUESTIONS

(A) Answer the following questions in not exceeding 4 lines each :

(*Each Carries two Marks*)

(1) What do you mean by dissolution?

(2) What is the difference between dissolution of partnership and dissolution of partnership firm?

(*B'lore, Oct., 1981*)

(3) What is realisation account? When is it opened?

(*B'lore, May, 1981*)

(4) What is realisation account? Why is it prepared?

(*Kar., April, 1995*)

(5) How you treat "Unrecorded Asset" in dissolution of a firm?

(*B'lore, April, 1980 & 1983*)

(6) Give the entry to close realisation account.

(*B'lore, April,1984*)

(7) Mention the methods of preparing the realisation account.

(8) How do you treat a contingent liability arised on dissolution of a firm? (*B'lore, April, 1991*)

(9) How do you treat unrecorded liabilities at the time of dissolution of a firm? (*B'lore, April, 1998*)

(B) Answer the following questions/problems :

(*Each Carries eight Marks*)

(1) What is dissolution of a partnership firm? What are the circumstances under which a partnership firm is dissolved ?

(*Shivaji, Oct., 1989*)

(2) Distinguish between dissolution of partnership and dissolution of firm.

(*Madurai, Oct., 1991*)

(3) Discuss the various modes of dissolution of a firm.

(*Berhampur April, 1992*)

(4) Give the journal entries to close the books of accounts of dissolution of the firm. (*Calcutta, Oct.,1993*)

(5) How do you treat the following at the time of dissolution of partnership firm :

(a) When a partner agrees to discharge a liability of the firm?

(b) When a Partner's Capital Account shows debit balance?

(*M.K.U., Oct., 1993*)

(6) A, B and C are partners sharing-profits and losses in the ratio of 4 : 3 : 3. Their balance sheet as on 31-12-1993 when they decide to dissolve the firm was as follows :

Liabilities		Rs.	Assets	Rs.
Sundry Creditors		5,000	Cash at Bank	1,000
Partners' Capitals :			Sundry Assets	30,000
A	12,000		Profit & Loss A/c	4,000
B	9,000			
C	9,000	30,000		
		35,000		35,000

The sundry assets realised Rs. 10,500 and the expenses of dissolution amounted to Rs. 1,000. Creditors were paid off Rs. 4,500 in full satisfaction. Prepare realisation account.

(*Bangalore, Oct., 1994*)

Ans. : Realisation Loss : 'A' Rs. 8,000; 'B' Rs. 6,000 and 'C' Rs. 6,000.

(7) X, Y and Z were partners sharing profits equally. They decided to dissolve the firm on 31-12-1991. Their Balance Sheet on that date was as under :

Liabilities		Rs.	Assets	Rs.
Creditors		5,000	Building	25,000
Capitals :			Machinery	7,000
X	30,000		Furniture	3,000
Y	20,000		Stock	21,000
Z	10,000	60,000	Debtors	8,000
			Cash	1,000
		65,000		65,000

The assets were realised as follows :

Debtors Rs. 6,400; Stock Rs. 22,500; Furniture Rs. 2,500; Machinery Rs. 6,000 and Buildings Rs. 33,000.

Creditors were paid in full. The expenses of realisation amounted to Rs. 400.

Pass the journal entries to close the books of the firm.

(*M.K.U., April, 1992*)

Ans. : Realisation profit Rs. 6,000 (2,000 + 2,000 + 2,000)
Repayment of capitals : X—Rs. 32,000; Y—Rs. 22,000 and Z—Rs. 12,000.

(8) X, Y and Z were partners sharing profits and losses in proportion to their capitals which on 31st August, 1993 stood at Rs. 3,000, Rs. 2,000 and Rs. 1,000 respectively. On that date in addition to Z's loan of Rs. 1,200 there were liabilities of the firm amounting to Rs. 3,000. The partners dissolved the firm on 31st August, 1993. They realised Rs. 14,400 from assets.

Prepare the partners' capital accounts. (*Bangalore, Oct.,1993*)

Ans. : Realisation profit : Rs. 4,200; Final payments : X— Rs. 5,100; Y— Rs. 3,400 and Z— Rs. 1,700.

(9) P, Q and R are partners having capitals of Rs. 20,000; Rs. 15,000; and Rs. 10,000 respectively. They share profits and losses in 2 : 2 : 1 respectively.

On 1-1-98, the firm was dissolved. After having paid off all the liabilities at a discount of 10% for Rs. 4,500 but before paying realisation expenses amounting to Rs. 500, the cash balance was found to be Rs. 39,500.

Prepare Realisation Account and Partners' Capital Account.

(*Kar., April, 1998*)

Ans. : Book value of sundry assets : Rs. 50,000 (20,000 + 15,000 + 10,000 + 5,000 *i.e.*, 4,500 × 100/90); Book value of sundry liabilities Rs. 5,000 (4,500 × 100/90); Assets realised Rs. 44,000; Realisation loss : P—Rs. 2,400; Q—Rs. 2,400; R—Rs. 1,200; Final payment : P—Rs. 17,600; Q—Rs. 12,600 and R—Rs. 8,800.

(C) Solve the following problems : (*Each Carries 16 Marks*)

(1) Ashok, Basavaraj and Chintamani are in partnership sharing profits and losses in the ratio of 4 : 3 : 3. Their balance sheet as on 31-12-1985 when they decided to dissolve the firm was as follows :

Liabilities	Rs.	Assets	Rs.
Sundry Creditors	5,000	Cash in Bank	1,000
Partners' Capitals :		Sundry Assets	30,000
Ashok	12,000	Profit & Loss A/c	4,000
Basavaraj	9,000		
Chintamani	9,000		
	35,000		35,000

The sundry assets realised Rs. 10,500 and the expenses of dissolution amounted to Rs. 1,000

The creditors were paid off Rs. 4,500 in full satisfaction.

Prepare the necessary ledger accounts to close the books of the firm.

(*Kar., Oct., 1976*)

Ans. : Realisation loss : Ashok Rs. 8,000; Basavaraj Rs. 6,000 and Chintamani Rs. 6,000. Repayment of capitals : Ashok Rs. 2,400, Basavaraj Rs. 1,800 and Chintamani Rs. 1,800. Cash Account total Rs. 11,500.

(2) Kishore and Nakul are partners sharing profits and losses equally. Their Balance Sheet on 30th September, 1990 is as follows :

Liabilities	Rs.	Assets		Rs.
Creditors	11,200	Cash		3,500
Bills Payable	1,800	Stock		17,800
Kishore's Loan	5,000	Debtors	13,800	
Reserve Fund	6,000	*Less* : Provision	1,400	12,400
Capital A/cs :		Furniture		2,800
Kishore	15,000	Machinery		22,500
Nakul	20,000			
	59,000			59,000

They decided to dissolve the firm. The assets realised as follows :

Stock	Rs. 18,200
Debtors	Rs. 10,600
Furniture	Rs. 1,800
Plant and Machinery	Rs. 19,000

Creditors allowed a discount of 2% and expenses of realisation amounted to Rs. 544.

Give journal entries and the necessary ledger accounts to close the books of the firm.

(*Shivaji, April, 1983*)

Ans. : Realisation loss : Kisore Rs. 3,110 and Nakul Rs. 3,110;
Repayment of Capitals : Kishore Rs. 14,890 and Nakul Rs. 19,890;
Cash Account Total : Rs. 53,100.

(3) A, B and C are partners sharing profit and losses in the proportion of 1/2, 1/3 and 1/6 respectively. They decide to discontinue the business and dissolve partnership on 1st January, 1985 on which date the Balance Sheet of the firm was as follows :

Liabilities		Rs.	Assets	Rs.
Capitals :			Premises	25,650
A	20,000		Machinery	10,800
B	12,000	32,000	Stock	8,420
Contingency Reserve		6,000	Sundry Debtors	15,830
Sundry Creditors		20,260	Bills Receivable	850
Bank Loan		5,120	C's Account	1,250
			Cash at Bank	580
		63,380		63,380

The assets realised the following amounts :

Premises Rs. 15,500; Machinery Rs. 8,000; Stock Rs. 9,300; Debtors Rs. 14,630; Bills Receivable Rs. 850. The goodwill was sold for Rs. 2,500.

Discounts amounting to Rs. 320 were allowed by creditors while paying their claims. The expenses of realisation amounted to Rs. 450.

During the course of dissolution, a liability, under an action for damages was settled for Rs. 12,000 against Rs. 10,000 provided in the books of the firm.

Prepare the accounts necessary to show the result of realisation and the cash distribution among the partners.

(*Mysore April, 1972*)

Ans. : Realisation loss: A—Rs. 6,450, B—Rs. 4,300 & C—Rs. 2,150; Cash brought by C—Rs. 2,400; Cash paid to A—Rs. 16,550 and B—Rs. 9,700; Bank Account Total—Rs. 53,760. Payment made to creditors (20,260 + 2,000 – 320) Rs. 21,940.

(4) The Balance Sheet of A, B and C sharing profits and losses as 3 : 2 : 1 respectively stood as follows on 30th June, 1990 :

Liabilities		Rs.	Assets	Rs.
Creditors		50,400	Cash at Bank	3,700
Joint Life Policy Reserve		10,000	Stock	20,100
Reserve Fund		12,000	Debtors	62,600
Capital Accounts :			Investments	16,000
A	30,000		Furniture	6,500
B	20,000		Buildings	23,500
C	10,000	60,000		
		1,32,400		1,32,400

The firm was dissolved as on that date. For the purpose of dissolution, the investments were valued at Rs. 18,000 and took at Rs. 17,500. A agreed to take over the investments and B to take over the stock. C took over the furniture at book value. Debtors and Buildings realised Rs. 57,000 and Rs. 25,000 respectively. Expenses of realisation amounted to Rs. 450. In addition one bill for Rs. 500 under discount was dishonoured and had to be taken up by the firm.

Give journal entries and necessary ledger accounts to close the books of the firm.

(*B.Com., Panjab, April, 1981*)

Ans. : Realisation Profit : A—Rs. 2,175; B—Rs. 1,450 and C—Rs. 725. Repayment of Capital : A—Rs. 20,175; B—Rs. 7,950 and C—Rs. 6,225.
Bank Account Total : Rs. 85,700.

(5) Vishal and Kushal were in partnership sharing profits and losses in the proportion of 9/16 and 7/16 respectively. The following was their balance sheet as on 31-3-1985 :

Liabilities	Rs.	Assets	Rs.
Creditors	10,000	Cash	3,000
Capital Accounts :		Debtors	9,400
Vishal	7,000	Stock	4,600
Kushal	5,500	Furniture	100
Current Account :		Current Account :	
Vishal	600	Kushal	2,000
		Property	4,000
	23,100		23,100

It was decided to dissolve the firm on the above date. Property realised Rs. 3,000; Bad Debts and Discount amounted to Rs. 1,050; Stock realised Rs. 5,000; Furniture was taken over by Kushal at an agreed price of Rs. 50 and Creditors were paid less Rs. 100 for discount.

Pass the necessary journal entries to close the books of the firm and show Cash Account and Partners' Capital Accounts.

(*Kar., March, 1966*)

Ans. : Realisation loss : Vishal Rs. 900 and Kushal Rs. 700.

Repayment of Capitals : Vishal Rs. 6,700 and Kushal Rs. 2,750.

(6) X, Y and Z sharing profits in the proportion of 3 : 2 : 1 decided to dissolve partnership on 31st December, 1990 on which date their Balance Sheet was as under :

Liabilities		Rs.	Assets		Rs.
Capital Accounts :			Goodwill		20,000
X	30,000		Leasehold Buildings		12,500
Y	10,000		Machinery		30,520
Z	10,000	50,000	Stock-in-trade		7,556
Bank Loan		11,500	Investments		6,330
Leashold Redemption Fund		6,000	Joint Life Policy		12,000
Life Policy Fund		12,000	Sundry Debtors	5,800	
Sundry Creditors		16,206	*Less* : R.D.D.	500	5,300
			Cash at Bank		1,500
		95,706			95,706

The life policy is surrendered for Rs. 10,000. The investments are taken over by Y for Rs. 8,000. X agreed to discharge the Bank loan. The remaining assets are sold for Rs. 86,706. The expenses of realisation amounted to Rs. 850.

Show the necessary ledger accounts including final accounts of the partners.

(*Bangalore, April, 1984 and B.Com., Nagpur*)

Ans. : Realisation Profit : X—Rs. 13,825; Y—Rs. 9,217 and Z—Rs. 4,608. Repayment of Capital : X— Rs. 55,325; Y— Rs. 11,217; and Z— Rs. 14,608; Bank Account Total Rs. 98,206.

(7) B and C who share profit and losses in the proportion of 5 and 3 respectively agreed to dissolve the partnership on 30th June, 1995. The position was :

Liabilities	Rs.	Assets	Rs.
Creditors	9,316	Goodwill	4,000
B's Loan A/c	2,884	Fixtures	1,000
B's Capital A/c	8,000	Machinery	2,400
C's Capital A/c	5,400	Stock	9,200
B's Current A/c	800	Debtors	10,000
C's Current A/c	400	Bank	200
	26,800		26,800

In the course of realisation, it was found a liability to Brown and Co. of Rs. 160 for stock purchased had been omitted from the Balance Sheet and the goods included in the stock on hand.

The assets realised : Goodwill Rs. 2,000; Fixtures Rs. 800; Machinery Rs. 2,100; Stock Rs. 8,500; Debtors Rs. 9,200.

Sundry expenses amounted to Rs. 150; Rs. 9,290 was paid to the Creditors in full settlement.

Pass entries to close the books and show the Realisation Account, Cash Account and Capital Accounts.

(*Mysore, April, 1962*)

Ans. : Realisation Loss : B— Rs. 2,677.50 and C— Rs. 1,606.50. Repayment of Capitals : B—Rs. 6,122.50 and C—Rs. 4,193.50. Bank Account Total Rs. 22,800.

Note : **Liabilities to Brown & Co. Rs. 160 should not be transferred to realisation account, because only those liabilities given in the Balance Sheet should be transferred. But while paying the liabilities, liability to Brown & Co. also should be paid and debited to realisation account.**

(8) Ram, Krishna and Hari entered into partnership on 1-1-1993 sharing profits and losses in the ratio of 4 : 4 : 2 and contributing capitals of Rs. 60,000 Rs. 40,000 and Rs. 20,000 respectively.

Their assets and liabilities on 31-12-1993 were as follows :

Furniture Rs. 2,000; Debtors Rs. 56,000; Bills Receivable Rs. 10,000; Stock Rs. 90,000; Creditors Rs. 60,000 and Bills Payable Rs. 8,000. The profit and loss account showed a debit balance of Rs. 30,000.

On the above date they agreed to dissolve the firm on the following terms:

(i) Krishna agreed to take over the debtors at a discount of 20% and to pay off the creditors.

(ii) Ram agreed to take over the stock at a discount of 10% and to pay off bills payable.

(iii) Hari agreed to take over bills receivable at Rs. 9,500 and furniture at a depreciation of 10%.

Prepare the Realisation Account, Partners' Capital Accounts and Bank Account.

(*Kar., April, 1975 mod.*)

Ans. : Realisation Loss : Ram Rs. 8,360; Krishna Rs. 8,360 and Hari Rs. 4,180.
Cash brought in by Ram Rs. 33,360 and Hari Rs. 1,480.
Cash paid to Krishna Rs. 34,840.
Bank Account Total Rs. 34,840.

(9) Black, White and Yellow were equal partners in a firm which was dissolved on 31-3-1992. On the date of dissolution the capitals of the partners were : Black Rs. 18,000 (Cr.), White Rs. 16,000 (Cr.) and Yellow Rs. 5,000 (Dr.). There were also creditors of Rs. 5,000, bank overdraft of Rs. 3,000 and reserve fund of Rs. 1,500 at the time of dissolution.

The sundry assets realised Rs. 35,000. Of the creditors Rs. 200 were not to be paid and the rest were paid off at a discount of Rs. 100. The bank overdraft was discharged together with Rs. 150 for interest. Expenses of dissolution came to Rs. 400.

Show the necessary ledger accounts to close the books of the firm.

(*Kar., April, 1990 & Gulbarga, April, 1996*)

Ans. : Realisation Loss : Black Rs. 1,250; White Rs. 1,250 & Yellow Rs. 1,250.
Cash paid to Black Rs. 17,250 and White Rs. 15,250.
Cash received from Yellow Rs. 5,750.
Cash Account Total Rs. 40,750.
Book Value of Assets Rs. 38,500 (43,500 – 5,000).

(10) Balraj, Kamraj and Hansraj are three partners having capital of Rs. 40,000, Rs. 30,000 and Rs. 20,000 respectively. On 1-1-1988 the firm was dissolved. After having paid off all the liabilities at a discount of Rs. 5% for Rs. 9,500, except the realisation expenses amounting to Rs. 800 and cash balance was found to be Rs. 70,800. The partners were sharing profits and losses in the ratio of 2 : 2 : 1.

(*Kar., Oct., 1979 and 1986*)

Show the Realisation Account, Partners' Capital Accounts and Cash Accounts.

Ans. : Realisation Loss : Balraj Rs. 8,000; Kamraj Rs. 8,000 and Hansraj Rs. 4,000.
Repayment of Capitals : Balraj Rs. 32,000; Kamraj Rs. 22,000 and Hansraj Rs. 16,000.
Cash A/c : Total Rs. 80,300.
Book Value of Assets : Rs. 1,00,000 (40,000 + 30,000 + 20,000 + 10,000).

(11) Naveen and Vishal have been in business together for last three years ending 31st December, 1990 at which date they agree to dissolve. The capital at the commencement of the business was Rs. 30,000 and Rs. 20,000. Profits and losses were shared in the ratio of 3 : 2. The results of three years before allowing 10% interest on capitals were :

1988 Profit Rs. 30,000
1989 Profit Rs. 22,200
1990 Loss Rs. 5,380

Drawings of each partner were : Rs. 4,000 per year. Creditors on the date of dissolution were Rs. 16,400. The assets realised Rs. 75,000. Expenses of dissolution amounted to Rs. 550. Give the necessary accounts to close the books of the firm.

(*B.Com., Bombay and I.C.W.A. Inter*)

Ans. : Realisation Loss : Naveen Rs. 8,862 and Vishal Rs. 5,908.
Repayment of Capitals : Naveen Rs. 37,478 and Vishal Rs. 20,572.
Bank Account : Total Rs. 75,000; Book Values of Assets : Rs. 89,220.

(12) A, B and C are partners in a firm sharing profits and losses in the ratio of 3 : 2 : 1. They dissolve the partnership and B decided to continue the business by taking over the goodwill of the firm at Rs. 10,000. Their Balance Sheet as on the date of dissolution stood as follows :

Liabilities	Rs	Assets	Rs.
Creditors	8,400	Bills Receivable	9,000
Bills Payable	5,600	Goodwill	6,000
Capitals :		Book Debts	19,600
A	34,000	Investments	12,600
B	40,000	Machinery	15,000
C	19,200	Motor-van	13,000
		Stock-in-trade	24,600
		Cash at Bank	7,400
	1,07,200		1,07,200

A takes over investments for Rs. 11,000 and the Motor-van for Rs. 14,000. All other assets and also liabilities are taken over by B on the bases of a revaluation as follows :

Machinery Rs. 16,400
Stock-in-trade Rs. 21,000

Book Debts and Bills Receivable are taken over at book value. B brings in cash to pay A and C.

Write up the ledger accounts to close the books of the firm and draw the initial Balance Sheet of 'B'.

(*Shivaji, April, 1985 & Madurai, Oct., 1986*)

Ans. : Realisation Profit : A–Rs. 600; B–Rs. 400 and C–Rs. 200; Cash paid to: A–Rs. 9,600 and C–Rs. 19,400; Cash brought in by B–Rs. 21,600 Bank Account Total : Rs. 76,000; Balance Sheet Total : Rs. 76,000.

Note :

Dr. **B's Capital Account** Cr.

	Rs.		Rs.
Realisation (Business taken over 10,000 + 16,400 + 21,000+ 19,600 + 9,000 – 14,000 *i.e.*, 8,400 + 5,600)	62,000	By Balance b/d	40,000
		By Realisation A/c (Share of profit)	400
		By Bank A/c	21,600
	62,000		62,000

Initial Balance Sheet of B

	Rs.		Rs.
Creditors	8,400	Goodwill	10,000
Bills Payable	5,600	Machinery	16,400
B's Capital A/c	62,000	Stock-in-trade	21,000
		Book Debts	19,600
		Bills Receivable	9,000
	76,000		76,000

(13) The partnership between Ram and Mohan was dissolved on 31-3-1984 on that date the partners' capital accounts were : Ram Rs. 50,000 and Mohan Rs. 30,000. Rs. 10,000 were owed by Mohan to the firm, Rs. 20,000 were owed by the firm to Ram and Rs. 15,000 were due to the creditors.

The firm was dissolved and the assets realised Rs. 90,000 exclusive of Rs. 10,000 owed by Mohan. Creditors were paid in full. In addition one bill for Rs. 1,000 under discount was dishonoured and had to be taken up by the firm. Expenses of realisation came to Rs. 1,200.

Prepare the necessary ledger accounts.

(*Karnatak, April, 1992*)

Ans. : Realisation Loss : Rs. 17,200 (8,600 + 8,600).
Repayment of Capitals : Ram Rs. 16,400 and Mohan Rs. 11,400.
Bank Account Total : Rs. 90,000 and Book Value of Assets Rs. 1,05,000.

Notes : (1) Profit sharing ratio is equal.
(2) Liability of bill dishonoured Rs. 1,000 is debited to realisation account and credited to bank account.
(3) Initial Balance Sheet.

	Rs.		Rs.
Capitals :		Advance to Mohan	10,000
Ram	50,000	Sundry Assets	1,05,000
Mohan	30,000	(Balancing figure being	
Advance from Ram	20,000	value of assets)	
Sundry Creditors	15,000		
	1,15,000		1,15,000

(14) Anil, Bharat and Chandru were partners sharing profits and losses equally. Their Balance Sheet on 31-3-1990, the date of dissolution was as follows :

Liabilities	Rs.	Assets	Rs.
Creditors	45,000	Cash at Bank	52,500
Bills Payable	40,000	Debtors	1,25,000
Bank Loan	25,000	Stock	1,75,000
Capitals :		Investments	50,000
Anil	1,55,000	Furniture	2,500
Bharat	1,20,000		
Chandru	20,000		
	4,05,000		4,05,000

Bharat agreed to take over investments at Rs. 80,000 and Anil takes over stock at Rs. 1,40,000 and furniture at book value.

The debtors realised Rs. 1,18,000. The creditors were paid Rs. 42,000 in full satisfaction of their claims. Bills payable and bank loan were paid in full.

Prepare realisation account, bank account and partners' capital accounts.

(Mysore, April, 1992)

Ans. : Realisation Loss : Rs. 9,000 (3,000 + 3,000 + 3,000).
Repayment of Capitals : Anil Rs. 9,500, Bharat Rs. 37,000 and Chandru Rs. 17,000.
Bank Account Total : Rs. 1,70,500.

(15) Ramesh and Suresh agreed to dissolve their partnership firm on 31-12-1991, on which date their balance sheet was as follows :

Liabilities	Rs.	Assets	Rs.
Creditors	8,000	Bank	4,000
Suresh's Loan	6,000	Debtors	6,000
Capital Accounts :		Stock	20,000
Ramesh	20,000	Furniture	4,000
Suresh	15,000	Plant and Machinery	18,000
Reserve Fund	6,000	Goodwill	3,000
	55,000		55,000

The assets realised as follows :

Stock Rs. 28,000; Furniture Rs. 3,700; Debtors Rs. 5,800, Plant & Machinery Rs. 17,000.

The creditors were paid off at 5% discount. The cost of dissolution amounted to Rs. 500.

Show the Realisation A/c, Bank A/c and Partners' Capitals A/cs.

(Karnatak, April, 1995 and M.K.U., Oct., 1998)

Ans. : Realisation : Profit Rs. 3,400 (1,700 + 1,700).
Repayment of Capitals: Ramesh Rs. 24,700 and Suresh Rs. 19,700.
Bank Account Total : Rs. 58,500 and Suresh Loan paid Rs. 6,000.

Note : The profit sharing is equal.

9

INSOLVENCY OF A PARTNER

When a partner owes some money to a partnership firm, that should be paid by the partner to the partnership firm to settle his account. But if such a partner is insolvent (*i.e.*, if a partners' estate is not sufficient to pay off his dues, he is considered as insolvent partner), he is unable to pay the entire amount owed by him to the partnership firm. The deficiency or unrecoverable debit balance of insolvent partner will be treated as a loss to other solvent partners. This additional loss is to be borne by the solvent partners. But the question arises, in what ratio such a loss should be shared between the solvent partners. The loss is to be shared by the solvent partners as per the decision in *Garner* Vs. *Murray*, only if there is no specific agreement among the partners about the ratio in which the loss should be shared.

Decision in *Garner* Vs. *Murray*

In this case Garner, Murray and Wilkins were equal partners of a partnership firm in England. The firm was dissolved. At the time of dissolution, Wilkins's Capital Account showed a debit balance, Wilkins became insolvent and could not contribute anything to make good the debit balance in his capital account which was to be borne by Garner and Murray who were solvent partners. But dispute arose between Garner and Murray over the ratio in which the loss should be shared arrising from the insolvency of a partner. Garner wanted to share this loss with Murray in their profit-sharing ratio. Because, before the decision in *Garner* Vs. *Murray* was given, the loss arising from the insolvency of a partner was considered as an ordinary loss (*i.e.*, trading loss), therefore, and it had to be shared between the solvent partners in their profit-sharing ratio. But Murray didn't agree and argued that such loss being an extra-ordinary loss (*i.e.*, capital loss) and as such it should be borne by the solvent partners in their last agreed 'capital ratio' and not in their profit-sharing ratio. Garner filed a suit against Murray. But the decision given by the learned Judge (Justice Joyce) was in the favour of Murray.

As per the decision in the case of *Garner* Vs. *Murray* it was ruled that "in the absence of any agreement to the contrary, the loss arising out of the insolvency of a partner should be borne by the other solvent partners in proportion to their last agreed capitals after each solvent partner has brought in cash equal to his share of loss on realisation".

The points of the above decision are as follows :

(1) The decision is applied only when at least one partner is insolvent and at least two partners are solvent. If there is only one solvent partner, the entire loss has to be borne by the one solvent partner.

(2) Solvent partners should bring cash equal to their share of loss on realisation. Realisation loss should be shared by all the partners in their respective profit-sharing ratio.

(3) Deficiency or loss of the insolvent partner should be shared by the solvent partners in the ratio of last agreed capitals.

Last Agreed Capitals

Last agreed capitals are those capitals, which are appearing in the Balance Sheet of a partnership firm just prior to dissolution. In this case first we have to know what the term "capital" means for the purpose of application of decision in *Garner* Vs. *Murray*. For this purpose, the capitals of partners can be divided into two kinds *viz.*, (1) Fixed Capitals and (2) Fluctuating Capitals.

(1) Fixed Capitals of the Partners : If the capital accounts and also current accounts of the partners are given in the Balance Sheet, the capitals of the partners are to be considered as fixed. When the capitals are fixed, for the purpose of decision in *Garner* Vs. *Murray*, the term 'capital' means only the opening capitals of the partners as given in the Balance Sheet. Therefore, last agreed capitals are opening capitals of the partners as given in the Balance Sheet. Hence, the deficiency of the insolvent partner is to be borne by the solvent partners on the ratio of their fixed capitals (opening capitals) as appearing in the Balance Sheet of the firm. If there are any accumulated and undistributed profits in the form of general reserve, reserve fund, credit balance of profit and loss account etc., and accumulated losses in the form of debit balance of profit and loss account in the Balance Sheet of the firm, they should be transferred directly to the current account of the partners in their profit-sharing ratio and not to their capital accounts since their capitals are fixed.

(2) Fluctuating Capitals of the Partners : If there are only capital accounts and not current accounts of partners in the Balance Sheet, the capital accounts of partners are to be considered as fluctuating. When the capitals are fluctuating, the last agreed capital means capitals obtained after adjusting there in drawings up to the date of dissolution, interest on drawings, interest on capitals, salary or remuneration due to any partner, reserves, accumulated profits and losses and profit and loss account balance given in the Balance Sheet.

Procedure to Workout the Problems on *Garner* Vs. *Murray*

The following procedure is to be followed while working out the problems on *Garner* Vs. *Murray*:

(1) The realisation account should be prepared in the usual manner.

(2) The profit or loss on realisation should be transferred to the capital accounts of the partners in their profit-sharing ratio.

(3) If there is a loss on realisation, the solvent partners have to bring cash equal to their share of realisation loss. The entry will be, debit the Cash or Bank Account and credit the Capital or Current Accounts of Solvent Partners.

(4) All the adjustments given in the problem regarding reserves, Profit and Loss Account balances, salary of partner, interest on capital, interest on drawings etc., should be made in the partners capital account.

(5) The net capital deficiency of an insolvent partner is to be found out and the deficiency of an insolvent partner should be shared by the solvent partners in ratio of last agreed capital as already explained. The entry will be : debit the Solvent Partners' Account and credit the Insolvent Partners' Capital Account.

(6) At last, final payment will be made to the solvent partners according to the balance shown by their capital accounts. The entry will be : debit the Solvent Partners' Capital Account with the amount paid to them and credit the Bank or Cash Account.

Some Points in Connection with the Decision in *Garner* Vs. *Murray*

(1) If there are Firm Debts and Private Debts : If there are debts of partnership firm, the assets of the firm will be sold off and any amount realised from the sale of assets of the firm is utilised first in payment of the debts of the partnership firm and surplus amount if any, will be paid to the partners in their profit sharing ratio. Similarly, if there are private debts of the partners in their individual capacity, the assets of the partners will be sold off and any amount received from the sale of private assets of the partner is utilised first for paying off his private liabilities and surplus amount if any, is paid to the firm for meeting the deficit of the firm. In case if the private liabilities of any partner are more than his private assets, nothing is to be paid by him to the firm for meeting the deficit of the firm.

(2) When there is only one Solvent Partner : The decision in *Garner* Vs. *Murray* is applied only when at least two partners are solvent and at least one partner is insolvent. If there is only one solvent partner, the decision in *Garner* Vs. *Murray* cannot be applied. In such a case, the entire deficiency of all the insolvent partners has to be borne by the one solvent partner.

(3) If the Capital Account of Solvent Partner shows a Debit Balance before the Dissolution of the Firm : If the partner is solvent and his capital account shows a debit balance before the dissolution of the firm, he will not have to bear the deficiency of the insolvent partners. Because, as per the decision given in the *Garner* Vs. *Murray*, the deficiency of the insolvent partners is to be borne by the solvent partners in proportion of their last agreed capitals.

(4) If there is no Specific Instruction in the Problem regarding the Insolvency or Solvency of a Partner : If the partner's capital account shows a debit balance and there is no instruction in the problem regarding the insolvency and solvency of such a partner, we assume that he is a solvent partner. He should bring necessary cash to make good the deficit in his capital account.

Applicability of Decision in *Garner* Vs. *Murray*

Some people in India believed that *Garner* Vs. *Murray* decision is not applicable to India. But there is nothing in the Indian Partnership Act, 1932 which goes against the rule laid down in *Garner* Vs. *Murray*. Similarly, no court of law in India is not given any decision either to uphold or to invalidate the decision in *Garner* Vs. *Murray*. Therefore, the decision in *Garner* Vs. *Murray* would be safe to follow in India until an Indian Court decides against the application of the decision in *Garner* Vs. *Murray*.

Illustration 1

A, B and C are in partnership sharing profits and losses in the ratio of 2 : 2 : 1. They dissolved their partnership on 31st December, 1990. Their Balance Sheet after realisation of assets and payment of liabilities is as follows :

Liabilities		Rs.	Assets	Rs.
Capital Accounts :			Cash in Hand	15,000
A	22,000		Realisation Losses	16,000
B	14,000	36,000	Capital Account:	
Reserve Fund		5,000	'C'	10,000
		41,000		41,000

'C' becomes insolvent and is unable to contribute anything. Give the necessary ledger accounts :

(A) By applying the practice followed before the decision in *Garner* Vs. *Murray* and

(B) By applying the decision in *Garner* Vs. *Murray*.

Solution :

(A) By applying the practice followed before the decision in *Garner* Vs. *Murray*

Dr. **Solvent Partners' Capital Accounts** Cr.

	A Rs.	B Rs.		A Rs.	B Rs.
To Realisation Loss	6,400	6,400	By Balance b/d	22,000	14,000
To C's Capital A/c.	6,100	6,100	By Reserve Fund	2,000	2,000
To Cash or Bank (Balance paid)	11,500	3,500			
	24,000	16,000		24,000	16,000

Dr. **C's Capital Account** Cr.

	Rs.		Rs.
To Balance b/d	10,000	By Reserve Fund	1,000
To Realisation A/c (Loss)	3,200	By A's Capital A/c	6,100
		By B's Capital A/c	6,100
	13,200		13,200

Dr. **Cash or Bank Account** Cr.

	Rs.		Rs.
To Balance b/d	15,000	By A's Capital A/c	11,500
		By B's Capital A/c	3,500
	15,000		15,000

Notes : (i) Before the decision in *Garner* Vs. *Murray*, the solvent partners need not bring cash to the extent of their respective loss of realisation.

(ii) Before the decision in *Garner* Vs. *Murray*, the deficiency of insolvent partner should be shared by the solvent partners in their profit-sharing ratio. In this problem the profit-sharing ratio of solvent partners is equal (2 : 2).

(B) By applying the decision in *Garner* Vs. *Murray*

Dr. **Solvent Partners' Capital Accounts** Cr.

	A Rs.	B Rs.		A Rs.	B Rs.
To Realisation Loss	6,400	6,400	By Balance b/d	22,000	14,000
To C's Capital A/c	7,320	4,880	By Reserve Fund	2,000	2,000
To Cash or Bank (Balance paid)	16,680	11,120	By Bank (Cash brought)	6,400	6,400
	30,400	22,400		30,400	22,400

C's Capital Accounts

Dr.	Rs.	Cr.	Rs.
To Balance b/d	10,000	By Reserve Fund	1,000
To Realisation A/c	3,200	By A's Capital A/c	7,320
(Loss)		By B's Capital A/c	4,880
	13,200		13,200

Cash or Bank Accounts

Dr.	Rs.	Cr.	Rs.
To Balance b/d	15,000	By A's Capital A/c	16,680
To A's Capital A/c	6,400	By B's Capital A/c	11,120
To B's Capital A/c	6,400		
	27,800		27,800

Notes : (i) As per decision of *Garner* Vs. *Murray*, the solvent partners should bring cash equal to their share of loss on realisation.

(ii) The deficiency of insolvent partner is to be shared by the solvent partners in their last agreed capital ratio. Last agreed capital ratio is calculated as under :

	A	B
Capital as per Balance Sheet	22,000	14,000
Add : Share in accumulated reserve	2,000	2,000
Capital just before dissolution	24,000	16,000

Therefore, last agreed capital ratio is 6 : 4.

Illustration 2

A, B and C are equal partners and following is the position of the firm soon after dissolution :

		Rs.		Rs.
Capital Accounts :			Cash at Bank	7,900
A	12,000		Losses	27,000
B	8,000			
C	2,900	22,900		
Profit and Loss A/c		12,000		
		34,900		34,900

Assuming that 'C' is totally insolvent and is unable to contribute anything. Prepare the necessary ledger accounts :

(a) If the Capitals are Fixed Units and

(b) If the Capitals are Fluctuating Units.

Solution :

(a) When the Capitals are Fixed Units

Dr. **Solvent Partners' Current Accounts** Cr.

	A Rs.	B Rs.		A Rs.	B Rs.
To Realisation Loss	9,000	9,000	By P&L A/c	4,000	4,000
To C's Capital A/c.	1,260	840	By Cash or Bank (Cash brought)	9,000	9,000
To Solvent Partners' Capital A/c (Transfer)	2,740	3,160			
	13,000	13,000		13,000	13,000

Dr. **Solvent Partners' Capital Accounts** Cr.

	A Rs.	B Rs.		A Rs.	B Rs.
To Bank (Final settlement)	14,740	11,160	By Balance b/d	12,000	8,000
			By Solvent Partners' Current A/c (Transfer)	2,740	3,160
	14,740	11,160		14,740	11,160

Dr. **C's Current Account** Cr.

	Rs.		Rs.
To Realisation A/c (Loss)	9,000	By P & L A/c	4,000
		By C's Capital A/c	5,000
	9,000		9,000

Dr. **C's Capital Account** Cr.

	Rs.		Rs.
To C's Current A/c	5,000	By Balance b/d	2,900
		By A's Current A/c (3/5)	1,260
		By B's Current A/c (2/5)	840
	5,000		5,000

Dr. **Bank Account** Cr.

	Rs.		Rs.
To Balance b/d	7,900	By A's Capital A/c	14,740
To A's Current A/c	9,000	By B's Capital A/c	11,160
To B's Current A/c	9,000		
	25,900		25,900

(b) When the Capitals are Fluctuating Units

Partners' Capital Accounts

Dr.	A Rs.	B Rs.		A Rs.	B Rs. Cr.
To Realisation Loss	9,000	9,000	By Balance b/d	12,000	8,000
To C's Capital A/c	1,200	900	By P&L A/c	4,000	4,000
To Bank A/c (Balance paid)	14,800	11,100	By Cash or Bank (Cash brought)	9,000	9,000
	25,000	21,000		25,000	21,000

C's Capital Account

Dr.	Rs.		Rs. Cr.
To Realisation A/c (Loss)	9,000	By Balance b/d	2,900
		By P&L A/c	4,000
		By A's Capital A/c (4/7)	1,200
		By B's Capital A/c (3/7)	900
	9,000		9,000

Bank Account

Dr.	Rs.		Rs. Cr.
To Balance b/d	7,900	By A's Capital A/c	14,800
To A's Capital A/c	9,000	By B's Capital A/c.	11,100
To B's Capital A/c	9,000		
	25,900		25,900

Notes : (i) When the capitals of the partners are fixed for the purpose of sharing the deficiency of the insolvent partner, the term "Capitals" means only opening capitals of the partners as given in the Balance Sheet.

(ii) When the capitals of the partners are fluctuating, the term 'Capital' means capital after adjusting reserve fund, P & L A/c balance etc. given in the Balance Sheet. Therefore, the partners' capital will be :

	A Rs.	B Rs.
Opening Capital	12,000	8,000
Add : P&L A/c balance	4,000	4,000
	16,000	12,000

(iii) When there is no instruction regarding the apply of decision in *Garner* Vs. *Murray*, it is advisable to apply the decision in *Garner* Vs. *Murray*.

Illustration 3

Ram, Sham, Vijay and Ajay were equal partners. The original capital was : Ram Rs. 20,000; Vijay Rs. 14,000; Sham Rs. 8,000 and Ajay Rs. 10,000; but by agreement amongst the partners the drawings had been merged in the capital accounts and balances at the date of dissolution were as shown in the following Balance Sheet :

Balance Sheet

Liabilities		Rs.	Assets		Rs.
Creditors		20,000	Cash at Bank		1,000
Capitals :			Sundry Assets		25,000
Ram	15,000		Capitals :		
Vijay	5,000	20,000	Sham	9,000	
			Ajay	5,000	14,000
		40,000			40,000

On the date they dissolved their firm. The assets realised Rs. 10,000. Dissolution expenses amounted to Rs. 1,000. The creditors were paid in full. Ajay brought in cash equal to his deficiency. But Sham became insolvent and he was therefore unable to bring in full amount to make up the deficiency of his capital.

However, 50 paise per rupee was recovered from his private estate. Prepare the necessary ledger accounts showing the final settlement.

(Kar., Board & Madras, B.Com.)

Solution :

Dr. **Realisation Account** Cr.

	Rs.			Rs.
To Sundry Assets	25,000	By Creditors		20,000
To Bank (Creditors paid)	20,000	By Bank (Assets sold)		10,000
To Bank (Paid realisation expenses)	1,000	By Partners' Capital A/cs : (Losses)		
		Ram	4,000	
		Vijay	4,000	
		Sham	4,000	
		Ajay	4,000	16,000
	46,000			46,000

Solvent Partners' Capital Accounts

Dr.	Ram Rs.	Vijay Rs.		Ram Rs.	Vijay Rs. Cr.
To Realisation Loss	4,000	4,000	By Balance b/d	15,000	5,000
To Sham's Capital A/c	4,875	1,625	By Bank	4,000	4,000
To Bank (Balance paid)	10,125	3,375	(Cash brought)		
	19,000	9,000		19,000	9,000

Partners' Capital Accounts (Including Insolvent)

Dr.	Sham Rs.	Ajay Rs.		Sham Rs.	Ajay Rs. Cr.
To Balance b/d	9,000	5,000	By Bank	6,500	9,000
To Realisation A/c	4,000	4,000	(Cash brought)		
(Loss)			By Ram's Capital A/c	4,875	—
			By Vijay's Capital A/c	1,625	—
	13,000	9,000		13,000	9,000

Bank Account

Dr.	Rs.		Rs. Cr.
To Balance b/d	1,000	By Realisation A/c	20,000
To Realisation A/c	10,000	(Creditors paid)	
(Sale of Assets)		By Realisation A/c	1,000
To Ram's Capital A/c	4,000	(Realisation exp. paid)	
To Vijay's Capital A/c	4,000	By Ram's Capital A/c	10,125
To Ajay's Capital A/c	9,000	(Final settlement)	
(Cash brought to make up his deficiency)		By Vijay's Capital A/c	3,375
		(Final settlement)	
To Sham's Capital A/c	6,500		
(50 paise per rupee was recovered from his private estate)			
	34,500		34,500

Notes : (i) Last agreed Capital Ratio is 3 : 1 (15,000 : 5,000).

(ii) Only the solvent partners should share the deficiency of capital of insolvent partner. Therefore, the balance in Sham's Account has been debited to Ram and Vijay in their last agreed capital ratio.

(iii) While calculating the last agreed capital ratio, we have to consider only the solvent partners' capital account balances given in the Balance Sheet, and not the original capitals of solvent partners.

Illustration 4

Alpa, Kalpa, and Chalpa decided to dissolve their partnership on 31st Dec., 1990, on which date the balance was as follows :

Balance Sheet

Liabilities		Rs.	Assets		Rs.
Creditors		20,000	Land and Buildings		20,000
Reserve Fund		10,000	Plant & Machinery		10,000
Bills Payable		2,000	Debtors	15,000	
Capital Accounts :			*Less* : Provisions	5,000	10,000
Alpa	15,000		Stock		12,000
Kalpa	10,000		Furniture		6,000
Chalpa	2,000	27,000	Cash		1,000
Current Accounts :			Chalpa's Current A/c		3,000
Alpa	2,000				
Kalpa	1,000	3,000			
		62,000			62,000

The partners are sharing profits and losses in the ratio of 2 : 2 : 1. The assets realised as follows :

	Rs.
Land and Buildings	21,000
Plant & Machinery	8,000
Debtors	10,000
Stock	9,000
Furniture	4,000

Chalpa became insolvent and the expenses of realisation amounted to Rs. 2,000.

Prepare necessary accounts to close the books of the firm.

Solution :

Dr. **Realisation Account** Cr.

		Rs.			Rs.
To Land & Building		20,000	By Creditors		20,000
To Plant & Machinery		10,000	By Bills Payable		2,000
To Debtors		15,000	By Provisions		5,000
To Stock		12,000	By Bank A/c :		
To Furniture		6,000	Land & Buildings	21,000	
To Bank :			Plant & Machinery	8,000	
Creditors	20,000		Debtors	10,000	
Bills Payable	2,000	22,000	Stock	9,000	
To Bank		2,000	Furniture	4,000	52,000
(Realisation expenses paid)			By Partners' Current A/c		
			(Losses) :		
			Alpa	3,200	
			Kalpa	3,200	
			Chalpa	1,600	8,000
		87,000			87,000

Dr. **Solvent Partners' Current Accounts** Cr.

	Alpa	Kalpa		Alpa	Kalpa
To Realisation Loss	3,200	3,200	By Balance b/d	2,000	1,000
To Chalpa's Capital A/c	360	240	By Reserve Fund	4,000	4,000
To Solvent Partners'			By Bank	3,200	3,200
Capital A/c	5,640	4,760	(Cash brought)		
	9,200	8,200		9,200	8,200

Dr. **Solvent Partners' Capital Accounts** Cr.

	Alpa	Kalpa		Alpa	Kalpa
To Bank	20,640	14,760	By Balance b/d	15,000	10,000
(Balance paid)			By Solvent Partners'		
			Current A/c	5,640	4,760
	20,640	14,760		20,640	14,760

Dr. **Chalpa's Current Account** Cr.

	Rs.		Rs.
To Balance b/d	3,000	By Reserve Fund	2,000
To Realisation A/c (Loss)	1,600	By Chalpa's Capital A/c	2,600
	4,600		4,600

Dr. **Chalpa's Capital Account** Cr.

	Rs.		Rs.
To Chalpa's Current A/c	2,600	By Balance b/d	2,000
		By Alpa's Current A/c	360
		By Kalpa's Current A/c	240
	2,600		2,600

Dr. **Bank Account** Cr.

	Rs.		Rs.
To Balance b/d	1,000	By Realisation A/c	20,000
To Realisation A/c	52,000	(Creditors paid)	
(Sale of Assets)		By Realisation A/c	2,000
To Alpa's Current A/c	3,200	(Bills payable paid)	
(Cash brought)		By Realisation A/c	2,000
To Kalpa's Current A/c	3,200	(Realisation exp. paid)	
(Cash brought)		By Alpa's Capital A/c	20,640
		By Kalpa's Capital A/c	14,760
	59,400		59,400

Notes : (i) Last agreed Capital Ratio of solvent partners is 3 : 2.

(ii) Even though the problem has not clearly stated about the actual amount paid for the liabilities, we can assume that the liabilities are paid in full.

Illustration 5

A, B and C were partners in a firm. They had been sharing profits and losses in the ratio of 3 : 2 : 1. They dissolved the firm. At the time of dissolution, capitals of 'A' and 'B' were Rs. 10,000 and Rs. 6,000 respectively. 'C' had overdrawn Rs. 2,000. The firm's liabilities were—creditors Rs. 12,000 and loan from 'B' Rs. 8,000. The assets were sold for Rs. 30,000. The realisation expenses were Rs. 800. 'C' subsequently became bankrupt.

Write the ledger accounts of the firm on the completion of the dissolution.

Solution :

In this problem, the book value of assets is not given. Therefore, we can find out the book value of assets by preparing the Balance Sheet of the firm as at the date of dissolution.

Balance Sheet

Dr. Cr.

Liabilities		Rs.	Assets	Rs.
Creditors		12,000	Sundry Assets	34,000
Loan from 'B'		8,000	(Balancing figure)	
Capital Accounts :			(Book Value)	
A	10,000		C's Capital Account	2,000
B	6,000	16,000	(Overdrawn)	
		36,000		36,000

Realisation Account

Dr. Cr.

	Rs.			Rs.
To Sundry Assets	34,000	By Creditors		12,000
To Bank	12,000	By Bank		30,000
(Creditors paid)		(Asset realised)		
To Bank	800	By Capital Accounts of		
(Realisation expenses paid)		Partners (Losses) :		
		A	2,400	
		B	1,600	
		C	800	4,800
	46,800			46,800

Partners' Capital Accounts

Dr. Cr.

	A Rs.	B Rs.		A Rs.	B Rs.
To Realisation Loss	2,400	1,600	By Balance b/d	10,000	6,000
To C's Capital A/c.	1,750	1,050	By Bank	2,400	1,600
To Bank	8,250	4,950	(Cash brought)		
(Balance paid)					
	12,400	7,600		12,400	7,600

C's Capital Account

Dr. Cr.

	Rs.		Rs.
To Balance b/d	2,000	By A's Capital A/c (5/8)	1,750
To Realisation Loss	800	By B's Capital A/c (3/8)	1,050
	2,800		2,800

Dr. **Bank Account** Cr.

	Rs.		Rs.
To Realisation A/c (Assets realised)	30,000	By Realisation A/c (Creditors paid)	12,000
To A's Capital A/c (Cash brought)	2,400	By Realisation A/c (Realisation exps. paid)	800
To B's Capital A/c (Cash brought)	1,600	By B's Loan A/c	8,000
		By A's Capital A/c	8,250
		By B's Capital A/c	4,950
	34,000		34,000

Illustration 6

Brahma, Kshatriya, Vaishya and Shudra were partners sharing profits and losses in the ratio of 3 : 3 : 2 : 2 respectively. The following is the Balance Sheet at the 31st December, 1990.

Liabilities		Rs.	Assets		Rs.
Creditors		31,000	Cash in Hand		4,000
Brahma's Loan		20,000	Debtors	32,000	
Capital Accounts :			*Less* : R.D.D.	1,000	31,000
Brahma	40,000		Stock		20,000
Kshatriya	30,000	70,000	Furniture		8,000
			Car		14,000
			Capital Accounts :		
			Vaishya	12,000	
			Shudra	32,000	44,000
		1,21,000			1,21,000

It was decided to dissolve the firm with effect from 31st December, 1990 and Kshatriya was appointed to liquidate the assets and pay the creditors. He was entitled to receive 5% commission on the amounts finally paid to other partners towards capitals. He was to bear the expenses of realisation, which amounted to Rs. 500. The assets realise Rs. 5,400 excluding cash on hand, creditor were paid in full. In addition a sum of Rs. 5,000 was also paid to staff on retrenchment in full settlement of their claim.

Shudra was insolvent and the partners accepted Rs. 7,400 from his estate in settlement.

Prepare the necessary Ledger Accounts of the firm.

(*Adapted from C.A.*)

Solution :

Realisation Account

Dr.		Rs.			Cr. Rs.
To Stock		20,000	By R.D.D.		1,000
To Furniture		8,000	By Creditors		31,000
To Car		14,000	By Bank (Assets realised)		54,000
To Debtors (Gross amount)		32,000	By Partners' Capital A/cs (Losses) :		
To Bank :			Brahma	7,200	
Creditors paid	31,000		Kshatriya	7,200	
Staff on retrenchment paid	5,000	36,000	Vaishya	4,800	
			Shudra	4,800	24,000
		1,10,000			1,10,000

Solvent Partners' Capital Accounts

Dr.	Brahma Rs.	Kshatriya Rs.	Cr.	Brahma Rs.	Kshatriya Rs.
To Realisation Loss	7,200	7,200	By Balance b/d	40,000	30,000
To Bank (Realisation exps. paid by Kshatriya)	—	500	By Bank (Cash brought to meet realisation loss)	7,200	7,200
To Shudra's Capital A/c (Deficiency in Shudra's Capital)	16,800	12,600	By Brahma's Capital A/c (Remuneration due from Brahma)	—	762
To Kshatriya's Capital A/c (Remuneration due to Kshatriya)	762	—			
To Bank (Balance paid)	22,438	17,662			
	47,200	37,962		47,200	37,962

Partners' Capital Accounts (Including Insolvent)

Dr.	Vaishya Rs.	Shudra Rs.	Cr.	Vaishya Rs.	Shudra Rs.
To Balance b/d	12,000	32,000	By Bank (Cash brought) to meet realisation loss)	4,800	—
To Realisation Loss	4,800	4,800	By Bank (Private estate realised)	—	7,400
			By Bank (Cash brought to meet his deficiency)	12,000	—
			By Brahma's Capital A/c (Share of Shudra's deficiency)	—	16,800
			By Kshatriya's Capital A/c (Share of Shudra's deficiency)	—	12,600
	16,800	36,800		16,800	36,800

Dr. **Bank Account** Cr.

	Rs.			Rs.
To Balance b/d	4,000	By Realisation A/c.:		
To Realisation A/c	54,000	Creditors	31,000	
(Assets realised)		Claim to Staff	5,000	36,000
To Brahma's Capital A/c	7,200	By Kshatriya's Capital A/c		500
To Kshatriya's Capital A/c	7,200	(Cash paid by him to		
To Vaishya's Capital A/c	4,800	meet realisation exp.)		
To Shudra's Capital A/c.	7,400	By Brahma's Loan A/c		20,000
To Vaishya's Capital A/c	12,000	By Brahma's Capital A/c		22,438
		By Kshatriya's Capital A/c		17,662
	96,600			96,600

Notes : (i) Vaishya's capital account shows a debit balance, hence he need not bear any deficiency of insolvent partner. The deficiency of Shudra (Rs. 29,400) should be borne by only Brahma and Kshatriya in the ratio of last agreed capitals i.e., 40,000 : 30,000 or 4 : 3.

(ii) Kshatriya's remuneration is calculated as below :

Kshatriya's remuneration (commission) is 5% on the amount finally paid to the others partners. Amount finally payable to other partners is as under:

	Rs.
Amount payable to Brahma before charging Kshatriya's commission (40,000 – 7,200 = 32,800 – 16,800)	16,000
Amount payable to Vaishya and Shudra	Nil
Amount payable before charging commission	16,000
Therefore, Kshatriya's commission will be (16,000 × 5/105)	762

(iii) It is assumed that Kshatriya paid the realisation expenses by using the firm's cash. Therefore, it is debited to his capital account and credited to Bank account. Suppose the realisation expenses are paid by Kshatriya out of his own funds, it should not be recorded in the books of the firm.

Illustration 7

P, Q and R are partners sharing profits and losses in the proportion of one half, one third and one sixth respectively. The partnership was dissolved on 31st March, 1990 on which date the Balance Sheet of the firm was as under :

	Rs.		Rs.
P's Capital	8,415	Sundry Assets	6,750
Q's Capital	5,916	Sundry Debtors	3,415
Reserves	3,600	Bills Receivable	2,518
Sundry Creditors	14,982	Stock	4,516
		R's Account	12,500
		Cash on Hand	3,214
	32,913		32,913

The lives of the partners were insured severally for : P Rs. 10,000, Q Rs. 5,000 and R Rs. 6,000. The premiums were charged to the P & L A/c. On the date of the dissolution, the surrender value of each of the policies was 30% of the sum assumed. 'P' took over his policy, but the policies of Q and R were surrendered. In the course of realisation it was found :

(i) That a liability of Rs. 1,500 for purchase of goods in 1988-89 had been omitted from the Balance Sheet and that the goods had been included in the value of stock.

(ii) That bills receivable amounting to Rs. 3,500 which were discounted by the firm were dishonoured and not proved to be valueless. The firm pays the amount to the Bank.

(iii) 'P' agreed to takeover the goodwill of the firm at Rs. 2,500. The bills receivable were retired by the acceptors for Rs. 2,400. The remaining assets realised Rs. 10,399. The expenses of realisation amounted to Rs. 600. 'R' is insolvent, but his estate paid Rs. 2,100.

Prepare the final accounts of the partners closing the books of the firm and show the results of the dissolution.

(*Adapted from B.Com., Mysore & Mangalore, April, 1997*)

Solution :

Dr. **Realisation Account** Cr.

		Rs.			Rs.
To Sundry Debtors		3,415	By Sundry Creditors		14,982
To Sundry Assets		6,750	By Bank :		
To Bills Receivable		2,518	Q's Life Policy	1,500	
To Stock		4,516	(5,000 × 30/100)		
To Bank :			R's Life Policy	1,800	
Creditors	16,482		(6,000 × 30/100)		
(Including the amount			Bills Receivable	2,400	
omitted Rs. 1,500)			Remaining Assets	10,399	16,099
Liability on dishonoured			By P's Capital A/c		5,500
discounted bill	3,500	19,982	(Life Policy Rs. 3,000		
To Bank		600	& Goodwill Rs. 2,500		
(Realisation exps.)			taken over)		
			By Partners' Capital A/cs		
			(Losses) : P - Rs. 600,		
			Q - Rs. 400 & R - Rs. 200		1,200
		37,781			37,781

Dr. **Solvent Partners' Capital Accounts** Cr.

	P Rs.	Q Rs.		P Rs.	Q Rs.
To Realisation A/c (Life Policy and Goodwill taken over)	5,500	—	By Balance b/d	8,415	5,916
			By Reserve	1,800	1,200
			By Bank (Cash brought to meet realisation loss)	600	400
To Realisation Loss	600	400			
To R's Capital A/c (R's Deficiency)	5,894	4,106	By Bank (Cash brought to meet his deficiency)	1,179	—
To Bank (Balance paid)	—	3,010			
	11,994	7,516		11,994	7,516

Dr. **R's Capital Account** Cr.

	Rs.		Rs.
To Balance b/d	12,500	By Reserve	600
To Realisation Loss	200	By Bank (Private estate realised)	2,100
		By P's Capital A/c (Share of R's deficiency)	5,894
		By Q's Capital A/c (Share of R's deficiency)	4,106
	12,700		12,700

Dr. **Bank Account** Cr.

		Rs.			Rs.
To Balance b/d		3,214	By Realisation A/c :		
To Realisation A/c :			Creditors	16,482	
Bills Receivable	2,400		Liability on dishonoured discounted bill	3,500	19,982
Q's Policy A/c	1,500				
R's Policy A/c	1,800				
Remaining Assets	10,399	16,099	By Realisation A/c (Realisation exp. paid)		600
To P's Capital A/c		600	By P's Capital A/c (Final payment)		3,010
To Q's Capital A/c		400			
To R's Capital A/c		2,100			
To P's Capital A/c		1,179			
		23,592			23,592

Note : R's deficiency Rs. 10,000 should be shared between P & Q in the ratio of last agreed capitals. Last agreed capital ratio is calculated as below :

	P	Q
Capital Account balance as per Balance Sheet	8,415	5,916
Add : Share in accumulated reserve	1,800	1,200
	10,215	7,116

So the ratio is 10,215 : 7,116 or 3,405 : 2,372.

When all Partners Except One Become Insolvent :

Sometimes, all the partners except one partner become insolvent. In such a case, the decision in *Garner* Vs. *Murray* cannot be applied. Because, for application of decision in *Garner* Vs. *Murray* there must be at least two solvent partners. Therefore, when all partners except one partner become insolvent, the debit balances of capital accounts or capital deficiency of all the insolvent partners will be borne by the one solvent partner.

Illustration 8

Kavita, Sunita and Savita are partners sharing profits and losses in the proportion of 1 : 2 : 3 respectively. Their Balance Sheet on the date of dissolution (31-12-90) was as under :

Balance Sheet

Liabilities		Rs.	Assets	Rs.
Sundry Creditors		25,000	Cash	8,000
Bank Overdraft		2,000	Plant & Machinery	10,000
Bank Loan on the Security			Buildings	20,000
of Plant & Machinery		15,000	Debtors	5,000
Capitals :			Stock	10,000
Kavita	7,000		Profit and Loss A/c	12,000
Sunita	8,000		Advance to Kavita	2,000
Savita	10,000	25,000		
		67,000		67,000

The firm's assets were realised as follows :

Plant and Machinery	Rs. 5,000	Building	Rs. 10,000
Debtors	Rs. 2,000	Stock	Rs. 7,000

Kavita paid off the bank overdraft. Realisation expenses amounted to Rs. 600. Kavita has a private estate which is valued at Rs. 12,000. Sunita and Savita became bankrupt, the estate of the former partner paying 40 paise in the rupee and latter 20 paise in the rupee.

Show the necessary Ledger Accounts.

Realisation Account

Dr.		Rs.	Cr.		Rs.
To Plant & Machinery		10,000	By Sundry Creditors		25,000
To Building		20,000	By Bank Overdraft		2,000
To Debtors		5,000	By Bank Loan		15,000
To Stock		10,000	By Bank :		
To Advance to Kavita		2,000	Plant & Machinery	5,000	
To Bank :			Buildings	10,000	
Realisation Exps.	600		Debtors	2,000	
Creditors	25,000		Stock	7,000	
Bank Loan	15,000	40,600	Advanced to Kavita	2,000	26,000
To Kavita's Capital A/c		2,000	(Recovered)		
(Bank O/D taken over)			By Partners' Capital A/cs :		
			(Losses)		
			Kavita	3,600	
			Sunita	7,200	
			Savita	10,800	21,600
		89,600			89,600

Solvent Partner Capital Account (Kavita's Capital A/c)

Dr.	Rs.	Cr.	Rs.
To Profit & Loss A/c	2,000	By Balance b/d	7,000
To Realisation Loss	3,600	By Realisation A/c	2,000
To Sunita's Capital A/c	1,920	(Bank O/D taken over)	
(Deficiency)		By Bank	3,960
To Savita's Capital A/c	5,440	(Cash brought to meet	
(Deficiency)		deficiency)	
	12,960		12,960

Insolvent Partners' Capital Accounts

Dr.	Sunita Rs.	Savita Rs.	Cr.	Sunita Rs.	Savita Rs.
To Profit & Loss A/c	4,000	6,000	By Balance b/d	8,000	10,000
To Realisation Loss	7,200	10,800	By Bank (40 paise in a rupee recovered)	1,280	—
			By Bank (20 paise in a rupee recovered)	—	1,360
			By Kavita's Capital A/c	1,920	5,440
	11,200	16,800		11,200	16,800

Dr. **Bank or Cash Account** Cr.

	Rs.		Rs.
To Balance b/d	8,000	By Realisation	40,600
To Realisation A/c	26,000	(Liabilities paid)	
(Assets realised)			
To Kavita's Capital A/c	3,960		
To Sunita's Capital A/c	1,280		
To Savita's Capital A/c	1,360		
	40,600		40,600

Notes : (i) Advance to Kavita is an asset. So it is transferred to Realisation Account.

(ii) Kavita has a private estate valued at Rs. 12,000. It means Kavita is able to pay the dues upto Rs. 12,000. Therefore, the advance given to her is recovered and recorded in the Realisation Account.

Illustration 9

The following Balance Sheet is presented to you as on 31-12-1990.

Liabilities		Rs.	Assets		Rs.
Creditors		20,000	Sundry Assets		30,000
B's Loan		5,000	Cash at Bank		1,000
Capitals :			Loss		15,000
A	10,000		Drawings :		
B	6,000		B	2,000	
C	6,000		C	2,000	4,000
D	3,000	25,000			
		50,000			50,000

The partners shared profits and losses as A : 2/10, B : 3/10, C : 3/10 and D : 2/10. The firm was dissolved on 31-12-1990. The position of the partners on 31-12-1990 was as follows :

	Private Estate	Private Liabilities
	Rs.	Rs.
A	10,000	15,000
B	20,000	6,000
C	5,000	4,000
D	8,000	9,000

The assets realised Rs. 26,000 and expenses of dissolution came to Rs. 1,000. Prepare ledger accounts giving effect to the dissolution.

(B.Com., Mysore and Panjab)

Solution :

Realisation Account

Dr.		Rs.			Cr. Rs.
To Sundry Assets		30,000	By Creditors		20,000
To Bank :			By Bank (Assets realised)		26,000
Realisation Exps.	1,000		By Partners' Capital A/cs :		
Creditors	20,000	21,000	(Losses)		
			A	1,000	
			B	1,500	
			C	1,500	
			D	1,000	5,000
		51,000			51,000

A's Capital Account

Dr.	Rs.		Cr. Rs.
To Profit & Loss A/c.	3,000	By Balance b/d	10,000
To Realisation Loss	1,000		
To C's Capital A/c (C's Deficiency)	1,000		
To D's Capital (D's Capital A/c)	1,000		
To Bank (Balance paid)	4,000		
	10,000		10,000

B's Capital Account

Dr.	Rs.		Cr. Rs.
To Profit & Loss A/c	4,500	By Balance b/d	6,000
To Drawings	2,000	By Bank (Cash brought to meet his deficiency)	2,000
To Realisation Loss	1,500		
	8,000		8,000

C's Capital Account

Dr.	Rs.		Cr. Rs.
To Profit & Loss A/c	4,500	By Balance b/d	6,000
To Drawings	2,000	By Bank (Cash received from his private estate to meet his deficiency)	1,000
To Realisation Loss	1,500		
		By A's Capital A/c	1,000
	8,000		8,000

D's Capital Account

Dr.	Rs.		Cr. Rs.
To Profit & Loss A/c	3,000	By Balance b/d	3,000
To Realisation Loss	1,000	By A's Capital A/c.	1,000
	4,000		4,000

Bank Account

Dr.	Rs.		Cr. Rs.
To Balance b/d	1,000	By Realisation A/c (Creditors and realisation expenses paid)	21,000
To Realisation A/c (Assets realised)	26,000		
To B's Capital A/c	2,000	By B's Loan	5,000
To C's Capital A/c	1,000	By A's Capital A/c	4,000
	30,000		30,000

Notes : (i) The private estates of the partner are utilised first in paying the private liabilities and the excess if any, is utilized for the payment of firm's debts.

(ii) A and B are solvent partners. But B, though solvent, does not have any credit balance in his capital account after making all the adjustments on the date of dissolution. Therefore, he need not bear any portion of deficiencies of C and D. The entire deficiencies of C and D is to be borne by 'A' whose capital account shows a credit balance.

When all the Partners become Insolvent

When all the partners become insolvent, it is said to be insolvency of a partnership firm. In such a case, the decision in *Garner* Vs. *Murray* cannot be applied. When cash available with the firm (after meeting the realisation expenses) together with the amount brought by the partners from their private estate is not sufficient to pay off liabilities like creditors, bills payable, etc. in full, we can conclude that the partnership firm is insolvent. If the partnership firm is insolvent, it is not possible to the firm to pay the liabilities in full. Therefore, the liabilities of the firm are paid proportionately based on their claims. If there are secured creditors, they will be paid in full to the extent of the securities held by them and the remaining balance of creditors will be paid with other liabilities proportionately based on their claims.

Accounting Procedure

There are mainly two methods of recording the transactions of insolvency of a partnership firm. They are as follows :

(A) First Method

Under this method, three accounts are to be prepared *viz.*, the Realisation Account. Partners' Capital Accounts and Bank Account.

(1) The Realisation Account is prepared in the usual manner. All the assets and liabilities are transferred to the Realisation Account at their book values. The assets realised, liabilities paid and realisation expenses are also recorded in the Realisation Account. The profit or loss in the Realisation Account is transferred to all the partners' capital accounts, in their profit-sharing ratio.

(2) While preparing the Partners' Capital Accounts, their old balances appearing in the Balance Sheet, the profit or loss in the Realisation Account and any amount brought by the partners from their private estate should be recorded in the capital accounts. Thereafter, the partners' capital accounts will be closed. While closing the partner's capital accounts, the following two points should be remembered in the mind :

(i) the debit balance in the partner or partners' capital accounts is transferred to the capital accounts of the partners showing credit balances in the ratio of capitals (*i.e.*, opening capitals) on the date of dissolution.

(ii) the deficit arising in the partner or partners capital accounts from the above transfer is again transferred to the capital accounts of the other partner or partners showing the credit balances in the ratio of their capitals on the date of dissolution.

(3) While preparing the Bank Account, the old bank balance, the amount realised from the sale of assets and the amount brought in by the partners from their private estates should be debited and the amount paid for the realisation expenses should be credited. The balance remaining after making all these entries is to be utilised for the payment of creditors and all the liabilities and is recorded in the Bank Account as "By Realisation Account". Because, the balance of cash available is to be paid to creditors through realisation account.

(B) Second Method

Under this method, in addition to the Realisation Account, Partners' Capital Accounts and Bank Account, two more accounts such as Liabilities Account and Deficiency Account are to be prepared.

(1) While preparing the Realisation Account, the liabilities are not transferred to the Realisation Account under this method. Only assets are transferred to the Realisation Account. Realisation of assets and payment of realisation expenses are to be recorded in the Realisation Account. Whatever, the amount is paid to the liabilities, it is paid directly to the liabilities and not

through the Realisation Account. The balance in the Realisation Account is to be transferred to the Partners' Capital Account.

(2) Capital Accounts of partners are prepared in the usual way. The opening balance of Partners' Capital Accounts and the balance in the Realisation Account are transferred to the Capital Accounts. If any amount is brought by the partners from their private estate, it is credited to the Partners' Capital Accounts. Finally, the balances in the Partners' Capital Accounts are transferred to the Deficiency Account.

(3) While preparing the Bank Account, the opening balance of bank or cash, the amount realised from the sale of assets and the amount brought in by the partners from their private estate is debited to the Bank Account. The amount paid for the realisation expenses is credited to the Bank Account. Finally, the balance remained in the Bank Account is utilised for the part payment to the liabilities.

(4) While preparing the Liabilities Accounts, the opening balance of liabilities (i.e., Creditors, Bills Payable etc.) are transferred to the Liabilities Accounts as "By Balance b/d" and the actual amount paid to the liabilities is debited to the Liabilities Accounts as "To Bank Account". Finally, the balance of Liabilities Accounts is transferred to the Deficiency Account.

(5) While preparing the Deficiency Account (i.e., Amount not Paid Account or Profit and Loss Account), the final balances in the Partners' Capital Accounts are transferred to the Deficiency Account and the amount not paid to the liabilities is credited to the Deficiency Account.

Illustration 10

Black, White and Red were partners in a partnership firm sharing profits and losses in the ratio of 2 : 2 : 1. They decided to dissolve the firm on 31-12-1992 on which date their Balance Sheet was as follows :

Balance Sheet

Liabilities		Rs.	Assets	Rs.
Creditors		50,000	Buildings	35,000
Bills Payable		30,000	Machinery	20,000
Capital Accounts :			Furniture	8,000
Black	20,000		Stock	22,000
White	10,000	30,000	Debtors	10,000
			Cash	1,000
			Red's Capital Account (Drawings)	14,000
		1,10,000		1,10,000

The assets were realised as follows :

(i) Building realised 80% of the book value

(ii) Machinery realised 25% less than the book value

(iii) Furniture realised Rs. 6,000

(iv) Stock realised Rs. 15,000

(v) Debtors realised 20% less than the book value.

Unfortunately all the partners become insolvent. However, the following amounts were recovered from the surplus of their private estates :

Black Rs. 4,600; White Nil; Red Rs. 1,000.

The cost of collecting and distributing the estate amounted to Rs. 1,000.

Prepare the necessary Ledger Accounts to close the books of the firm under both the methods.

Solution :

(A) When liabilities are passed through Realisation Account

Dr. **Realisation Account** Cr.

		Rs.			Rs.
To Building		35,000	By Creditors		50,000
To Machinery		20,000	By Bills Payable		30,000
To Furniture		8,000	By Bank (Assets Realised) :		
To Stock		22,000	Buildings	28,000	
To Debtors		10,000	Machinery	15,000	
To Bank (Liabilities paid) :			Furniture	6,000	
Creditors	48,500		Debtors	8,000	
Bills Payable	29,100	77,600	Stock	15,000	72,000
To Bank (Expenses paid)		1,000	By Partners' Capital A/cs : (Losses)		
			Black	8,640	
			White	8,640	
			Red	4,320	21,600
		1,73,600			1,73,600

Dr. **Partners' Capital Accounts** Cr.

	Black Rs.	White Rs.	Red Rs.		Black Rs.	White Rs.	Red Rs.
To Balance b/d	—	—	14,000	By Balance b/d	20,000	10,000	—
To Realisation Loss	8,640	8,640	4,320	By Bank (Surplus of private estate)	4,600	—	1,000
To Red's Capital A/c (Deficiency)	11,547	5,773	—	By Black's Capital A/c (Deficiency)	—	—	11,547
To White's Capital (Deficiency)	4,413	—	—	By White's Capital A/c (Deficiency)	—	—	5,773
				By Black's Capital A/c (Deficiency)	—	4,413	—
	24,600	14,413	18,320		24,600	14,413	18,320

Dr. **Bank Account** Cr.

	Rs.			Rs.
To Balance b/d	1,000	By Realisation A/c (Realisation exps. paid)		1,000
To Realisation A/c (Assets sold)	72,000	By Realisation A/c : (Liabilities paid)		
To Black's Capital A/c	4,600	Creditors	48,500	
To Red's Capital A/c	1,000	Bills Payable	29,100	77,600
		(Available cash *i.e.*, Balancing figure)		
	78,600			78,600

Notes : (i) The capital deficiency of partners is adjusted in the ratio of their capital on the date of dissolution (ratio 2 : 1)

(ii) Available cash paid to creditors is calculated as below :

Total amount of outside liabilities (50,000 + 30,000) 80,000

Cash available to pay the liabilities 77,600

(1,000 + 72,000 + 4,600 + 1,000 – 1,000)

Therefore, for liabilities of Rs. 80,000, available cash is Rs. 77,600,

then creditors will be paid for Rs. 48,500 $\left(\frac{50{,}000 \times 77{,}600}{80{,}000}\right)$.

Similarly bills payable will be paid for Rs. 29,100 $\left(\frac{30{,}000 \times 77{,}600}{80{,}000}\right)$.

(B) When liabilities are not passed through Realisation Account :

Realisation Account

Dr.	Rs.	Cr.		Rs.
To Buildings	35,000	By Bank : (Assets Realised)		
To Machinery	20,000	Buildings	28,000	
To Furniture	8,000	Machinery	15,000	
To Stock	22,000	Furniture	6,000	
To Debtors	10,000	Stock	15,000	
To Bank	1,000	Debtors	8,000	72,000
(Realisation expenses paid)		By Partners' Capital A/cs :		
		(Losses)		
		Black	9,600	
		White	9,600	
		Red	4,800	24,000
	96,000			96,000

Partners' Capital Accounts

Dr.	Black Rs.	White Rs.	Red Rs.	Cr.	Black Rs.	White Rs.	Red Rs.
To Balance b/d	—	—	14,000	By Balance b/d	20,000	10,000	—
To Realisation Loss	9,600	9,600	4,800	By Bank (Surplus of of their private estate)	4,600	—	1,000
To Deficiency A/c (transferred)	15,000	400	—	By Deficiency A/c (Transferred)	—	—	17,800
	24,600	10,000	18,800		24,600	10,000	18,800

Bank Account

Dr.	Rs.	Cr.	Rs.
To Balance b/d	1,000	By Realisation A/c (Realisation exps. paid)	1,000
To Realisation A/c (Assets sold)	72,000	By Creditors $\left(\frac{50,000 \times 77,600}{80,000}\right)$	48,500
To Black's Capital A/c	4,600		
To Red's Capital A/c	1,000	By Bill Payable $\left(\frac{50,000 \times 77,600}{80,000}\right)$	29,100
	78,600		78,600

Creditors Account

Dr.	Rs.		Cr. Rs.
To Bank (paid)	48,500	By Balance b/d	50,000
To Deficiency A/c. (Transferred)	1,500		
	50,000		50,000

Bills Payable Account

Dr.	Rs.		Cr. Rs.
To Bank (paid)	29,100	By Balance b/d	30,000
To Deficiency A/c. (Transferred)	900		
	30,000		30,000

Deficiency Account

Dr.	Rs.		Cr. Rs.
To Red's Capital A/c	17,800	By Black's Capital A/c	15,000
		By White's Capital A/c	400
		By Creditors A/c	1,500
		By Bills Payable A/c	900
	17,800		17,800

Illustration 11

X, Y and Z are partners sharing profits and losses in the ratio of 3 : 2 : 1. Below is their Balance Sheet as on 30th June, 1990 when they decided to dissolve the firm.

Liabilities	Rs.	Assets	Rs.
Sundry Creditors	51,000	Fixed Assets	50,000
Depreciation Fund	7,000	Current Assets	19,100
X's Loan	10,000	(Including cash Rs. 1,600)	
X's Capital Account	15,000	Z's Capital Account	3,900
Y's Capital Account	8,000	P & L A/c	18,000
	91,000		91,000

The assets realised Rs. 35,000. The position of the partners on the date of the dissolution was as follows :

	Private Estate Rs.	Private Liabilities Rs.
X	9,000	7,500
Z	4,000	5,000

'Y' was able to pay 20 paise in the rupee of what was payable on his account to the partnership. The expenses of realisation amounted to Rs. 500. Prepare ledger accounts.

(B.Com., Bombay and B.Com., Delhi)

Solution :

Dr. **Realisation Account** Cr.

	Rs.			Rs.
To Fixed Assets	50,000	By Depreciation Fund		7,000
To Current Assets (Excluding cash)	17,500	By Bank (Assets sold)		35,000
To Bank (Realisation exps. paid)	500	By Partners' Capital A/cs : (Losses)		
		X	13,000	
		Y	8,667	
		Z	4,333	26,000
	68,000			68,000

Dr. **Partners' Capital Account** Cr.

	X Rs.	Y Rs.	Z Rs.		X Rs.	Y Rs.	Z Rs.
To Balance b/d	—	—	3,900	By Balance b/d	15,000	8,000	—
To P&L A/c	9,000	6,000	3,000	By X's Loan A/c	10,000	—	—
To Realisation Loss	13,000	8,667	4,333	By Bank (Surplus from private estate)	1,500	—	—
To Deficiency A/c (Transferred)	4,500	—	—	By Bank $\left(\frac{6,667 \times 20}{100}\right)$	—	1,333	—
				By Deficiency A/c (Transferred)	—	5,334	11,233
	26,500	14,667	11,233		26,500	11,667	11,233

Dr. **Bank Account** Cr.

	Rs.		Rs.
To Balance b/d	1,600	By Realisation A/c (Expenses paid)	500
To Realisation A/c (Assets realised)	35,000	By Creditors (Creditors paid *i.e.*, Balancing figure)	38,933
To X's Capital A/c	1,500		
To Y's Capital A/c	1,333		
	39,433		39,433

Dr. **X's Loan Account** Cr.

	Rs.		Rs.
To X's Capital A/c (Transferred)	10,000	By Balance b/d	10,000
	10,000		10,000

Dr. **Creditors Account** Cr.

	Rs.		Rs.
To Bank (creditors paid)	38,933	By Balance b/d	51,000
To Deficiency A/c (Transferred)	12,067		
	51,000		51,000

Dr. **Deficiency Account** Cr.

	Rs.		Rs.
To Y's Capital A/c	5,334	By X's Capital A/c	4,500
To Z's Capital A/c	11,233	By Creditors A/c	12,067
	16,567		16,567

Note : Second method is widely used in the examination. Because, since the outside liabilities cannot be paid in full, the realisation account is to be prepared without transferring the outside liabilities. Therefore, students are advised to follow second method in the examination, unless they are specifically instructed to follow some other method.

EXAMINATION QUESTIONS

(A) Answer the following questions in not exceeding 4 lines each :

(*Each Carries two Marks*)

(1) What is insolvency?

(2) Who is solvent partner ? (*Kar., Oct., 1996*)

(3) Who is an insolvent partner ? (*Kar., April, 1995*)

(4) State the rule in *Garner* Vs. *Murray*.

(*B'lore, April, 1982*)

(5) State with reasons, whether the rule in *Garner* Vs. *Murray* is applicable in India.

(*B'lore, Nov., 1982*)

(6) In the absence of specific provision in the agreement can the ruling of the case *Garner* Vs. *Murray* be applied on dissolution.

(*B'lore, May, 1991*)

(7) How do you close the insolvent Partners' Capital Account ?

(*Kar., Oct., 1995*)

(8) Mention two circumstances when the decision in Garner Vs. Murray is not applicable or significant.

(9) How do you close capital accounts when all partners are insolvent ?

(*Kar., April, 1996*)

(10) What are the rulings of *Garner* Vs. *Murray* ?

(*Kar., April , 1998*)

(11) How do you close the Creditors Account when all the partners are insolvent ?

(*B'lore, April, 1998*)

(B) Answer the following questions/problems :

(*Each Carries eight Marks*)

(1) Explain the underlying principles of *Garner* Vs. *Murray* decision in dissolution of a firm.

(*Gulbarga, April, 1996*)

(2) What are the circumstances under which a decision in *Garner* Vs. *Murray* is applied ?

(*Shivaji, 1985*)

(3) Comment briefly on the decision in *Garner* Vs. *Murray*.

(4) What is the principle in the case of *Garner* Vs. *Murray*? When it is applicable?

(*M.K.U., April, 1992*)

(5) Capitals and creditors of a firm under dissolution were as under:

Capitals : A—Rs. 40,000 ; B—Rs. 25,000 and C—Rs. 5,000, Reserves Rs. 20,000 and Creditors Rs. 60,000.

The profits and losses are shared by partners A, B and C in the ratio of 2 : 1 : 1. The assets realised Rs. 80,000. 'C' was bankrupt.

Prepare the realisation account and partners' capital accounts applying the rule in "*Garner* Vs. *Murray*".

(*Karnatak, Oct., 1995*)

Ans. : Realisation loss Rs. 70,000 (35,000 + 17,500 + 17,500).
C's Capital deficiency of Rs. 7,500 is borne by A Rs. 4,688 and by 'B' Rs. 2,812.
Repayment of capital : A Rs. 45,312 and B Rs. 27,188.
Bank A/c Total Rs. 1,32,500 and Book value of assets Rs. 1,50,000.

Note : Capital ratio = 5 : 3 (*i.e.*, 50,000 : 30,000).

(6) A, B and C were partners in a firm under dissolution. Their respective capitals were Rs. 5,000, Rs. 3,000 and Rs. 1,000 and they shared profits and losses in the ratio of 2 : 2 : 1. Their undistributed profits were Rs. 2,500 and realisation loss amounted to Rs. 8,000.

Show the partners capital accounts assuming that 'C' was insolvent and was unable to contribute anything towards his deficiency.

Apply the rule of *Garner* Vs. *Murray*.

(*Gulbarga, April, 1993*)

Ans. : Capital deficiency of 'C' 100 borne by A Rs. 60 and B Rs. 40.
Repayment of capital : A Rs. 5,940 and B Rs. 3,960.
Share of loss brought in cash : A Rs. 3,200 and B Rs. 3,200.
Total of Cash A/c Rs. 99,000; Opening Cash Balance Total Rs. 3,500 *i.e.*, 11,500 – 8,000.

Note : Capital Ratio = 3 : 2 (6,000 : 4,000).

(7) X, Y and Z were partners sharing profits and losses equally. On the dissolution of their partnership, the Balance Sheet stood as follows :

Liabilities	Rs.	Assets	Rs.
X's Capital	50,000	Cash at Bank	48,000
Y's Capital	30,000	Z's Capital	8,000
		Losses	24,000
	80,000		80,000

Z become insolvent and was unable to contribute anything.

Prepare the partners' capital accounts by applying the decision in *Garner* Vs. *Murray*.

(*Bangalore, Oct., 1993*)

Ans. : Capital Deficiency of Z Rs. 16,000 borne by X Rs. 10,000 and Y Rs. 6,000 ; Bank Account Total Rs. 64,000. Repayment of Capitals : X Rs. 40,000 and Y Rs. 24,000.

Note : Capital Ratio : 5 : 3.

(8) A, B, C and D were equal partners in a firm. Their Balance Sheet after realisation of the assets was as under :

Liabilities	Rs.	Assets	Rs.
Creditors	20,000	Bank	68,000
Capital :		Capital (overdrawn) :	
A	30,000	C	20,000
B	20,000	D	6,000
Realisation Profit	24,000		
	94,000		94,000

Prepare the partners' capital accounts showing the final adjustments among the partners assuming that 'C' is insolvent.

(*Karnatak, April, 1996*)

Ans. : Capital Deficiency of 'C' Rs. 14,000 is borne by a A— Rs. 8,400 and B— Rs. 5,600; Capital Ratio : 3 : 2.
Repayment of Capitals : A— Rs. 27,600 and B— Rs. 20,400.
Bank Account Total Rs. 68,000.

Note : Rule of *Garner* Vs. *Murray* is applied.

(C) Solve the following problems :

(*Each Carries 16 Marks*)

(1) The following is the Balance Sheet of Ramesh, Suresh and Jagdeesh as on 31-12-1981 when the partners decide to dissolve the firm.

Liabilities	Rs.	Assets		Rs.
Creditors	9,000	Cash in Hand		1,000
General Reserve	3,000	Debtors	10,500	
Capital Accounts :		*Less* : Provision	500	10,000
Ramesh	28,000	Stock		15,000
Suresh	26,000	Furniture		2,000
Jagdeesh	2,000	Plant		40,000
	68,000			68,000

The assets realised as follows :

Debtors Rs. 6,000 ; Stock Rs. 10,000 ; Plant Rs. 32,000 and Furniture Rs. 500.

The realisation expenses amounted to Rs. 280. The creditors are paid off at a discount of 2%. Jagdeesh becomes bankrupt and is able to bring only Rs. 960 from his private assets.

Prepare : (i) Realisation A/c, (ii) Partners' Capital A/cs and (iii) Cash A/c (according to *Garner* Vs. *Murray* Principle) assuming that the capitals of partners are fluctuating.

(*Gulbarga, April, 1982*)

Ans. : Realisation loss Rs. 18,600; Final payment to : Ramesh Rs. 27,840 and Suresh Rs. 25,920; Capital deficiency of Jagdeesh Rs. 2,240; Last agreed capital ratio 29 : 27. Bank Account Total Rs. 62,860.

(2) The partners A, B and C were sharing profits and losses in the ratio of 5 : 3 : 2. As on 31-12-1985 their Balance Sheet appeared as follows :

Liabilities		Rs.	Assets		Rs.
Capitals : A	20,000		Debtors	40,000	
B	16,000		*Less* : Provision	2,000	38,000
C	3,000	39,000	Furniture		6,000
General Reserve		10,000	Stock		26,000
Creditors		23,000	Cash		2,000
		72,000			72,000

The firm was dissolved on that date and the assets realised as under :

Stock	Rs. 20,000
Furniture	Rs. 2,000
Debtors	Rs. 24,000

Rs. 1,000 was not paid to the creditors. The remaining amount was paid to the creditors at a discount of 5%. There was a liability of Rs. 6,100 for damages which had to be paid. The expenses came to Rs. 2,000.

'C' could contribute only Rs. 120.

Prepare the ledger accounts to close the books of the firm (assume that the capitals are fluctuating).

(*Gulbarga, Oct., 1986*)

Ans. : Realisation loss Rs. 30,000; Final payment to : A—Rs. 24,500 and B—Rs. 18,620; Capital deficiency of 'C' Rs. 880; Last agreed capital ratio 25 : 19; Bank Account Total Rs. 72,120.

(3) A, B and C were in partnership sharing profits and losses in proportion of 1/2, 1/3 and 1/6 respectively. The firm's balance sheet as on 30-9-1992 was as follows :

Liabilities	Rs.	Assets	Rs.
Creditors	3,15,000	Cash at Bank	1,40,000
Loan on Mortgage	45,000	Debtors	3,26,000
A's Capital	6,00,000	Stock	3,24,000
B's Capital	4,00,000	Fixed Assets	4,50,000
		C's Capital	1,20,000
	13,60,000		13,60,000

It was decided to dissolve the firm as on that date. The fixed assets and stock realised Rs. 7,50,000; bad debts and discount allowed amounted to Rs. 16,000. The mortgage loan was duly paid off. The creditors were paid less discount at 5%. There was a claim for damages pending against the firm which was settled at Rs. 56,000. The expenses of realisation amounted to Rs. 3,750. After realisation of the assets, 'C' was adjudicated as insolvent and a dividend of 25 paise in a rupee was received in respect of the firm's against his estate.

You are required to give the journal entries and ledger accounts so as to show the final distribution among partners.

(Gulbarga April, 1983)

Ans. : Realisation loss Rs. 84,000; Final payment to : A—Rs. 5,39,700 and B—Rs. 3,59,800; Capital deficiency of 'C' Rs. 1,00,500; Last agreed capital ratio 6 : 4; Bank Account Total Rs. 13,03,500.

Note : 'C' brings Rs. 33,500 being 25% of his capital deficiency. Realisation loss should be brought in cash by A & B.

(4) A, B and C are in partnership in a business sharing profits and losses equally. Their balance sheet is as follows :

Balance Sheet as at 31- 3-1982

Liabilities			Rs.	Assets		Rs.
Creditors			10,000	Furniture		2,100
Bills Payable			2,000	Stock		15,400
Capital's A/cs :	A	12,000		Debtors	18,000	
	B	9,000		*Less* : Provision	900	17,100
	C	1,000	22,000	Cash at Bank		1,400
Current A/cs :	A	2,000		Current Account :		
	B	2,000	4,000	C		5,000
Reserve Fund			3,000			
			41,000			41,000

'C' is insolvent and his private estate pays Rs. 1,800 to the firm. The partnership is consequently dissolved and the assets realised as follows :

Debtors Rs. 12,000 ; Stock Rs. 10,000 and Furniture Rs. 1,600. The Creditors were settled at Rs. 8,000.

Prepare the necessary ledger accounts to close the books of the firm in accordance with the decision in *Garner* Vs. *Murray*.

(*Sagar & Kar., April, 1984*)

Ans. : Realisation loss Rs. 9,000 ; Final payment to : A—Rs. 12,600 and B—Rs. 10,200; Capital deficiency of 'C' Rs. 4,200; Last agreed capital ratio 4 : 3; Bank Account Total Rs. 32,800.

(5) Raju, Ramu and Ratan were partners sharing profits and losses in the ratio of 3 : 2 : 1. Their Balance Sheet as on 31-12-94 was as follows :

Liabilities	Rs.	Assets		Rs.
Creditors	30,000	Cash		12,200
General Reserve	24,000	Debtors	50,000	
Capitals Accounts :		*Less :* Provision	2,000	48,000
Raju	69,000	Stock		60,000
Ramu	36,000	Furniture		18,000
		Profit and Loss A/c		6,000
		Capital A/c : Ratan		14,800
	1,59,000			1,59,000

They decide to dissolve the firm on the above date. The assets realised as follows :

Furniture Rs. 14,000, Debtors Rs. 40,000 and Stock Rs. 40,200. There is liability for rent amounting to Rs. 6,000, Patents of Rs. 4,000 which were written off previously realised Rs. 1,200.

The Creditors were paid off at a discount at 2%. Ratan became insolvent and only a dividend of 50 paise in a rupee was recovered from his private estate.

Prepare the necessary ledger accounts to close the books of the firm applying the rule in the decision in *Garner* Vs. *Murray*.

(*Gulbarga, Oct., 1988, April, 1990 & 1991*)

Ans. : Realisation loss Rs. 36,000; Final payment to : Raju Rs. 72,215 and Ramu Rs. 38,885; Capital deficiency of Ratan Rs. 8,900; Last agreed capital ratio 13 : 7; Bank Account Total Rs. 1,46,500.

(6) X, Y and Z commenced business on 1st January, 1987 with capitals of Rs. 50,000, Rs. 40,000 and Rs. 30,000 respectively. Profits and losses were shared as to X-1/2, Y-1/3 and Z-1/6. During the years 1987, 1988 and 1990 the firm earned Rs. 48,000, Rs. 60,000 and Rs. 36,000 profits. During the year 1989 the firm incurred a loss of Rs. 12,000. The partners withdrew on an average Rs. 3,000 per year. Z in addition had withdrawn Rs. 20,000.

On 31st December, 1990, they dissolved the firm. Creditors and bills payable amounting in all Rs. 78,000 were paid in full. The assets realised Rs. 1,36,000. Z was bankrupt and his estate could pay only Rs. 300.

Prepare the necessary ledger accounts and apply the principle of *Garner* Vs. *Murray*, assuming that partners' capital accounts are fixed.

(*Allahabad and Mysore, April, 1975 & 1982*)

Ans. : Realisation loss Rs. 1,38,000; Final payment to : X Rs. 1,02,500 and Y Rs. 70,800; Capital deficiency of Z Rs. 2,700; Last agreed capital ratio 5 : 4. Bank Account Total Rs. 2,51,300. Value of sundry assets Rs. 2,74,000.

Note : Profit credited to Current or Capital Account of X–Rs. 66,000 (1,32,000 × ½); Y–Rs. 44,000 (1,32,000 × 1/3); Z–Rs. 22,000 (1,32,000 × 1/6); Drawings debited to Current or Capital Account of X–Rs. 12,000 (3,000 × 4); Y–Rs. 12,000 (3,000 × 4); and Z–Rs. 32,000 (3,000 × 4 = 12,000 + 20,000).

(7) A, B and C are partners sharing profit and losses 40%, 30% and 30% respectively. They decide to dissolve and appoint B to realise the assets and distribute the proceeds. B is to receive 5% of the amounts realised from stock and debtors as his remuneration and is to bear all the expenses of realisation.

The following is the Balance Sheet prepared by the firm as on the date of the dissolution.

Liabilities		Rs.	Assets		Rs.
Creditors		59,000	Cash		1,500
Capital Accounts :			Debtors	45,500	
A	30,000		*Less:* R.D.D.	2,500	43,000
B	20,000	50,000	Stock		60,000
			C- Overdrawn		4,500
		1,09,000			1,09,000

B reports the result of realisation as follows :

Debtors realise	Rs. 35,000
Stock realise	Rs. 45,000
The goodwill is sold for	Rs. 2,000

Creditors were paid Rs. 57,500 in full settlement.

Outstanding creditor Rs. 500 have also been paid.

The expenses of realisation came to Rs. 600 which B met personally.

A and B agree to receive from 'C' Rs. 3,000 in full settlement of the firm's claim against him. Show Capital, Realisation and Cash Accounts.

(Berhampur, B.Com. Hons., 1985 & Mysore, April, 1970)

Ans. : B's Remuneration Rs. 4,000; Realisation loss Rs. 24,000; Final payment to : A–Rs. 24,780 and B–Rs. 19,920; Capital deficiency of 'C' Rs. 8,700; Last agreed capital ratio 3 : 2. Bank Account Total Rs. 1,03,300.

(8) The following is the Trial Balance as on December 31st, 1985 of M/s. A, B and C who had branches at different places and who shared profits and losses in the ratio of 2 : 2 : 1.

		Dr. Rs.	Cr. Rs.
Capitals : 1st Jan., 1985	A	—	14,000
	B	—	14,000
	C	—	2,000
Drawings :	A	1,572	—
	B	1,292	—
	C	816	—
Goodwill		2,400	—
Sundry Creditors		—	6,980
Profit and Loss A/c for the year (Before allowing interest at 5% on capitals)		4,000	—
Sundry Debtors :	Delhi	6,750	—
	Patna	3,250	—
	Kanpur	1,500	—
Furniture :	Delhi	1,000	—
	Patna	500	—
	Kanpur	600	—
Stock :	Delhi	4,600	—
	Patna	3,400	—
	Kanpur	5,300	—
		36,980	36,980

The firm was dissolved on the above date. A took over the Delhi Branch and B took over the Patna Branch, the assets being taken over at 10% less than the book values. Goodwill was value less but A agrees to pay Rs. 500 to B. The necessary adjustments being made in the Capital Accounts. The business at Kanpur was sold to a limited company which allotted 600 ordinary shares of Rs. 10 each in due proportion to A & B, credited as fully paid. To pay the liabilities, A & B introduced cash in the profit sharing ratios. The cost of winding up came to Rs. 400 for which A advanced cash. C is insolvent and can pay nothing. B received all the shares.

Give the necessary accounts to close the books of the firm. Assume the capital to be fluctuating. A & B settle accounts among themselves.

(*Shivaji & Utkal, April, 1979 & B'lore, Oct., 1992*)

Ans. : Realisation loss Rs. 6,150 ; Final payment to : B- Rs. 345; Cash brought by A to meet his deficiency by Rs. 345. Capital deficiency of 'C' Rs. 3,376 to be borne by A & B in their profit sharing ratio; Bank Account Total Rs. 7,725.

Note : In this problem the solvent partner sharing the deficiency of insolvent partner in their profit sharing ratio. Therefore, the decision in *Garner* Vs. *Murray* cannot be applied to this problem.

When all Partners except on become Insolvent :

(9) A, B and C were in partners in a firm sharing profits and losses in the proportion of 1/5, 3/10 and ½ respectively. The following was the balance sheet of the firm as on 30-6-1988 when they decided to dissolve their firm.

Liabilities		Rs.	Assets	Rs.
Creditors		12,000	Cash	1,000
Loan from Bank		14,000	Machinery	5,000
Capital's A/cs :			Debtors	20,000
A	3,000		Advance to A	2,000
B	4,000		Loss to date	8,000
C	3,000	10,000		
		36,000		36,000

The assets realised Rs. 20,000.

'A' has a private estate which is valued at Rs. 4,000. B is insolvent. From C's estate, a dividend of 50 paise in a rupee is recovered. Show the Partners' Capital Accounts and Bank Account of the firm assuming that all the entries relating to the dissolution are passed through the Realisation Account.

(*Kar., Oct., 1981 and Mysore, April, 1982*)

Ans. : Realisation loss Rs. 5,000; Capital deficiency of C Rs. 1,750 transferred to A Rs. 817 and B Rs. 933 in their capital ratio of 7 : 8 (1,400 : 1,600); B's deficiency of Rs. 933 transferred to A. Cash brought by A Rs. 1,250; Bank Account Total Rs. 26,000.

(10) J, G and M are partners sharing profits in the proportion of 2 : 3 : 1. They decided to dissolve the partnership on 31-12-90 and the Balance Sheet as on that date was as under :

Liabilities		Rs.	Assets		Rs.
Creditors		18,000	Freehold Property		8,000
Bank Overdraft		8,000	Plant & Machinery		14,400
(Guaranted by J)			Stock		9,600
Capital Accounts :			Debtors		2,400
J	4,800		Current Accounts :		
G	6,000		G	4,400	
M	4,000	14,800	M	5,200	9,600
Current A/c : J		3,200			
		44,000			44,000

The freehold property realised Rs. 5,600; Plant and Machinery Rs. 10,800; Stock Rs. 6,000 and the Debtors Rs. 2,400. J paid off the Bank overdraft. Expenses of realisation amounted to Rs. 480. G and M both became insolvent, the estate of the former paying 25 paise in the rupee and of the latter 10 paise in the rupee.

Draft the necessary journal entries and prepare the necessary accounts in the books of the partnership.

(*Mysore, April, 1969 and Poona, April, 1989*)

Ans. : Realisation loss Rs. 10,080; Capital deficiency of 'G' Rs. 2,580 and M Rs. 2,592 transferred to J; Bank Account Total Rs. 25,948.

When all Partners become Insolvent :

(11) A and B were equal partners and their Balance Sheet stood as under when the firm was dissolved :

Liabilities	Rs.	Assets	Rs.
Creditors	1,28,000	Cash	7,200
A's Capital Account	16,000	Stock	16,000
		Furniture	12,000
		Machinery	48,000
		Debtors	20,000
		B's Drawings	40,800
	1,44,000		1,44,000

The assets were realised as under :

Stock	Rs. 12,000
Furniture	Rs. 4,000
Debtors	Rs. 16,000
Machinery	Rs. 24,000

The expenses of realisation amounted to Rs. 5,600. A's private assets were insufficient to pay off his private debts. B is able to bring in cash Rs. 32,000 being the surplus from his private estate.

Show the necessary accounts to close the books of the firm.

(*Kar. and Sagar, Oct., 1988*)

Ans. : Realisation loss Rs. 45,600; Capital deficiency of A—Rs. 6,800 and B—Rs. 31,600; Paid to Creditors Rs. 89,600; Deficiency Account total Rs. 38,400; Bank Account total Rs. 95,200.

(12) Arun, Ravi and Sunil were partners in a firm sharing profits and losses in the ratio of 5 : 3 : 2. They incurred heavy losses in the last several years and hence they decided to dissolve the firm on 31-3-1992 on which date their balance sheet was as follows :

Liabilities		Rs.	Assets	Rs.
Creditors		2,50,000	Buildings	1,20,000
Bills Payable		1,00,000	Machinery	1,00,000
Capitals :			Stock	80,000
Arun	7,000		Debtors	50,000
Ravi	4,000		Cash	13,000
Sunil	2,000	13,000		
		3,63,000		3,63,000

The assets realised as follows :

(1) Buildings Rs. 1,10,000

(2) Machinery Rs. 70,000

(3) Debtors realised 25% less and

(4) Stock realised 50% of the book value

Unfortunately, all the partners become insolvent and their private estate realised as follows :

Arun Rs. 3,500; Ravi Rs. 2,000 and Sunil Rs. 500.

Prepare the necessary ledger accounts to close the books of the firm.

(*Kar., April, 1982*)

Ans. : Realisation loss Rs. 92,500; Capital deficiency of Arun Rs. 35,750, Ravi Rs. 21,750 and Sunil Rs. 16,000; Paid to Creditors Rs. 1,97,500 and paid for Bills Payable Rs. 79,000; Deficiency Account Total Rs. 73,500; Bank Account Total Rs. 2,76,500.

(13) X, Y and Z had the following balance sheet on 31-12-1980.

Liabilities		Rs.	Assets	Rs.
Creditors		80,000	Fixed Assets	80,000
Bank Loan		50,000	Debtors	48,000
(With charge on stock)			Stock	40,000
Capital Accounts :			Cash at Bank	2,000
X	40,000		Profit and Loss Account	60,000
Y	40,000			
Z	20,000	1,00,000		
		2,30,000		2,30,000

The partners decided to dissolve the firm. The assets were realised as follows :

Fixed Assets Rs. 40,000; Debtors Rs, 20,000 and Stock Rs. 20,000.

The position of the partners was as follows :

(a) X was having private assets worth Rs. 20,000 and also he was having private liabilities Rs. 30,000.

(b) Y was having private assets worth Rs. 17,000 and private liabilities Rs. 12,000.

(c) Z was able to pay Rs. 10,000 only on his account to the firm.

The partners share profits and losses in the ratio of 2 : 2 : 1. The loss on realisation is to be determined after considering the amount ultimately paid to creditors.

Show the necessary ledger accounts in the books of the firm.

(B'lore, April, 1989 & Kar., April, 1983 Mod.)

Ans. : Realisation loss Rs. 88,000; Capital balance of X–Rs. 19,200 (Dr.), Y–Rs. 14,200 (Dr.) and Z–Rs. 400 (Cr.) transferred to Deficiency Account. Paid to Creditors Rs. 56,000; Deficiency Account total Rs. 33,400.

Note : Calculation of cash available.

Dr. **Bank Account** Cr.

	Rs.		Rs.
To Balance b/d	2,000	By Bank Loan	20,000
To Realisation A/c	80,000	(To the extent of security)	
(Assets sold)		By Bank Loan (Remaining	21,000
To Y's Capital A/c	5,000	Bank loan of Rs. 30,000	
To Z's Capital A/c	10,000	*i.e.*, $\left(\frac{30,000 \times 77,000}{30,000 + 80,000}\right)$	
		By Creditors $\left(\frac{80,000 \times 77,000}{30,000 + 80,000}\right)$	56,000
	97,000		97,000

ADDITIONAL PROBLEMS

(14) X, Y and Z were the partners. The balance sheet of the firm stood as under on the date when the firm was dissolved :

Liabilities	Rs.	Assets	Rs.
Creditors	60,000	Sundry Assets	55,000
X's Capital Account	22,000	Profit and Loss Account	12,000
Z's Capital Account	10,000	Y's Capital Account	25,000
	92,000		92,000

The assets realised Rs. 40,000. The expenses of realisation amounted to Rs. 1,000. The position of the partners was as follows :

	Private estate Rs.	Private liabilities Rs.
X	18,000	20,000
Y	12,000	21,000
Z	12,000	10,000

Prepare the necessary ledger accounts to close the books of the firm.

(Karnatak, April, 1993)

Ans. : Realisation profit : Rs. 3,000 (1,000 + 1,000 + 1,000); Capital deficiency of Y Rs. 28,000 transferred to X–Rs. 21,000 and Z–Rs. 7,000; Ultimate capital deficiency of X– Rs. 2,000 is transferred to Z. Cash balance of Rs. 41,000 [40,000 + 2,000 (*i.e.*, 12,000 – 10,000) – 1,000] is paid to creditors.
Bank Account Total Rs. 42,000; Capital Ratio = 3:1 (18,000 : 16,000).

(15) Gampa, Maddi and Marula were equal partners in a firm. They decide to dissolve the firm on 31-12-1991 due to financial difficulties. Their Balance Sheet as on that date was as follows :

Liabilities	Rs.	Assets	Rs.
Creditors	15,400	Realisation Account (Loss)	18,400
Capital Accounts :		Profit and Loss Account	1,200
Gampa	16,000	Cash	23,800
Maddi	8,000		
Marula	4,000		
	43,400		43,400

At the time of dissolution, it was found that Marula was insolvent. At the end, the creditors agreed to allow a discount of Rs. 400. Assuming that Marula could not bring in anything towards his capital deficiency. Prepare the necessary ledger accounts if :

(i) *Garner* Vs. *Murray* rule is not applied

(ii) *Garner* Vs. *Murray* rule is applied

(a) When capitals are fixed

(b) When capitals are fluctuating. (*Bangalore, April, 1997*)

Ans. : (i) Realisation loss Rs. 18,000 (18,400 – 400 discount allowed by creditors); Solvent partners profit sharing ratio = 1 : 1; Final payment : Gampa Rs. 8,400 and Maddi Rs. 400; Capital deficiency of Marula Rs. 2,400.

(ii) (a) Realisation loss Rs. 18,000; Capital deficiency of Marula Rs. 2,400; Last agreed capital ratio = 2 : 1; Final payment : Gampa Rs. 14,000 and Maddi Rs. 6,800.

(b) Realisation loss Rs. 18,000; Capital deficiency of Marula Rs. 2,400; Last agreed capital ratio = 156 : 76 or 39 : 19; Final payment : Gampa Rs. 13,986 and Maddi Rs. 6,814.

Note : Realisation loss is brought in cash by solvent partners in accordance with the rule in *Garner* Vs. *Murray*.

(16) Ajay, Viswas and Vikas were partners sharing profits in the ratio 3:3:1. On 31st December, 1996 their Balance Sheet was as follows :

Liabilities	Rs.	Assets	Rs.
Sundry Creditors	30,000	Bank	9,500
Bills Payable	5,000	Stock	15,500
Ajay's Loan Account	6,000	Debtors	32,000
Reserve Fund	12,000	Furniture	5,000
Profit and Loss Account :	6,000	Machinery	21,000
Ajay	20,000	Drawings :	
Viswas	15,000	Ajay	4,000
		Viswas	1,000
		Vikas's Capital	6,000
	94,000		94,000

The assets realised as follows :

Stock Rs. 12,200; Debtors Rs. 30,100; Furniture Rs. 4,200; Machinery is taken over by Ajay at Rs. 18,000.

The expenses amounted to Rs. 1,200. Vikas is insolvent and his estate paid Rs. 1,900.

Prepare the necessary ledger accounts to close the books of the firm in accordance with the decision in *Garner* Vs. *Murray*.

(*Bangalore, April, 1990*)

Ans. : Realisation profit : Rs. 10,200 (4,372 + 4,371 + 1,457); Capital deficiency of Vikas (Rs. 2,985) should be shared by Ajay (Rs. 1,558) and Viswas (Rs. 1,427) in their capital ratio of 23,714 : 21,714; Final payment : Ajay Rs. 4,156 and Viswas Rs. 20,287; Bank Account Total Rs. 66,643.

Note : Calculation of Capital ratio :

	Ajay Rs.	Viswas Rs.
Opening credit balance of capital A/c	20,000	15,000
Add : Proportionate share in reserve fund	5,143	5,143
Add : Proportionate share in P & L balance	2,571	2,571
	27,714	22,714
Less : Drawings	4,000	1,000
Ratio	23,714	21,714

(17) Ramesh, Dinesh and Suresh were partners sharing profits and losses in the ratio 1/2, 1/3 and 1/6 respectively. Their Balance Sheet as on 31-12-1996 was as follows :

Liabilities	Rs.	Assets	Rs.
Creditors	31,500	Bank	14,000
Mortgage Loan	4,500	Debtors	32,600
Ramesh's Capital	30,000	Stock	22,400
Dinesh's Capital	20,000	Fixed Assets	15,000
		Suresh's Capital	2,000
	86,000		86,000

They dissolved the partnership. Fixed assets and stock realised Rs. 35,000. Bad debts and discounts to debtors amounted to Rs. 1,600. Mortgage loan was paid. Creditors were paid at a discount of 5%. Outstanding expenses Rs. 5,600 were also paid. Expenses of realisation was Rs. 375. Suresh was insolvent and a dividend of 25 paise in the rupee was received from his estate. Close the books of the firm in accordance with the decision in *Garner* Vs. *Murray* case.

(*Bangalore, April, 1992*)

Ans. : Realisation loss: Rs. 8,400 (4,200 + 2,800 + 1,400); Capital deficiency of Suresh (Rs. 2,550) should be shared by Ramesh (Rs. 1,530) and Dinesh (Rs. 1,020) in their capital ratio of 3 : 2; Final payment : Ramesh Rs. 28,470 and Dinesh Rs. 18,980; Bank A/c Total Rs. 87,850; Liabilities paid Rs. 40,025 (29,925 + 4,500 + 5,600); Suresh's deficiency Rs. 2,550 (2,000 + 1,400 – 850 *i.e.*, 3,400×1/4).

(18) A, B, C and D are partners sharing profit in the ratio of 2 : 2 : 1 : 1. Their Balance Sheet as on 31-12-90 was as follows :

Liabilities		Rs.	Assets	Rs.
Capital Accounts :			Fixed Assets	20,000
A	14,000		Debtors	10,000
B	12,000		Cash at Bank	2,000
C	2,000		Profit and Loss A/c	12,000
D	1,600	29,600		
Creditors		12,000		
Bills Payable		2,400		
		44,000		44,000

On 1st Jan., 1991 the firm was dissolved. All the assets except cash were realised for Rs. 24,800. Realisation expenses were Rs. 200. All the liabilities were discharged at book values. 'D' became insolvent and he could not bring anything from his private estate. Prepare the dissolution accounts applying *Garner* Vs. *Murray* decision.

(*Bangalore University, Nov., 1994*)

Ans. : Realisation profit: Rs. 5,400; Capital deficiency of 'D' (Rs. 1,300) is shared by A and B (722 and 578) in their last agreed capital ratio under fluctuating capital method;
Final payment : A– Rs. 9,278 and B– Rs. 7,422.

Note : 'C' did not take part in the deficiency of 'D' as his capital account showed a debit balance, though he is solvent.

(19) Ram, Shyam and Shesh were partners sharing profits in the ratio 2 : 1 : 2. They appointed Shesh to realise the assets and distribute the proceeds. Shesh is to receive 5% remuneration on all the realisations other than amount received from partners and is to bear all expenses. The Balance Sheet of the firm on 31-12-88 was as follows :

Liabilities		Rs.	Assets		Rs.
Sundry Creditors		30,000	Goodwill		3,000
Outstanding Expenses		1,200	Debtors	31,500	
Capitals :	Ram	20,000	*Less* : Reserve	1,500	30,000
	Shyam	1,000	Stock		35,200
	Shesh	16,000			
		68,200			68,200

Shesh reports the result of realisation as follows: Debtors Rs. 21,500; Stock Rs. 27,000 and Goodwill Rs. 200. Creditors were paid at a discount 2%. Besides, outstanding expenses of Rs. 1,200 and outstanding creditors not provided for Rs. 825 were also paid. Shyam was insolvent and his estate yields only Rs. 500. Prepare Realisation Account, Capital Accounts and Bank Account (Follow the principle in *Garner* Vs. *Murray* decision).

(Bangalore, May, 1993 and Oct., 1995)

Ans. : Realisation loss : Rs. 22,160 (8,864 + 8,864 + 4,432); Shesh's remuneration Rs. 2,435 (5% on Rs. 48,700); Capital deficiency of Shyam (Rs. 7,364) is shared by between Ram (4,091) and Shesh (3,273) in their capital ratio 5 : 4.

Final payment : Ram Rs. 15,909 and Shesh Rs. 15,162; Bank Account Total 62,496.

Note : There should not be any entry in the books of the firm for realisation expenses as they are to be borne by Shesh.

(20) A, B, C and D had been carrying on business in partnership sharing profits in the ratio 3 : 2 : 1 : 1. They decided to dissolve the firm when their Balance Sheet stood as follows :

Liabilities		Rs.	Assets		Rs.
Capitals :			Office Premises		60,000
A	50,000		Furniture		10,000
B	30,000	80,000	Office Equipment		10,000
General Reserve		28,000	Motor Car		20,000
Development Reserve		7,000	Stock		30,000
Creditors		10,000	Debtors		20,000
Loan of Mortgage of Office Premises		40,000	Cash		4,000
			Capitals :		
			C	5,000	
			D	6,000	11,000
		1,65,000			1,65,000

(a) The assets realised as under :

Office premises Rs. 45,000; Office equipment Rs. 3,500; Stock Rs. 20,000; Furniture Rs. 8,000; Motor car Rs. 10,000; Debtors Rs. 12,000.

(b) Expenses of realisation amounted to Rs. 2,000.

(c) Further creditors not shown in books — Rs. 6,000 had to be paid.

You are required to draw up the Realisation Account, Partners' Capital Accounts and Cash Account, assuming that C became insolvent and only Rs. 100 was realised from his private estate. Apply the principles of *Garner* Vs. *Murray*.

(Bangalore, Oct., 1991 and April, 1995)

Ans. : Realisation loss : Rs. 59,500 (25,500 + 17,000 + 8,500 + 8,500); Capital deficiency of 'C' is shared in between A (5,200) and B (3,200) in their capital ratio 13 : 8; Final payment : A– Rs. 59,800 and B–Rs. 36,800; Final debit balance brought in by D Rs. 1,000; Liabilities paid Rs. 56,000 (16,000 + 40,000); Cash Account Total Rs. 1,54,600.

Notes : (i) Development reserve should be credited to all the partners' capital account in their profit share ratio.

(ii) D is solvent. Before adjusting the realisation loss, his capital account shows a debit balance. Hence, he need not bear the deficiency of C.

(iii) Calculation of capital ratio :

	A	B
Opening credit balance of capital	50,000	30,000
Add : Share of general reserve and development reserve	15,000	10,000
Ratio = 13 : 8	65,000	40,000

(21) M, N, O and P are partners in a firm sharing profits and losses in the ratio of 4 : 3 : 2 : 1. The following is their Balance Sheet as on 31-12-1995.

Liabilities	Rs.	Assets	Rs.
Capitals :		Sundry Assets	60,000
O	12,000	Bank	20,000
P	12,000	Capitals :	
Q's Loan A/c	6,000	M	8,000
Reserve	10,000	N	2,000
Creditors	50,000		
	90,000		90,000

On 31-12-1995 the partners decided to dissolve the firm under the following conditions :

1. Sundry assets realised Rs. 40,000.
2. Creditors were paid at a discount of 5%. In addition, unrecorded creditors of Rs. 1,500 were also paid.
3. There was an unrecorded assets of Rs. 500 which was taken over by 'O'
4. Expenses of dissolution amounted to Rs. 1,500.
5. 'M' became insolvent and only Rs. 4,000 were realised from his estate.

Prepare the necessary ledger accounts to close the books of the firm.

(*Mangalore University, BBM, April, 1996*)

Ans. : Realisation loss : Rs. 29,500; Deficiency of M (Rs. 7,900) transferred to O : Rs. 4,077 & P : Rs. 3,823; Cash to be brought in by N : Rs. 3,950.

(22) From the following Balance Sheet of M and N, prepare accounts in the books of the firm.

Balance Sheet of M and N

Liabilities		Rs.	Assets	Rs.
Creditors		56,000	Sundry Assets	62,000
Partners' Capital :			Cash	4,000
M	5,000			
N	5,000	10,000		
		66,000		66,000

Sundry assets were realised for Rs. 24,000. Both partners were insolvent. The private property and assets of the partners were as under :

	Private Property Rs.	Private Liability Rs.
M	10,000	12,000
N	4,000	3,000

(*Karnatak, April, 1998*)

Ans. : Realisation loss : Rs. 38,000 (19,000 + 19,000); Capital deficiency of M Rs. 14,000 and N Rs. 13,000; Surplus from private estate of N Rs. 1,000; Paid to creditors Rs. 29,000; Bank Account Total Rs. 29,000 and Deficiency Account Total Rs. 27,000.

(23) A, B and C were carrying business on sharing profits and losses equally. Their Balance Sheet on 31st Dec., 1997 stood as follows :

Liabilities	Rs.	Assets	Rs.
S. Creditors	80,000	Cash	2,000
A's Loan	20,000	Stock	48,000
Gen. Reserve	6,000	Debtors	40,000
Capital :		Furniture	6,000
A	10,000	Profit and Loss A/c.	3,000
B	6,000	C's Capital A/c	23,000
	1,22,000		1,22,000

Owing to the inability to meet the demands of the creditors the firm was dissolved. 'B' and 'C' cannot pay anything whereas 'A' can contribute only Rs. 3,000 from his private estate. The assets were realised as follows :

Stock Rs. 30,000, Debtors Rs. 28,000 and Furniture Rs. 2,000. Expenses amounted to Rs. 2,000. Show the necessary accounts assuming that all partners are insolvent. (*Bangalore, April, 1998*)

Ans. : Realisation loss : Rs. 36,000; Capital deficiency of B– Rs. 5,000 and C– Rs. 34,000; Paid to creditors Rs. 63,000; Bank Account Total Rs. 65,000 and Deficiency Account Total Rs. 39,000.